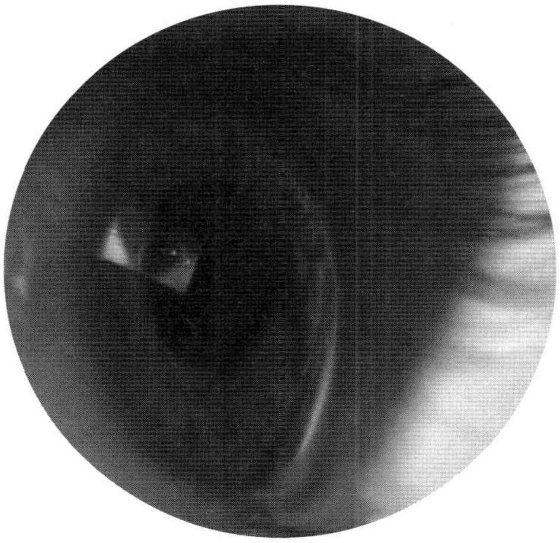

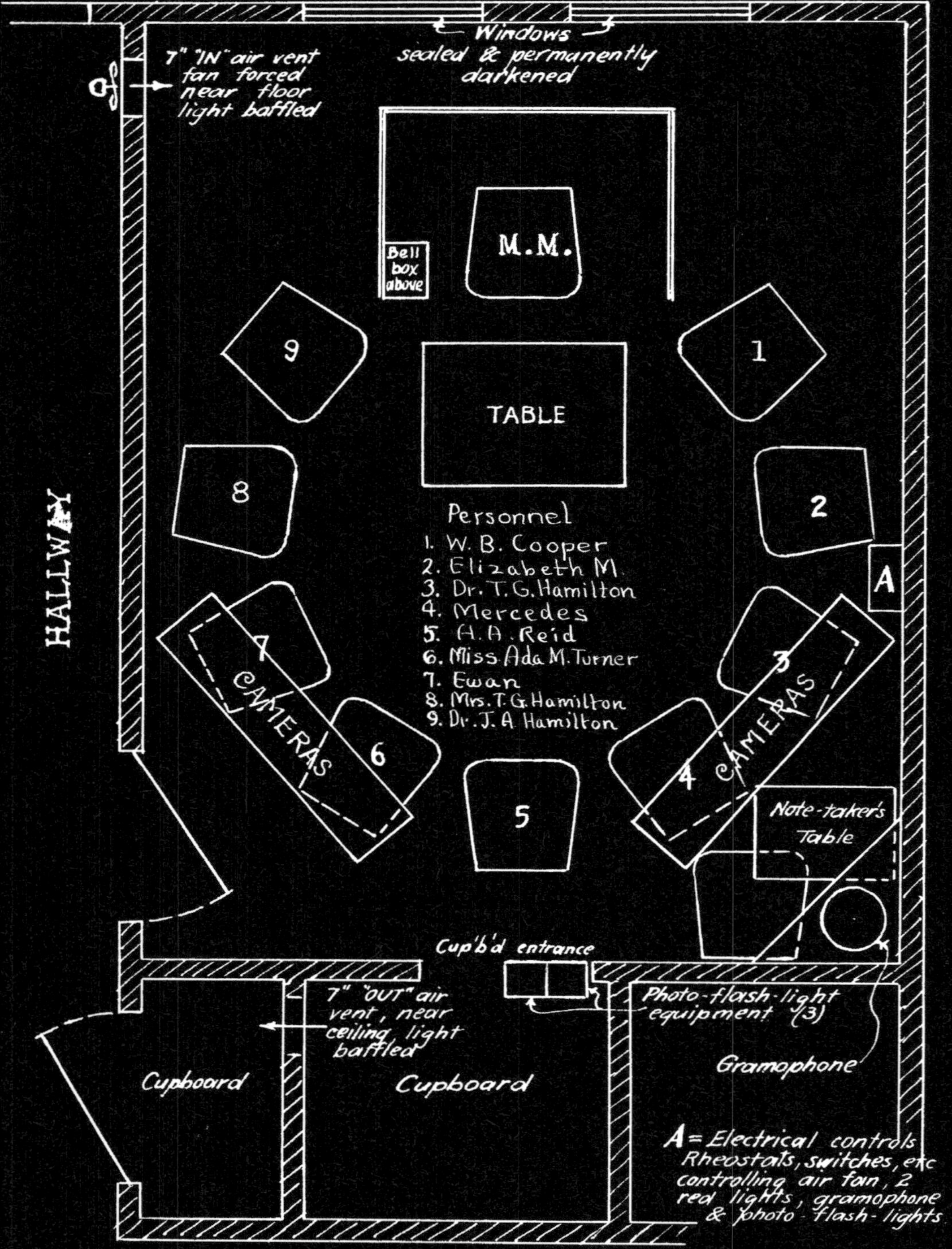

FRONT COVER:
Dermo Optics, 2006, Video, Colour, Stereo, 4mins 9secs

PREVIOUS PAGE:
After Image, 2002, Video, Black and White, Colour, Stereo, 4mins 30secs

THIS PAGE AND PAGES 4, 5, 8, 9, 12, 13:
Hamilton Family fonds, University of Manitoba Archives & Special Collections (PC 12, A. 79–41)

SUSAN MacWILLIAM

REMOTE VIEWING

EDITED BY KAREN DOWNEY

arts council of Northern Ireland

BRITISH COUNCIL

Department of Culture, Arts and Leisure www.dcalni.gov.uk

la Biennale di Venezia 53. Esposizione Internazionale d'Arte Eventi collaterali

black dog publishing london uk

35

MAY 29, 1931

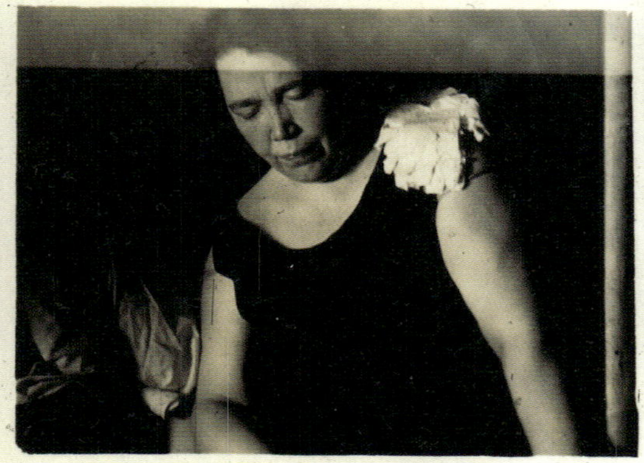

FLAT HAND"

35 MAY 29, 1931

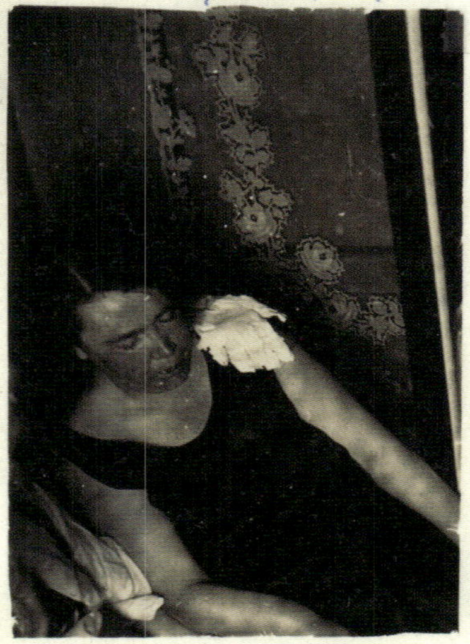

FLAT HAND

36

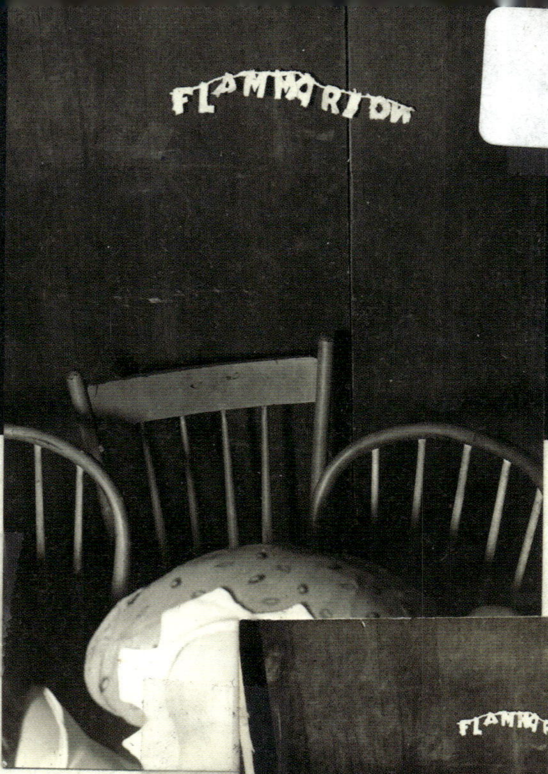

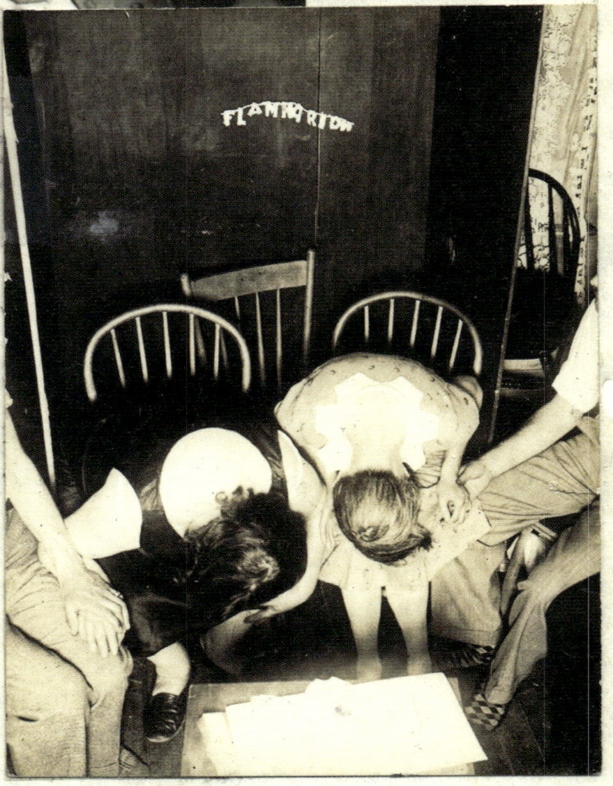

37

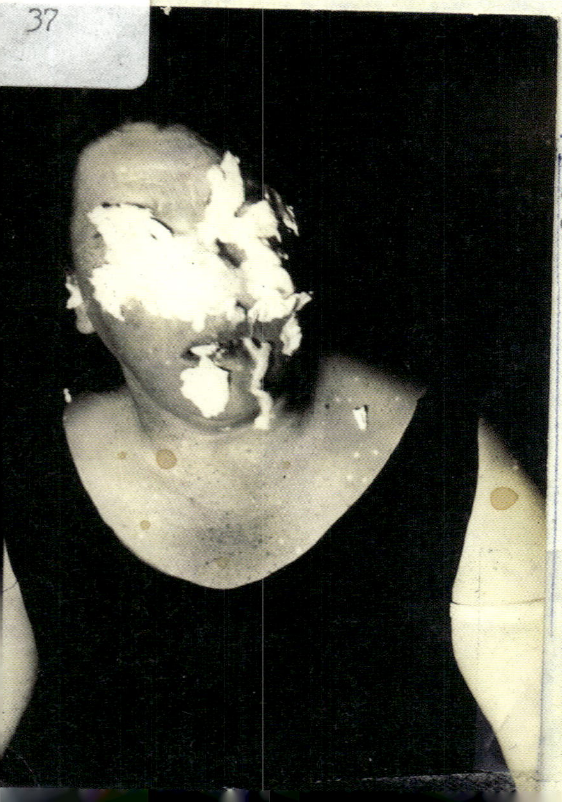

No.36. June 10/31. Teleplasmic letters. Flammarion, the French astronomer & pioneer psychic researcher gave much mental evidence in 1927 through Elizabeth M. L.H.

No. 37. June 12, 1931. Teleplasmic spots. At this time Dawn (Mrs. Marshall) was very tired, and emotionally unstable. Her nervous condition appeared to interfere with the production of the materialising substance. L.H.

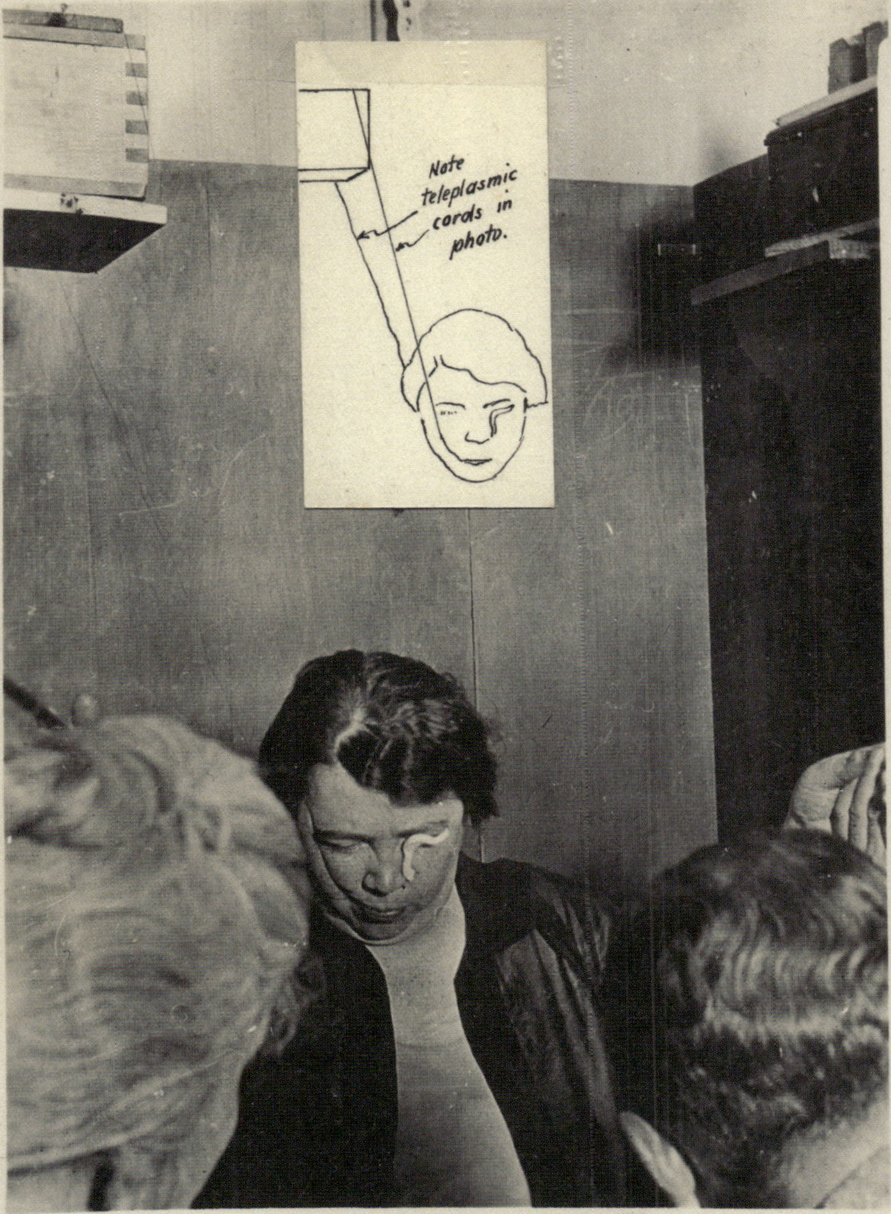

E

Enlargement of Sept. 23. 1928

The cord issuing from the medium's mouth may be seen at its upper portion as it passes over the edge of the bell-box. The second cord is visible as it descends from the distant and lower edge of the box and disappears in the shadow behind the medium's head. Again the bell was ringing at the moment the photograph was taken, again providing proof that teleplasm is a factor in telekinesis.

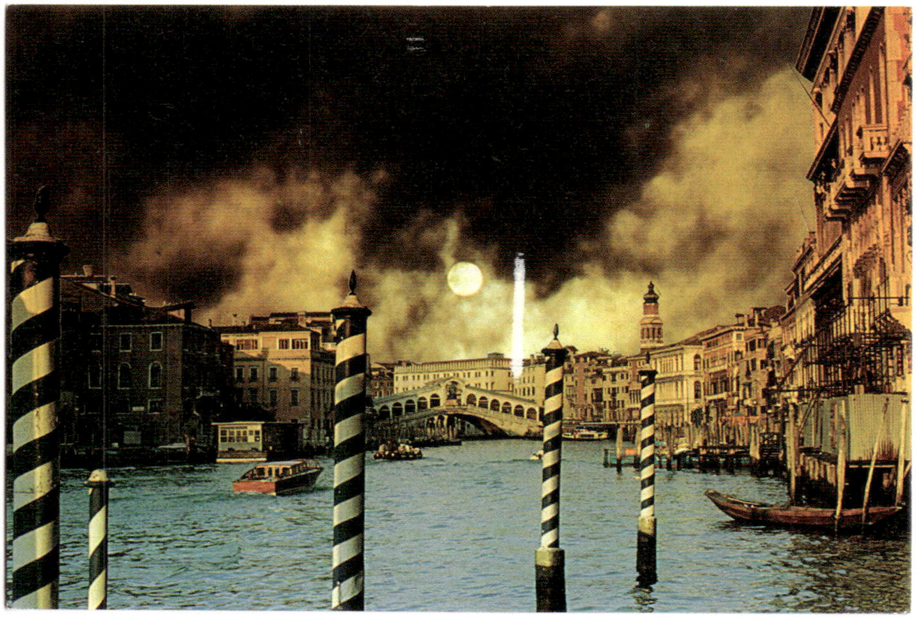

Ectoplasm over Venice, Postcard from the artist to Ciaran Carson

FOREWORD

Susan MacWilliam is one of the leading artists to emerge from Northern Ireland in the last decade. She is now carving out a notable reputation for herself amongst the ranks of international contemporary visual arts. Her solo exhibition at the 2009 Venice Biennale presents a unique opportunity to increase exposure for her important work on an unprecedented world-wide scale.

The Arts Council of Northern Ireland, in partnership with the British Council Northern Ireland, has commissioned the exhibition team of Susan MacWilliam and curator Karen Downey to represent the best of current Northern Irish visual arts at the Biennale.

Susan's exhibition at the 53rd Venice Biennale is Northern Ireland's third successive presentation at the world's oldest, most attended and highest-profile international contemporary visual arts event. Our first, in 2005, saw a group exhibition by the exciting new generation of artists to emerge from this region. Their participation reflected Northern Ireland's growing 'internationalism', and many of these artists have gone on to achieve major recognition beyond our shores.

The second presentation, in 2007, of cutting-edge video installations by Willie Doherty, an artist already established at the very forefront of international contemporary visual art, built on the success of the first exhibition and attracted more than 40,000 visitors.

Remote Viewing, a solo exhibition with new work by Susan MacWilliam, marks a seminal moment in the artist's rising international career. Her richly complex and multi-layered work, mediating between the worlds of art and psychical research will receive in Venice the serious critical and commercial attention it unquestionably merits.

The strange and enigmatic narratives from other worlds and other times that inhabit *Remote Viewing* will live on in the viewer's memory long after the present Biennale ends.

Susan's exhibition at the 53rd Venice Biennale reinforces Northern Ireland's status on the world stage as a creative nation capable of consistently producing artists whose work can stand alongside the best in the world.

Rosemary Kelly, OBE
Chairman
Arts Council of Northern Ireland

Brian Hanna
Chair
British Council Northern Ireland
Advisory Committee

2nd Cloud of Teleplasm

March 10, 1929

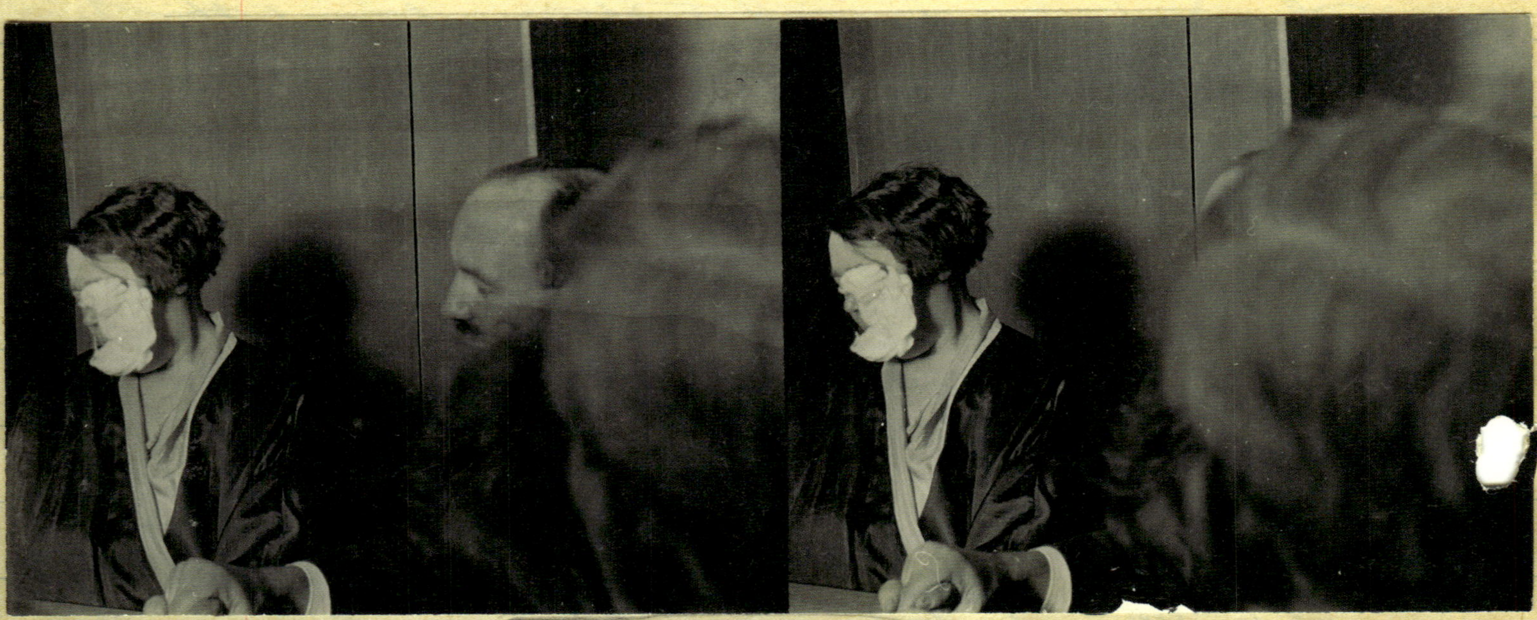

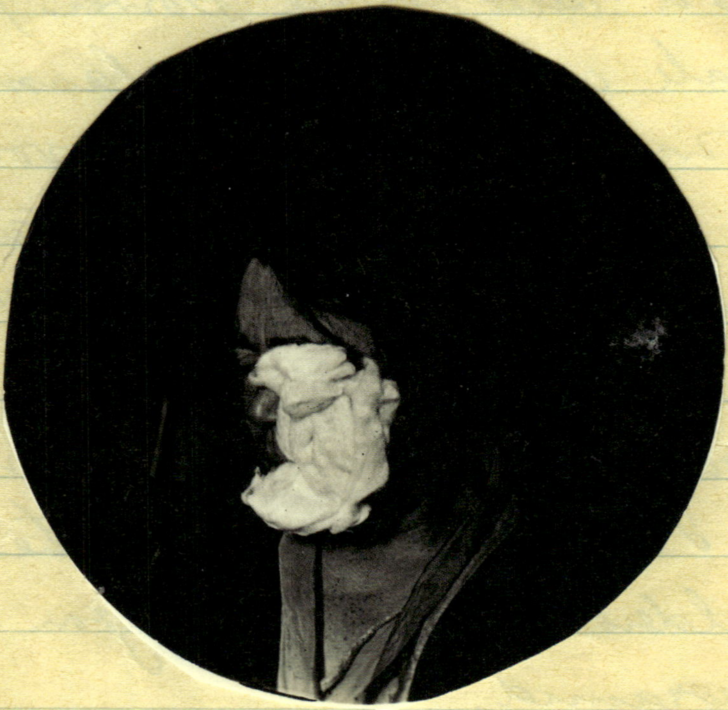

36. THE TELEPLASMIC MANIFESTION
JUNE 10 1931

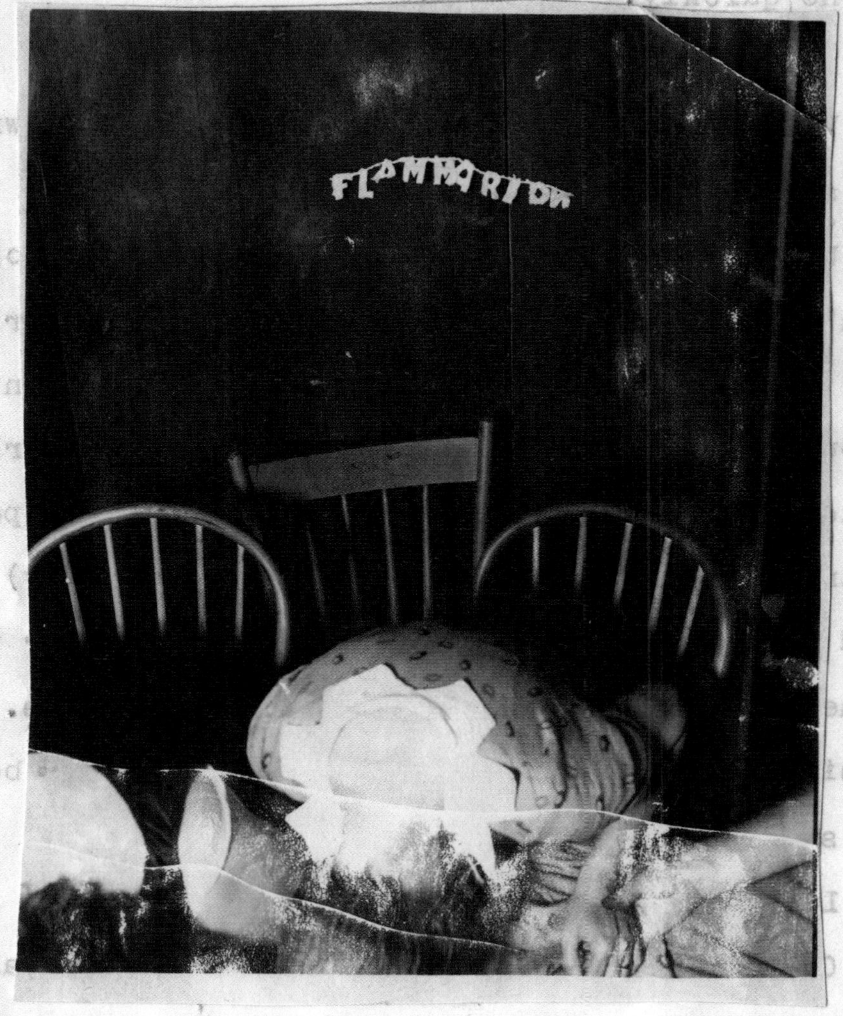

The name "written" in teleplasm — "Flammarion" the noted French astronomer and pioneer researcher. Claimed to communicate through the trance state of Elizabeth M. see his books. "Psychic Force" "At the moment of death" & others.

CONTRIBUTORS

KAREN DOWNEY has worked as Exhibitions Director at Belfast Exposed Photography since 2000 developing the archive, exhibition and publishing programmes. In 2008 she was UK curator for the European Central Bank Photography Award and she curated Northern Ireland's presentation at the 53rd Venice Biennale.

BRIAN DILLON is UK Editor of *Cabinet* magazine and a Research Fellow at the University of Kent. His memoir, *In the Dark Room*, 2005, won the Irish Book Award for non-fiction. His *Tormented Hope: Nine Hypochondriac Lives* is published this year. He writes regularly for such publications as *Frieze*, *Modern Painters*, *Art Review*, *The London Review of Books*, *The Times Literary Supplement*, *The Irish Times* and *The Dublin Review*.

CIARAN CARSON is Professor of Poetry at Queen's University, Belfast. He is the author of nine collections of poems, including *Belfast Confetti*, *First Language*, and *Breaking News*. His prose works include *Last Night's Fun*, *The Star Factory*, *Fishing for Amber: A Long Story*; and a novel, *Shamrock Tea*. His translation of Dante's *Inferno* won the 2002 Oxford Weidenfeld Translation Prize, and a translation of the Old Irish epic *Táin Bó Cuailnge* was published in 2007. His *Collected Poems* were published in 2008 and a new book of poems, *On the Night Watch*, is due in 2009, as is a novel, *The Pen Friend*. Among the prizes he has won are the TS Eliot Prize, the Irish Times Irish Literature Prize, the Cholmondeley Award, and the Forward Prize.

MARINA WARNER is a writer specialising in mythology and fairy-tales, with an emphasis on the part women play in them. Her recent books include *Fantastic Metamorphoses*; *Other Worlds*, 2002, and *Phantasmagoria: Spirit Visions, Metaphors, and Media*, 2006. Award-winning books include *Alone of All Her Sex: The Myth and the Cult of the Virgin Mary*, 1976, *Joan of Arc: The Image of Female Heroism*, 1982, *Monuments & Maidens*, 1985, *From the Beast to the Blonde*, 1994, and *Monsters of Our Own Making*, 1998. She is now writing a book on magic and Arabian Nights. Marina Warner is Professor in the Department of Literature, Film, and Theatre Studies at the University of Essex. She was awarded a CBE in 2008.

DR SLAVKA SVERAKOVA is a writer on art. She has worked at universities in the former Czechoslovakia, England, Scotland and Northern Ireland, supervising MFA and PhD degrees in art history and practice. Her research interests cover movements in architecture and art from the fifteenth and twentieth centuries. She has written catalogue essays and chapters in edited books and monographs. She writes for such journals as *Inter* (Quebec), *Sculpture* (USA) and *Circa* (Belfast/Dublin).

MARTHA LANGFORD is an associate professor and Concordia University Research Chair in Art History at Concordia University in Montreal. Major works include *Suspended Conversations: The Afterlife of Memory in Photographic Albums*, 2001, and *Scissors, Paper, Stone: Expressions of Memory in Contemporary Photographic Art*, 2007, as well as an edited collection, *Image & Imagination*, 2005, all from McGill-Queen's University Press. Langford is a contributing editor for *Border Crossings* (Winnipeg), *Exit* (Madrid) and *Photography & Culture* (London); she is a regular book reviewer for *Source* (Belfast). An active independent curator, she was artistic director of the international biennale, Le Mois de la Photo à Montréal 2005. She is currently writing an intellectual biography of Michael Snow.

CONTENTS

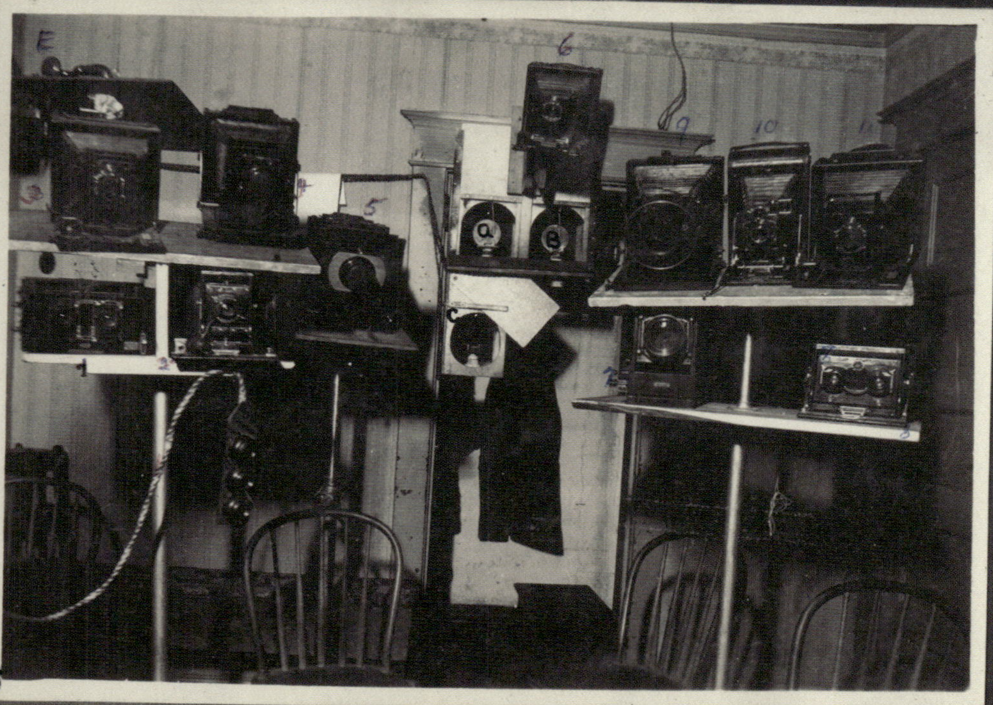

A,B,C,flash-powder devices
D. 3 push-buttons for exploding flash electrically
E. Repeater-phonograph, controlled by electric switch.

Cameras

1. Goerz Stereo, plats/films
2. 5x7 Rapid Rectilinear
3. ,, ,, ,,
4. $4\frac{1}{4}$x$6\frac{1}{2}$ Thornton Picard Portrait.
5. 5x7 Quartz lens camera
6. 5x7 Wide angle lens camera
7. 5x7 Seneca Portrait ,,
8. Woollensak Stereo
9. Doppel Anastigmat 5x7
10. 5x7 Zeiss Anastigmatic, roll film or plate
11. 5x7 Rapid Rectilinear.

View of photographic equipment: A, B, C, flash-light boxes; D, electric push-buttons which explode the three flashes respectively.

Note stereoscopic cameras - one at either side.
Later - flash bulbs were used.

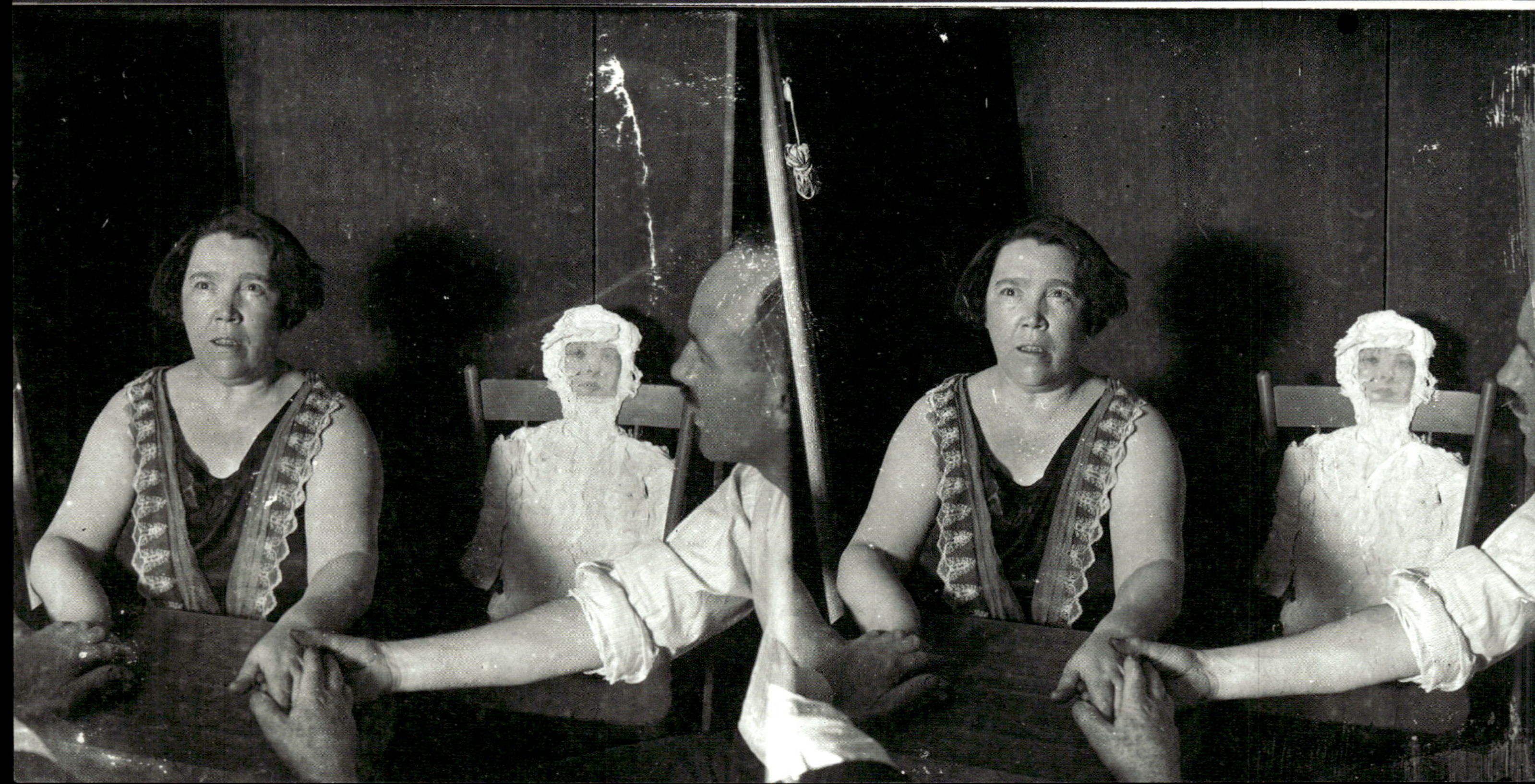

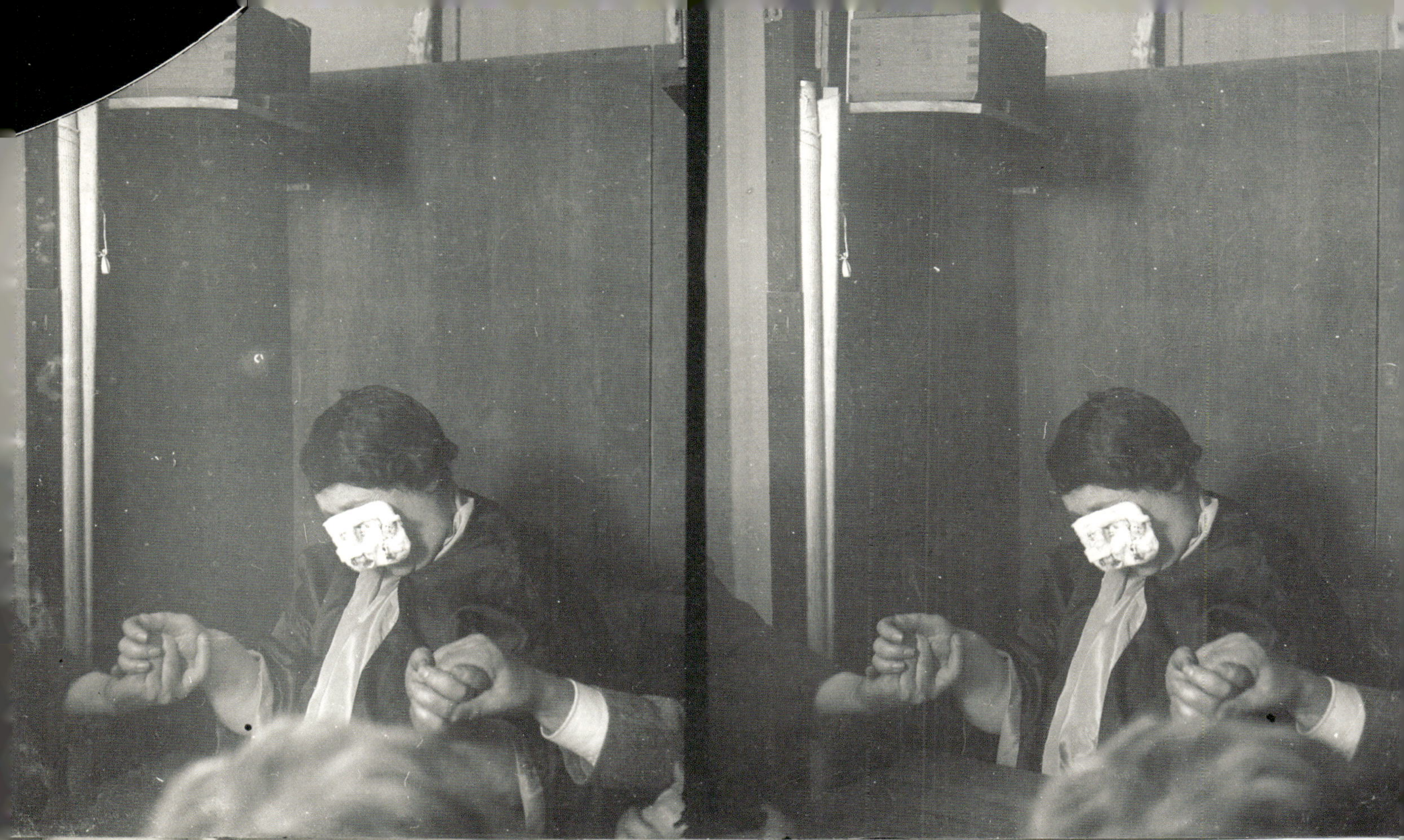

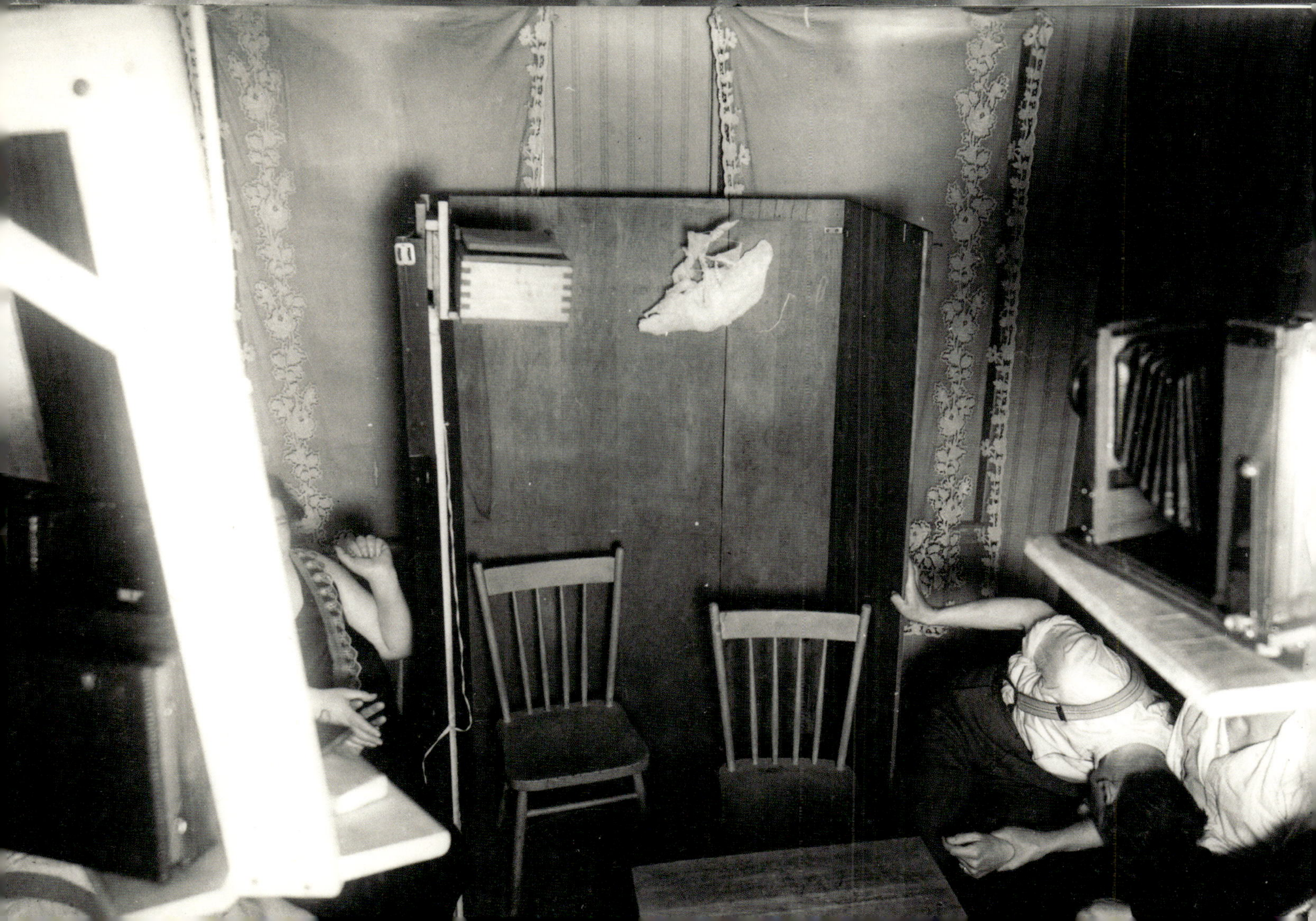

INTRODUCTION

Remote Viewing is the first significant published volume of work by Susan MacWilliam, an artist who has spent over ten years exploring cases of paranormal activity. The subject of her art is the psychic and the supernatural, as well as the field of psychical research—more recently known as parapsychology—which has been applied to the study of these phenomena. The scope of MacWilliam's work is wide, exploring cases of materialisation and trance mediums, x-ray vision, optograms and dermo-optical perception. She uses video, photography and sculptural installation to investigate these accounts in a way that examines forms of portraiture and storytelling.

Remote Viewing features three significant works: a major new work entitled *F-L-A-M-M-A-R-I-O-N,* 2009, *Eileen,* 2008, a three-channel video piece and *Dermo Optics,* 2006, a video and sculptural installation, all of which will be exhibited as Northern Ireland's presentation at the 53rd Venice Biennale of Art. These works are presented in the context of a series of commissioned and selected texts, archival material, video stills and photographs from earlier related works.

The opening sequence of the book introduces a set of intriguing images from the Thomas Glendenning Hamilton Spirit Photograph Archive in Winnipeg, where MacWilliam conducted early research for *F-L-A-M-M-A-R-I-O-N*. A number of the photographs and technical notes relate to a particular séance event, recorded by Hamilton in 1931, where a 'teleplasmic' manifestation of the word "Flammarion" appeared at the back of the séance cabinet. The selected photographs feature a number of significant elements: the 'teleplasmic lettering' and other ectoplasmic manifestations, the medium, séance participants and a bank of cameras.

MacWilliam's early interest in spirit photography and the documented relationship between the medium and researcher informs much of her work. In his essay, Brian Dillon positions occult photography in the context of nineteenth century developments in modern technology and medical science. Under the scrutiny of the psychic investigator and his photographic apparatus, the séance room transforms into a laboratory, a site of scientific enquiry and rationalisation. Both the medium and the researcher become engaged in acts of translation, articulating their experience in words and images.

This idea of translation, or mediation, carries significant meaning in *F-L-A-M-M-A-R-I-O-N,* where MacWilliam deftly employs language, both as a spoken and visual medium, to explore the space between perception and description. The work features parapsychologist and poltergeist investigator Dr William G Roll and poet and writer Ciaran Carson. In his essay *Words from the Cabinet,* Carson reflects on his experience of participating in the work, of performing and being directed, of speaking and 'being spoken' by language. *Remote Viewing* includes a second essay by Carson written in response to MacWilliam's video work *Library,* 2008, a subtle meditation on the space of reading and research.

Also featured in the *F-L-A-M-M-A-R-I-O-N* section of the book are extracts from Marina Warner's *Phantasmagoria*, a rich text exploring ideas of spirit and soul. The selected writings are presented as a series of titled vignettes, like snapshots from an archive. They are textual references that resonate with some of the metaphorical meanings underlying MacWilliam's practice. Through Warner's contribution the relationship between the medium and the camera is further explored, where the medium is viewed as a metaphor for photography itself, preserving and transmitting people, places and things through time.

Analogies between the medium and the artist, the séance and the art-making process are also significant. Slavka Sverakova, whose essay was written in correspondence with MacWilliam, quotes her in saying: "I have always thought the process of manifestations and materialisations in the séance room to be similar to the realisation of ideas and objects in the studio." Many of MacWilliam's important early works, *The Last Person*, 1998, *Experiment M*, 1999, *After Image*, 2002, *Kuda Bux*, 2003, and *Headbox*, 2004, were studio productions. In recent years, MacWilliam has adopted what could be described as a fieldwork approach, conducting social research among the international parapsychology community.

MacWilliam has worked closely with a number of well-known parapsychologists and psychical research institutions and has developed strong, reciprocal relationships with many of her subjects. Both Sverakova and Dillon comment on the way MacWilliam complicates and subverts conventional researcher/subject relationships. By shifting her role between the positions of artist-as-researcher and artist-as-medium, MacWilliam both directs and performs her art. Even when she is not visible in the work, she is a palpable presence.

Taking both the archive and the interview as a starting point, MacWilliam applies a variety of approaches to her art. Frequently using multiple-person, and psychological narrative modes, she presents a dense weave of image and anecdote, to explore particular personal and social histories. *Eileen* is one of five works produced as a portrait of the famous Irish medium, Eileen J Garrett, 1893–1970. Based on extended interviews with family and friends, MacWilliam conjures Garrett's private and social worlds through a series of layered and fascinating episodes. Martha Langford describes *Eileen* as "an electronic choral work" and remarks on how the work "exquisitely captures the layered storage, random retrieval, and verbal rehearsals of memory that we call 'storytelling'".

Dermo Optics, the final work featured in *Remote Viewing*, is significant in that it marks MacWilliam's departure from the studio and the beginnings of her direct engagement with the sites and scholars of parapsychology. It is an account of MacWilliam's visit to the Dermo Optical Laboratory of Dr Yvonne Duplessis in Paris, where she participated in experiments testing 'fingertip vision' (or eyeless sight). The work thwarts narrative expectation revealing little about the scientific process and the individual researchers. Instead, MacWilliam manipulates the footage in order to reintroduce something of the randomness, 'simultaneity' and intensity of her experience at the laboratory.

Following *Dermo Optics*, Martha Langford's essay discusses the variety of forms and processes that make up MacWilliam's oeuvre. She discusses a number of works and the range of strategies employed in their production: "Her strategies include recreation, appropriation and materialisation —each method of mediation carefully constructed in form and process, and rigorously disciplined, with unsettlingly compelling results." Langford's text appears to echo MacWilliam's work, in that it is a rich weave of observations and recurrent themes. She provides the reader with strong insight into the work and some sense of the pleasure and intrigue of her own encounter with it.

Remote Viewing can be regarded as a series of encounters, between the artist and her subjects, between the writers and artworks, between the reader and the text. MacWilliam's work is essentially a study in human interaction and the way that ideas are transferred from one person to another. This book provides us with an opportunity to follow MacWilliam into the dark spaces between perception and language, past and present, the visible and invisible, as she pursues her preoccupation with the possibilities and limits of vision, narrative and representation.

Karen Downey

Brian Dillon

SOME JEALOUSY OF GHOSTLY BEINGS

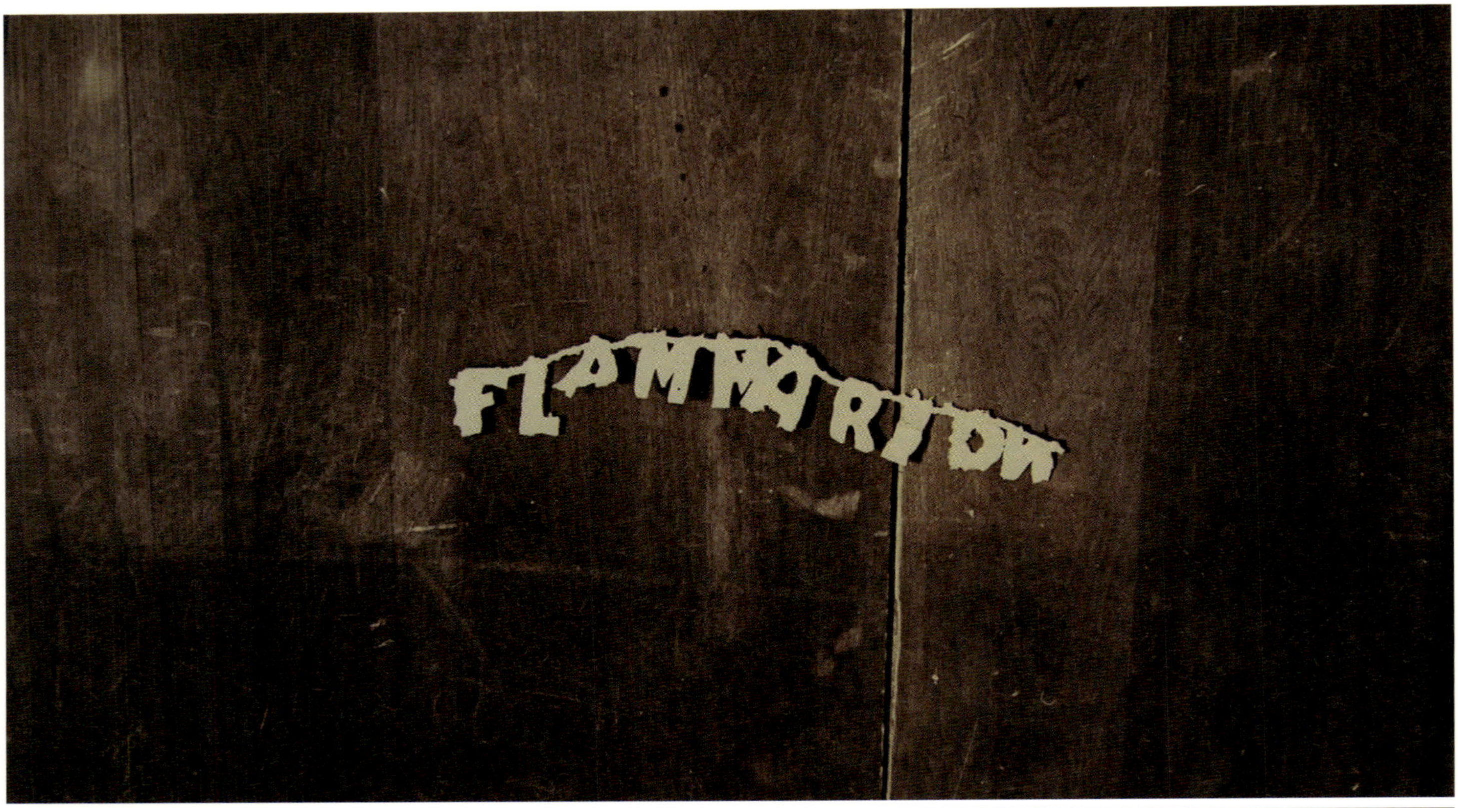

F-L-A-M-M-A-R-I-O-N, 2009, Video, Colour, Stereo

Bank of Cameras. Courtesy Hamilton Family fonds, University of Manitoba Archives

After Image, 2002, Video, Black and White, Colour, Stereo, 4mins 30secs

The historical episode that animates Susan MacWilliam's *F-L-A-M-M-A-R-I-O-N* exists, like much of the artist's own work, at the meeting point of a number of disciplines and media. It is first of all a photographic phenomenon: the materialisation of a spectral word—"Flammarion", the surname of a prominent French astronomer and psychical researcher —during a séance carried out by Dr Thomas Glendenning Hamilton in Winnipeg, Canada, in June 1931. The 'teleplasm' in question is reputedly the only such materialisation to take the form of a text; it is secondly, then, a written emanation, a script apparently expressed from one realm into another, a language both bodily and abstract. It is also a part of the historical record of occult research, a spirited fragment from the archives that returns, recognisable but repurposed, in MacWilliam's work. And it is finally a matter of a body enclosed, surveyed and studied, a palpable person whose physical reality is transformed into narrative, speech and imagery. *F-L-A-M-M-A-R-I-O-N* is a work alive—if that is the word—with several registers, voices and substances at once.

Since the late 1990s, MacWilliam has been making videos and installations that reanimate certain resonant moments in the history of séances, spirit photography and other varieties of psychical research. Her work is in no sense merely an archaeology of those events, nor simply an effort to exploit the considerable metaphorical potential of an art based on spectres, apparitions and voices from elsewhere. Instead, she enters into these histories in the most intimate fashion, collaborating with psychical researchers or their descendents, becoming herself the object or protagonist of the restaged scene of apparition or materialisation, hazing the distinction between subject and investigator—which is also to say between the predominantly male perspective of occult research and its female object. In *F-L-A-M-M-A-R-I-O-N*, all of these categories are in play, and all of them subtly involuted in the course of MacWilliam's oblique meditation on what occurred in the séance cabinet, before Hamilton's battery of a dozen cameras, in 1931.

F-L-A-M-M-A-R-I-O-N has deep roots in MacWilliam's knowledge of the history of occult photography. The spectral nature of the photograph was established early in the history of the medium. The Romantic autobiographer Thomas De Quincey, whose *Confessions of an English Opium-Eater*, 1821, was already a study in the intimacy of light, space,

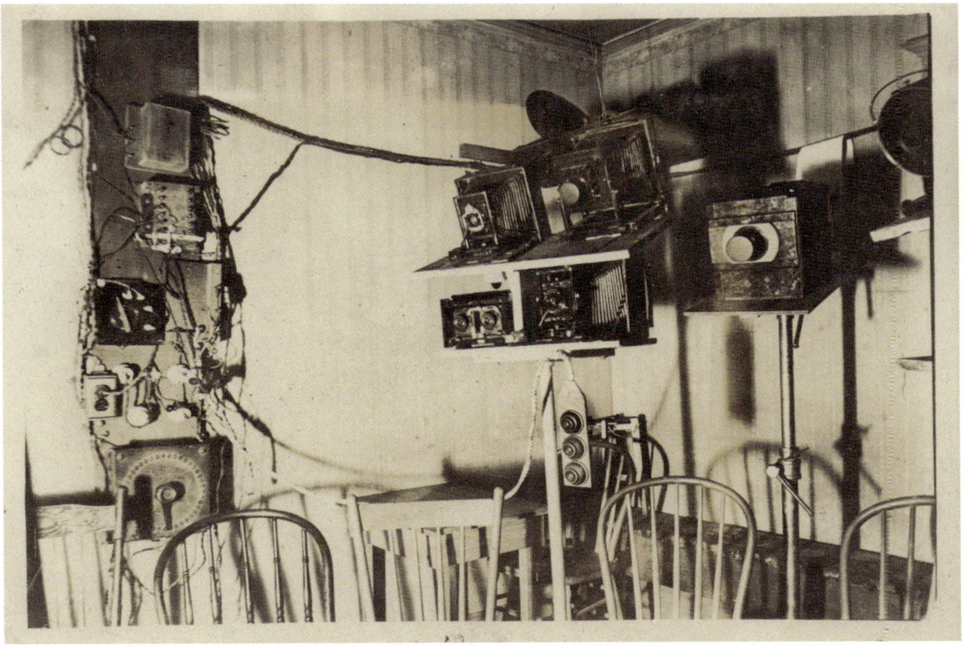

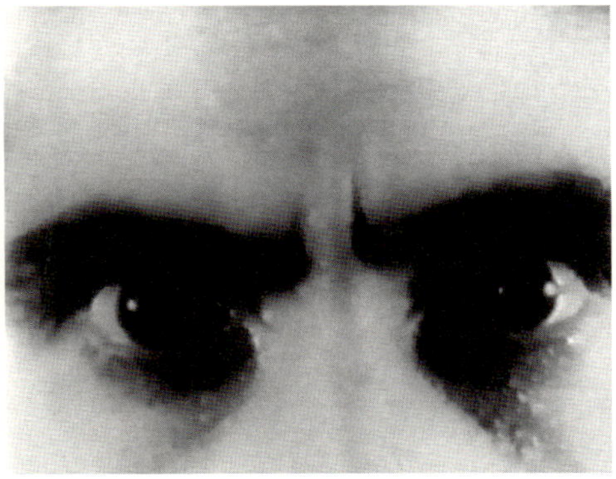

memory and mourning, turned in 1845 to consider the visionary new technology. In the opening pages of his *Suspiria De Profundis*, the aged De Quincey regretted the recent advent of the railway and of novel and more deadly forms of artillery. The Daguerreotype, however, seemed a more ambiguous innovation; in putting "light under harness as a slave for man", photography had conjured certain vexing phantoms: "the eye of the calmest observer is troubled; the brain is haunted as if by some jealousy of ghostly beings moving amongst us".[1] As the melancholy De Quincey knew too well, such ghosts were not easy to dismiss, and the urge to commune with spectres was a profound one for his technologically advanced century.

A canon of celebrated photographic revenants was established in the 1870s. In the middle of that decade, Édouard Isidore Buguet produced images in which the shades of Balzac and Napoleon III may be seen hovering above his sitters.[2] (Following his exposure as a fraud, Buguet would contrive a series of amusing self-portraits in which he is menaced by the devilish spirit of Paganini and appears to levitate items of furniture by 'mediumnic attraction'.) But for the most part the images and motivations are more urgent, more intimate and more mysterious: the spirit photography proper of the succeeding decades purports to show manifestations of the deceased that were invisible to the naked eye. A familiar typology of apparently immaterial, semi-transparent domestic spirits is swiftly established, along with certain photographic conventions such as the *carte de visite* showing its sitter oblivious to a looming phantomic presence.

And yet, the most profound and troubling forms of mediumistic photography are perhaps not those

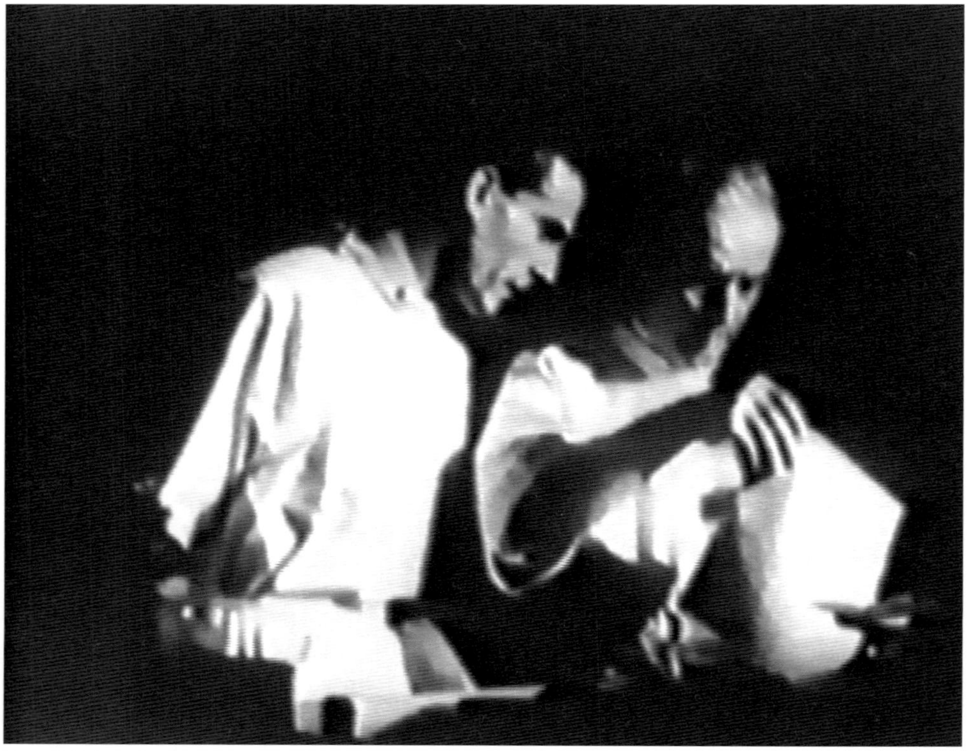

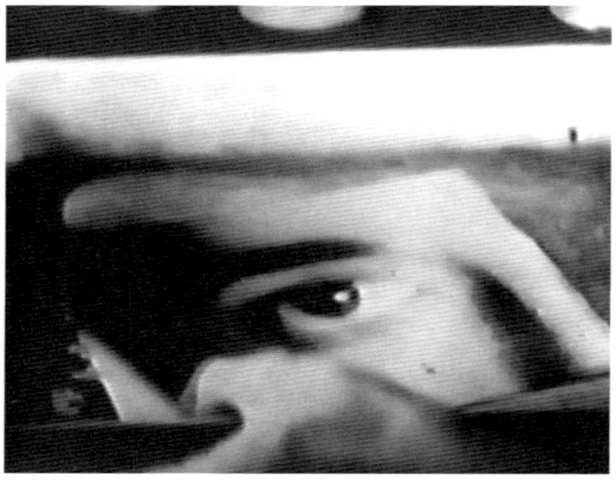

After Image, 2002, Video, Black and White, Colour, Stereo, 4mins 30secs

F-L-A-M-M-A-R-I-O-N, 2009, Video, Colour, Stereo

'Katie King' manifests at the home of Sir William Crookes Courtesy Mary Evans Picture Library

that affect to capture the evanescent or invisible ghost but those that frame a more tangible visitation: the appearance of a physical body, or the obscure emanation of a body, within the carefully stage-managed precincts of the séance room or cabinet. It is these more palpable apparitions, seen or even touched by those present, that appear to express more clearly the quasi-scientific logic of photography in the late nineteenth century and well into the twentieth. That is to say, occult photography becomes a matter of circumscribing and recording 'real' bodies —and most especially female bodies—rather than spirited images of the beyond. In this sense, a clear continuum is established between mediumistic photography and the abstracting gaze of medical science.

A case in point is the extraordinary series of photographs taken by the scientist Sir William Crookes of the English medium Florence Cook. In a curtained-off cubbyhole or 'spirit cabinet' at her parent's home in Hackney, London, Cook was said to have manifested the form of one Katie King, the daughter of a seventeenth century buccaneer who had been dispatched to convince the world of the truth of spiritualist doctrines. In the earliest photographs of Cook, taken by Frederick Hudson, Katie King is a conventional spirit, unseen except by the revelatory apparatus of the camera; at a séance on the Isle of Wight in 1872, however, she manifested herself to those present for the first time. In subsequent photographs, taken the following year, King is clearly visible while the medium remains shut up in the spirit cabinet. On one such occasion, she is said to have inspected the camera and declared it "a queer machine".

Crookes' intervention in this exemplary occult controversy—Florence Cook having been widely suspected of fraud, he launched an 'experimental campaign' in her defence—was in part a matter of the evidentiary machinery he brought to bear upon the bodies of the medium and the manifestation alike. A battery of five cameras and an array of electric and magnesium lamps were trained on the scene. But the more telling innovation is perhaps the way in which Crookes' photographs and his written accounts of his experiments are so immediately concerned with the physicality of what occurred in front of the cameras. A séance is the occasion for Crookes (in whose images Katie King's gestures are especially striking) of a certain physical encounter: "Holding one of Miss Cook's hands in mine... I passed the lamp up and

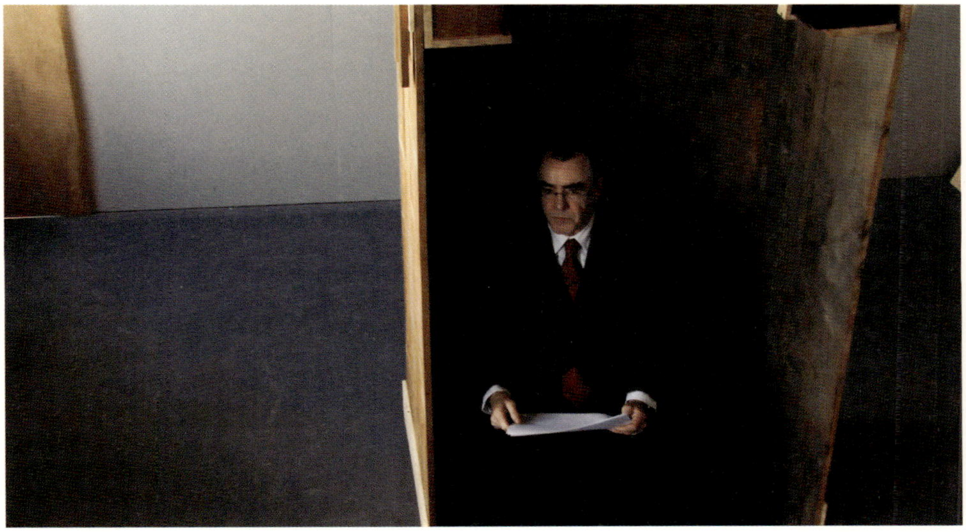

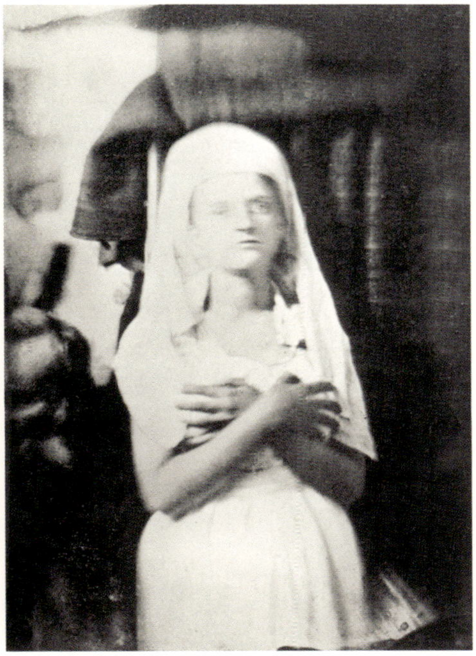

down so as to illuminate Katie's whole figure and satisfy myself that I was really looking at the veritable Katie whom I had clasped in my arms a few minutes before and not at the phantasm of a disordered brain."[3]

In this sense, Crookes' experiments are of a piece with the history of occult materialisations in the late nineteenth and early twentieth centuries—increasingly the spirit cabinet is the space in which (almost exclusively) female bodies either manifest whole or, in the case of the medium's body itself, issue forth in expressive gestures and actual bodily productions. The most celebrated photographic oeuvre in this respect is that of Albert von Schrenck-Notzing. The genius of his *Phenomena of Materialization*, published in 1914, was to posit—in the form of palpable ectoplasmic 'pseudopods' —a direct physical extrusion of one realm into another, the conduit being the body of the medium. The enigmatic artefacts photographed by Schrenck-Notzing —an ectoplasmic 'veil' over the head of the medium Eva C, a vegetal lattice strung between her breasts, a great spume of something white emerging from the mouth of another woman—are accompanied by an elaborate repertoire of physical attitudes: the medium's prostration during her trance state, or her complex movements of veiling and unveiling at the threshold of the spirit cabinet.

It is this focus on the legible order of female gestures that most readily links occult photography to the broader history of photographic surveillance of women's bodies in this period. In the most well documented instance of the latter, the French psychiatrist Jean-Martin Charcot, director of the Salpêtrière clinic in Paris, subjected his hysterical patients to a strict photographic regime, contriving a kind of spectacular (not to say phantasmagoric) evidence for the reality of the condition in question. In the words of Albert Londe, director of the clinic's photographic department in the 1880s, the photographic plate was nothing less than "the scientist's true retina"; in training the camera closely on the racked and somatising body of the hysteric, the researcher purported both to capture what was visible to the naked eye and to peer into a deeper stratum of truth. Like the occult researcher, he surrounded the woman's body with a complex scenography of truth-telling, "a staging aimed at knowledge, knowledge aiming at the *what* (rather than the who) of bodies".[4]

Susan MacWilliam's extended and elaborate engagement with the history of occult practice and

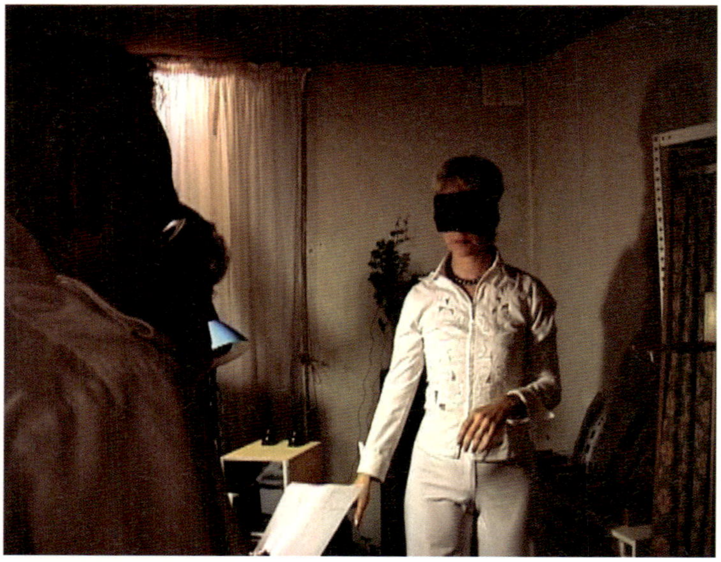

Dermo Optics, 2006,
Video, Colour, Stereo,
4mins 9secs

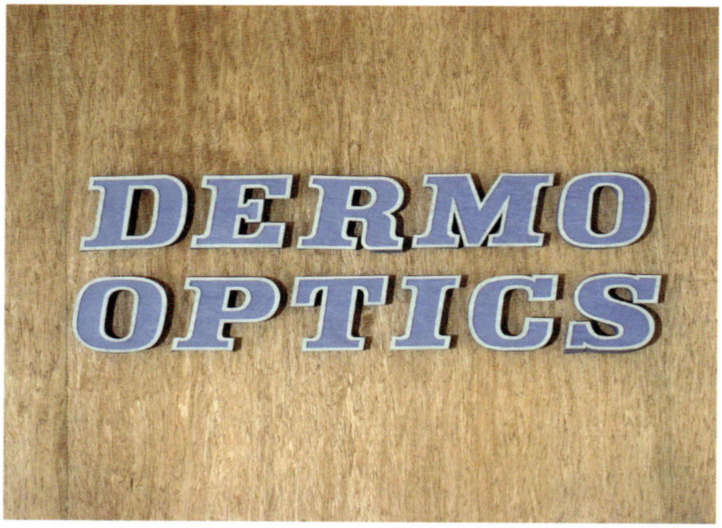

Dermo Optics, 2006
Installation detail
Wall text

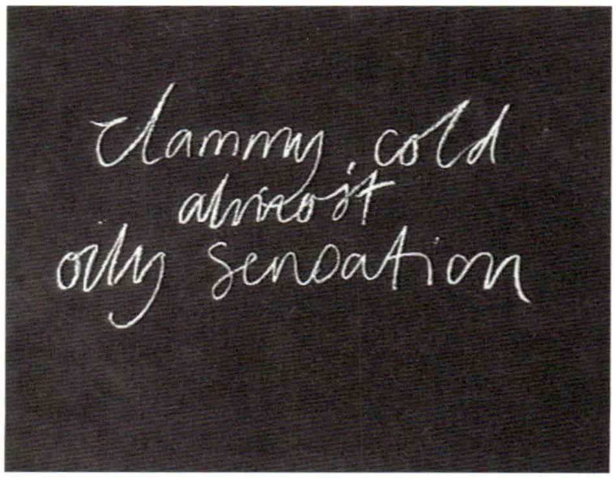

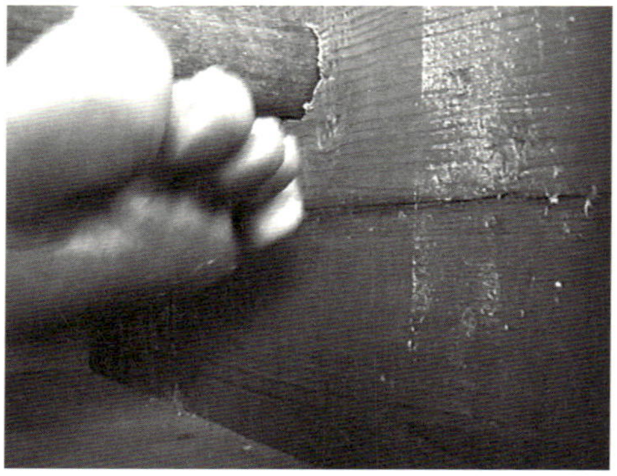

Experiment M, 1999,
Video, Black and White,
Silent, 5mins 43secs

research is only in part concerned with this particular strand of mediumistic photography and its scientific (or pseudo-scientific) counterparts. Other phenomena—other regimes of knowledge and types of spectacle—are also explored in her work: in *After Image*, 2002, the supposed persistence on the retina of the last image seen before death; in *Kuda Bux*, 2003, the theatrical performance of 'eyeless sight'. This last phenomenon is the subject too of *Dermo Optics*, her 2006 video in which Madame Duplessis, a venerable researcher at the Centre d'Information de la Couleur in Paris, investigates 'fingertip vision' in her cellar laboratory. The delicate relationships between mediums and researchers are the subject of several videos and installations: relationships into which the artist intrudes herself with consummate tact, tracing personal as well as professional networks of influence and affinity in such works as *Eileen*, 2008, in which the aged daughter of the celebrated Irish medium Eileen Garrett recalls key episodes from her mother's life. But the central encounter between the body of the medium and the photographic apparatus remains for MacWilliam an abiding concern.

In 1999, she completed *Experiment M*, an installation and two-screen video piece that in several senses sets the scene for the rigour and fascination of the present work. *Experiment M* draws on research undertaken by William J Crawford in Belfast between 1914 and 1920. Crawford's subjects, the Goligher family, conducted séances during which the youngest daughter, Kathleen, was observed to levitate tables; in his written account, "psychic rods or columns" of ectoplasm are said to have issued from between her

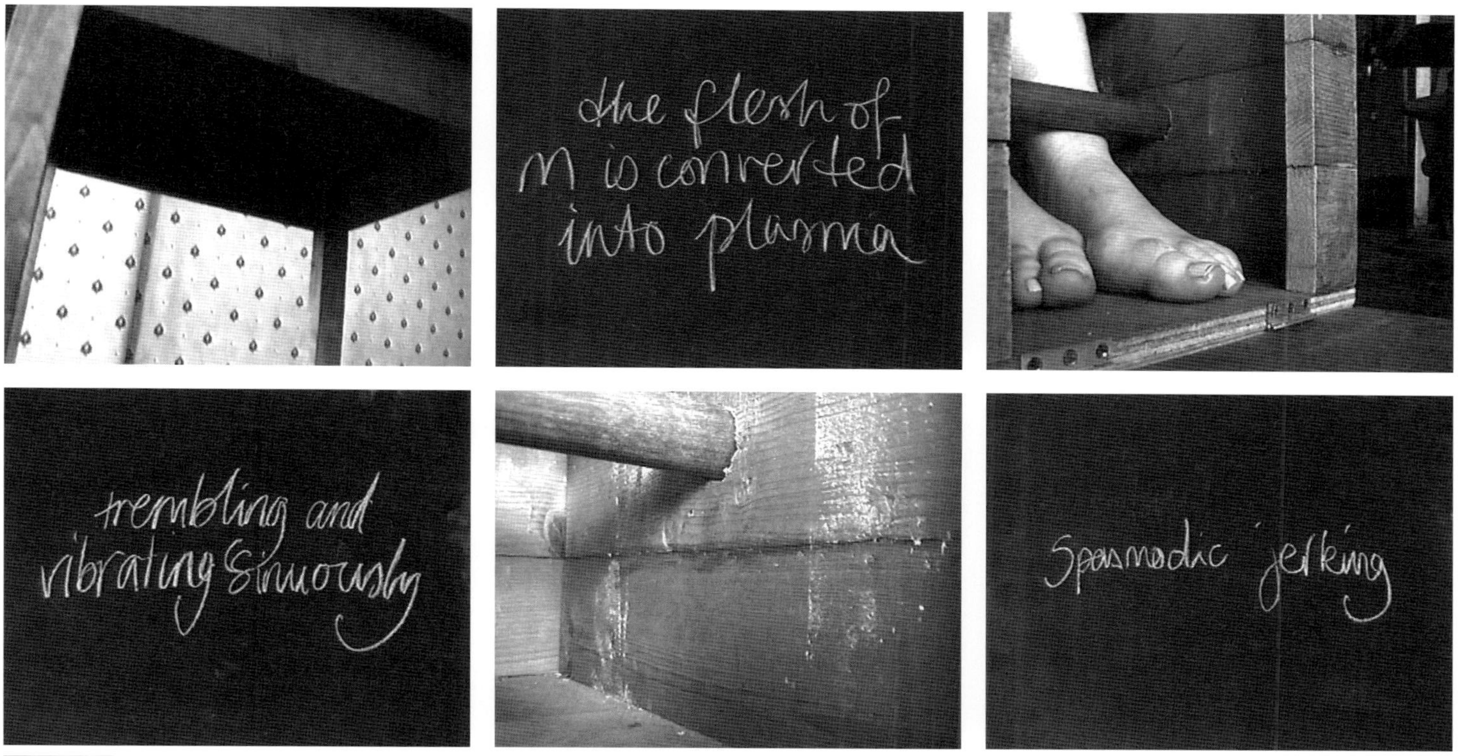

legs. What exercises MacWilliam in this case is precisely the junction and disparity between the physicality of the scene—the restricted and writhing female body reproduced on screen—and the researcher's intimate account of that body. Phrases excerpted by the artist from Crawford's *The Psychic Structures at the Goligher Circle* and *The Reality of Psychic Phenomena* include "intermittent muscular jerking", "ejection or injection of the psychic stuff" and "medium wore clean white knickers". In sum, *Experiment M* is a study in the textual and photographic representation of a body that pulses with meaning.

F-L-A-M-M-A-R-I-O-N is in part an advance on that investigation. Once again we are invited to enter imaginatively into the space of the séance cabinet, to bear witness to a body at the moment it is translated—where 'translated' has its archaic sense of physical reinvention—into words and images. The Winnipeg 'teleplasm' is in one sense an allegory for what happens to the mediumistic or the hysteric body before the implacable regard of the camera: that is, the body is translated into words. (In the regime at Salpêtrière, for example, the photograph is an intermediate stage in the rendering of the woman's body into a written account by Charcot himself or one of his subordinates.) Where the appearance of a teleplasmic 'ship' during one of Hamilton's séances, and the revelation of 'a finger of Katie King' during another session, are alarming but conventional, the hovering legend "FLAMMARION" introduces another order into the space of the séance. It reveals that the spirited body is above all a legible body and that both mediums and researchers are engaged in acts of translation.

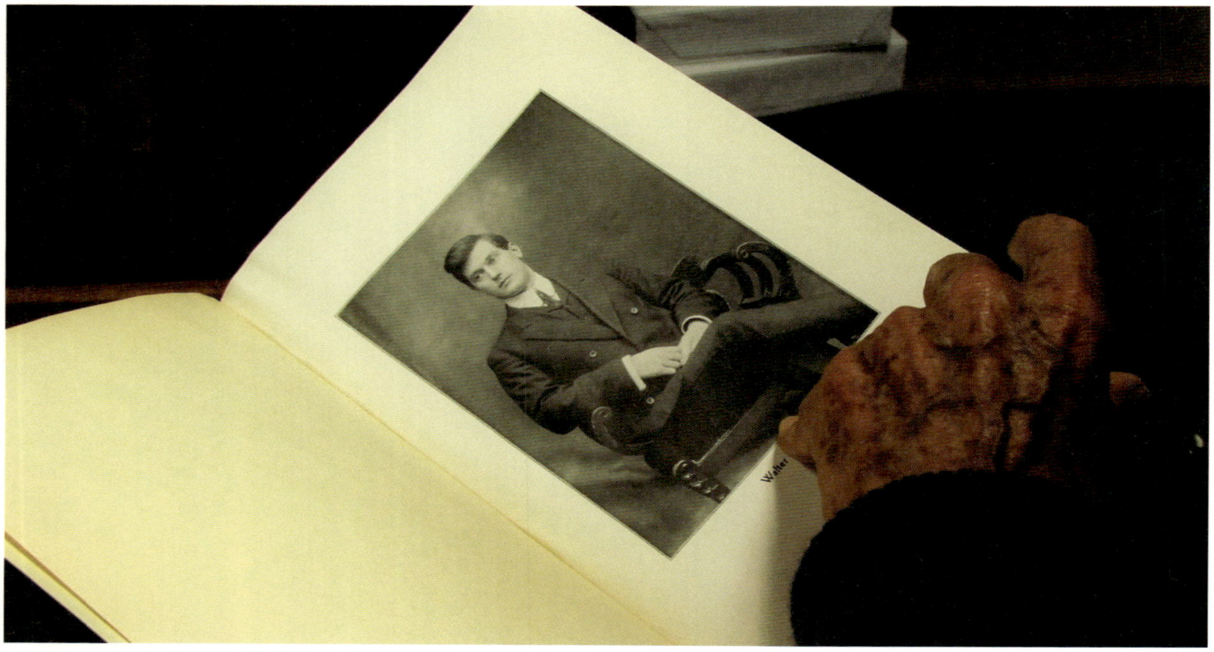

F-L-A-M-M-A-R-I-O-N, 2009, Video, Colour, Stereo

F-L-A-M-M-A-R-I-O-N, 2009, Video, Colour, Stereo

For the most part, the 'text' to be read and interpreted in the séance cabinet was the body of a woman, though the spirit channeled or expressed by that body could well be male. In Winnipeg, for example, the medium Mary Marshall materialised the images of William Gladstone, Arthur Conan Doyle and the Victorian evangelist Charles Haddon Spurgeon, while the guiding spirit of many of the sessions was named Walter. In *F-L-A-M-M-A-R-I-O-N*, MacWilliam disrupts the process of translation, becoming herself the researcher who records a male voice that speaks not from the spirit realm but from out of the histories of spirit photography and filmmaking. The writer Ciaran Carson intones words and phrases from the lexicons of photography and film—"cross-cutting, cut away, cyclorama, definition, depth of field, diaphragm"—while the parapsychologist William Roll repeats the name of Camille Flammarion and reflects on the events in Winnipeg in 1931. In a curious reversal, the two men—both interpreters of sorts, both committed to 'hearing voices' from other places and times—are made to embody, as if unconsciously, the abstractions of word and narrative. MacWilliam, in turn, has come to resemble the psychic investigator or the inquisitive physician, the figure who (like Crookes or Charcot) commands the body to speak.

What remains in *F-L-A-M-M-A-R-I-O-N* of the early experiments in spirit photography, then, is this sense of an enclosed and vocalising or (in the case of the textual teleplasm) silently signaling body, intently scrutinised by artist and audience alike. In MacWilliam's work, however, the distinction between

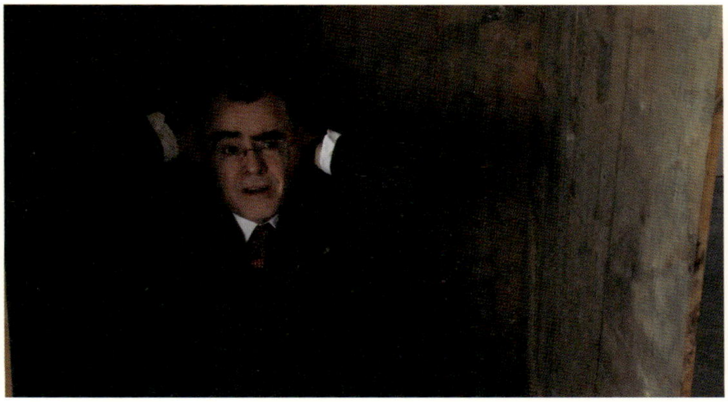

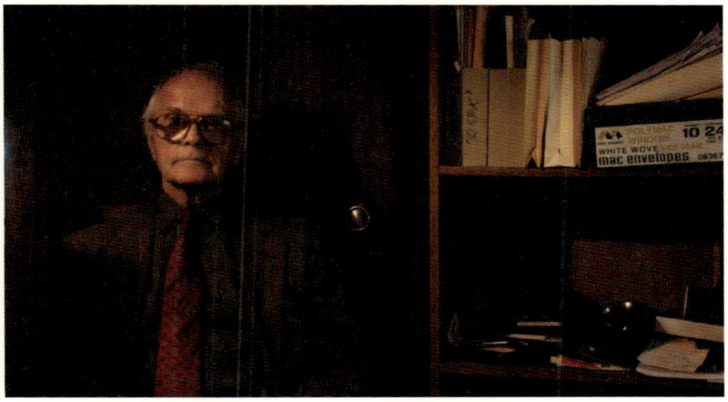

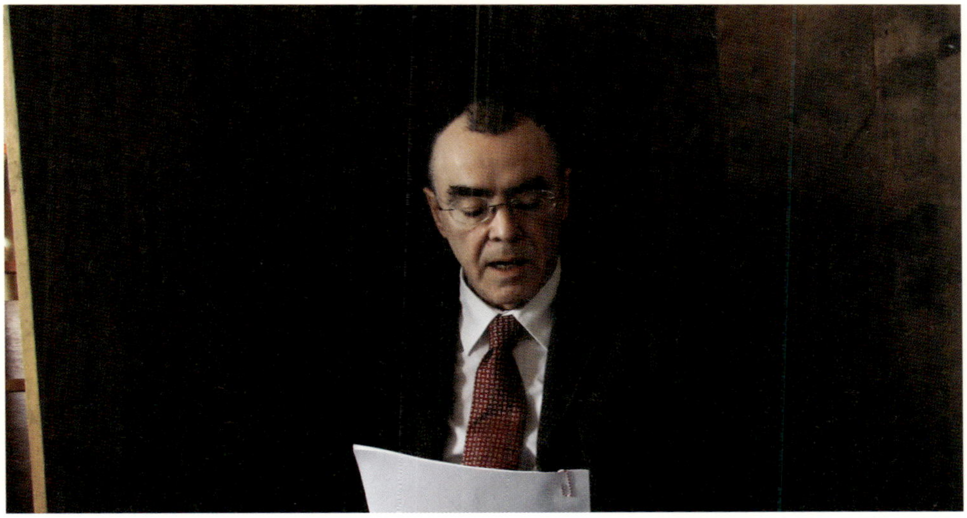

spirit and spectator is hard to maintain: the researcher becomes the subject of the research, the writer is overwritten or ventriloquised by the history he affects to recount. Photography, as De Quincey knew, is a way of visualising and invigilating spectres; but the traffic of phantom meanings is never only in one direction. As MacWilliam's open and collaborative practice reveals, the darkened chambers of the séance cabinet and the camera itself are spaces where not only is the spirit world said to transmute into material reality, but the solid observer feels himself or herself dissolve in a medium made of word, image and voice.

1. De Quincey, Thomas, *Suspiria De Profundis*, in *Confessions of an English Opium-Eater*, London: Macdonald, 1956, p. 447.

2. Chéroux, Clément, Andreas Fischer et al, *The Perfect Medium: Photography and the Occult*, New Haven: Yale University Press, 2005, pp. 56ff.

3. Crookes, Sir William, "Spirit Forms", quoted in *The Perfect Medium*, p. 173.

4. Didi-Huberman, Georges, *Invention of Hysteria: Charcot and the Photographic Archive of the Salpêtrière*, trans., Alisa Hartz, Cambridge, MA: MIT Press, 2003, p. 32 and passim.

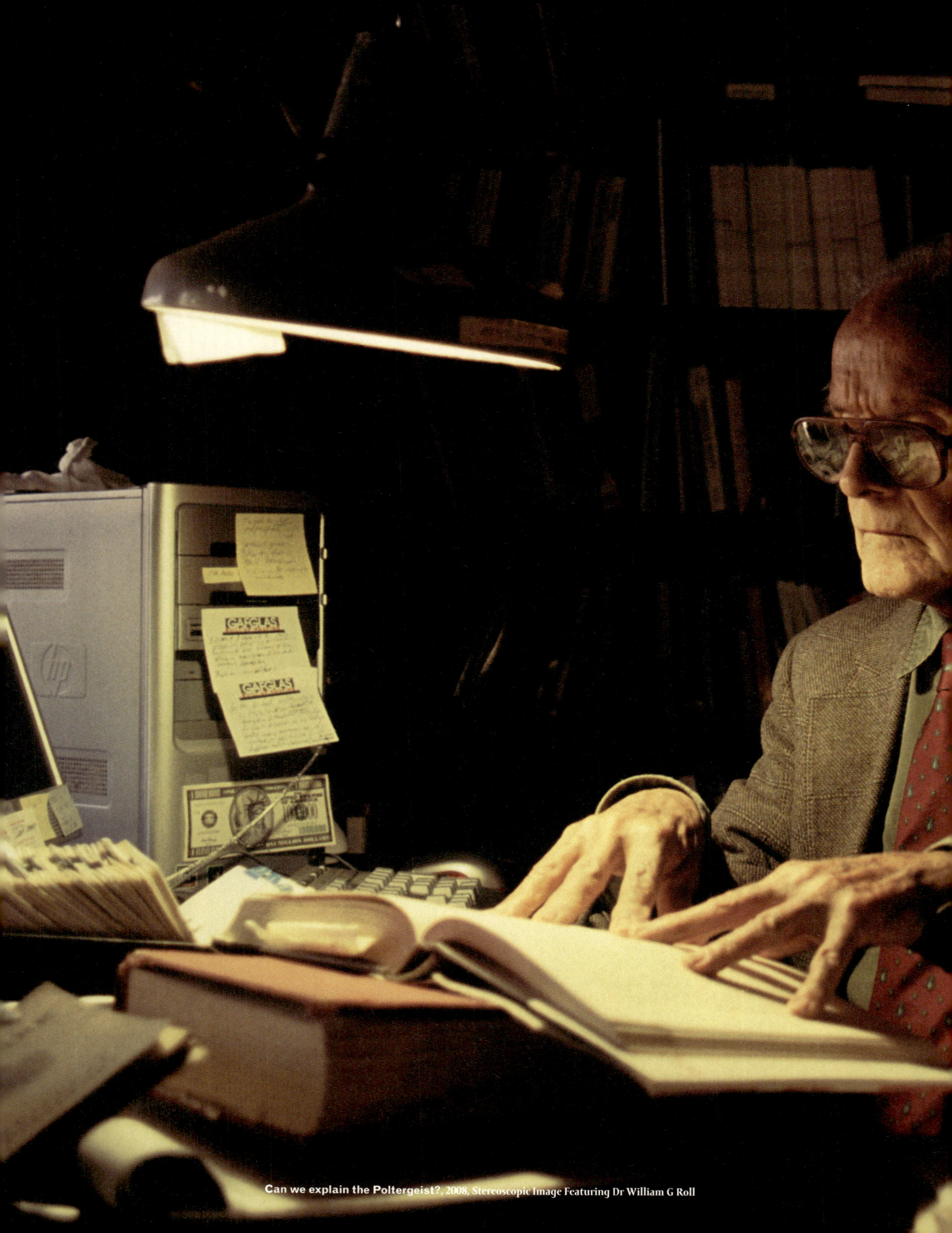

Can we explain the Poltergeist?, 2008, Stereoscopic Image Featuring Dr William G Roll

2009, Video, Colour, Stereo

F-L-A-M-M-A-R-I-O-N

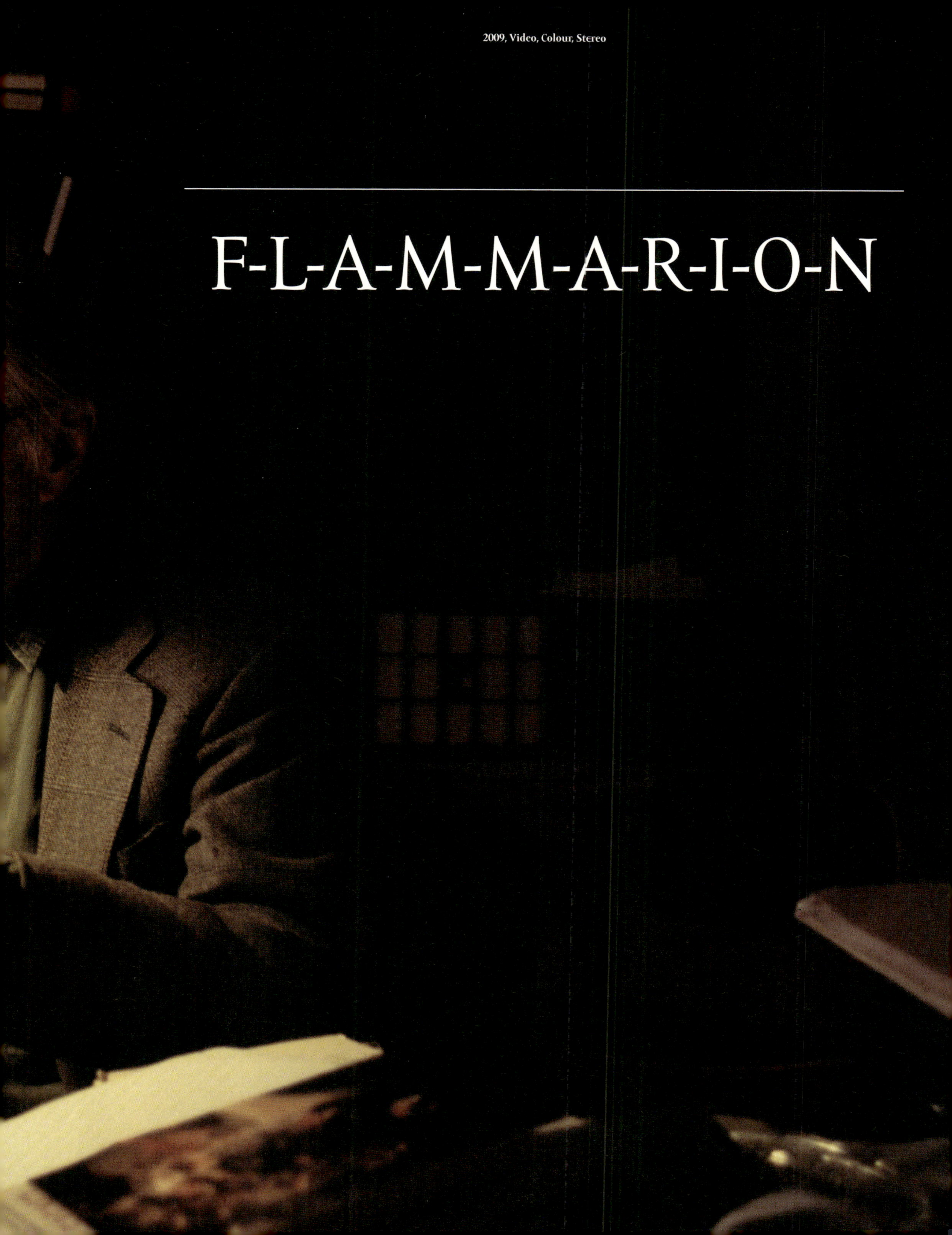

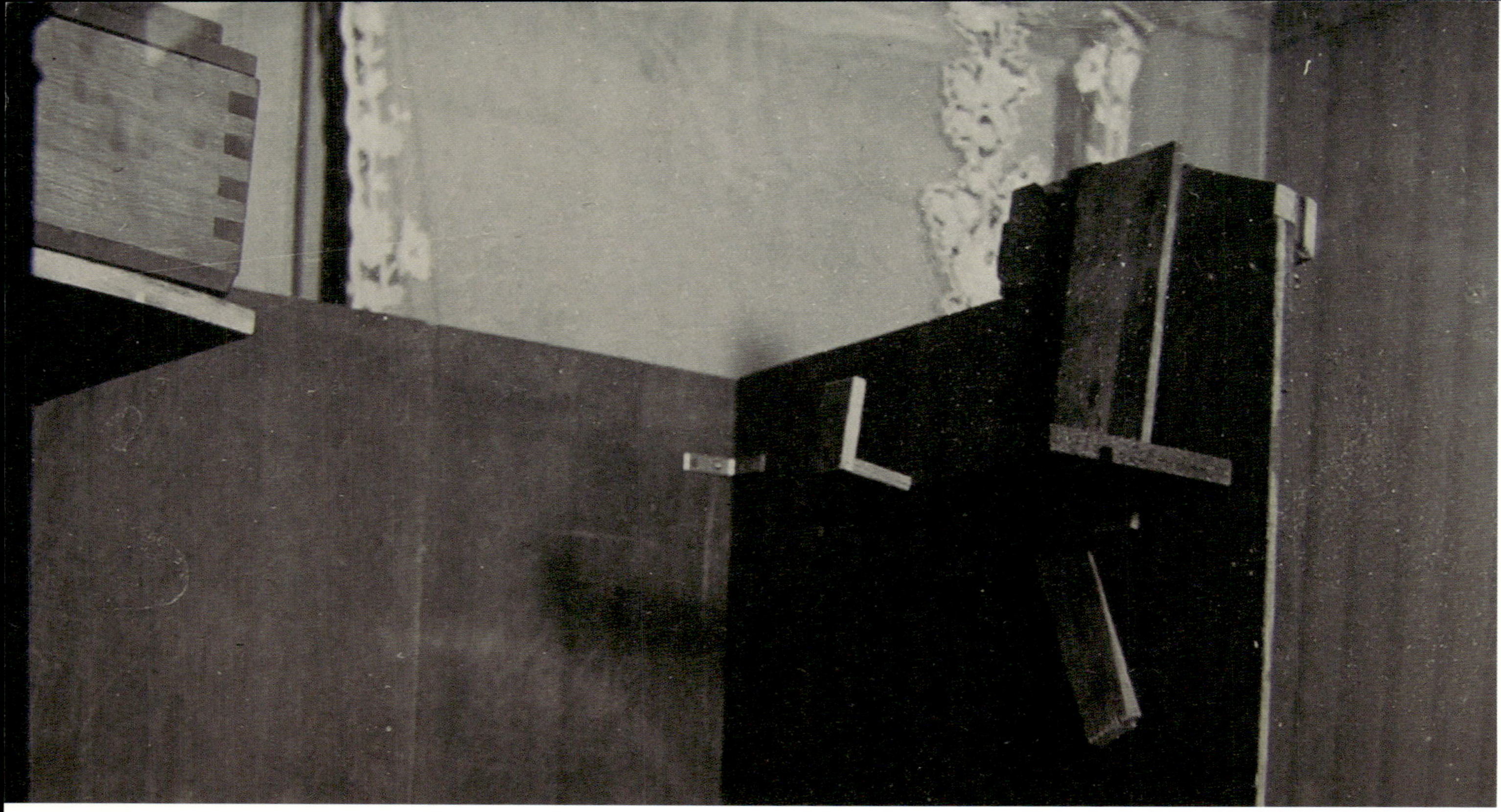

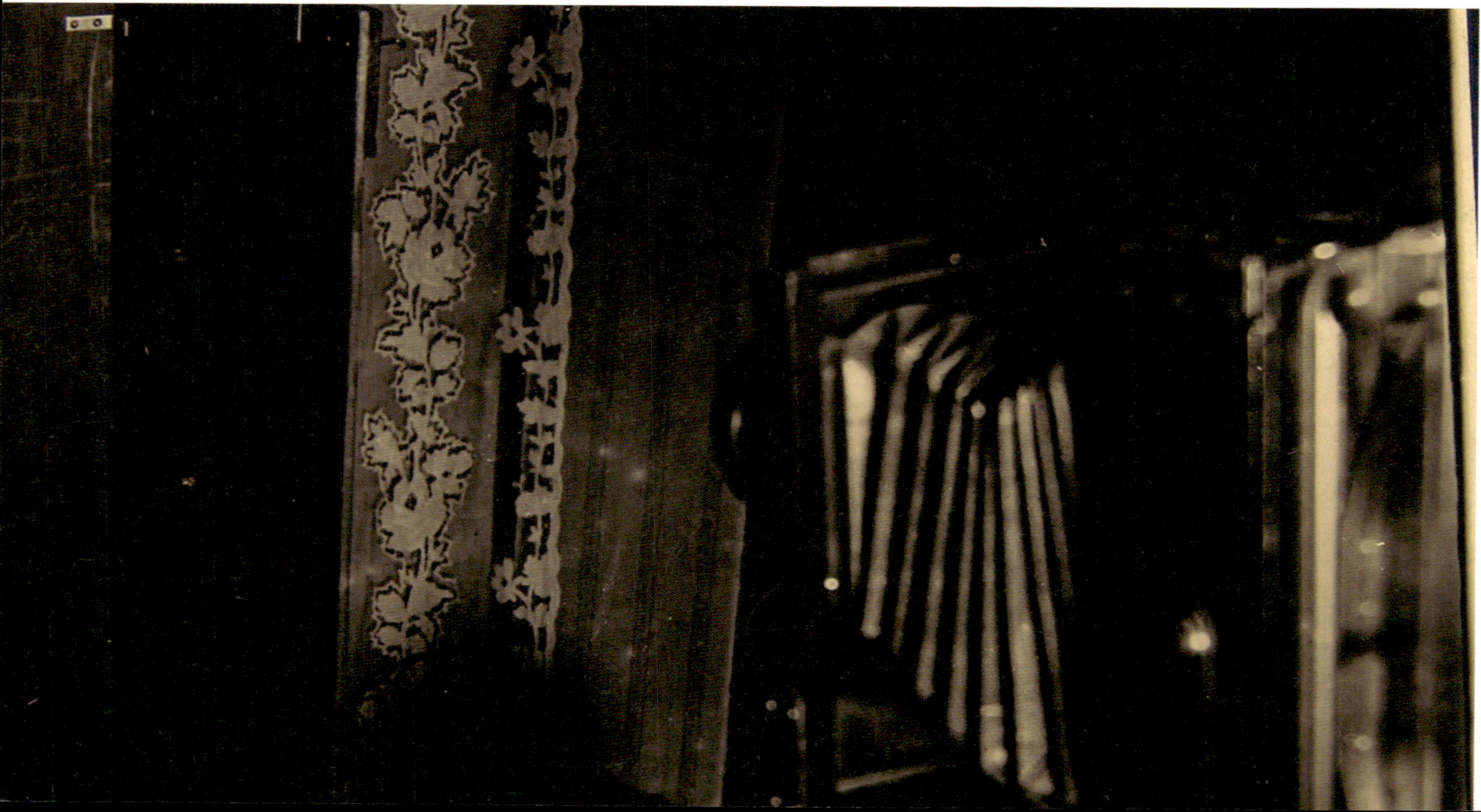

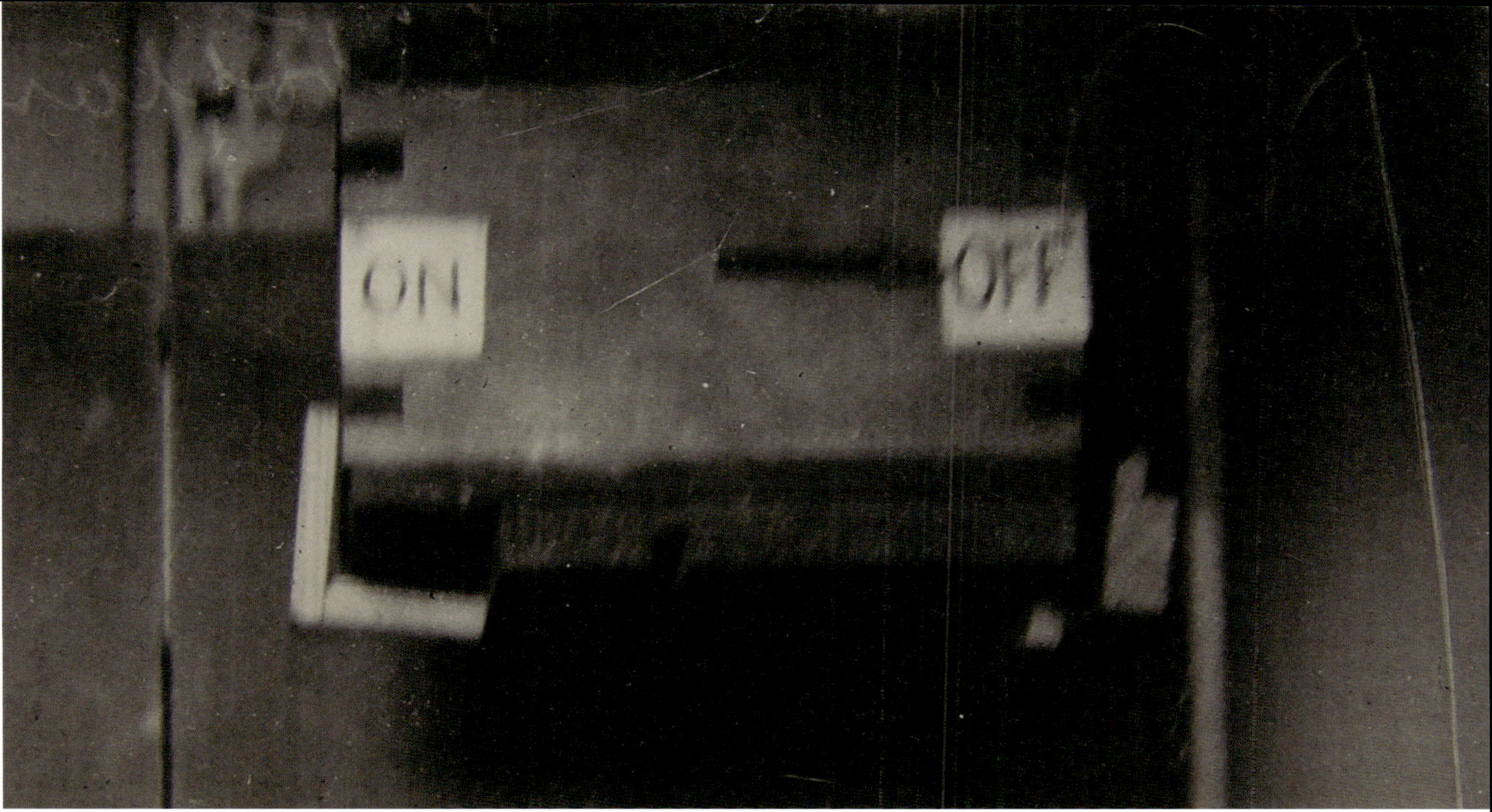
ON
OFF

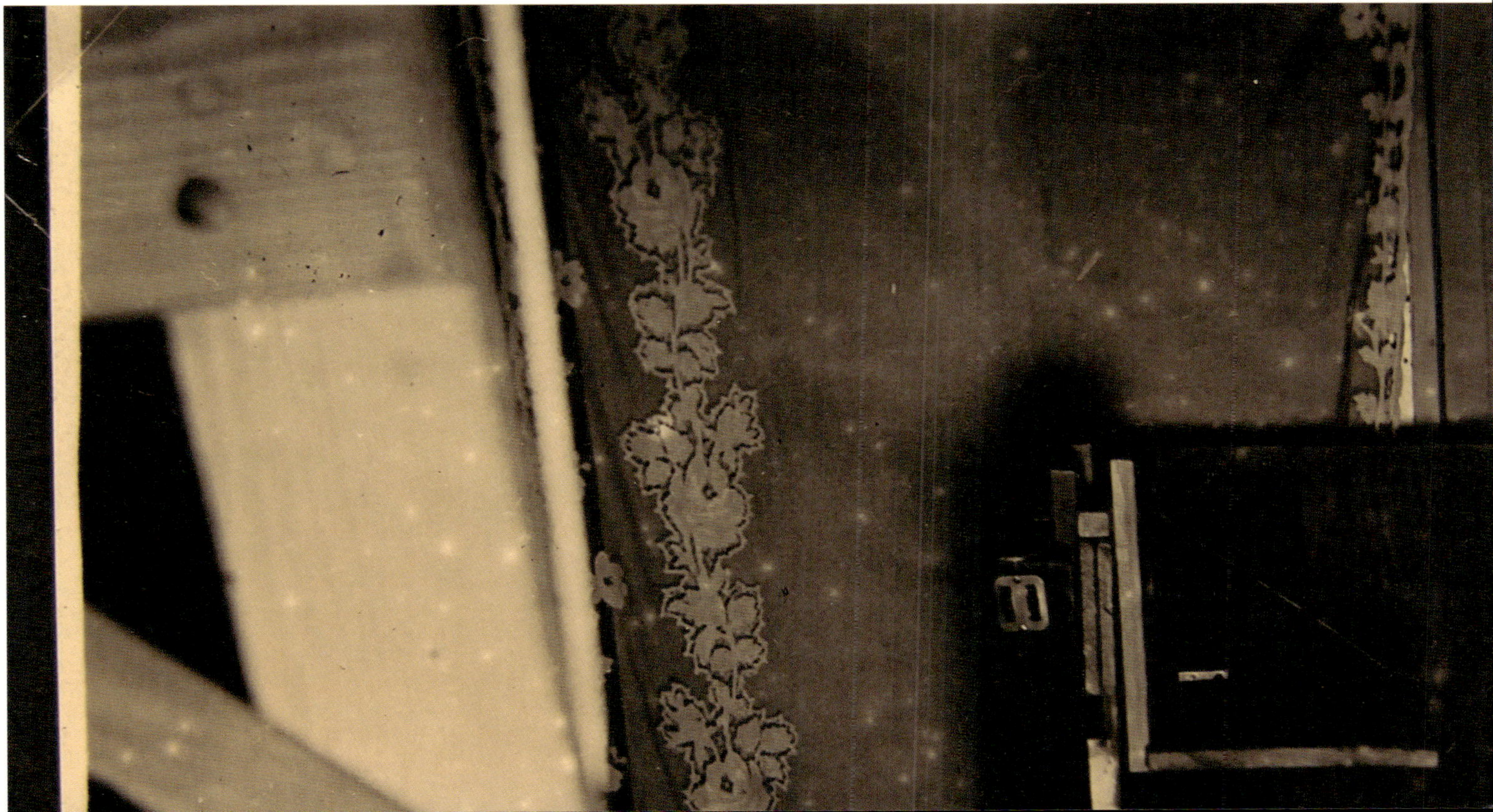

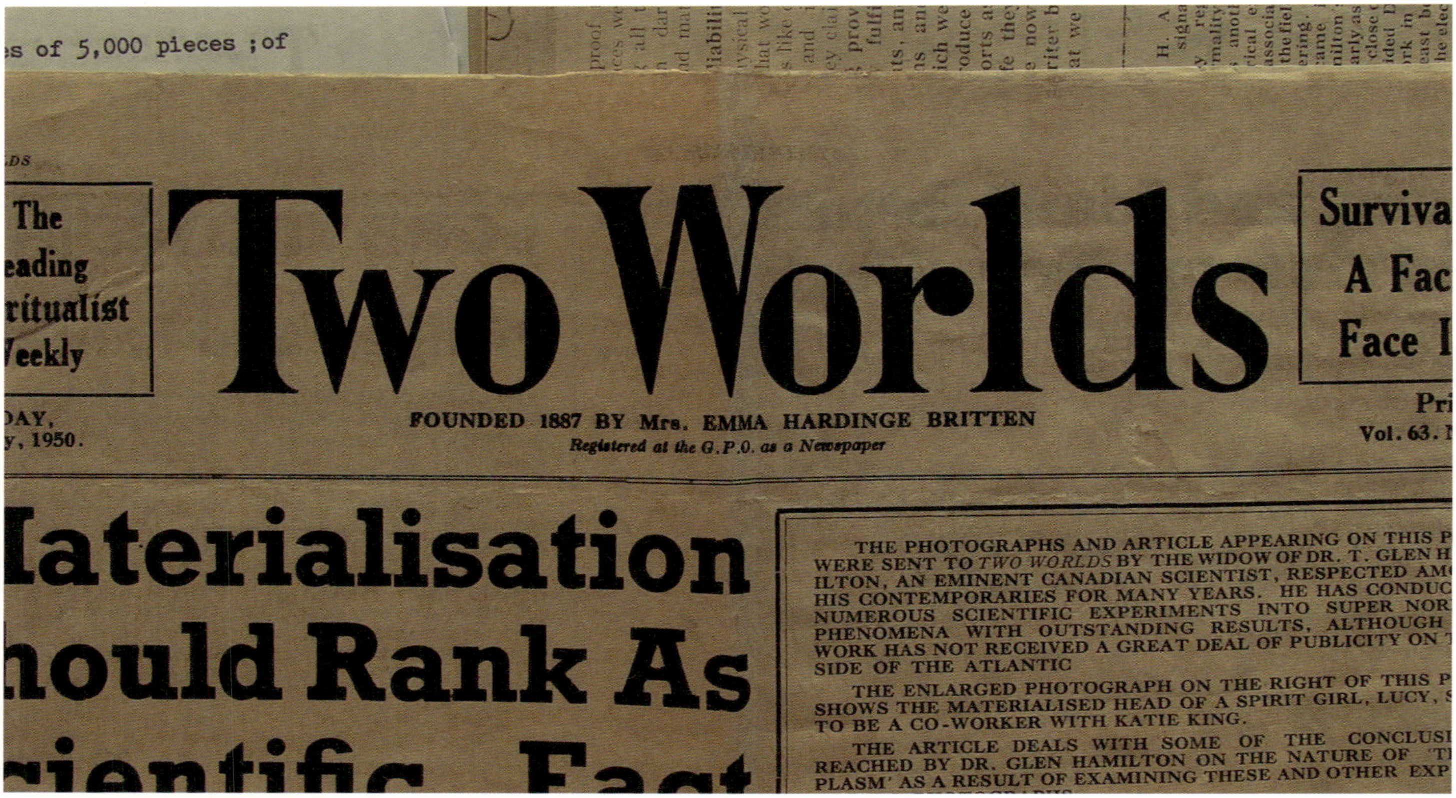

es of 5,000 pieces ;of

The Leading Spiritualist Weekly

Two Worlds

Survival A Fact Face I

DAY, y, 1950.

FOUNDED 1887 BY Mrs. EMMA HARDINGE BRITTEN

Registered at the G.P.O. as a Newspaper

Pri Vol. 63.

Materialisation Should Rank As Scientific Fact

THE PHOTOGRAPHS AND ARTICLE APPEARING ON THIS P WERE SENT TO *TWO WORLDS* BY THE WIDOW OF DR. T. GLEN H ILTON, AN EMINENT CANADIAN SCIENTIST, RESPECTED AMO HIS CONTEMPORARIES FOR MANY YEARS. HE HAS CONDUC NUMEROUS SCIENTIFIC EXPERIMENTS INTO SUPER NOR PHENOMENA WITH OUTSTANDING RESULTS, ALTHOUGH WORK HAS NOT RECEIVED A GREAT DEAL OF PUBLICITY ON T SIDE OF THE ATLANTIC

THE ENLARGED PHOTOGRAPH ON THE RIGHT OF THIS P SHOWS THE MATERIALISED HEAD OF A SPIRIT GIRL, LUCY, S TO BE A CO-WORKER WITH KATIE KING.

THE ARTICLE DEALS WITH SOME OF THE CONCLUSI REACHED BY DR. GLEN HAMILTON ON THE NATURE OF 'T PLASM' AS A RESULT OF EXAMINING THESE AND OTHER EXP

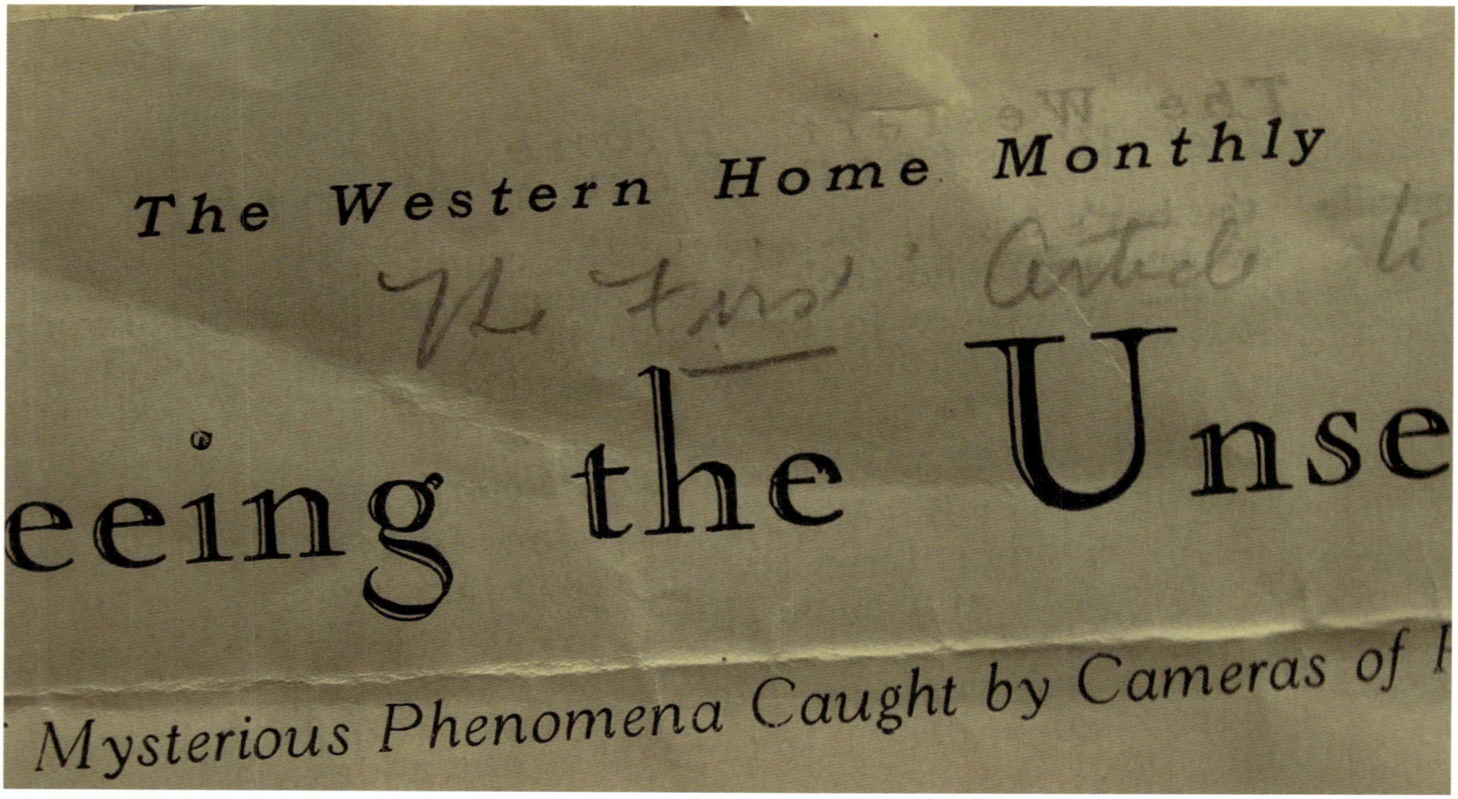

The Western Home Monthly

The first article

Seeing the Unse

Mysterious Phenomena Caught by Cameras of

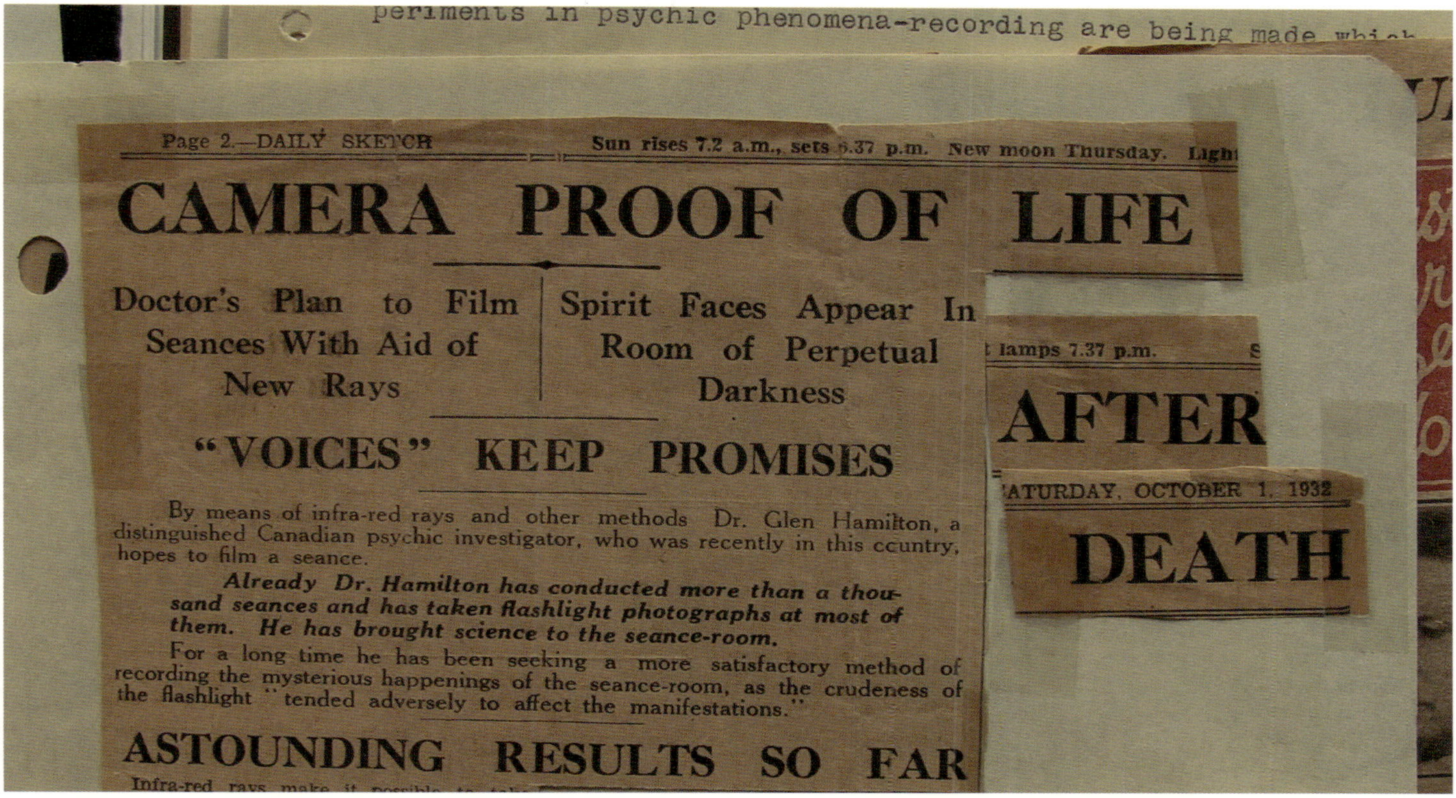

periments in psychic phenomena-recording are being made which

Page 2.—DAILY SKETCH — Sun rises 7.2 a.m., sets 6.37 p.m. New moon Thursday. Light

CAMERA PROOF OF LIFE

Doctor's Plan to Film Seances With Aid of New Rays

Spirit Faces Appear In Room of Perpetual Darkness

"VOICES" KEEP PROMISES

By means of infra-red rays and other methods Dr. Glen Hamilton, a distinguished Canadian psychic investigator, who was recently in this country, hopes to film a seance.

Already Dr. Hamilton has conducted more than a thousand seances and has taken flashlight photographs at most of them. He has brought science to the seance-room.

For a long time he has been seeking a more satisfactory method of recording the mysterious happenings of the seance-room, as the crudeness of the flashlight "tended adversely to affect the manifestations."

ASTOUNDING RESULTS SO FAR

Infra-red rays make it possible to take

t lamps 7.37 p.m.

AFTER

SATURDAY, OCTOBER 1, 1932

DEATH

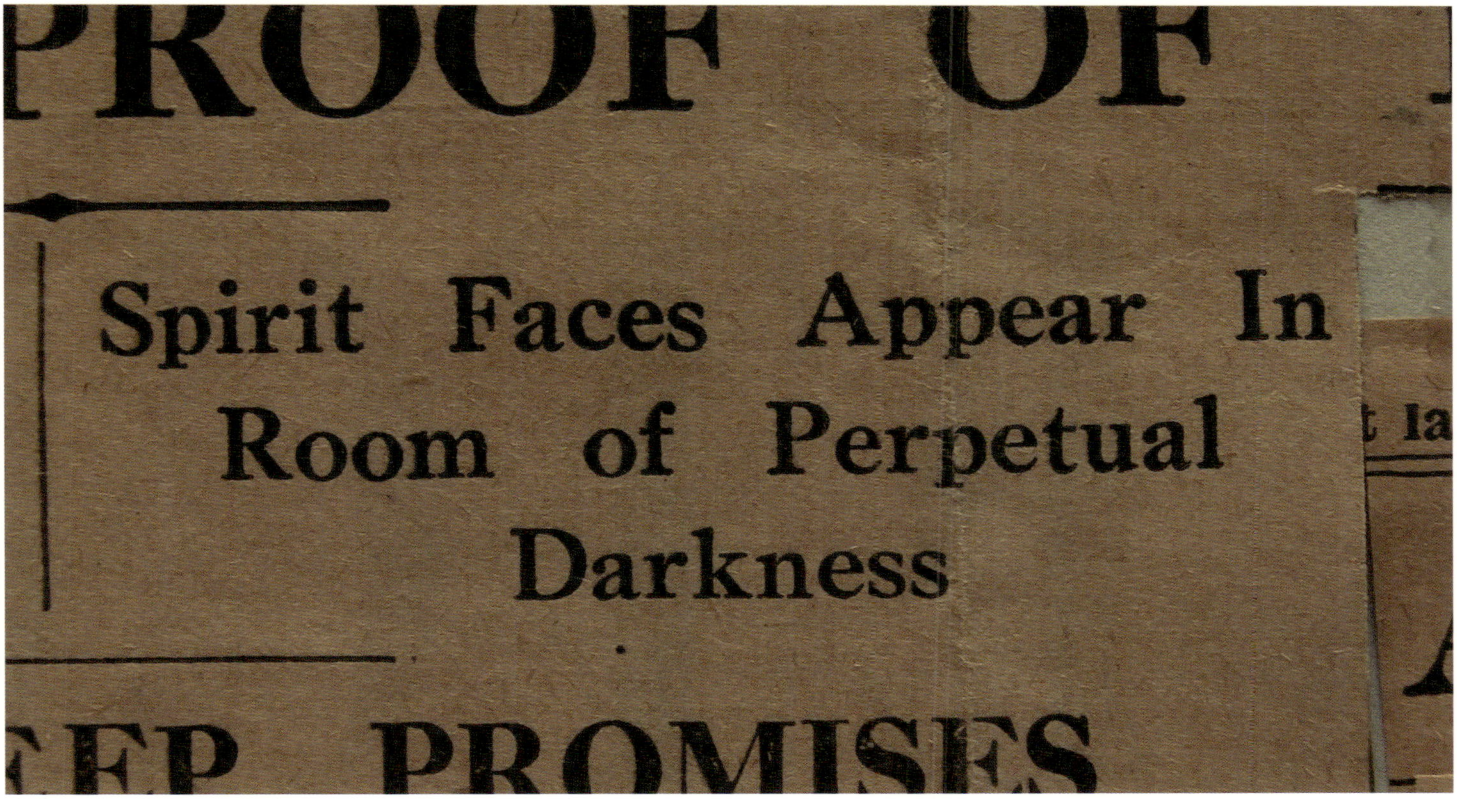

PROOF OF

Spirit Faces Appear In Room of Perpetual Darkness

EEP PROMISES

t la

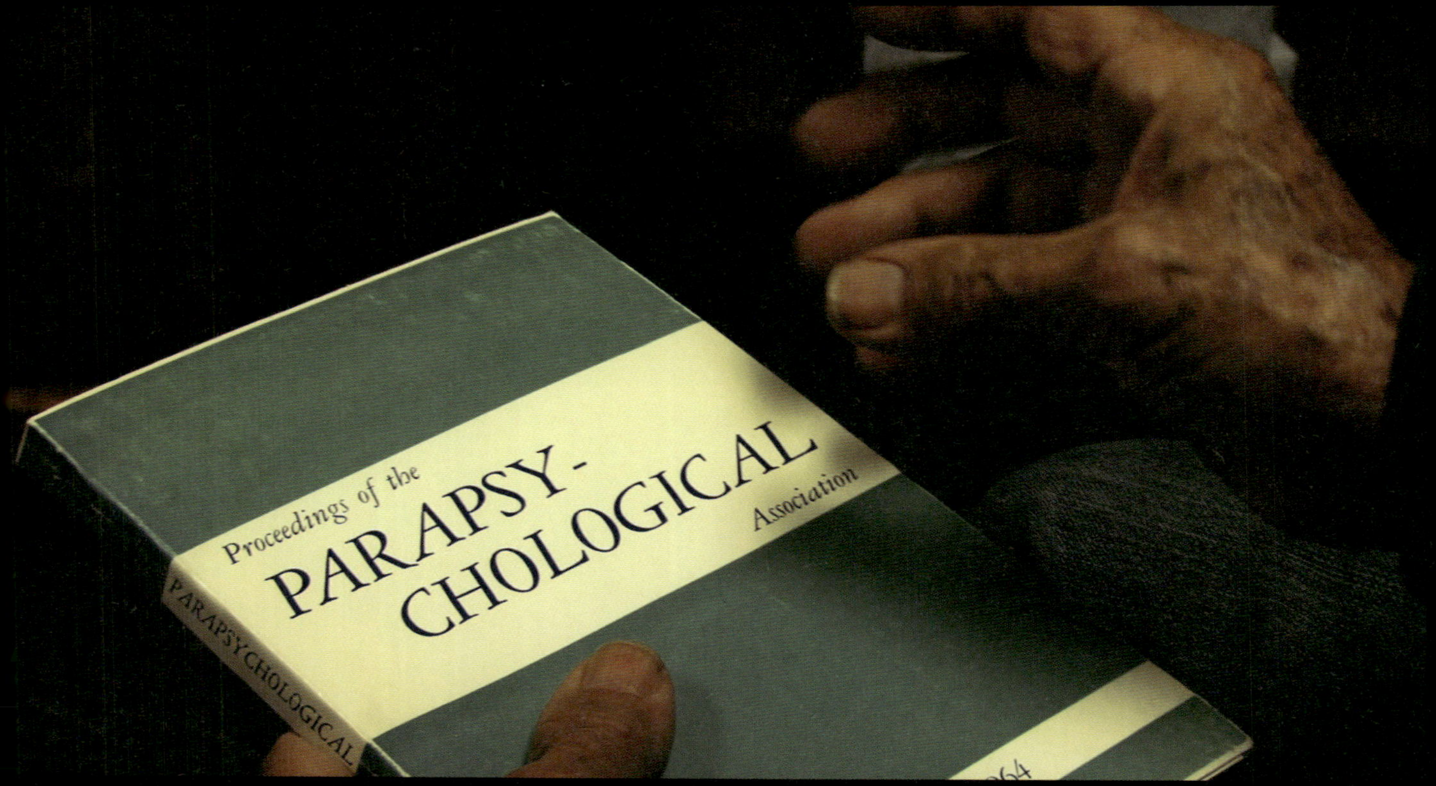
Proceedings of the
PARAPSY-
CHOLOGICAL
Association
PARAPSYCHOLOGICAL

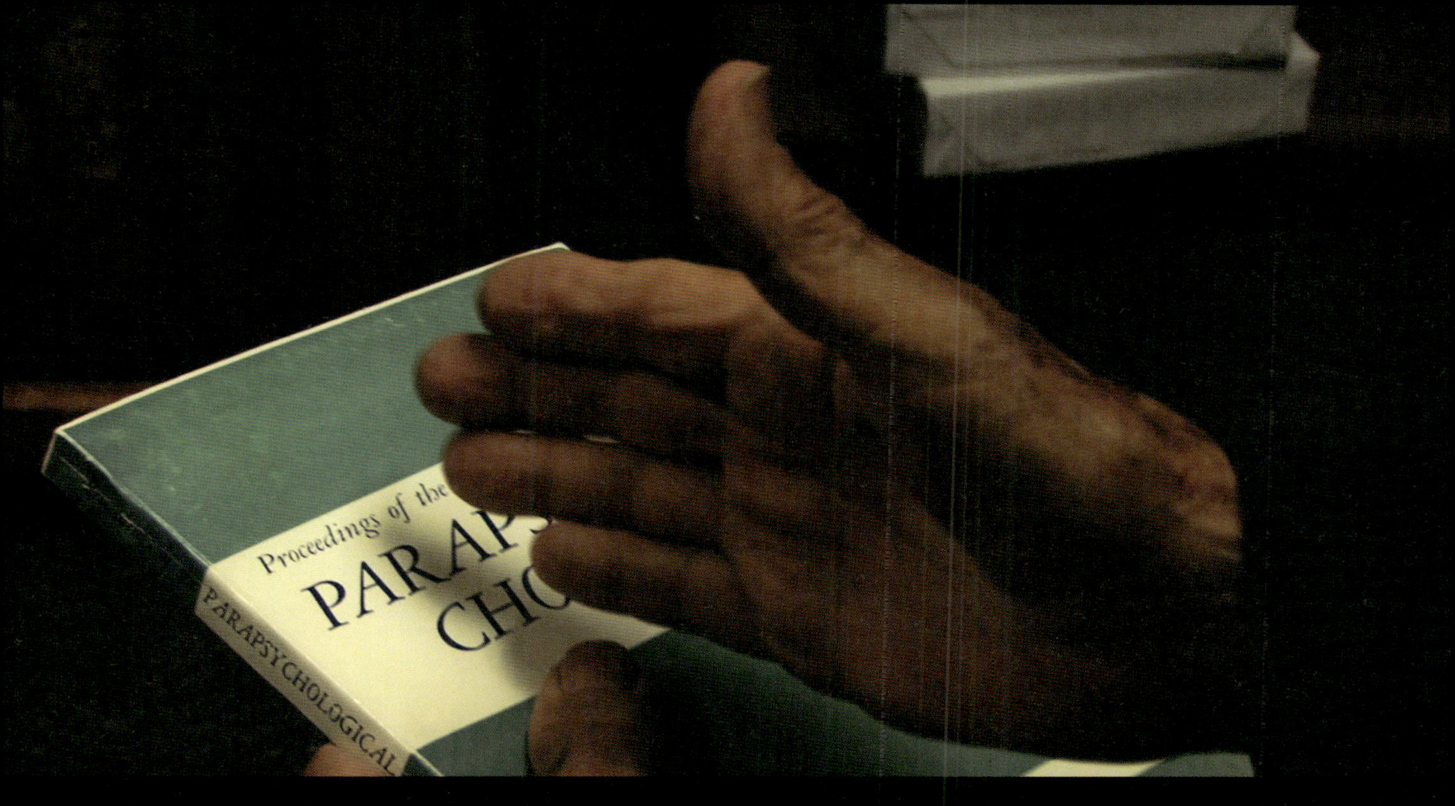
Proceedings of the
PARAPSYCHOLOGICAL

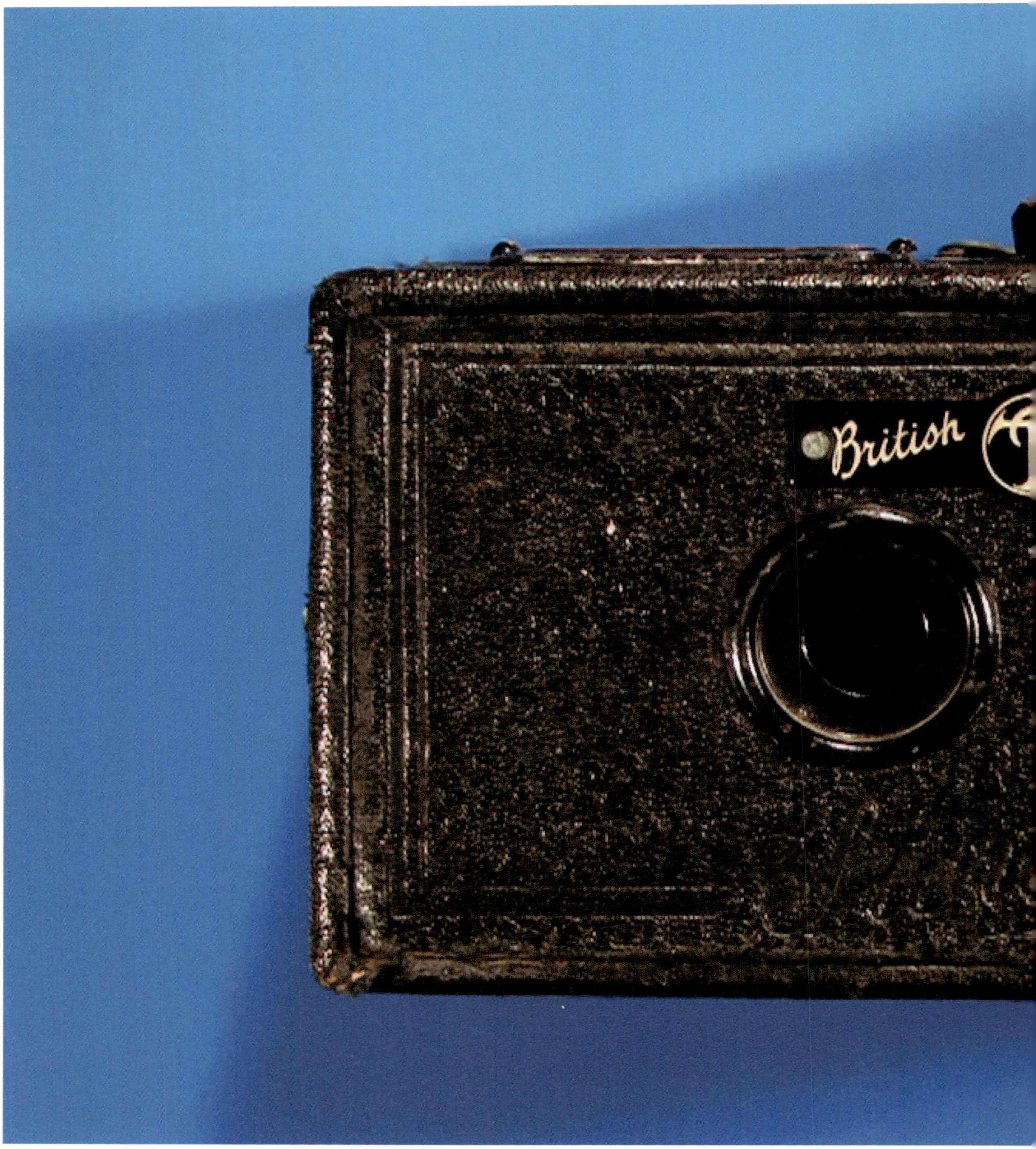
British

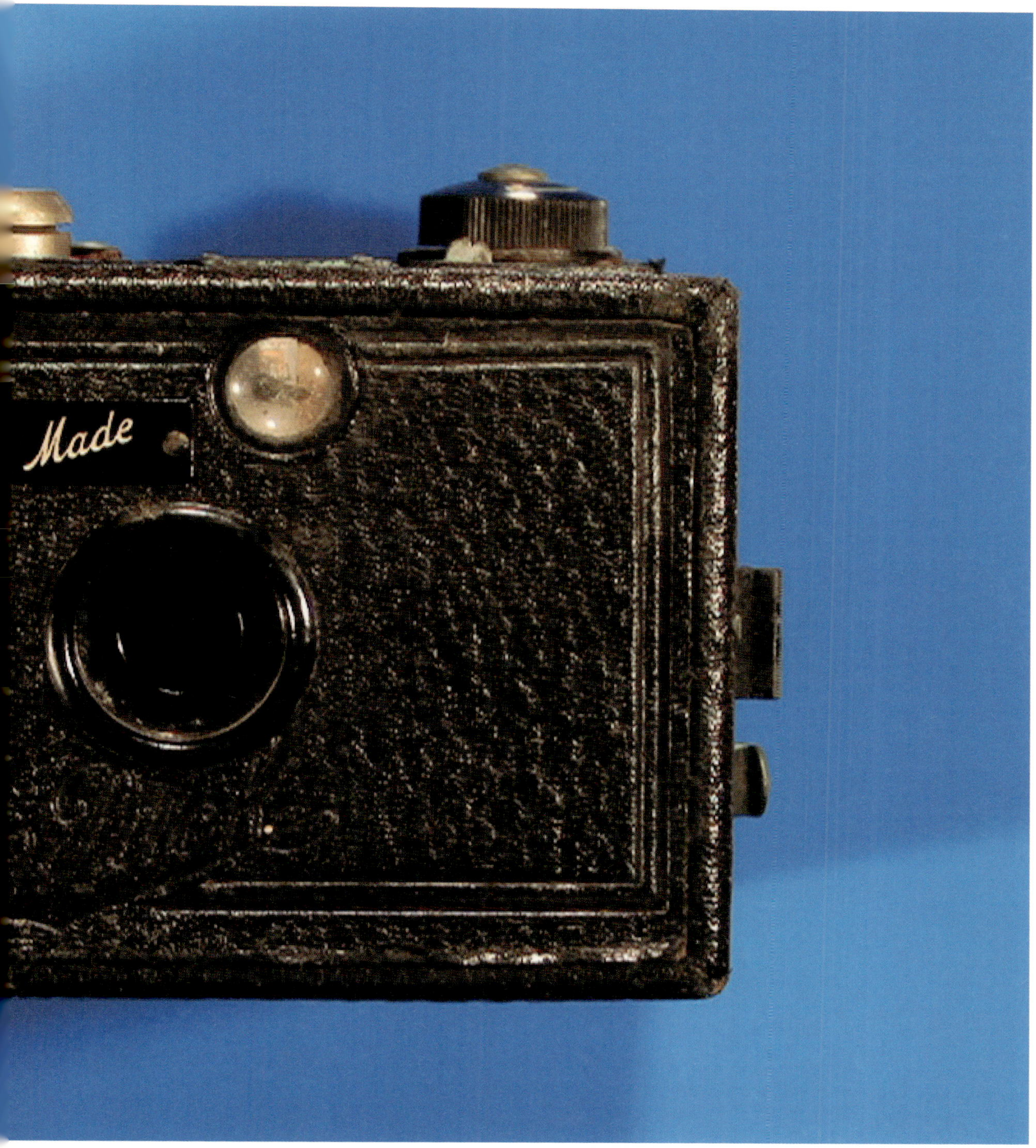
Made

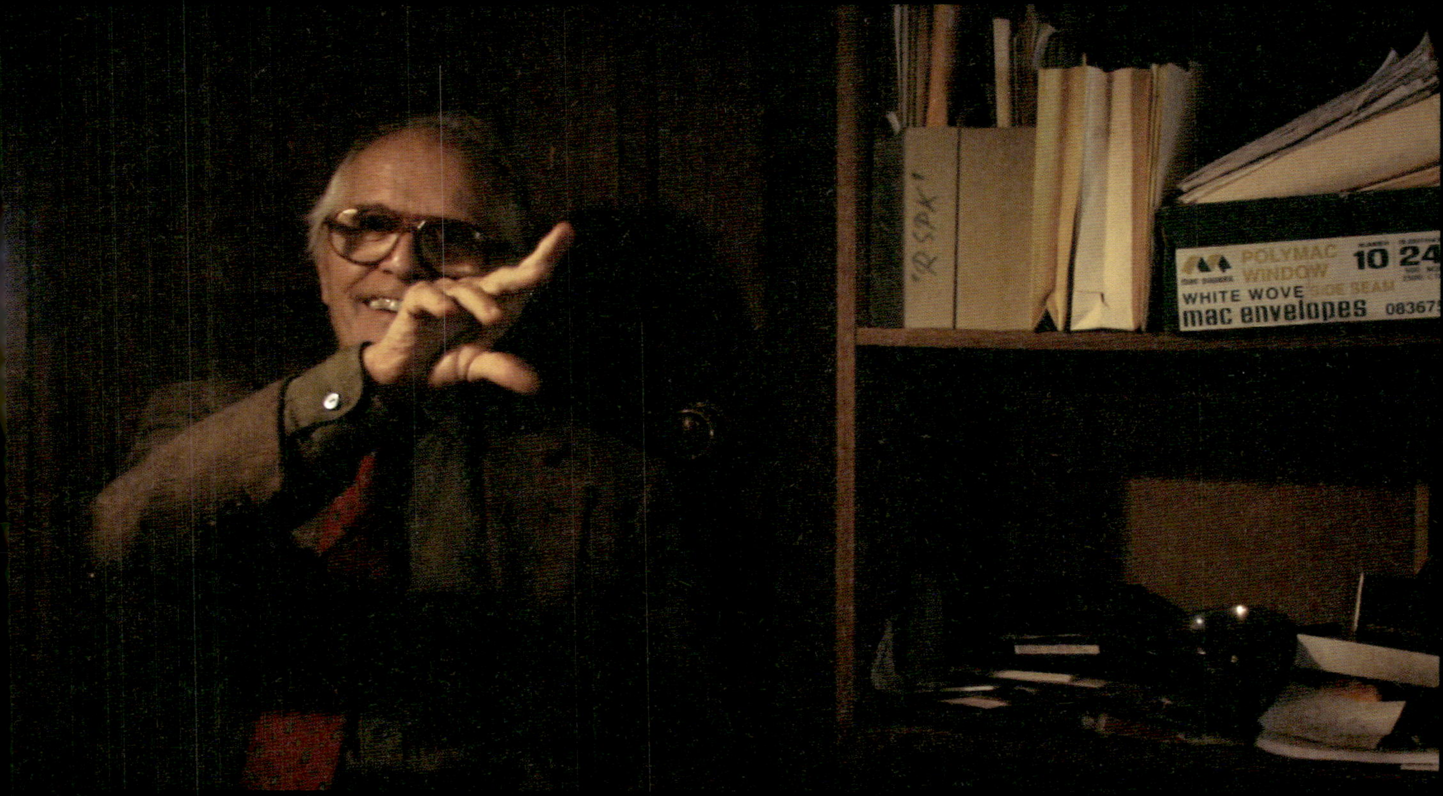
POLYMAC
WINDOW
10
WHITE WOVE SIDE SEAM
mac envelopes

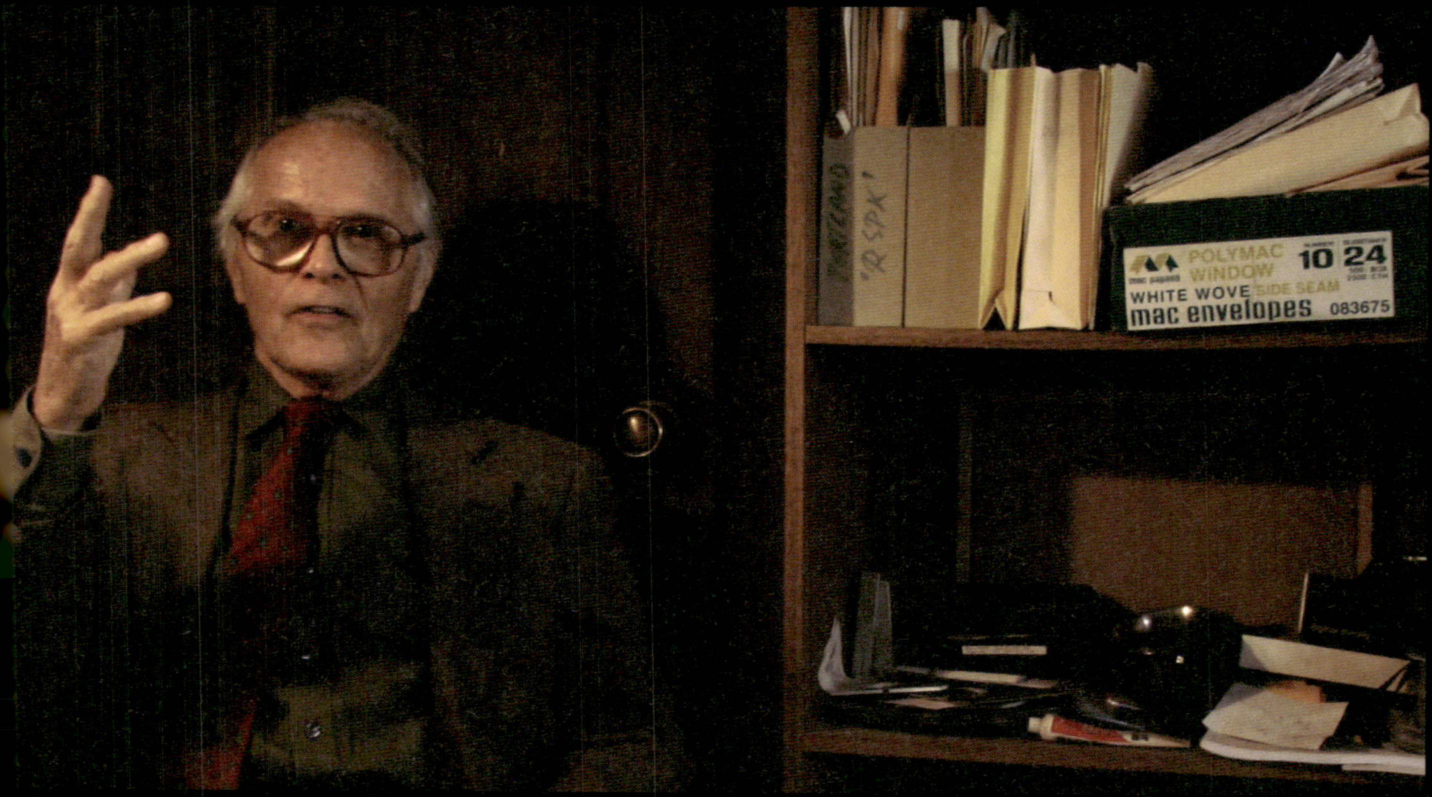
POLYMAC
WINDOW
10 24
WHITE WOVE SIDE SEAM
mac envelopes 083675

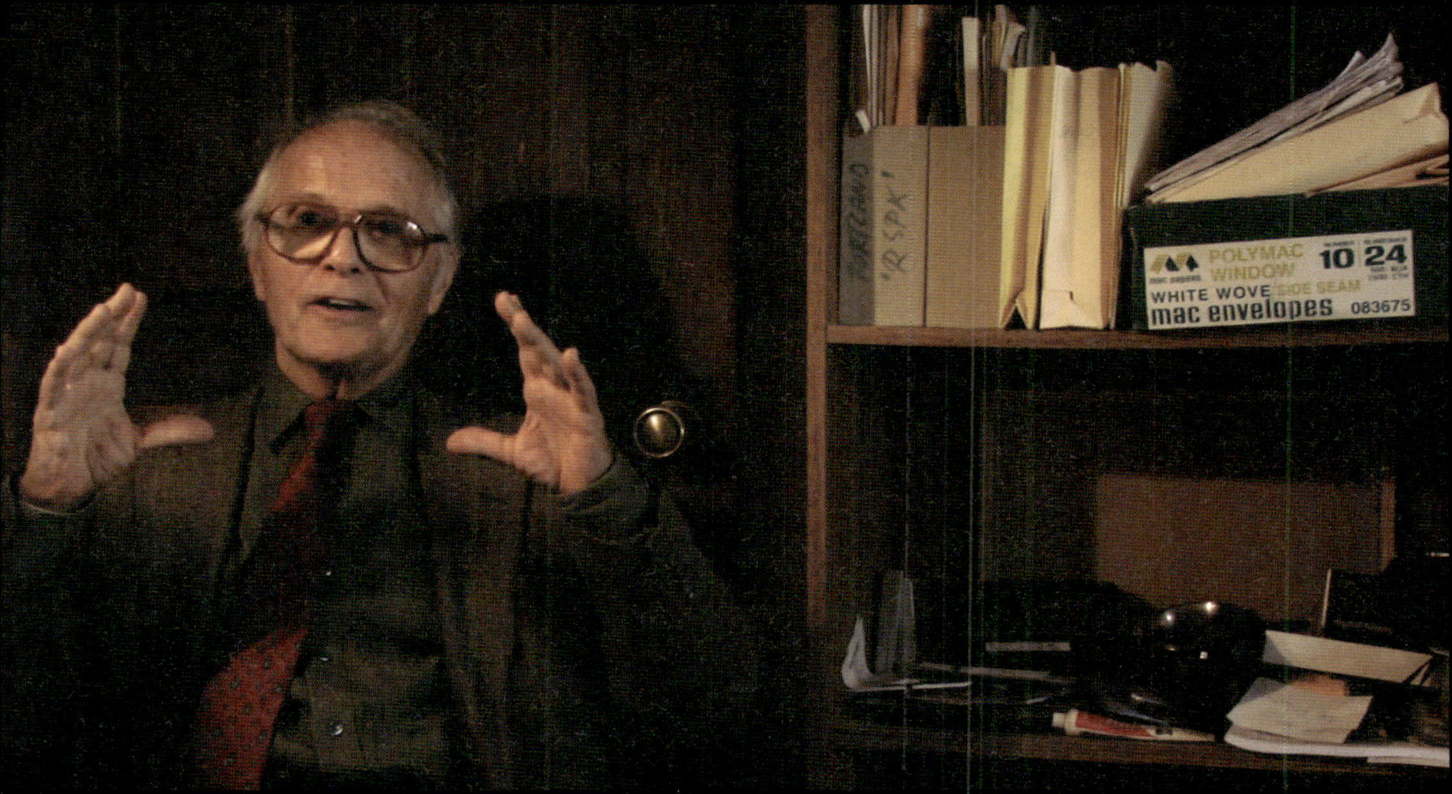
"RSPK"
POLYMAC
WINDOW
10
24
WHITE WOVE
SIDE SEAM
mac envelopes
083675

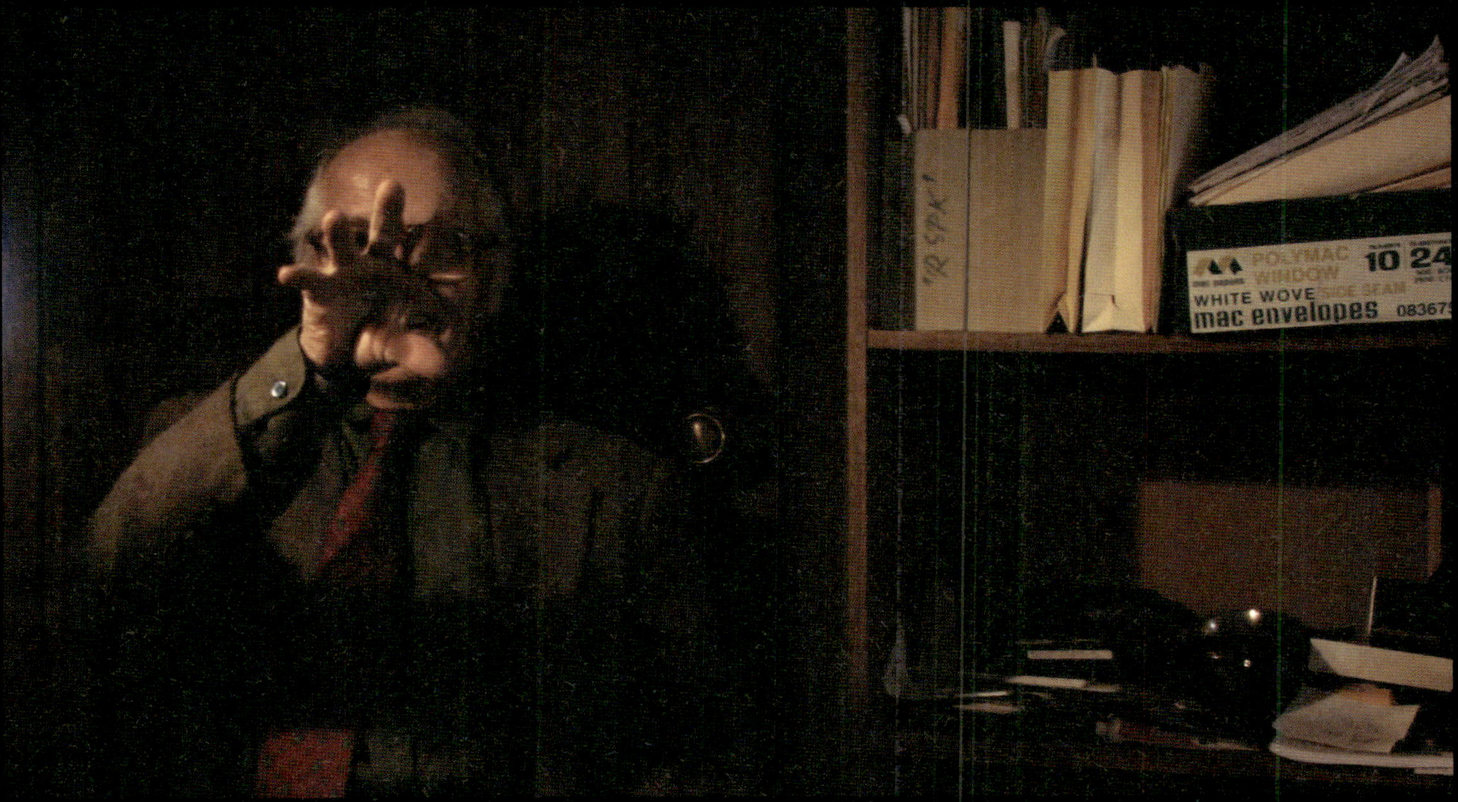
"RSPK"
POLYMAC
WINDOW
10
24
WHITE WOVE
SIDE SEAM
mac envelopes

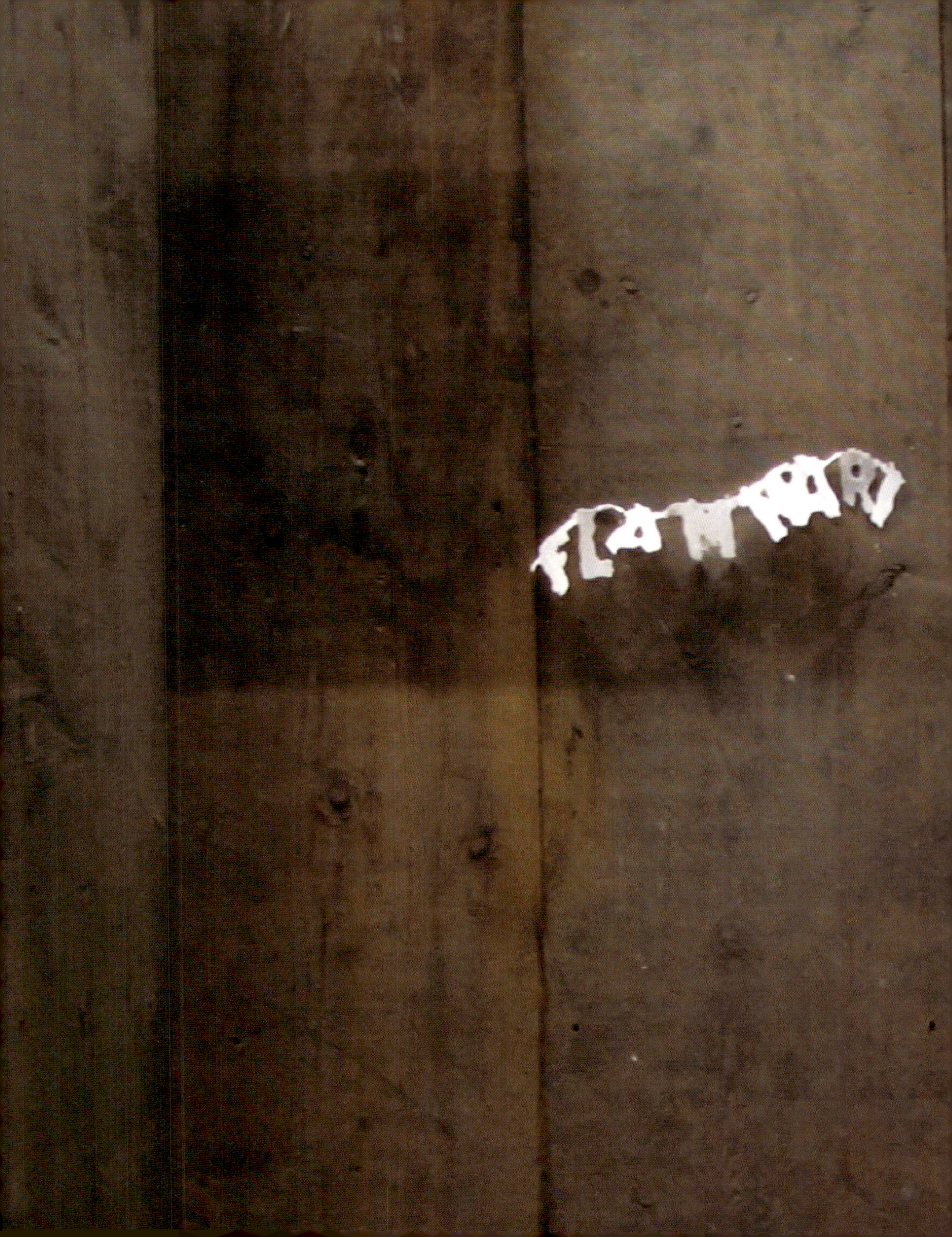

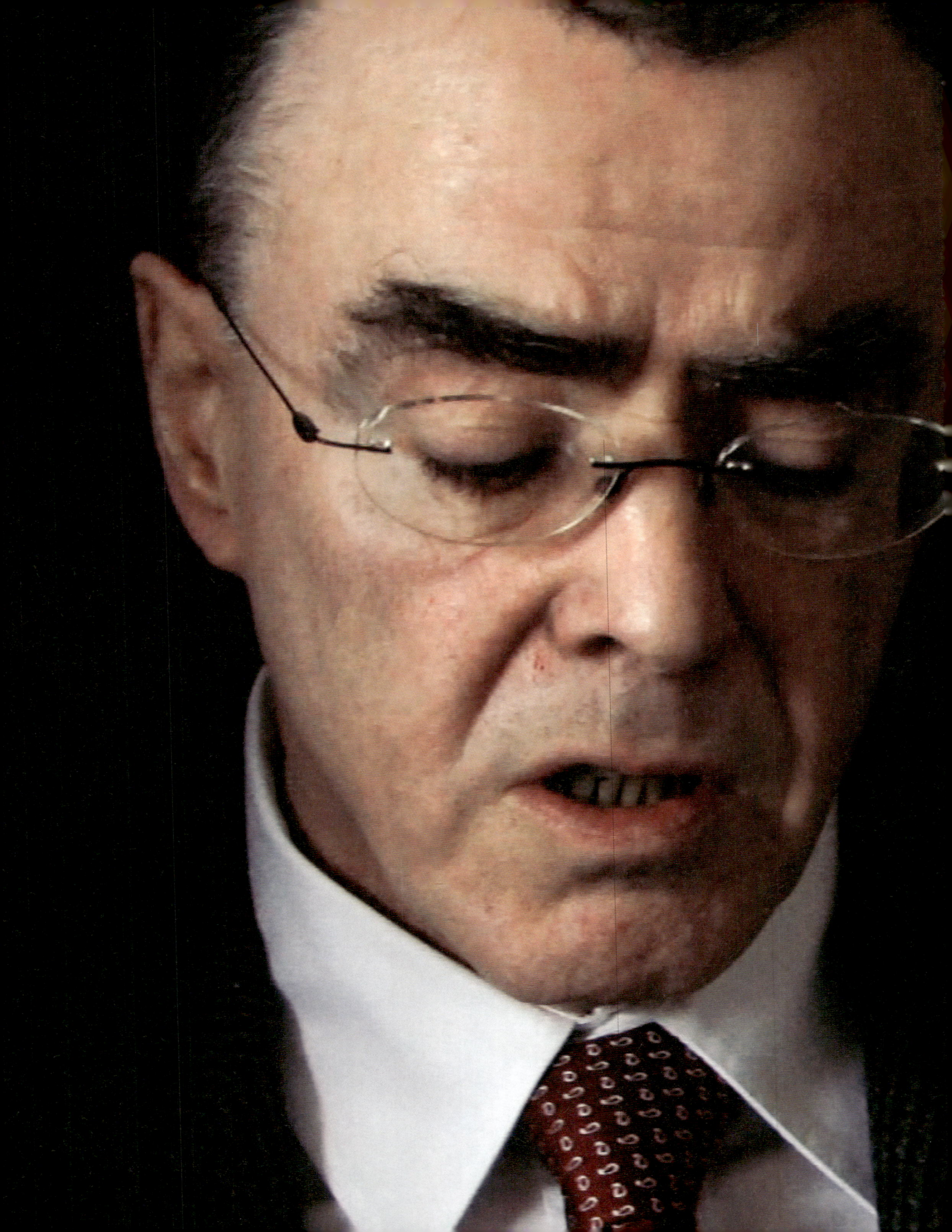

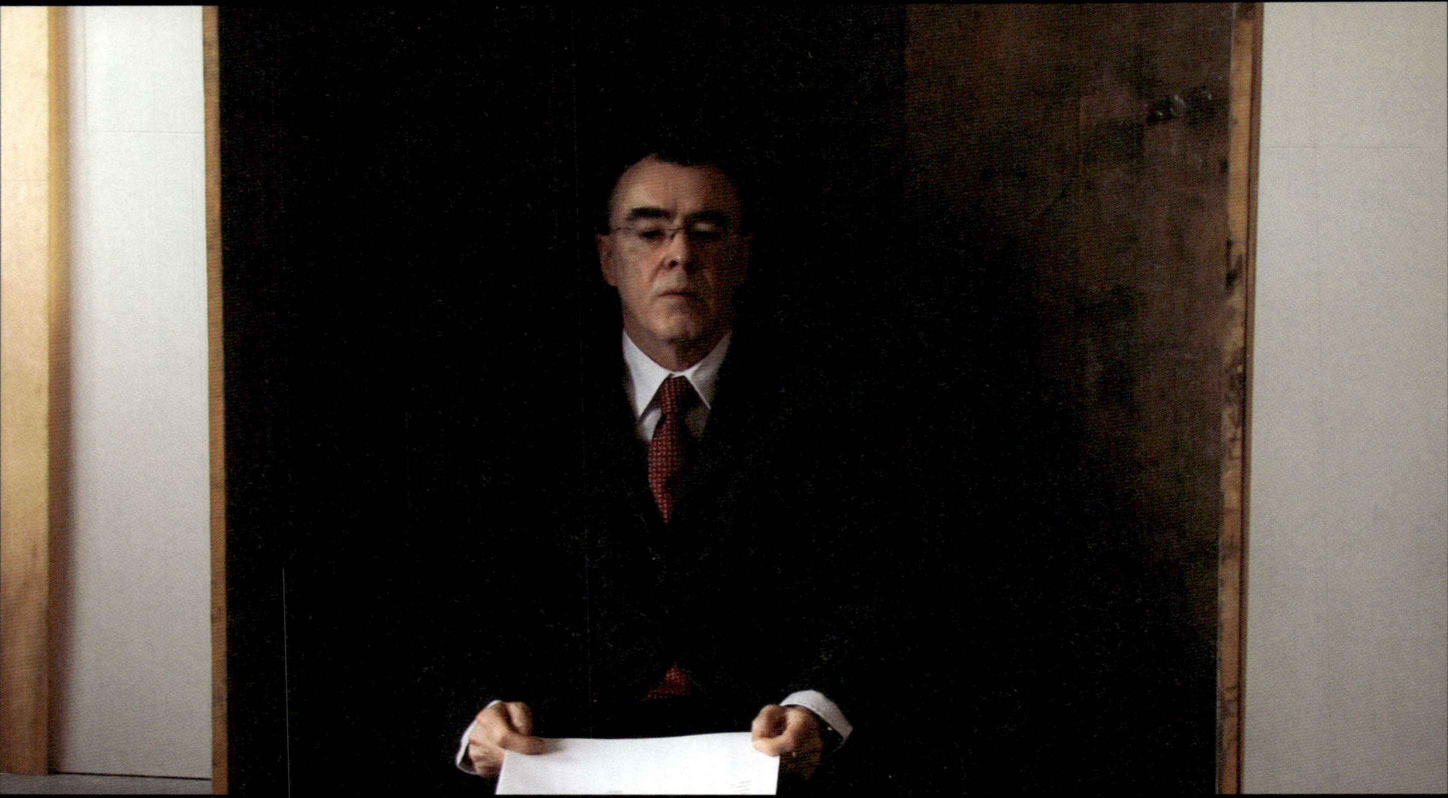

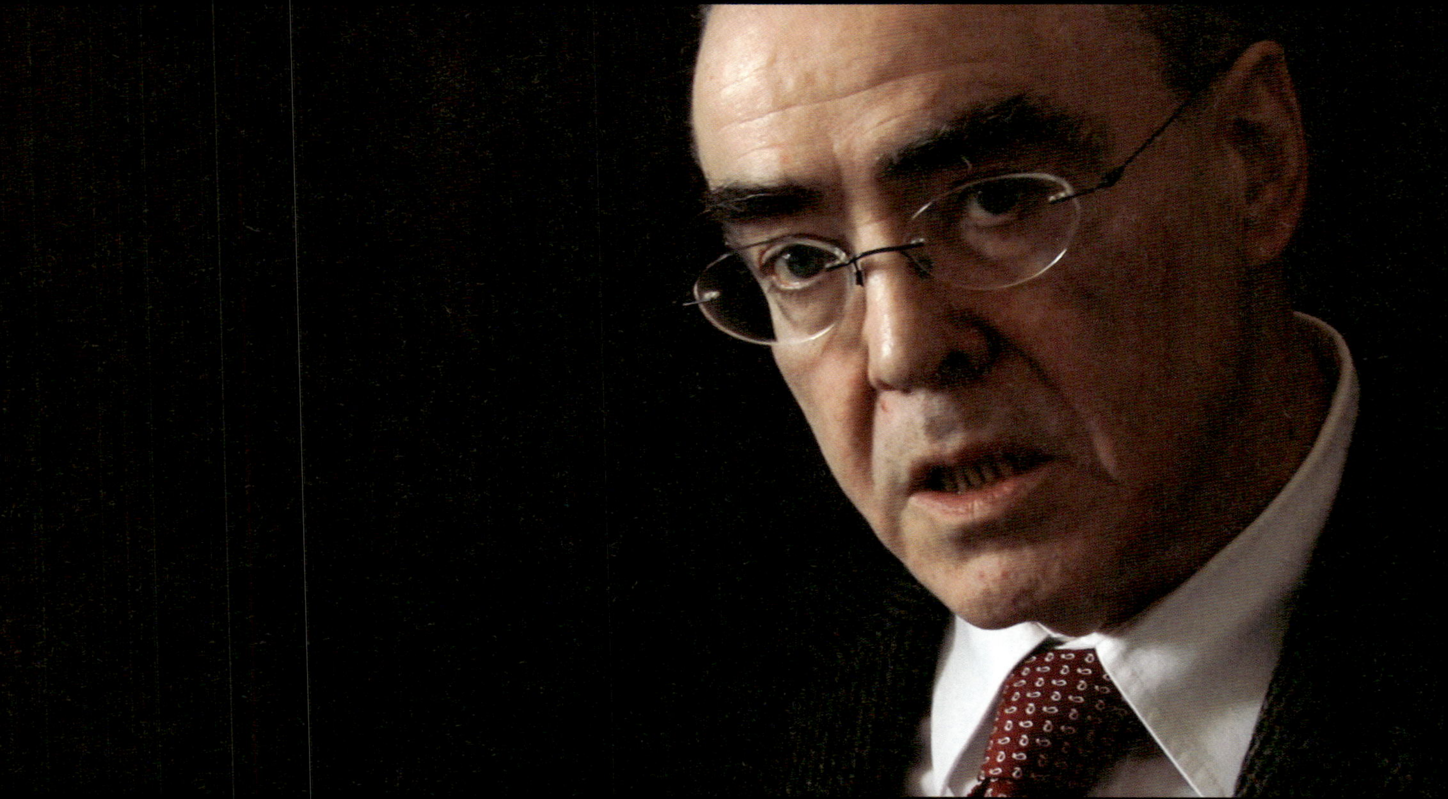

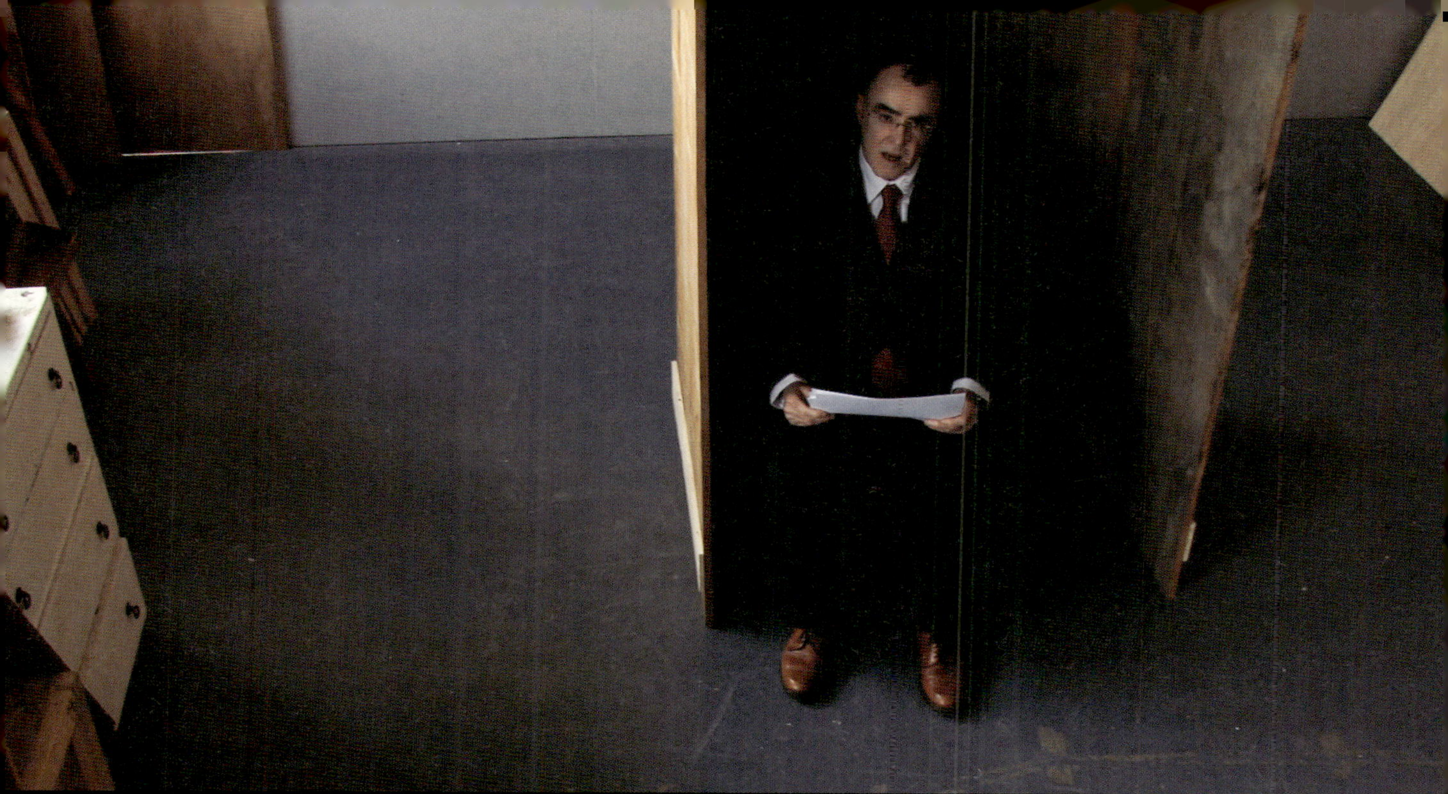

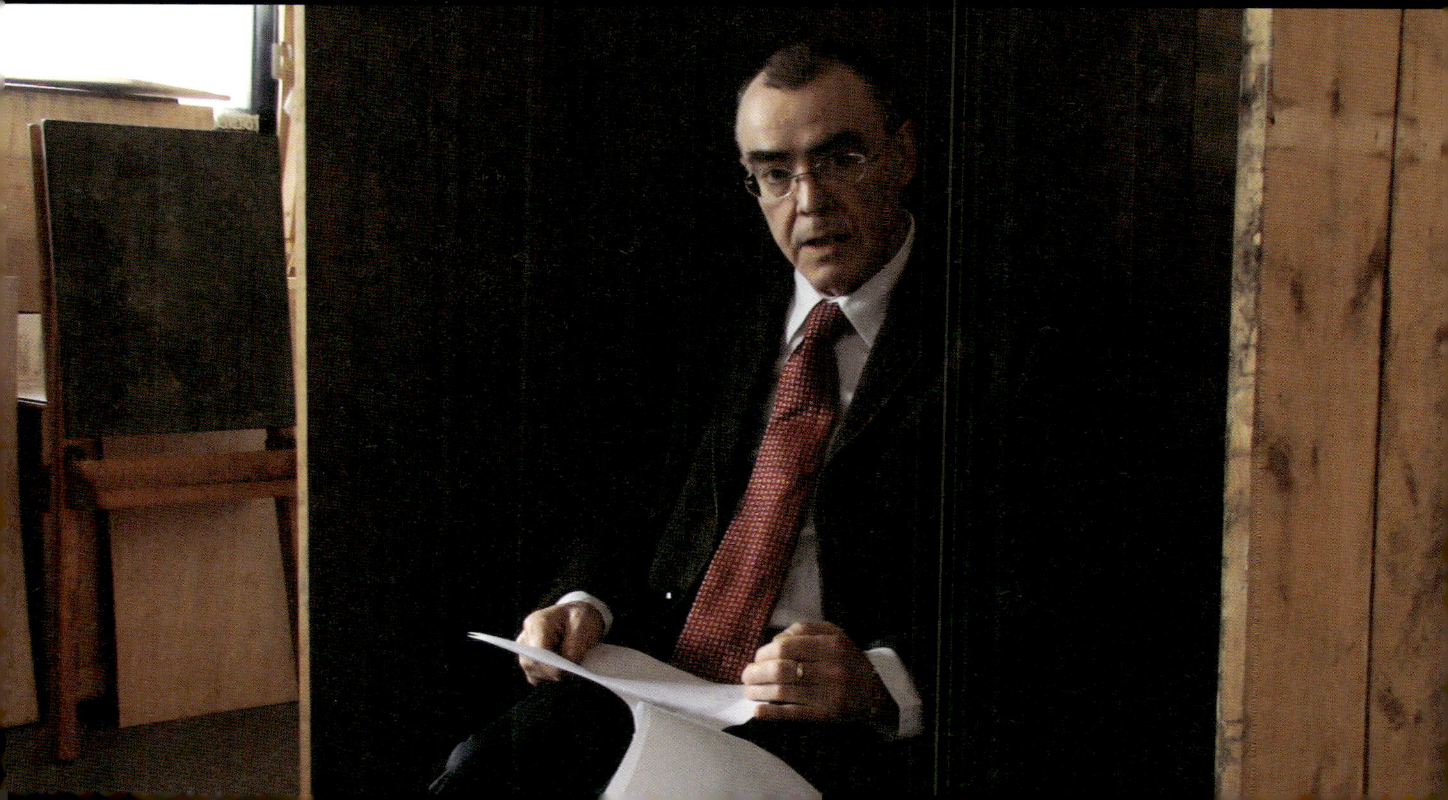

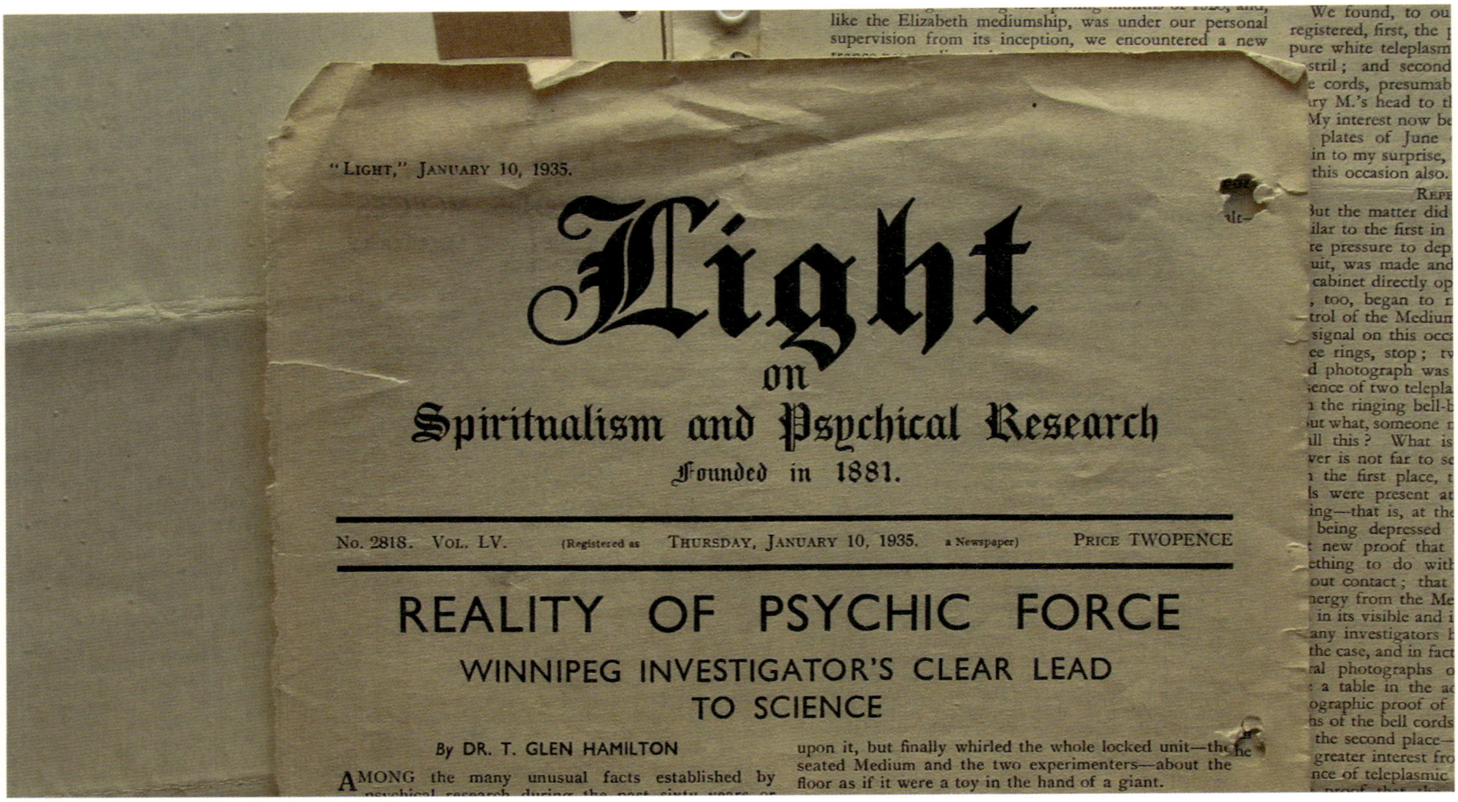

"LIGHT," JANUARY 10, 1935.

Light
on
Spiritualism and Psychical Research
Founded in 1881.

No. 2818. VOL. LV. (Registered as THURSDAY, JANUARY 10, 1935. a Newspaper) PRICE TWOPENCE

REALITY OF PSYCHIC FORCE
WINNIPEG INVESTIGATOR'S CLEAR LEAD TO SCIENCE

By DR. T. GLEN HAMILTON

AMONG the many unusual facts established by

upon it, but finally whirled the whole locked unit—the seated Medium and the two experimenters—about the floor as if it were a toy in the hand of a giant.

like the Elizabeth mediumship, was under our personal supervision from its inception, we encountered a new

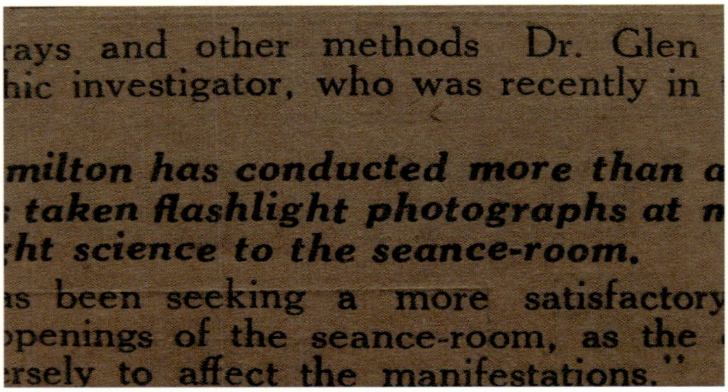

rays and other methods Dr. Glen
hic investigator, who was recently in
milton has conducted more than a
taken flashlight photographs at m
ht science to the seance-room.
s been seeking a more satisfactory
ppenings of the seance-room, as the
ersely to affect the manifestations."

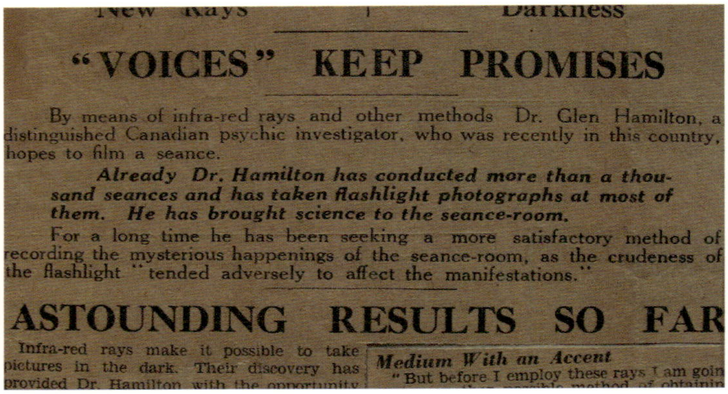

"VOICES" KEEP PROMISES

By means of infra-red rays and other methods Dr. Glen Hamilton, a distinguished Canadian psychic investigator, who was recently in this country, hopes to film a seance.

Already Dr. Hamilton has conducted more than a thousand seances and has taken flashlight photographs at most of them. He has brought science to the seance-room.

For a long time he has been seeking a more satisfactory method of recording the mysterious happenings of the seance-room, as the crudeness of the flashlight "tended adversely to affect the manifestations."

ASTOUNDING RESULTS SO FAR

Infra-red rays make it possible to take pictures in the dark. Their discovery has provided Dr. Hamilton with the opportunity

Medium With an Accent

"But before I employ these rays I am going

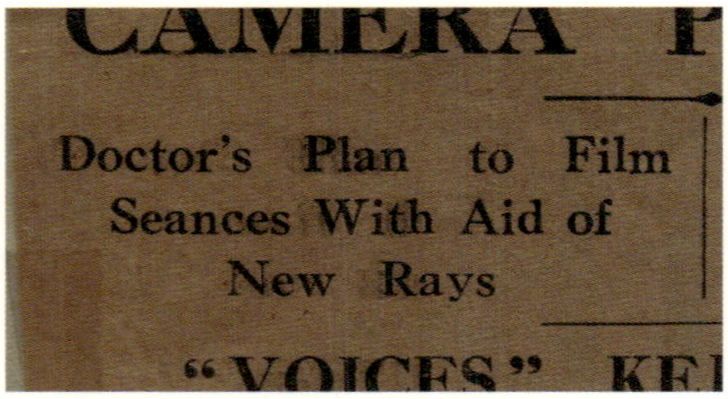

CAMERA P

Doctor's Plan to Film Seances With Aid of New Rays

"VOICES" KE

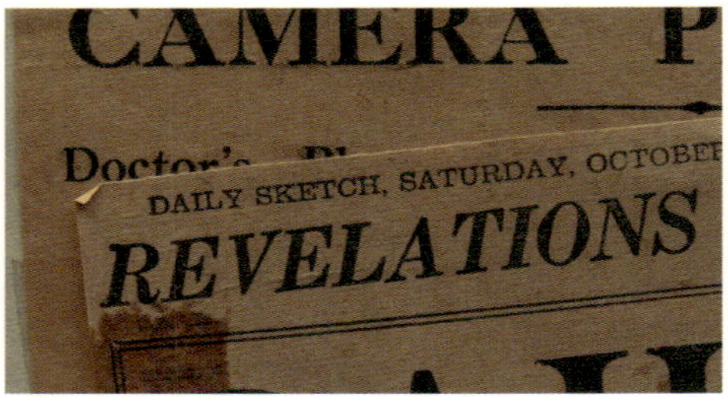

CAMERA P

DAILY SKETCH, SATURDAY, OCTOBER

REVELATIONS

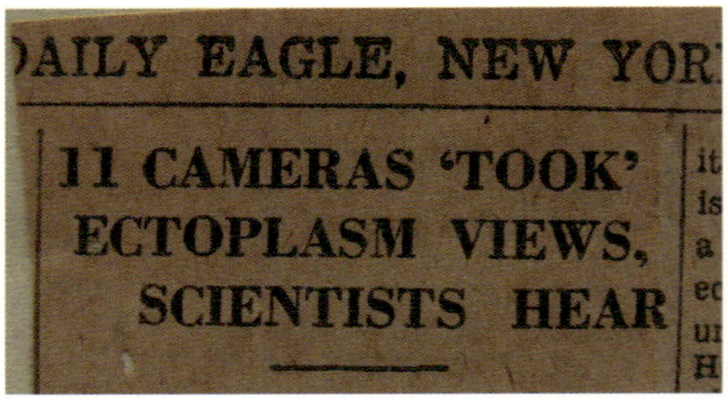

DAILY EAGLE, NEW YOR

11 CAMERAS 'TOOK' ECTOPLASM VIEWS, SCIENTISTS HEAR

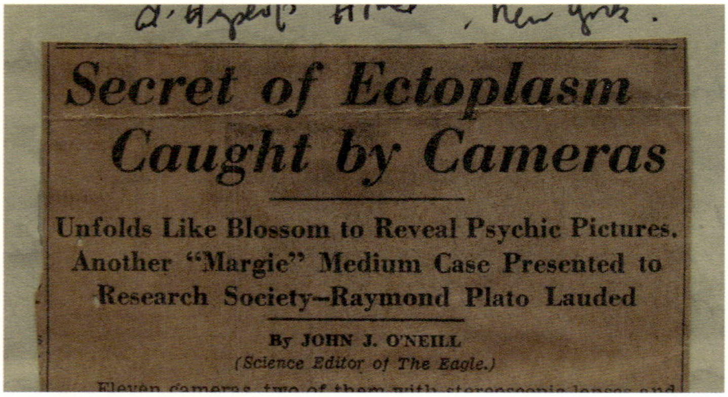

Secret of Ectoplasm Caught by Cameras

Unfolds Like Blossom to Reveal Psychic Pictures. Another "Margie" Medium Case Presented to Research Society—Raymond Plato Lauded

By JOHN J. O'NEILL
(Science Editor of The Eagle.)

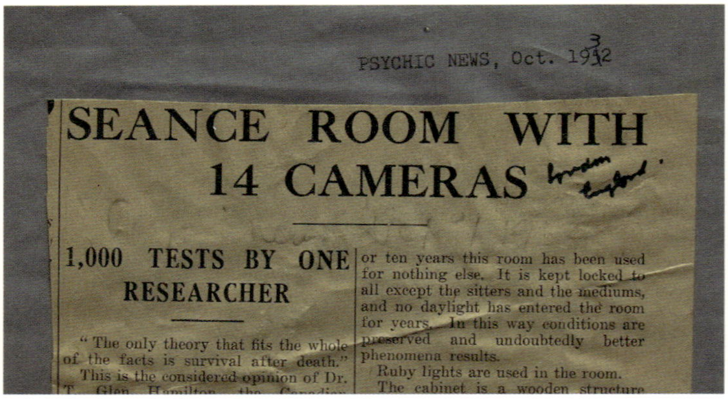

PSYCHIC NEWS, Oct. 1932

SEANCE ROOM WITH 14 CAMERAS

1,000 TESTS BY ONE RESEARCHER

"The only theory that fits the whole of the facts is survival after death."

This is the considered opinion of Dr.

or ten years this room has been used for nothing else. It is kept locked to all except the sitters and the mediums, and no daylight has entered the room for years. In this way conditions are preserved and undoubtedly better phenomena results.

Ruby lights are used in the room.

The cabinet is a wooden structure

ngs of the seance-room, as the crudeness of to affect the manifestations."

RESULTS SO FAR

take y has tunity Having every rtly to which

Medium With an Accent

"But before I employ these rays I am going to try another possible method of obtaining a moving picture of the seance happenings. That is the use of the Sasha system of sudden illumination from an electric bulb—a method which is replacing the old flash for newspaper work.

Studies Teleplasm

From the experiments in telekensis, involving table lifting and turning, Dr. Hamilton moved on to a study of teleplasm, or etoplasm, the mysterious emanation from the body of the medium during a state of deep trance.

Thin cords of ectoplasm were

Secrets Caught by Came

"From the beginning," h always insisted on applying scientific methods to these e example, the room in my hou seances are held is used for r six or seven years it has alwa

1,000 TESTS BY ONE RESEARCHER

"The only theory that fits the whole of the facts is survival after death."

This is the considered opinion of Dr. T. Glen Hamilton, the Canadian psychic researcher, after a thousand sittings under rigid test conditions.

Dr. Hamilton has now returned to Winnipeg after spending six weeks in London, during which time he gave addresses and showed slides of the remarkable photographs he has taken of physical phenomena.

or ten years th for nothing els all except the s and no daylight for years. In preserved and phenomena resu

Ruby lights a

The cabinet with no curtain, in full sight of range of the there is no top is six feet high. mediums.

A large n used, someti

"More than once my cameras have caught a table floating in the air, upside down, or being flung from one part of the room to the other.

"Faces, some of which have, apparently, been identified; materialised forms; teleplasm, and other things have been caught by these cameras again and again.

"Although the results, photographically, are striking, we have missed some wonderful pictures owing to the force and crudeness of the flash exploded in the room. Hence my determination to use the infra-red ray to obtain moving as well as still pictures.

r all, there have been ical researchers hout the ages, and of their efforts are to nd in many historical Saul was one when guised himself before nce with the Witch of Croesus was one when sted the oracles of , and, coming nearer vn time and our own , we find such men as n Ewart Gladstone, Balfour, Sir William es, Sir Oliver Lodge, Stead, Camille Flam-, the great French omer, Conan Doyle, t Blatchford—men of inquiring minds that it them material re- all keenly interested in cal phenomena, and, t cases, actually spend- considerable part of ives in adding to their nd the world's scanty edge of these phenom-

re are few families that not something "uncan- mysterious and never actorily explained, in records, and perhaps it be as well if, before ng properly on this arti- e writer were to explain e has no preconceptions regarding the source nomena of this nature. While admitting that

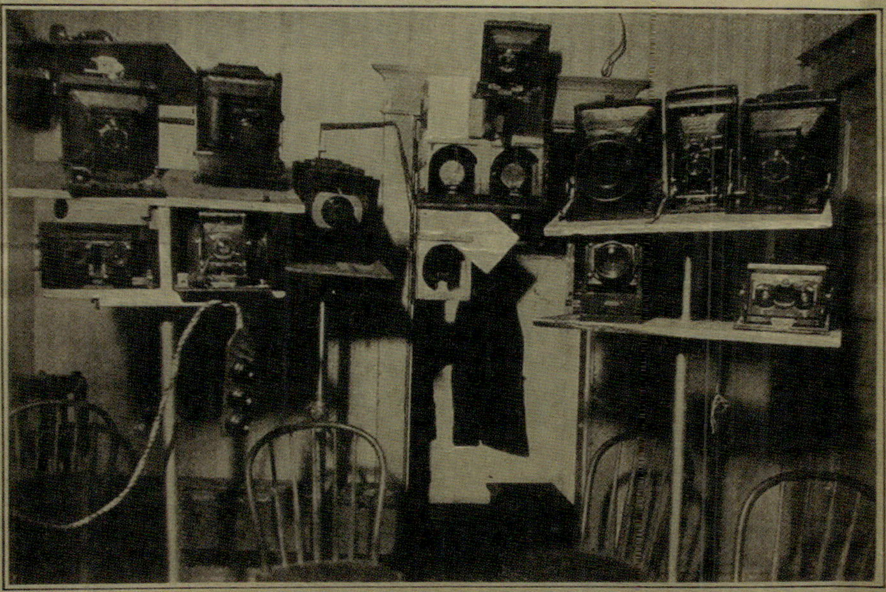

The cameras used at the seances held in Dr. Hamilton's laboratory number as many as twelve, two of them stereoscopic, enabling a three-dimensional photograph to be taken, when a teleplasmic experiment is under way.

really something tangible to be investigated, had made chemistry his hobby, he was interested in

or part of her clothing, depending on the nature of the experiment, immediately before a sitting, in an

ment. The flashlight, by which the picture is taken, is fired by electricity from a push button in the doctor's hand.

The bell boxes used—the mechanisms through which it is claimed that the "controls," or disembodied spirits, manifest their presence by rings—have been constructed on the lines laid down by the Scientific American as most suited to the investigation of psychical phenomena.

Now, with a picture of the personnel of the group and of the room and its arrangements in your mind's eye, we shall take you to a seance at Dr. Hamilton's house. But first give us just a minute while we tell of the precautions taken to ensure that the room is not entered by unauthorized persons or by anyone at the wrong time. "The room is always locked in the intervals between work," Dr. Hamilton avers, "and it is bolted on the inside when work is in progress. Mediums and sitters never enter this room between experiments. The medium with whom the teleplasmic structures are visibly connected removes the whole

times fall into a trance so that at one seance there are, sometimes, several 'mediumistic sources.'

"I bring to my investigations not only my experience as a medical man, but also my knowledge of photography and electricity, which I have carefully studied.

"With regard to the hundreds of photographs secured at these seances, I can vouch for their absolute genuineness. The impressions made on the photographic plates come from sources external to the camera, not from inside the camera, as in the case of what are commonly called spirit photographs.

SACRED SEANCE ROOM

Then other mediums in the circle developed too. They found that their phenomena, resulting from a combination of all the mediums, grew stronger still.

They began to get teleplasmic structures, which they saw and photographed.

Dr. Hamilton's circle naturally went through various changes, but eventually the sitters became regular and the doctor fitted up a séance room which was used only for sittings. For nine

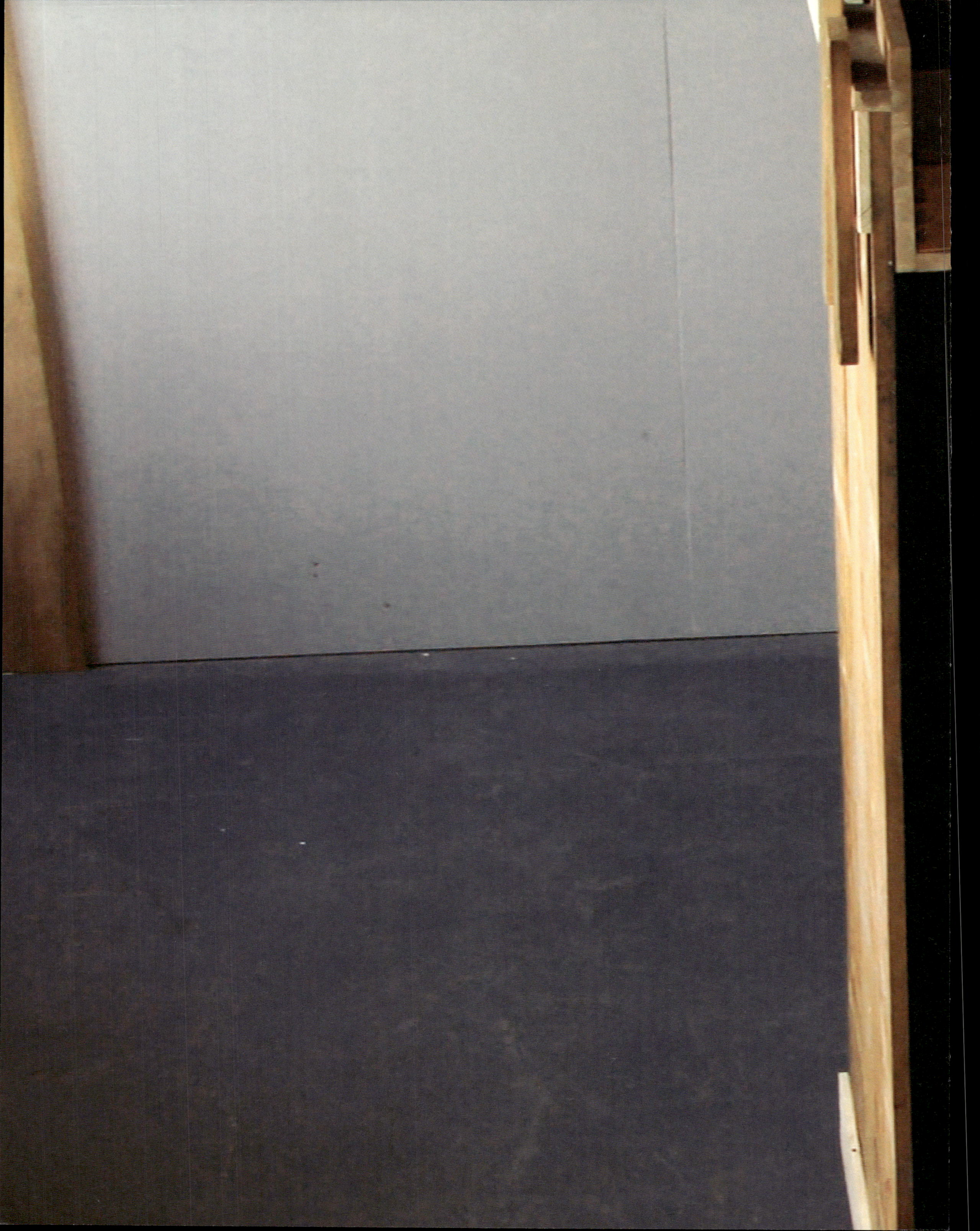

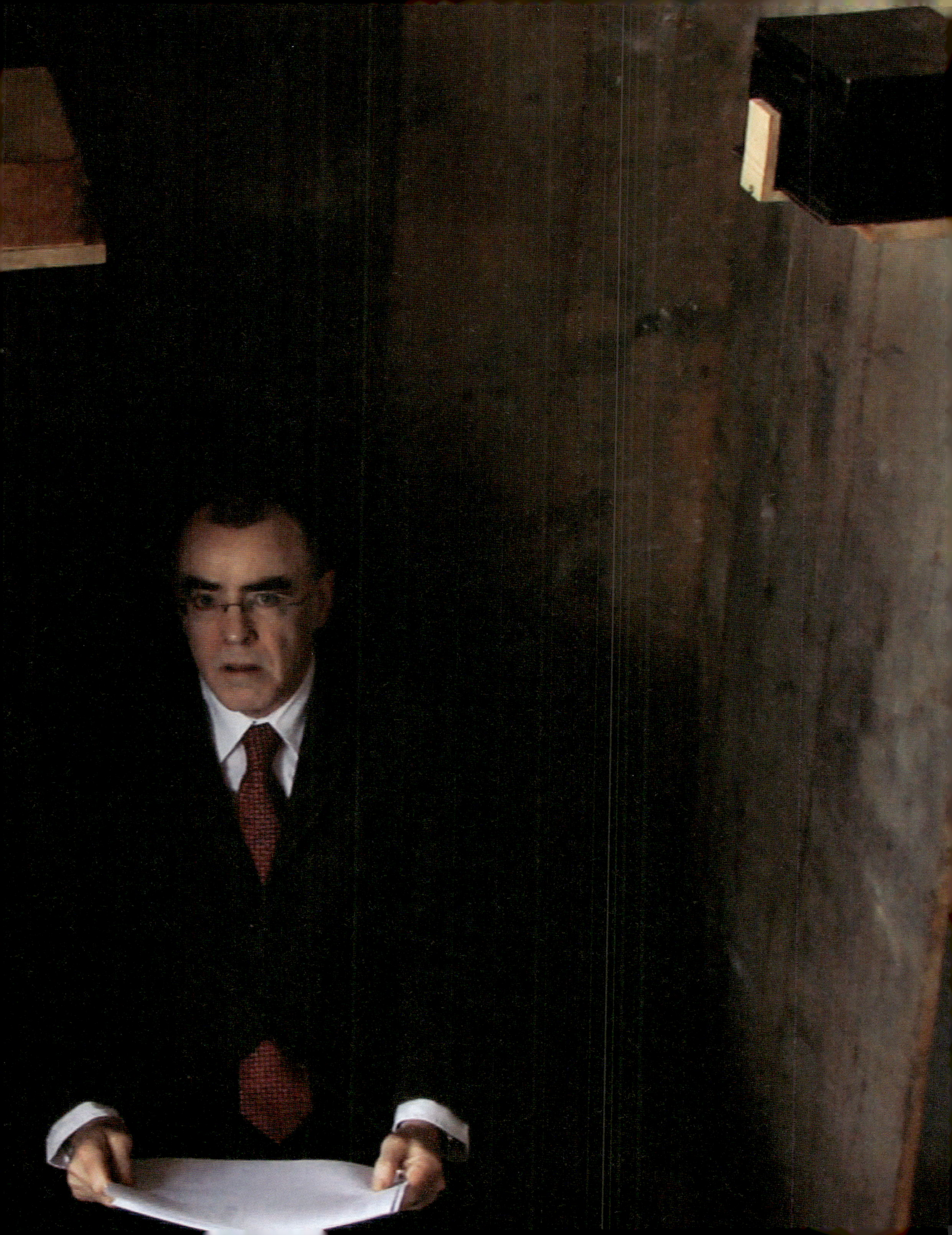

WORDS FROM THE CABINET

It takes a while to get to the cabinet. En route I'm thinking of the postcard of Venice I received from Susan MacWilliam this morning, Tuesday 17 February 2009. Post from Italy is notoriously slow, yet this, postmarked the 14th—St Valentine's Day—has taken a mere three days to wing its way to me over the weekend, as if delivered through some paranormal aperture in the spacetime continuum. There's something uncanny about the postcard itself, a view of the Grand Canal. Peculiar cloud formations boil in the sky as if painted by Turner, storm-cloud black and sepia. The sun appears like a full moon, dead centre low in the sky, a focal point. Maybe it is the moon, for the shadows slanting over the buildings suggest the sun is elsewhere. Maybe the sky is a decorative construct, a painted backdrop. Above the Rialto Bridge is what looks like a printing flaw, a vertical streak of light which is a near-doppelganger of the spectral column extending from the table-top in *Library*, or that in Crawford's photograph of the Goligher Circle. I turn the card over: "*Ectoplasm over Venice, Best wishes, Susan.*"

The possible manipulation of the image put me in mind of Italo Calvino's fiction, *Invisible Cities*, imaginary cities which are all Venice by another name. Searching for the book this morning in the semi-arbitrary arrangement of my library, I found wedged next to it some long-forgotten postcards of Verona, where I had been invited to read some years ago. The schedule had allowed me to spend two days in Venice, where I'd never been: folded in along with the postcards was my reservation for Casa Martini in the Cannaregio district for 14 and 15 October 2005. Then I remembered the cloudless blue of the sky, the dazzling facades of the *palazzi* and their shimmering reflections, the sounds of bells trembling over the water.

On my arrival I'd bought what seemed like a detailed map, but the more I wandered the city the more I found it difficult to locate myself, sometimes unaccountably doubling back on my steps or emerging from alleyways into courtyards, dead-ends or empty piazzas, and I abandoned myself to chance, for at ground level the city bore little resemblance to its cartographical delineation, a bird's eye view not available to the traveller on foot. Pleasantly bewildered, I was reminded of De Quincey's opium-driven excursions through a London "full of enigmatical entries, and alleys without soundings, and sphinx's riddles of streets, so intricate and unexplored that it was doubtful if they had yet been laid down in the modern charts".

So, as I travel to the cabinet, I am doubly disorientated, my memory of Belfast seeming to reflect my memory of Venice. I know Susan MacWilliam's studio is in the aptly named United Optical Laboratories building at the corner of Corporation Street and Great Patrick Street, and I have been there before, but I still find its whereabouts difficult to visualise; my mental map is still that of the 1960s, when I first got to know the district, and since then the four-lane roadway of the Dunbar Link has cut a traffic-laden diagonal swathe through it, obliterating the original layout. Most of the shops, dwellings and warehouses have disappeared, and with them the smell of meal, beer, rope and timber. Moreover, there is much building work in progress, Belfast is still under reconstruction, and what look like promising routes are barred by chain-link fencing. So it takes me a while to reconfigure where I am in this tangled node of urban fabric.

Eventually I get there, and take the six flights of stairs to the third floor. Wrong floor, wrong studio. I am directed down a floor. I knock, and Susan admits me to her studio. Here, too, one is disorientated, uncertain of what level is which—ground, upper or whatever—for the great windows of the long, high-ceilinged room give out directly on to the M3 flyover and the elevated railway link across the river Lagan, beyond which lie Belfast Lough, the docks, Harland & Wolff's shipyard, and the City Airport, all the means of entering or escaping Belfast, as Susan observes. Land, sea and air flood into the studio.

The cabinet is positioned slightly off-centre in the room. It is thought by those who believe in it that the cabinet attracts and conserves spiritual forces, enabling the production of manifestations by the medium who sits therein. It has been compared to a spiritual storage battery, releasing psychic energy throughout the séance. It looks like a roofless wooden outhouse open at one end, with a kitchen chair instead of a 'throne'. A water-closet, toilet, bog, loo or Waterloo, the john, the jacks, the privy, cloakroom, heads or thunderbox: there are so many euphemisms for this facility that it is sometimes difficult to know what to call it, or what its original name might have been, for no sooner is the word in currency than it becomes unspeakable for some, and one must add another entry to the thesaurus. It is also known as the library, because one often reads there when engaged in other necessary business. As it happens, my own water-closet is a mini-library: I've put up three shelves above the cistern. On the top shelf are some vintage travel books, Baedekers of London and Paris, Cook's Traveller's Handbook of the Rivieras of France & Italy, and the like; also, eight or nine volumes of the Thinker's Library published by the Rationalist Press in the1930s and 40s, among them *Natural Causes and Supernatural Seemings* by Henry Maudsley, *Fireside Science* by Sir E Ray Lankester, and *The Evidence for the Supernatural* by Ivor Ll Tuckett. Appropriately, the Library's logo is Rodin's sculpture *The Thinker*, seated with his fist supporting his chin like a man at stool.

It reminds me of my father telling me stories, back in 1951 or 1952. Sometimes he'd be taken short halfway through an episode, and he'd take me with him to the outside toilet, where I'd stand facing him in the cold and the dark while he continued his narrative, illustrating significant points with the lit blip of his cigarette, neon loops and spirals fading on the dark as instantly as written, yet persisting in our vision. "The human brain", says De Quincey, "is a natural and mighty palimpsest. Such a palimpsest is my brain; such a palimpsest, O reader! is yours. Everlasting layers of ideas, images, feelings, have fallen on your brain softly as light. Each succession has seemed to bury all that went before. And yet in reality not one has been extinguished."

I'm seated in the cabinet. Susan has constructed it from wooden boards reclaimed from the Orchid Studio, formerly the Orchid Ballroom in King Street, once a Mecca for the showbands of the 1960s. I had a notion that the building was still there; I could see its ornamental facade and high green cupola in my mind's eye, but when I went today to look at it I found it demolished. They're building an apartment block or office block in its stead, some such doomed speculation, and the Orchid exists now only in the memory. I wonder if the cabinet remembers its former life as the shelves of a drinks storeroom. It smells of dust and pine. I think of a coffin.

I begin to recite the wordlist Susan has given me to recite. Not a glossary, since no meanings are given. Just the bare words, the bare boards deprived of their contents. Terms relating to film, over 180 of them. Some of these are familiar to me. Some leave me guessing. Some others are beyond my ken. A random selection: Anamorphic lenses, Blow Down, Blimp, Cowboy Shot, Cyclorama, Dupe Negative, Edge Fog, Flex Fill, Grip, Halation, Intervalometer, Key Light, Light Leak, Minibrute, Pull Down Claw, Rack Focus, Sandbag, Slug, Sound Blanket, Sprocket, Stinger, Tail Slate, Undercrank, Vault Box, Xenon, Zoom.

When I was very young I would lie in bed on the verge of sleep, saying words over to myself. I was reared bilingually: Irish was the language of home, English the language of the street, the world beyond the home. It was a time when horse-drawn carts still operated on the streets of Belfast, and, hearing the clop and rumble of a cart passing beyond the window of my bedroom, I'd say the Irish for horse, "*capall*", rolling its syllables around my tongue, and then the more unfamiliar English "horse" , which, the more I said it, became all the more strange. And then *capall*, too, would suffer the same fate, becoming mere sound devoid of meaning, until I drifted off to sleep into a world beyond language. Sound Blanket. Clouds and stars.

We never fully know our language. My English is like the city in which I live. I know bits of it intimately, or so I think, because if asked to describe in detail the area in which I live, there will be inevitable hiatuses in my recollection. Edge Fog. Other bits—especially parts of East Belfast—are *terra incognita* to me. Other bits change unbeknownst to me until, visiting what I think is there, I find it gone. We dwell among clouds of unknowing. That is a necessary condition. Entering the language, we are forced to confront our own ignorance, to enter a zone where what we thought we knew becomes unfamiliar. Saying the words I am given in the cabinet, I begin to see them as a narrative, a journey into a dark forest perhaps, the path sometimes apparent in moonlit glades and then losing itself in the undergrowth. My guides, the words, do not explain themselves to me. I do not speak them, they speak me. I trust them. Words are full of stories of themselves and where they came from, and it is the business of the writer to follow them.

So, in the course of writing what you are reading, I Google "Minibrute" and find it is an amplifier. The Polytone model I've happened on has, among other specifications, a "Brute heavy-duty 15" speaker", a "3-Spring Hammond Reverb", "high and low gain inputs, effects loop, extension speaker jack, headphone jack, steel mesh speaker grill cover" and a "rugged black tolex covering". So I Google "tolex". Tolex was filed as a trademark on 30 August 1945 by the Textileather Corporation. It is currently registered as "a plastic sheet and film material for book binding and case covering for speakers and amplifiers". It was also used for coffin-case guitar cases. As for 30 August 1945, that was the day the Allied occupation of Japan began.

I'm back in the cabinet, thinking of a coffin. Or a den. A hidey-hole. A watchman's hut. A wardrobe in which children hide when playing hide-and-seek, the portal to another universe. Again I recite the words that have been given me. From time to time I take my eye off the list, memorising a few words in advance of speaking them to look into the lens of Susan's camera, addressing whomsoever might see me in the future as I am captured on video, not knowing who might reciprocate my gaze, knowing nothing of the future.

I open Invisible Cities and, looking for a clue as to what it all means, I come across this sentence: "Your gaze scans the streets as if they were written pages: the city says everything you must think, makes you repeat her discourse, and while you believe that you are visiting Tamara, you are only recording the names with which she defines herself and all her parts."

Another book about Venice, which I bought in Paris about ten years ago: *Les Balades de Corto Maltese—The Perambulations of Corto Maltese*, translated from the Italian of Guido Fuga and Lele Vianello. Corto Maltese is a comics series featuring an eponymous character, a raffish sailor-adventurer. It was created by the Italian Hugo Pratt in 1967, and the book in question —guidebook-cum-graphic-novel—is a tribute to both character and creator, an exploration of the topography and history of Venice. I bought it as much for its beautiful design as for its words, a palimpsest of text and drawing and historical reference. A sentence taken at random: "*Corto Maltese aimait venir à La Libreria Marciana, le matin, se perdre dans de labyrinthiques recherches.*" "Corto Maltese liked to come to the Library of St Mark of a morning, to lose himself in labyrinthine research." Besides being the patron of Venice, Mark is the patron of lawyers, prisoners, and glaziers. Among the holdings of the Library is the circular Map of the World drawn by Fra Mauro in 1459. It shows just Europe, Asia and Africa, though not quite as we know them. There are no Americas, no Australia: they have not yet been sailed to. Again I open the book at random and, at the beginning of a chapter, come across this epigraph from Hugo Pratt: "*Plus le rêve s'éloigne du réel, plus il devient vrai et prend son envol sans voile ni vent.*" "The more the dream drifts away from the real world, the more it becomes true and takes off without wind or sail."

Ciaran Carson

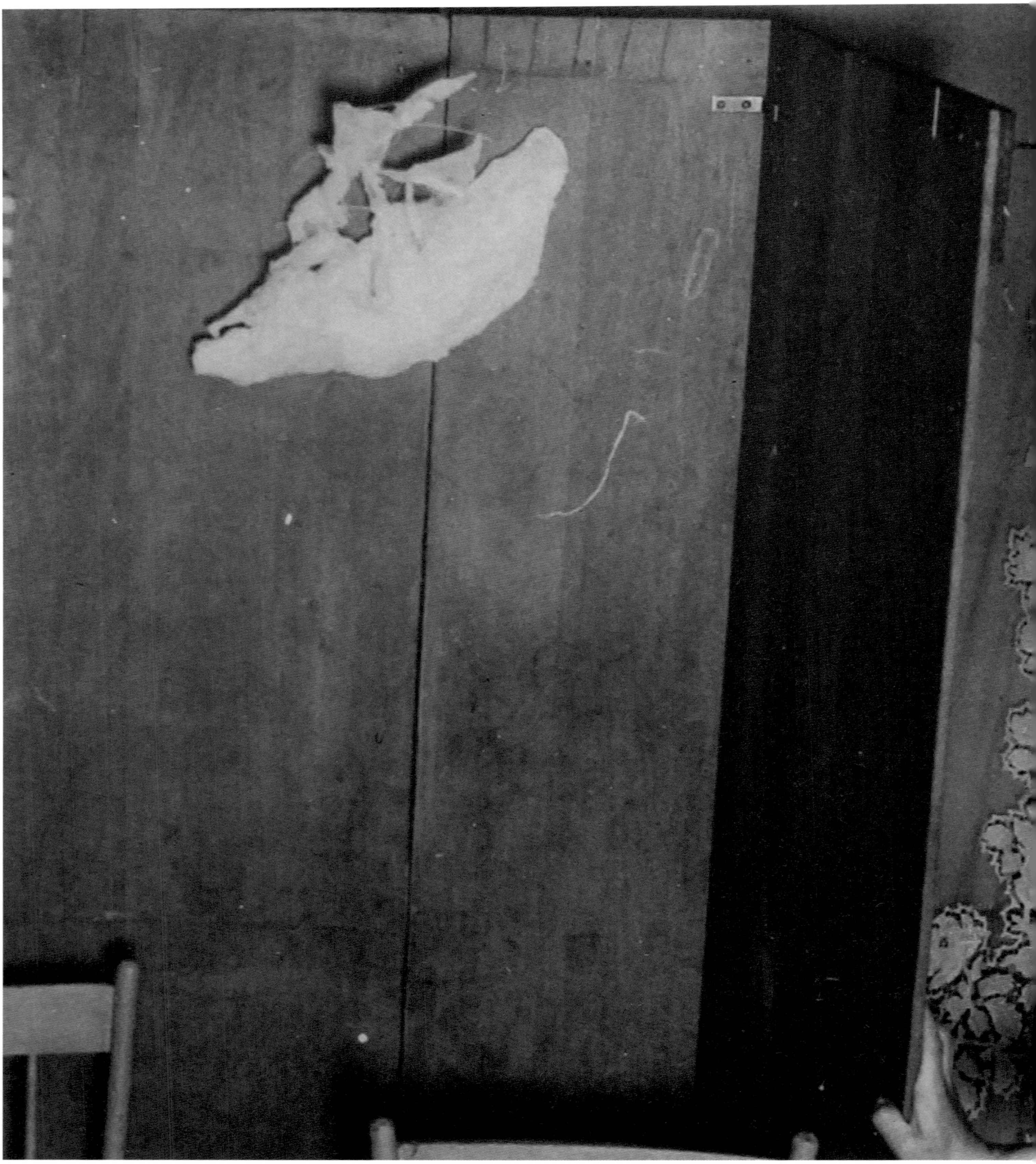

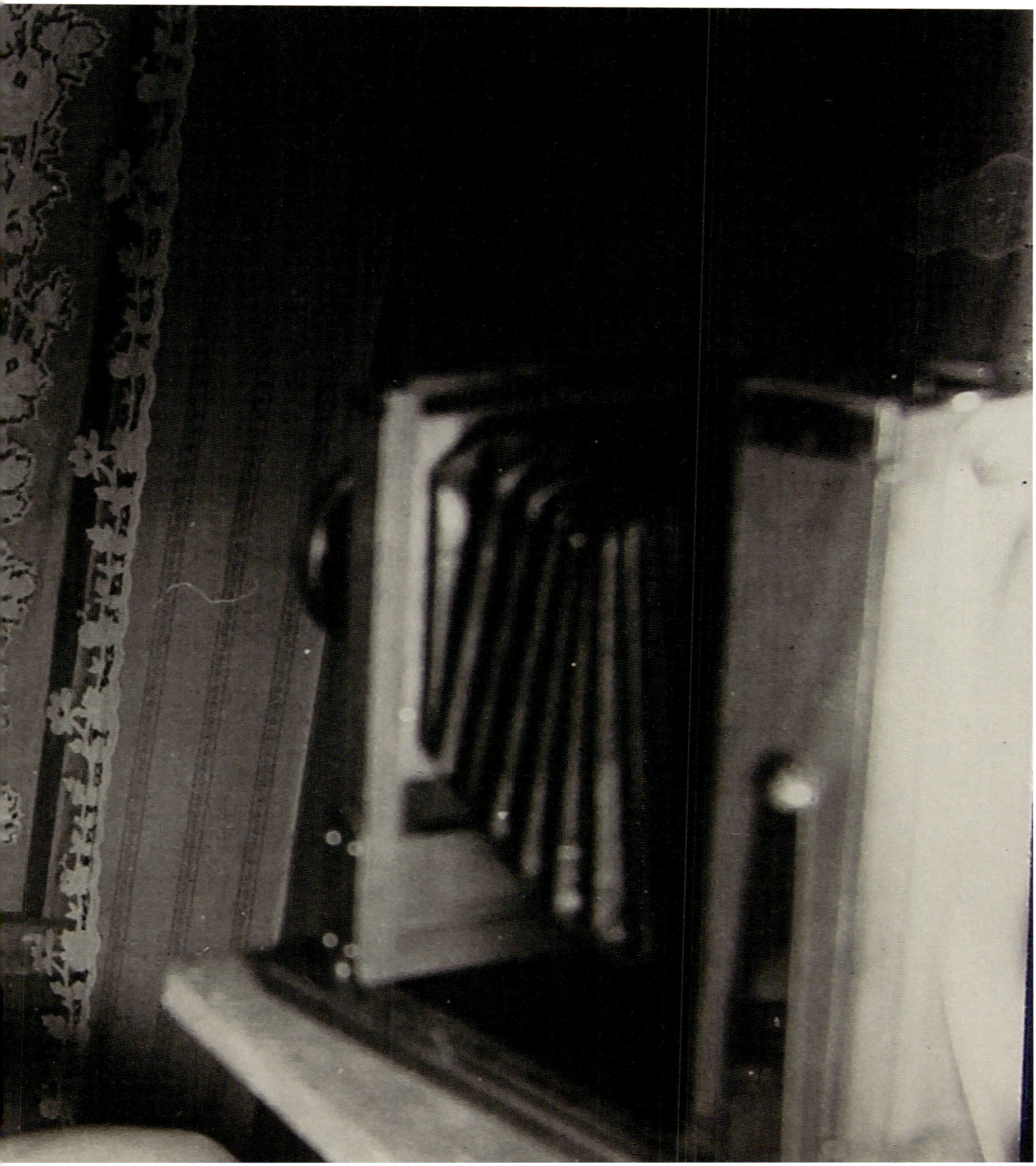

er exceÂlent

a flashlight

nt of the med

ectoplasm

i a photo

nd think

conditions of

photograph ta

um Mary M. in

so that

graph.'

that adv

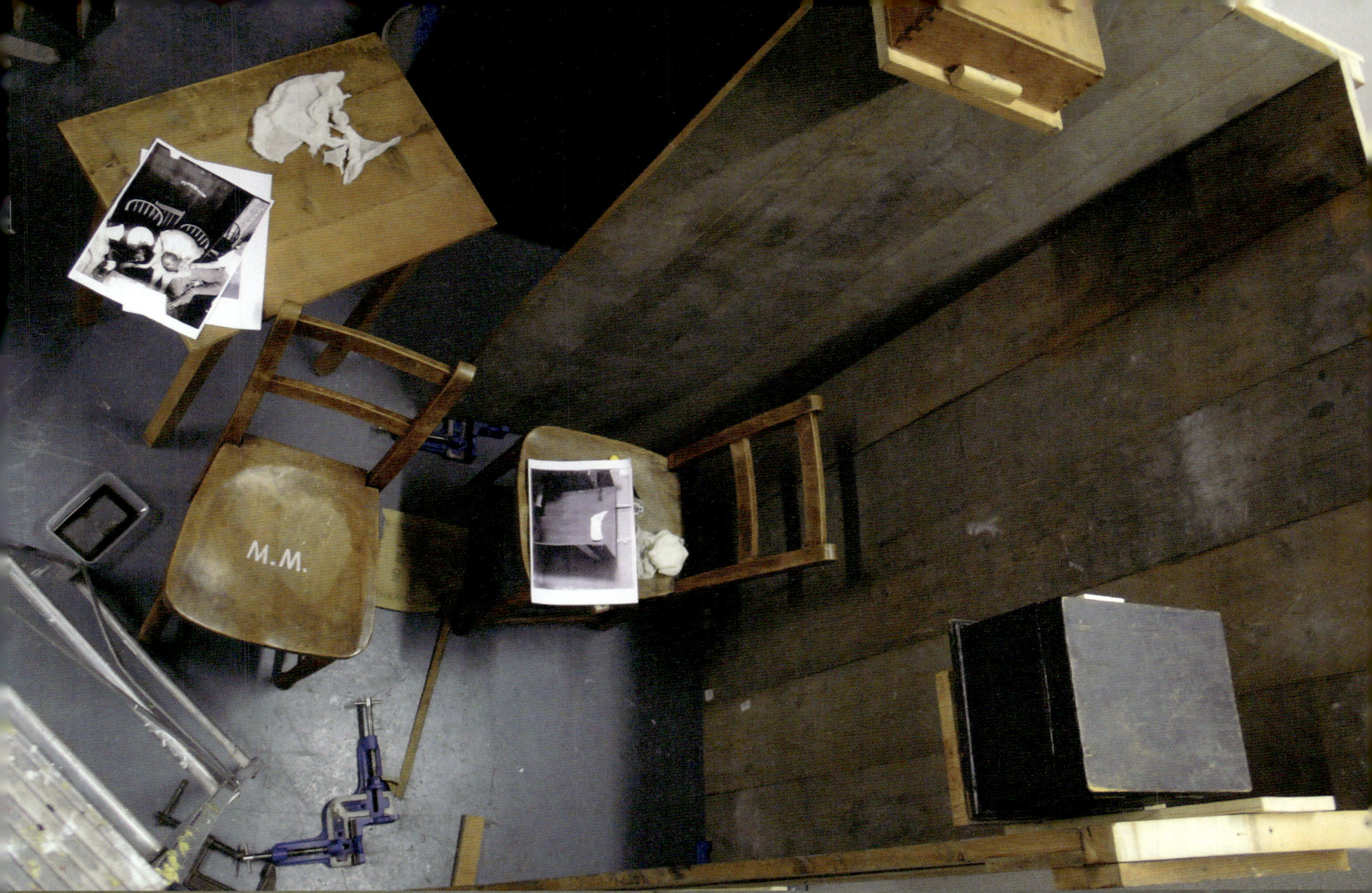
M.M.
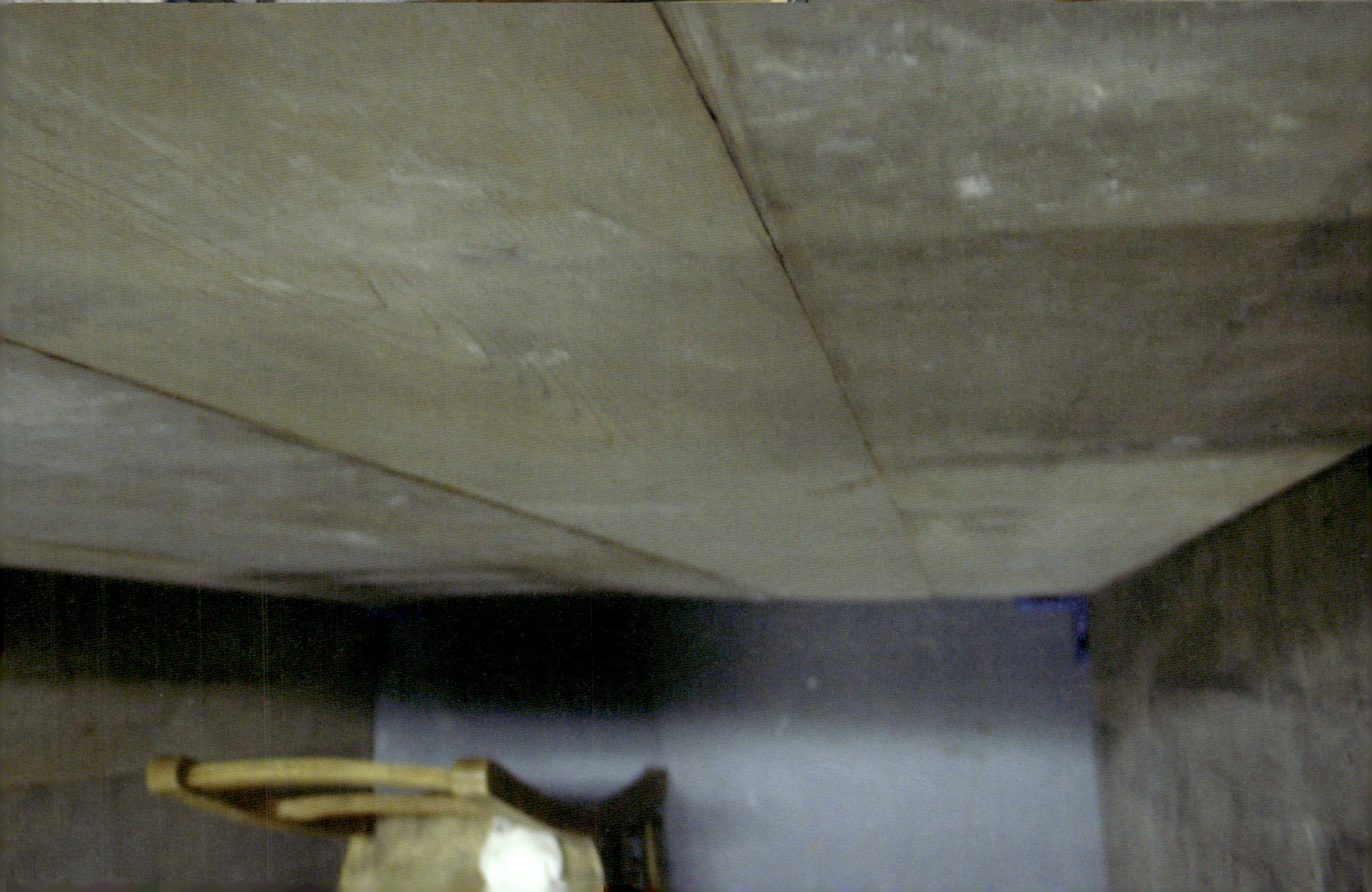

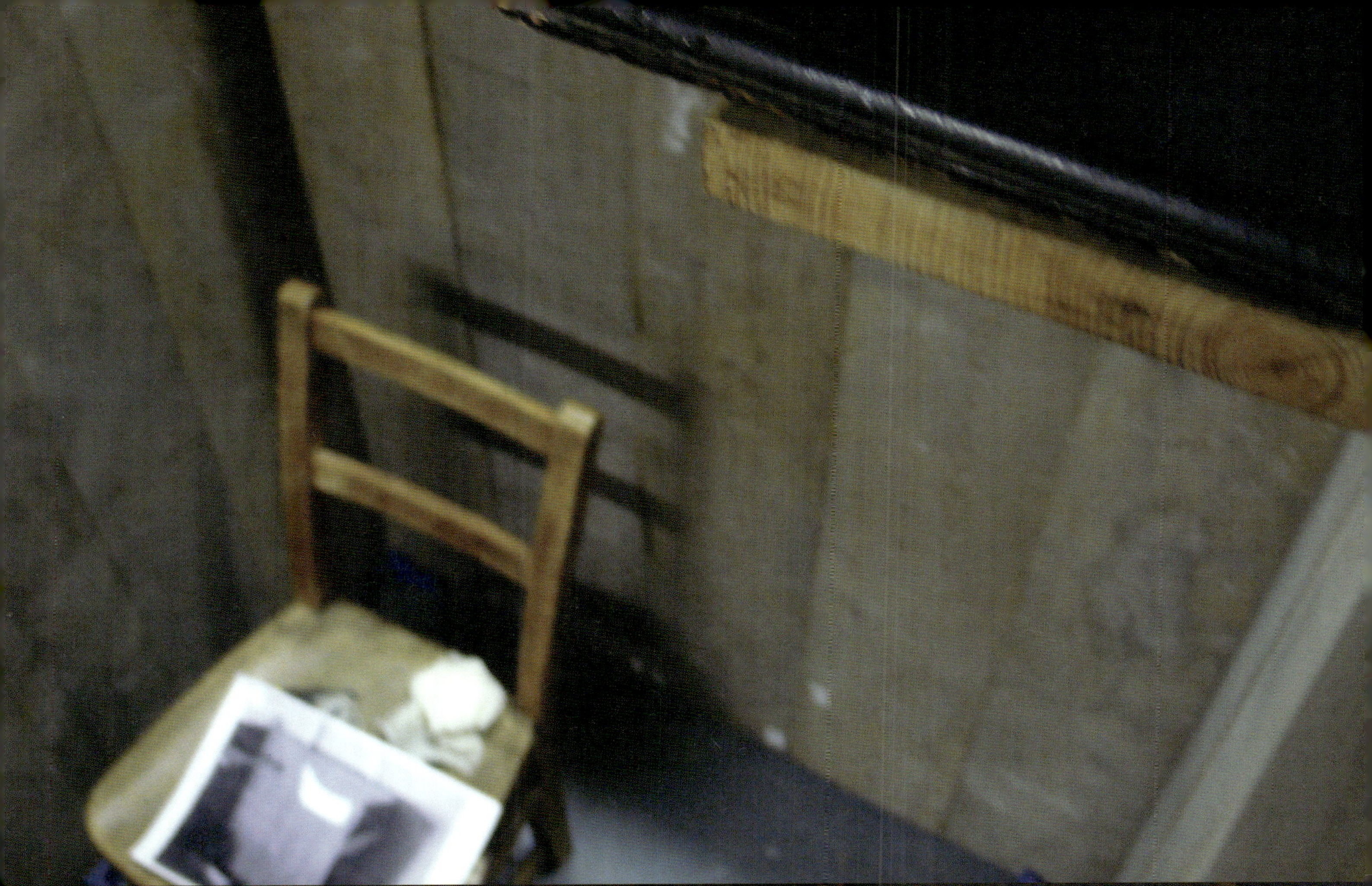
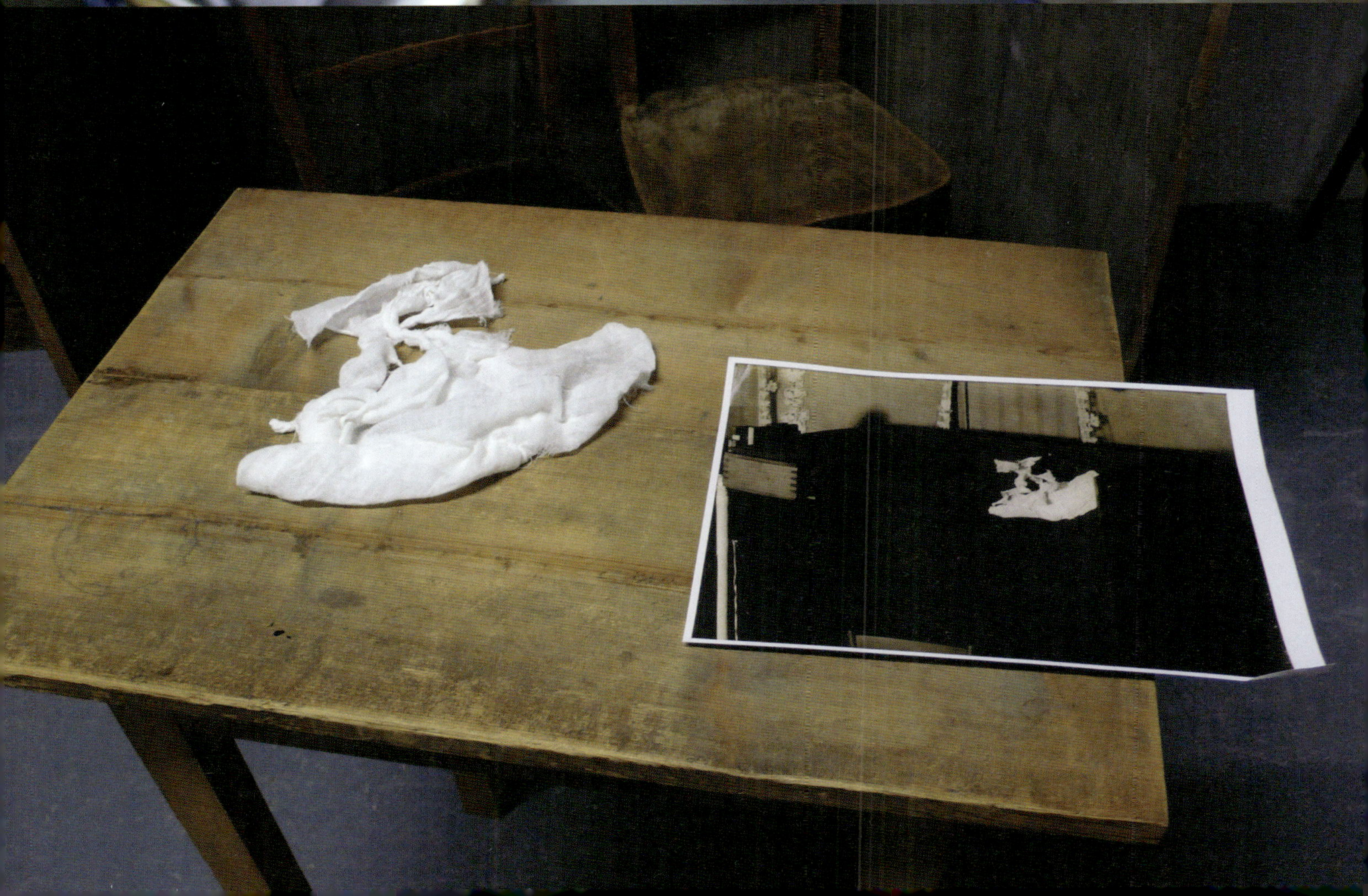

A FICTIONAL SPACE

The success of waxworks inspired another branch of popular public entertainment: the diorama, created by Louis Daguerre in Paris in 1825. This novel spectacle combined the craft skills of anatomists and model-makers, the detailed, haptic reality effects of religious statuary and waxworks, and the staging of a fictional space. Furthermore, the diorama leads directly to the coming of photography, since Louis Daguerre segued instinctively from his work with three-dimensional illusions to experiments with photography, and wrote a book about his two great inventions. The earliest daguerreotype shows the view from the roof of the diorama in the Boulevard du Temple. It is an eerie scene, for the length of the exposure caused everyone in the street below to disappear —with the exception of a customer's truncated boots and legs on a shoeshine's box. It was made in early January 1839, barely a month before Fox Talbot demonstrated his own successes in fixing an image—by a different method—to the Royal Society in London.

Movement eluded waxworks and the new photography alike, but animating a living likeness remained the deepest ambition of artists seeking to capture an image of life itself.

44

FOAM, FROTH, STEAM

Air, clouds, vapour, smoke, foam, froth, steam, and their spirituous, sublimed counterparts among airy and even gaseous substances (as Joyce noticed) have served to make manifest the invisible, supernatural, imponderable, and ineffable according to the promptings of belief and fantasy.

79 | 80

CLOUDS AND CLOUDINESS

Nebulousness has served to meet a need for expressing the bourne beyond which matter still materialises, but not a body, or, if within its bourne, the forms and shapes it takes. Clouds and cloudiness offer a magical passkey to the labyrinth of unknowable mysteries, outer and inner; they convey the condition of the ineffability that the unknown and the divine inhabit.

83

NATURE ABHORS A VACUUM

As Nature abhors a vacuum, so does the mind resist meaninglessness, invent stories to explain haphazard incidents, and provide reasons and origins; the amorphous, the inchoate, the formless, have beckoned irresistibly to the shaping powers of thought and imagination. Humans are polyglot creatures of language, and signs attract meanings, symbols stick to forms, verbal and visual. Pattern, design, system, significations—meaning—have accrued to every sort of natural phenomena.

106

WITHOUT PHANTASMS

"The soul never thinks without a mental image", declared Aristotle in *De Anima,* his book on the soul, using the word *psyche* for "soul" and *phantasma* for "mental image": in contemporary idiom, the psyche does not think without phantasms. How thought processes happen, where they take place in the mind, how the faculties are arranged, and what the character of mental images might be remain some of the most crucial puzzles about consciousness.

121

THE MIND'S EYE

Most famously of all, perhaps, the French philosopher René Descartes, in his meticulous examination of visual experience, decided that "It is the soul that sees, not the eye.... This is why maniacs and men asleep often see, or think they see, objects that are not before their eyes." He located the mind's eye in the pineal gland in the brain, the hyphen between body and spirit in his scheme, and illustrated the workings of this organ in several highly scientific-looking diagrams. Descartes also drew the picture of a blind man in order to illustrate how the brain makes pictures, not the eyes. Using two sticks to feel out the lie of the land around him, the blind man visualises his situation. Seeing and visualising bring personal consciousness into play, and demand active engagement, interpretation, and shaping, not passive receptivity.

121

OPTICAL SIMILE

One kind of mental image was described as "eidetic", referring to optical experiences that are retained in the mind's eye with hallucinatory intensity. It comes from *eidos,* used by Aristotle for that which is seen, or "form, shape, figure", both of something particular and of a generic kind of form, and it is related to *idein,* to see, and *eidolon,* a shape, image, spectre, or phantom, also an image in the mind, a vision or fancy. In Latin, the equivalent was *species,* confusingly, since this term's biological application has eclipsed the optical reference. For a long time, however, especially in seventeenth century Neoplatonist circles, *species* meant the appearance of something or someone, even a phantom, or double.

When the German psychologist ER Jaensch later attempted a strict definition, he reached for an optical simile: "They [eidetic images] may therefore be compared to the pictures produced by a magic lantern."

124

TERROR AND DREAD

The intrinsic subject-matter of the phantasmagoria turned to spectral illusion, morbid, frequently macabre, supernatural, fit to inspire terror and dread, those qualities of the sublime. It foreshadows the function of cinema as stimulant, and prepared the ground for the medium's entanglement with hauntings, possession, and spirit visions.

148

DOUBLE VISION

The Scottish scientist David Brewster, friend of Walter Scott, invented the kaleidoscope, 1819, which he named after the Greek word for beautiful. He also analysed binocularity, establishing its importance to human perception of depth, and accordingly applied it to another ingenious design—the stereopticon. It too became a hugely popular toy of the Victorian middle class, and helped popularise photography in the home.

Brewster was curious about legends of fairies, wonders, and superstitions, and collected examples in an anthropological spirit, publishing in 1832 an important series of public letters to Walter Scott, engaging that great exponent of ballads and fairy-tales in a rational discussion of the supernatural. In these Brewster sets out, among other things, the double mirror trick later dubbed "Pepper's Ghost": by angling planes of glass under and above the stage, a spectre can be beamed to hover in the air as large as life.

152 | 153

LITTLE SKIN

Images made of light and shadow cast by people, things, and places seem to preserve action at a distance: the transmission of the person through time. The metaphors adopted for the medium—including the word *pellicola,* little skin, for film itself in Italian—present a powerful instance of a figure of speech materialising into substance.

164

PERCEPTION AND FALLIBILITY

Soon after mid-century, photography was recording occurrences in the laboratory which the human eye could not see, and its evidence was increasingly relied on. But the invention of the medium coincides in time with the beginnings of Spiritualism, and this and later developments may not be quite as adventitious as has been assumed. The work on motion that Etienne-Jules Marey and Eadweard Muybridge undertook in the 1880s and AM Worthington's experiments in 1908 with high-speed photography, capturing splashes and other events hitherto imperceptible to the human eye, continued to widen the horizon of vision. The camera undid problems about human perception and fallibility—or so it was fervently believed. It could be trusted, because it did not have consciousness, and acted mechanically, objectively, and independently of the mind of its user. In its supposed objective character, photography was brought to bear on psychic possibilities: as there was no ghost in this machine, it must be true when one appeared.

222

INVISIBLE FORMS

The camera could perhaps apprehend this spirit body in a way that fallible human eyes could not. Spirit phenomena might also lie below the threshold of vision and beyond the frequency at which the brain registers light. The camera began to make visible another, transcendental variety of invisible forms: photography and phantoms are joined by elective affinities within the limits of knowledge.

223

CABINET

In many ways, the séance reproduces the camera obscura itself, and the relations with the invisible that it stages correspond to the relations between light and the photographic medium: spirits act like the equivalent of light, leaving a trace of their insubstantial passage in material form. Ghostly inhabitants of the other side, immaterial substances that informed the realm of the ether, impressed themselves on to the sensitive film of the here and now, through the lens of the medium seated inside a hooded and curtained alcove in a darkened chamber. Early camera obscuras were swathed in fabric with festoons and fringes of velvet and braid, and resemble very closely the draped cabinet of the séance, in which the medium was enclosed, and from which issued the 'phenomena'. Only the lens of the camera obscura and the void in its interior had been replaced—by the woman sitting inside the box. She operated in the place of a camera, or, later, in the place of the television cabinet itself.

230

ACTION UPON MATTER

This imitation of photography's processes was then itself authenticated by documentary images: psychic images taken with magnesium flares proved the prodigious character of the phenomena and the fleeting existence of ectoplasmic apparitions. These ways of generating spirit phenomena still cast the medium as a kind of camera, receiving and transmitting light's action upon matter.

230

IN THE MURK

The spirits' entrance and activities were also rendered persuasive through certain characteristics of the photographic medium: in black-and-white images taken during a séance, light traces appear phantasmic, conjuring the presence of wraiths, while other substances, the mysterious blobs and streaks that the mediums exuded, lose defining details of their appearance in the murk of the darkened chamber, illuminated only by a red bulb and the sudden dazzling flash of magnesium. They become as it were transubstantiated. Thus the pseudo-scientific aims and claims of the investigators and performers collide with the phantasmagoric manipulations of sense impressions and data in the séance.

243

FLAMMARION

A different experience of time began to be explored: in 1873, the versatile Flammarion wrote a curious Platonic dialogue about the possibilities of time-travel; in this early piece of science fiction, he personifies a comet called "Lumen", and imagines travelling through the ether all the way back through that beam's history to the beginning of the world, via the Battle of Waterloo and other events.

270

CONNECTION

Running through the myriad different approaches to spirits or psychic forces is a simple desire for connection, across time and space, within laws of mortality, separation and even decorum. The medium at the séance in some senses vanishes like the vanishing lady in the conjuring trick, because what matters are the voices and presences coming through her, and they are not enfleshed. This disembodiment is the patent condition of spirit, and in some unspoken way, the deepest and most ambiguous desideratum of the long experiment with psychic research.

272

PROBLEM OF IMPONDERABLES

The concept of ectoplasm grew out of Victorian physics and cognitive sciences and the post-Darwinian challenge to traditional faith. Ectoplasmic phenomena figured generic stuff of the spirit, not unique ghosts of dead souls. Ectoplasm did not *haunt* its believers: it offered a solution to the problem of imponderables, and embodied a postulated *prima materia.* From its first appearances in psychic experiments in the 1880s, ectoplasm was intensely pursued by scientifically minded researchers, who did not always believe in spirits as ghosts of the dead, and did not declare themselves to be Spiritualists. They were questing to know the structure of the universe.

Ectoplasm thus materialised phenomena from the world beyond the senses for its hopeful believers. It is "the substance from which spirits make themselves visible forms', but in itself it is shapeless, *informe* a kind of primordial paste—and to show itself as this, it borrows the metaphors of shapelessness, as with clouds and air and spirit bodies, as discussed earlier.... This new supernatural stuff approximates, awkwardly, to the *hyle* of matter in Aristotelian thought; it receives the stamp of the spirit conjured by the medium, and is extruded as form.

290

METAPHYSICS AND QUANTUM THEORY

But ectoplasm is an important chapter in the story of the spirit: it represents the final shake of the pieces that make up the traditional picture of ethereality. It offered its believers a wonderful proof of the existence of other states of matter, and as such, embodies a transition in the history of scientific inquiry between Christian metaphysics and quantum theory: it also, with regard to the argument of this book, materialises a long enduring metaphor at the most literal level, demonstrating the power of language in shaping experience.

300

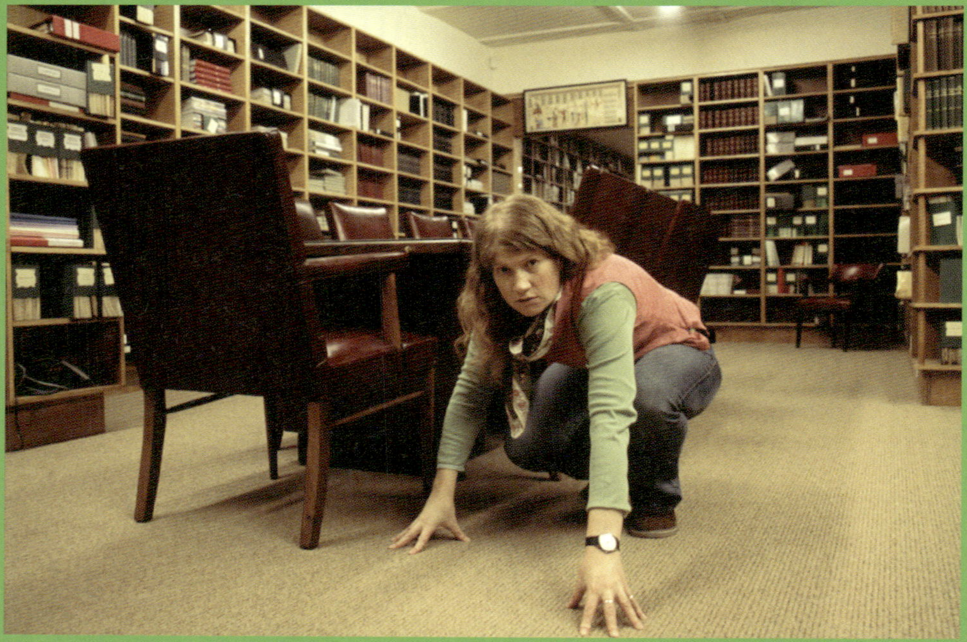

Artist as Medium, 2008, Stereoscopic Image, Eileen J Garrett Library, Parapsychology Foundation, New York

Ciaran Carson

NOTHING

BUT

THE

TRUTH

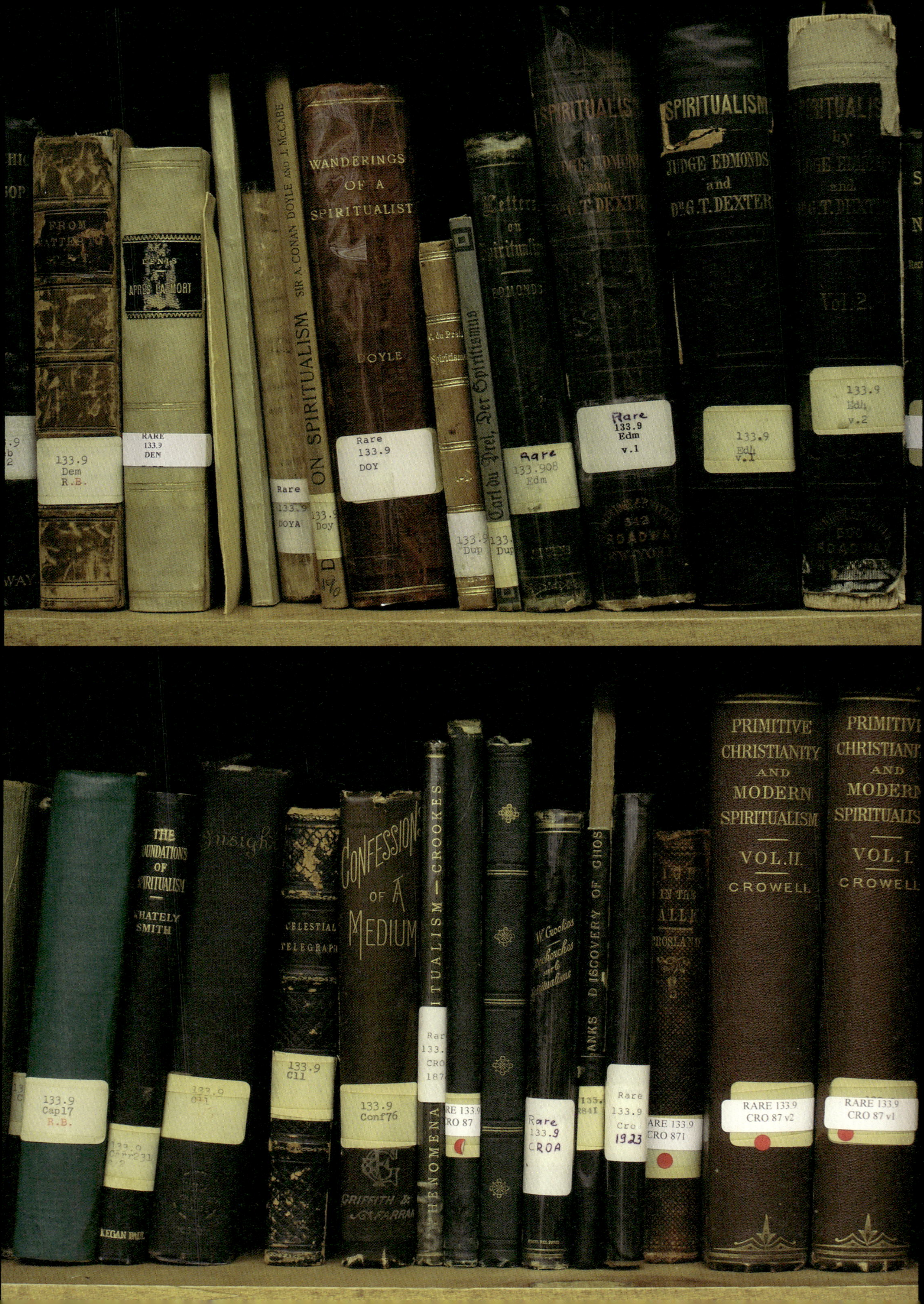

APRÈS LA MORT
SIR A. CONAN DOYLE AND J. McCABE
ON SPIRITUALISM
WANDERINGS OF A SPIRITUALIST
DOYLE
Carl du Prel, Der Spiritismus
Letters on Spiritualism
EDMONDS
SPIRITUALISM
by
JUDGE EDMONDS
and
Dr G. T. DEXTER
Vol. 2.
THE FOUNDATIONS OF SPIRITUALISM
WHATELY SMITH
KEGAN PAUL
CELESTIAL TELEGRAPH
CONFESSIONS OF A MEDIUM
GRIFFITH & FARRAN
PHENOMENA OF SPIRITUALISM — CROOKES
W. Crookes Researches in the Phenomena of Spiritualism
DISCOVERY OF GHOSTS
PRIMITIVE CHRISTIANITY AND MODERN SPIRITUALISM
VOL. II.
VOL. I.
CROWELL

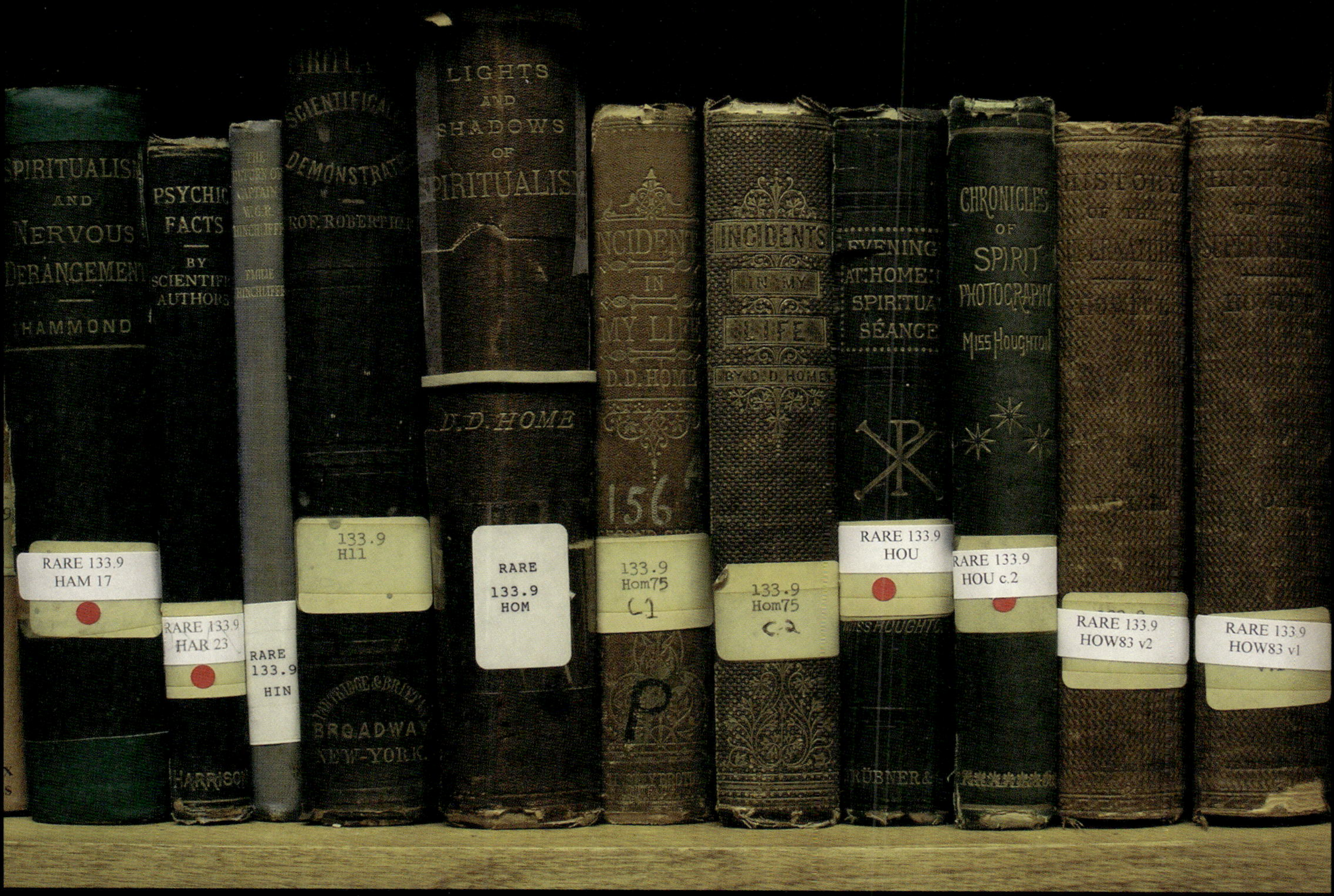
AND
NERVOUS
HAMMOND
RARE 133.9
HAM 17
FACTS
BY
AUTHORS
RARE 133.9
HAR 23
HARRISON
RARE
133.9
HIN
133.9
H11
BROADWAY
NEW-YORK
LIGHTS
AND
SHADOWS
OF
D.D. HOME
RARE
133.9
HOM
IN
D.D. HOME
133.9
Hom75
C1
INCIDENTS
LIFE
133.9
Hom75
c.2
EVENING
SÉANCE
RARE 133.9
HOU
CHRONICLES
OF
SPIRIT
PHOTOGRAPHY
MISS HOUGHTON
RARE 133.9
HOU c.2
RARE 133.9
HOW83 v2
RARE 133.9
HOW83 v1

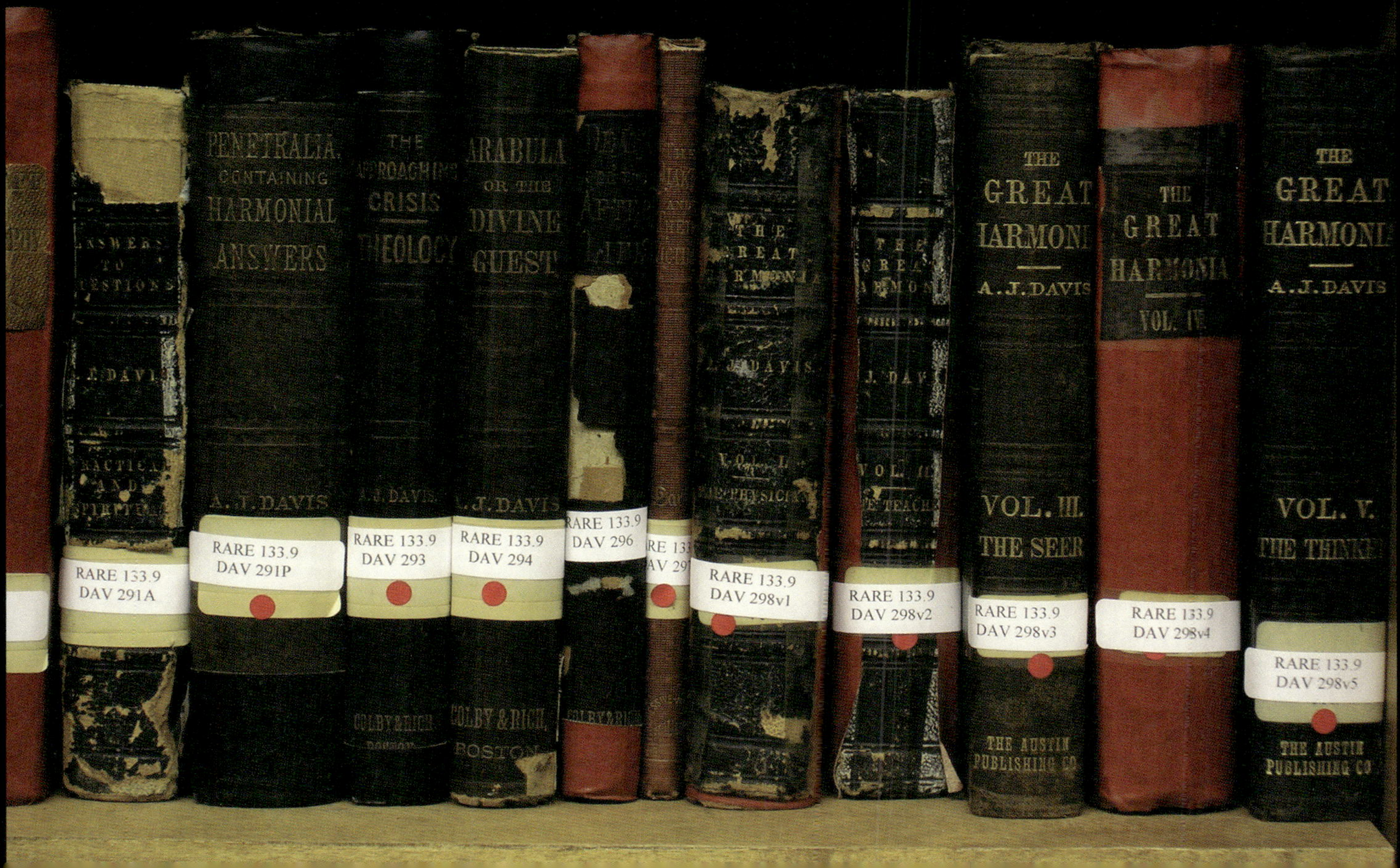
RARE 133.9
DAV 291A
PENETRALIA
CONTAINING
HARMONIAL
ANSWERS
A. J. DAVIS
RARE 133.9
DAV 291P
THE
CRISIS
THEOLOGY
A. J. DAVIS
RARE 133.9
DAV 293
COLBY & RICH
ARABULA
OR THE
DIVINE
GUEST
A. J. DAVIS
RARE 133.9
DAV 294
COLBY & RICH,
BOSTON
RARE 133.9
DAV 296
RARE 133.9
DAV 298v1
RARE 133.9
DAV 298v2
THE
GREAT
A. J. DAVIS
VOL. III.
THE SEER
RARE 133.9
DAV 298v3
THE AUSTIN
PUBLISHING CO
THE
GREAT
HARMONIA
VOL. IV
RARE 133.9
DAV 298v4
THE
GREAT
A. J. DAVIS
VOL. V.
RARE 133.9
DAV 298v5
THE AUSTIN
PUBLISHING CO

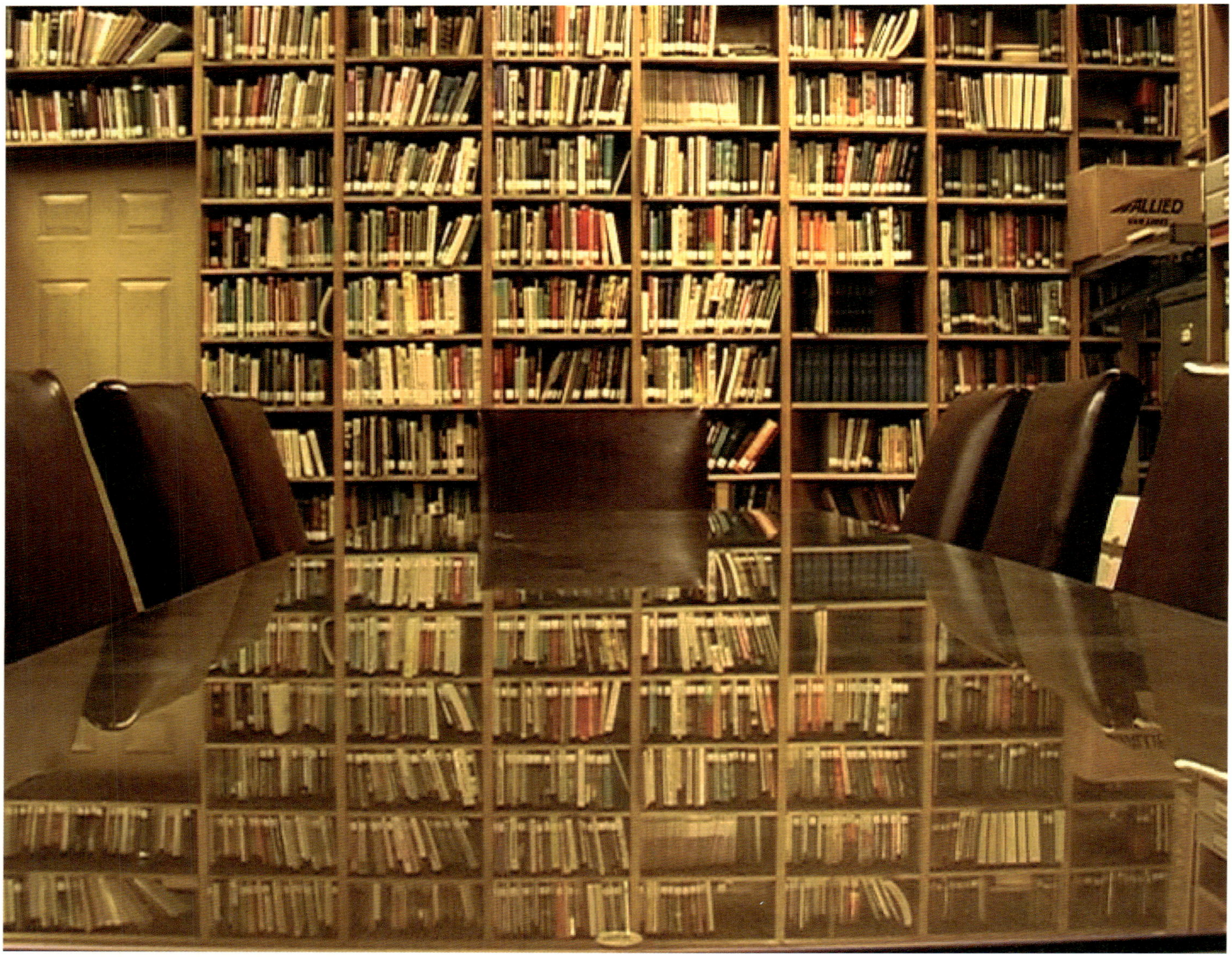

Library, 2008, Video, Colour, Stereo, 14mins, 10secs

It is quiet in the library. But, though seemingly devoid of human presence, it is not quite silent. I think I detect a faint mechanical hum, if only because the sleeve of the DVD states that "the air conditioner provides the soundtrack", and we are inclined to believe what we are told in such circumstances. Had my attention not been thus drawn to it, I wouldn't have noticed it, I think. Even now, given this information, it seems virtually indistinguishable from the normal, almost subliminal noise of the computer I am watching it on. Maybe it's DVD noise.

DVD stands for "Digital Versatile Disc" or "Digital Video Disc". Video is Latin for "I see" or "I am seeing". What am I seeing? Nothing moves in the room I am watching or looking into on the screen. It looks like a still, one paused frame of a motion picture, which is a series of still photographs played at speed in order to produce the illusion of motion, in the manner of a flicker-book or zoetrope. The picture shows a long rectangular polished table with a reading-lamp, behind whose pool of light reside spectral shelves of books. The scene runs for a full minute—a long time when nothing is happening—and I am beginning to think it is indeed a still—a still life perhaps—when the scene cuts suddenly to another. The same room (I believe it to be the same room, but that is an assumption) is shown from a different angle this time, from directly under the reading-lamp. It's one of those old-fashioned banker's lamps with a green glass shade and a chain-pull switch, and the chain-pull is swaying or vibrating ever so slightly, indicating that an unseen operator has just switched it on in the

PREVIOUS PAGES:
Rare Books, 2007, Photographs, Eileen J Garrett Library, Parapsychology Foundation, New York

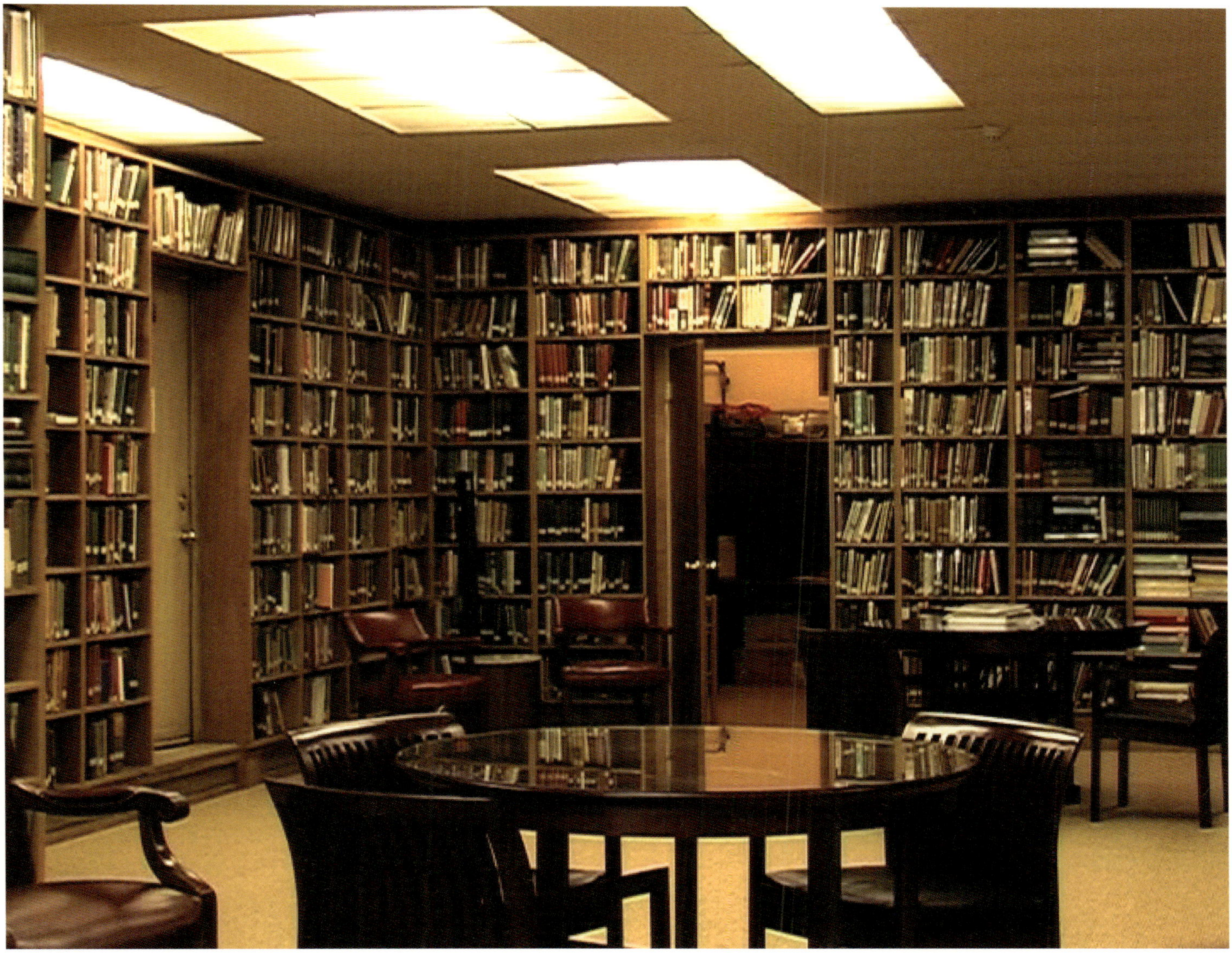

seemingly unpeopled room. Or perhaps the motion is caused by a draught: from this angle we see an open door leading to another room. In any event or at any rate it would seem to be happening in 'real' time, the time that it takes for the video to be taken.

The chain-pull is swinging minimally like a pendulum about to come to rest, except it never does come to rest for the 30 seconds' duration of this scene, but keeps on doing the same thing within the same tiny arc of motion. The room is more fully visible now, possibly because the light on in the other room is spilling into the main room, or maybe there is another, unseen light-source. The shelves of books are reflected in the polished surface of the table, and there is another table, a round one, in the background in front of the open door of the other room, in which there is a picture hanging on the wall in the manner of the paintings shown on the walls of Dutch genre interior paintings.

Cut. I am looking at the interior of another room, or maybe it is a different take on the same room. The light is much brighter here, and the room more cluttered. Books are heaped on a rectangular table and on the floor. There are brown cardboard storage boxes stacked in one corner. One set of bookshelves is neatly filled with books bearing white catalogue number labels on their spines; the other is in some disarray, many books piled horizontally, interspersed with random stacks of journals and pamphlets. It looks like the room is in the midst of a process, whether of ordering or disordering, renovation or dereliction I cannot tell.

Cut. A close-up of two stacks of books and other paper materials, the light emphasizing the deckled fore

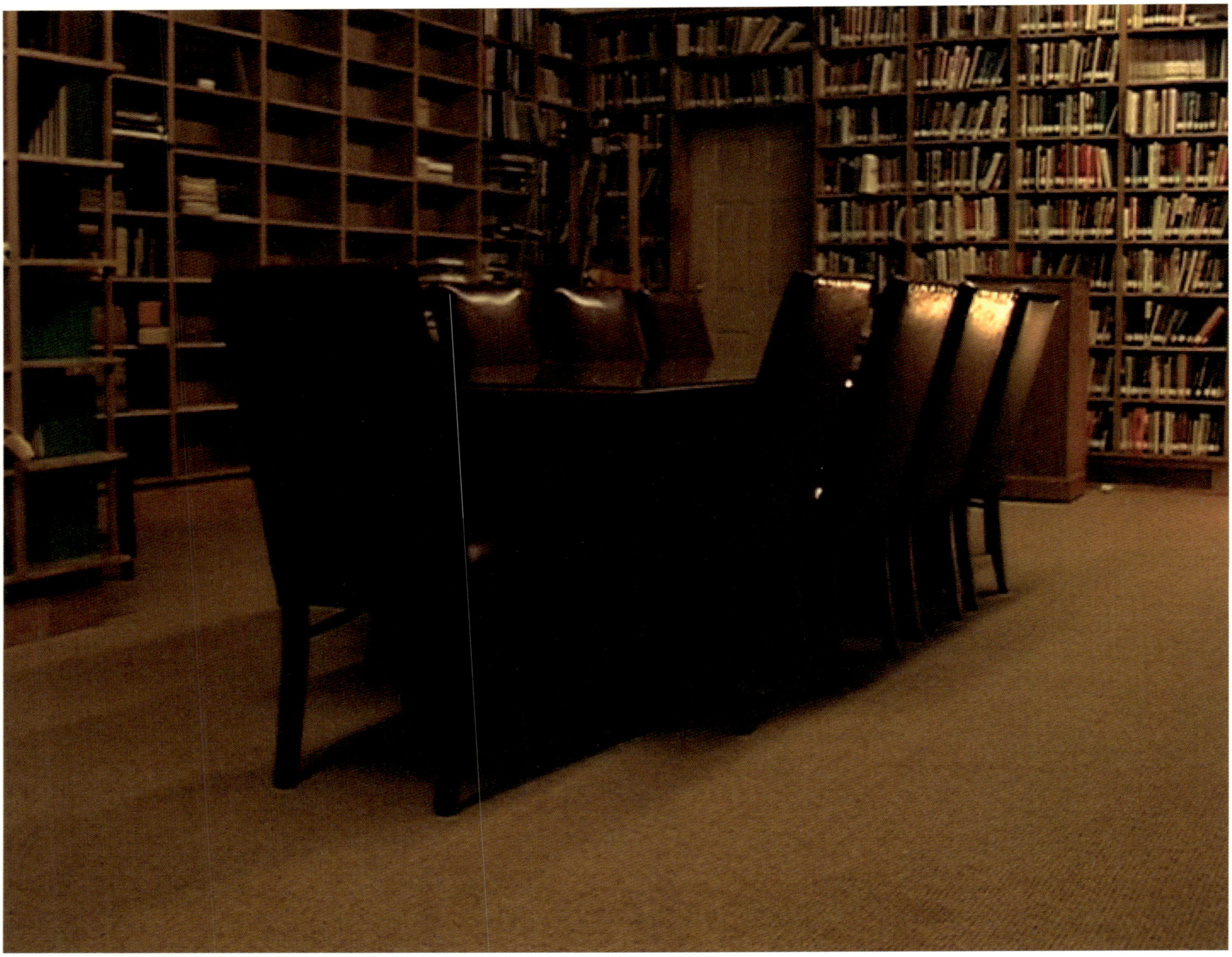

edges of their pages. Between them is a dark space, the threshold of a portal into another dimension, an unfathomable void. Cut. A brightly lit, spacious room, perhaps a different take on a previous room. Some of the shelves are empty and there is a step-ladder in one corner. Cut. Another close-up of two stacks of books with a dark tunnel in between. The top or bottom page edges of three of the books are stamped "Parapsychology Foundation Inc. Library". I imagine lifting one of them and riffling it in flicker-book mode so that the letters momentarily disintegrate, the ink a near-invisible blip of each of the page edges, before regaining their status quo as a badge of ownership. Cut.

Cut and cut and cut. A store-room or store-rooms piled with storage boxes and random clutter. Rooms with rectangular tables in them, or round tables, high leather-backed chairs, all of them unpeopled as the Marie Celeste. All those who occupied these chairs through time have gone into the void beyond the Library. Close-ups of books. *Chronicles of Spirit Photography. Essays from the Unseen. There is No Death. Spirit Intercourse. Nothing But the Truth.* Memoirs of many people. Susan MacWilliam's video *Library* consists of 53 segments, frames or scenes, and runs for just a little over 14 minutes. Yet the physical spaces represented in that space of time seem labyrinthine and endless, as in Jorge Luis Borges' *Library of Babel.*

It is difficult to tell at first viewing if the actual library consists of one or two rooms reiterated, or many rooms. Even if we assume that only one main room and one or two ancillary store-rooms, reading rooms or annexes are involved, it could be argued

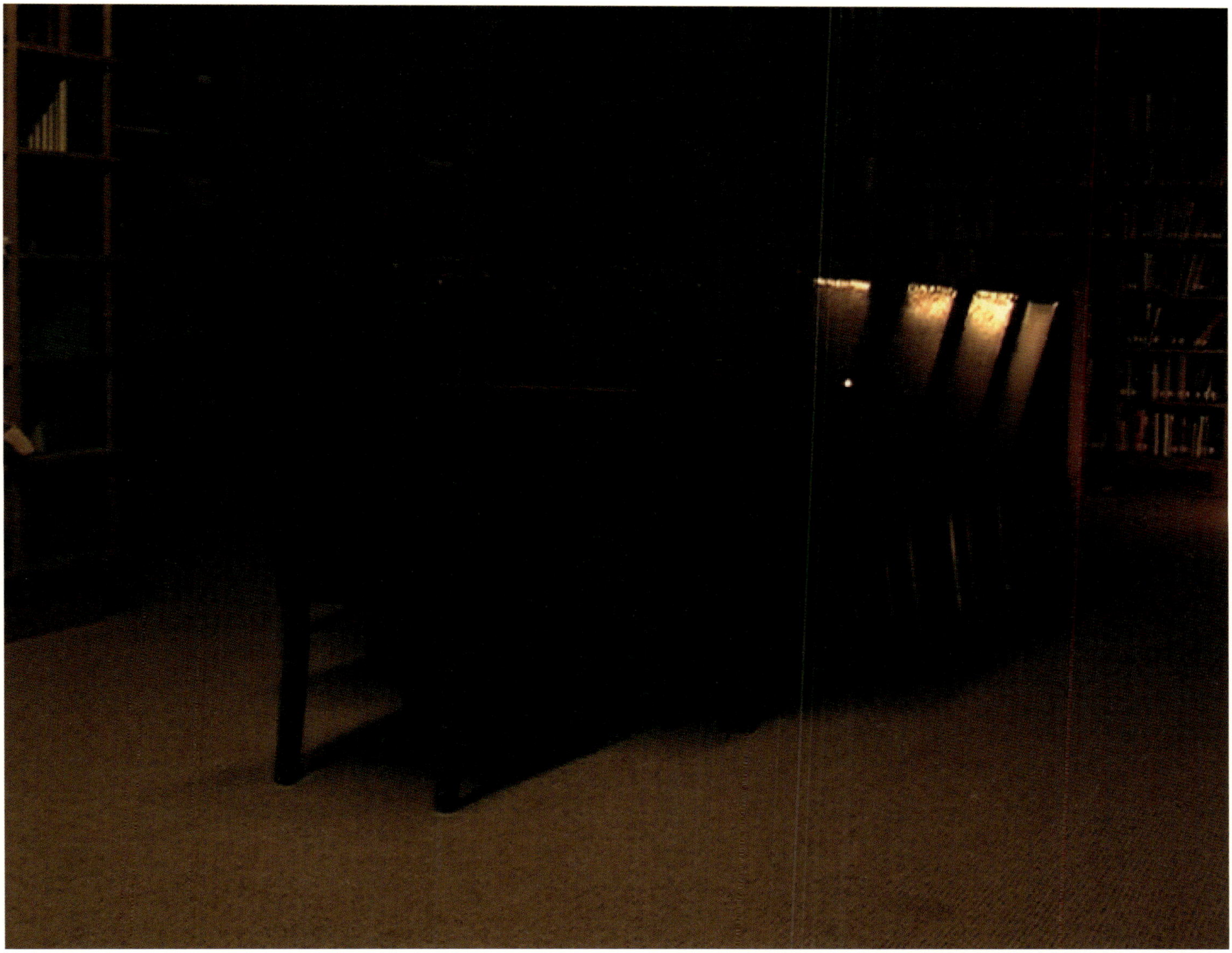

that different aspects of the same room are different experiences, and that the same room viewed differently is not the same room. Again, we are reminded of Borges and his fable of *Funes the Memorious,* who is blessed and cursed with so prodigious a memory that everything he experiences is unique, and that he is consequently incapable of general, Platonic ideas: "It was not only difficult for him to understand that the generic term dog embraced so many unlike specimens of differing sizes and different forms; he was disturbed by the fact that a dog at three-fourteen (seen in profile) should have the same name as the dog at three-fifteen (seen from the front). His own face in the mirror, his own hands, surprised him on every occasion."

When the video ends I go back to the beginning, this time pausing it from time to time to write down what I think I am seeing, or what I remembered from seeing the first time. Then I play it again. Only then does it occur to me to turn up the volume on the computer, and I realise what I have been missing. The ambient noise that accompanies each segment is different in pitch and volume: each room or aspect of a room has its own acoustic, different gradations of pitch and amplitude, fundamentals and overtones. Sounds like whispering, traffic, breathing, distant surf, the engines of an ocean liner bound for other shores. The noise of time passing.

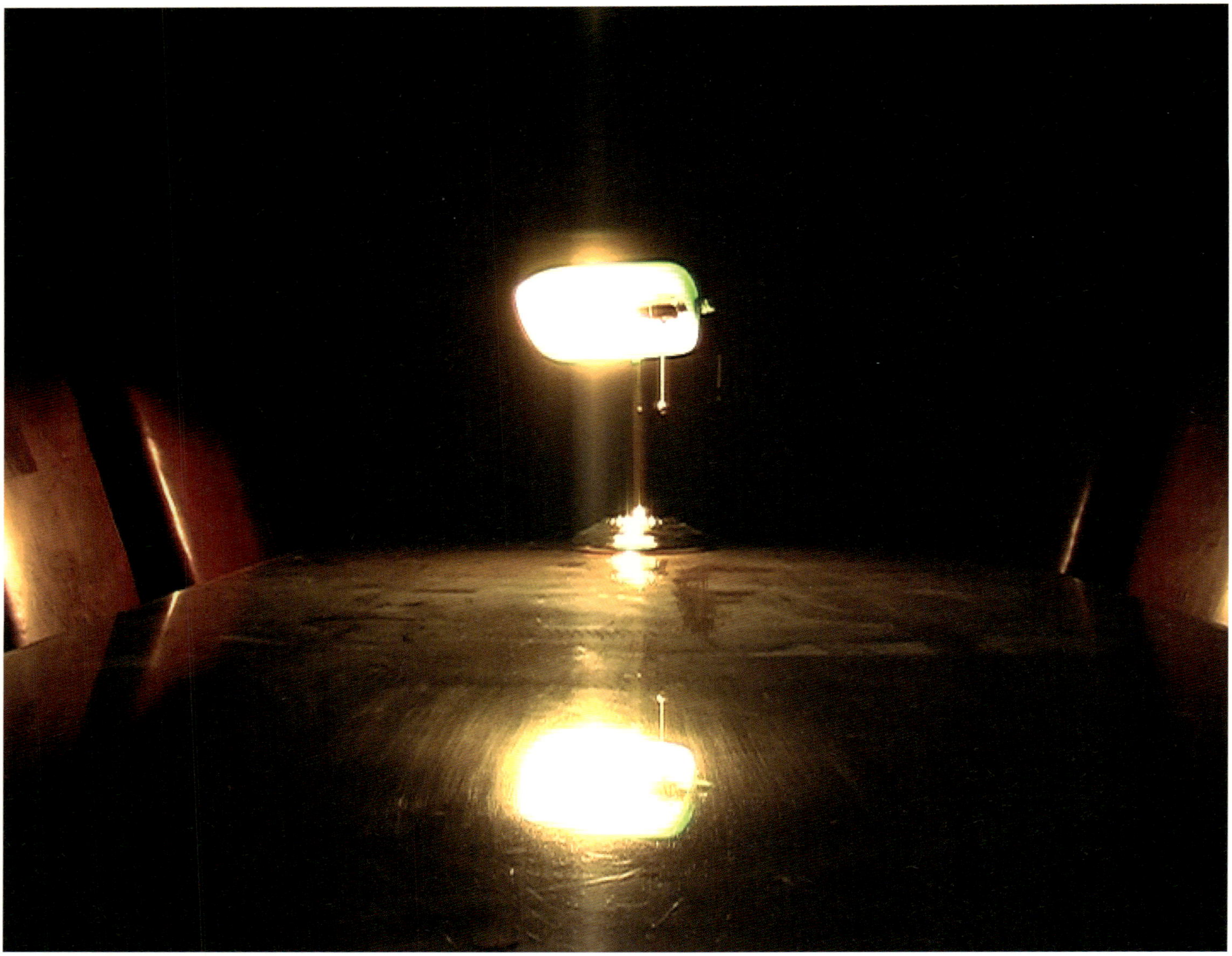

In the first segment of *Library* the light from the reading-lamp is brilliantly reflected in the polished table-top, and a curious side-effect is evident, a spectral column of light extending upwards from the table-top to the outer limit of the field of vision, caused, I assume, by the reflection. When I first saw it I was immediately reminded of a photograph associated with the work of the psychic investigator WJ Crawford.

In 1912, the year that the Titanic sank, Crawford, who had emigrated from New Zealand, became a lecturer in mechanical engineering at Queen's University, Belfast. Between 1915 and 1920 he conducted a series of experiments in the séance room of the eponymous circle centred around the medium Kathleen Goligher, as referenced by Susan MacWilliam's video *Experiment M*. The phenomena were of the usual kind—rappings, manipulation of objects, and levitations of a small table in a dimly lit attic. He established to his own satisfaction that Kathleen Goligher was indeed a powerfully gifted medium, and that the phenomena were caused by "psychic rods" extruded from the orifices of her body and controlled by mysterious "operators" in the world beyond the grave. Anxious to verify the physical existence of the rods, he made several attempts to photograph them using the then primitive technology of flash, since the Circle would allow him to photograph their proceedings only in the dark.

On 23 October 1915, as described by him in his book *The Reality of Psychic Structures*, he succeeded in obtaining an image which seemed to corroborate his theory. On the developed plate, plainly visible within

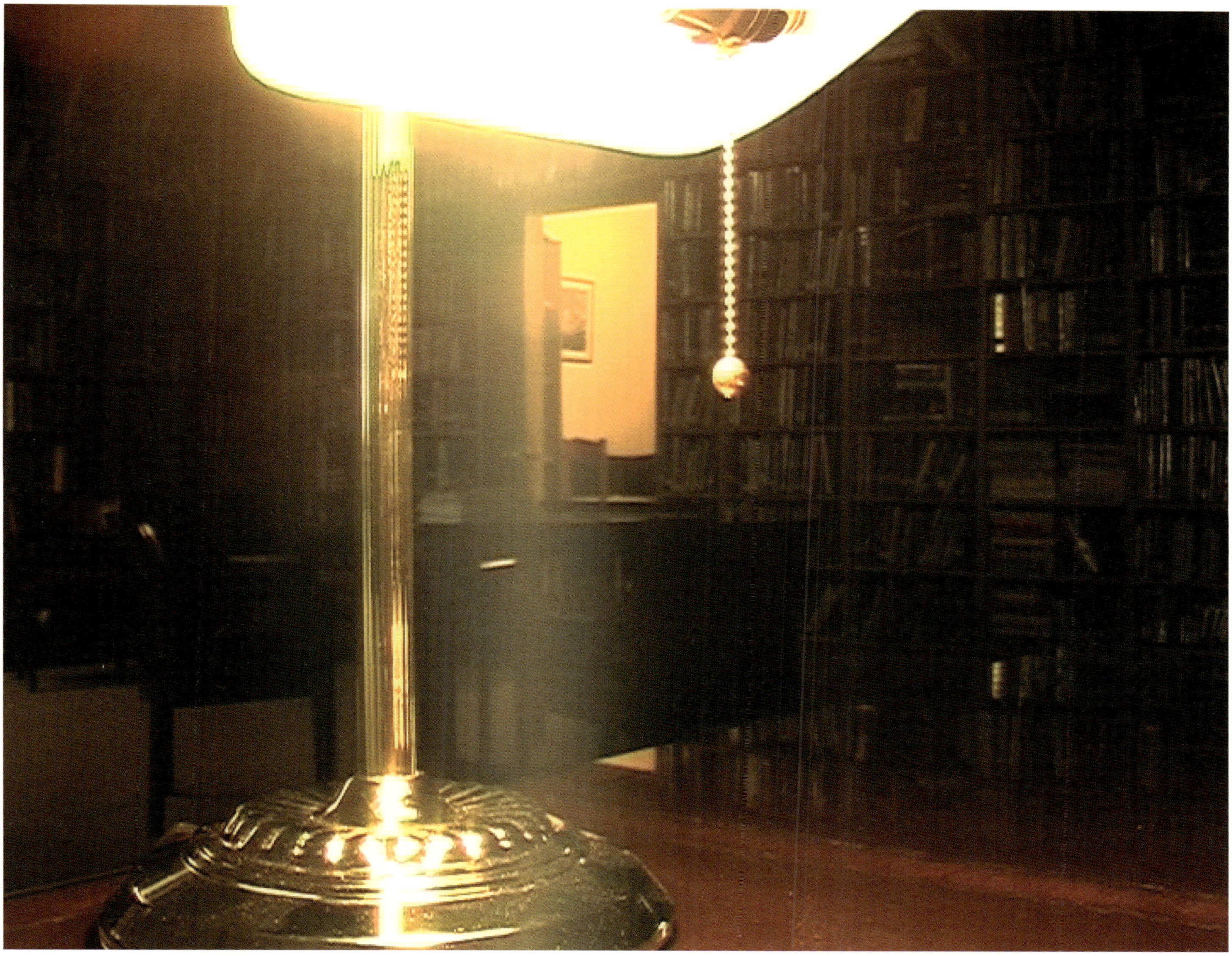

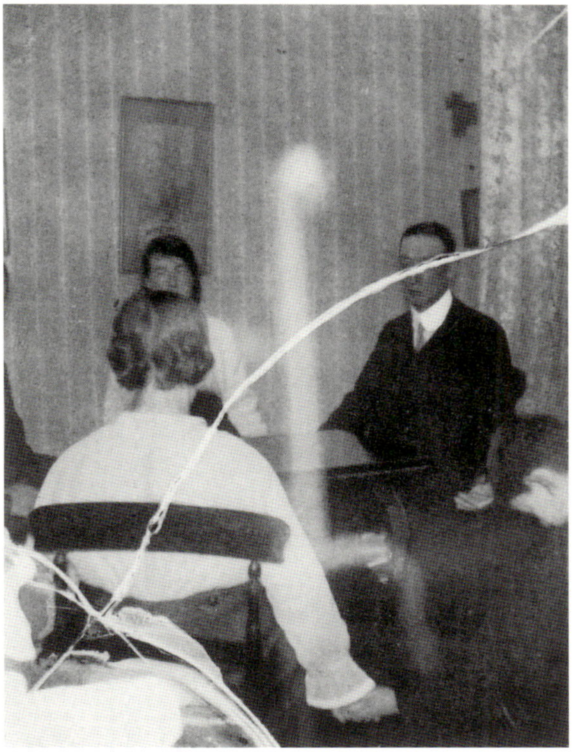

Psychic Structure, from *The Psychic Structures at the Goligher Circle*, by WJ Crawford, 1921, EP Dutton and Company. Courtesy Mary Evans Picture Library

the Goligher Circle, was a vertical column of whitish translucent material, about four inches in diameter and rising to a height of about five feet. The pattern of the wallpaper was quite easily seen through it, said Crawford. At its summit, however, it appeared quite opaque, as if the psychic stuff, issuing from its source, had exhausted its velocity at the top, and had doubled over on itself. The column, moreover, had several arms or branches, one of which appeared to terminate in or emanate from the chest of the medium. Others were joined to Miss Anna Goligher and Master S Goligher.

The whole photograph suggested to Crawford that the medium was in reality a psychic pump, with a complete pressure system. Perhaps, during levitation, the vertical column was under the table, in which case the pressure range would appear much greater. As it was,

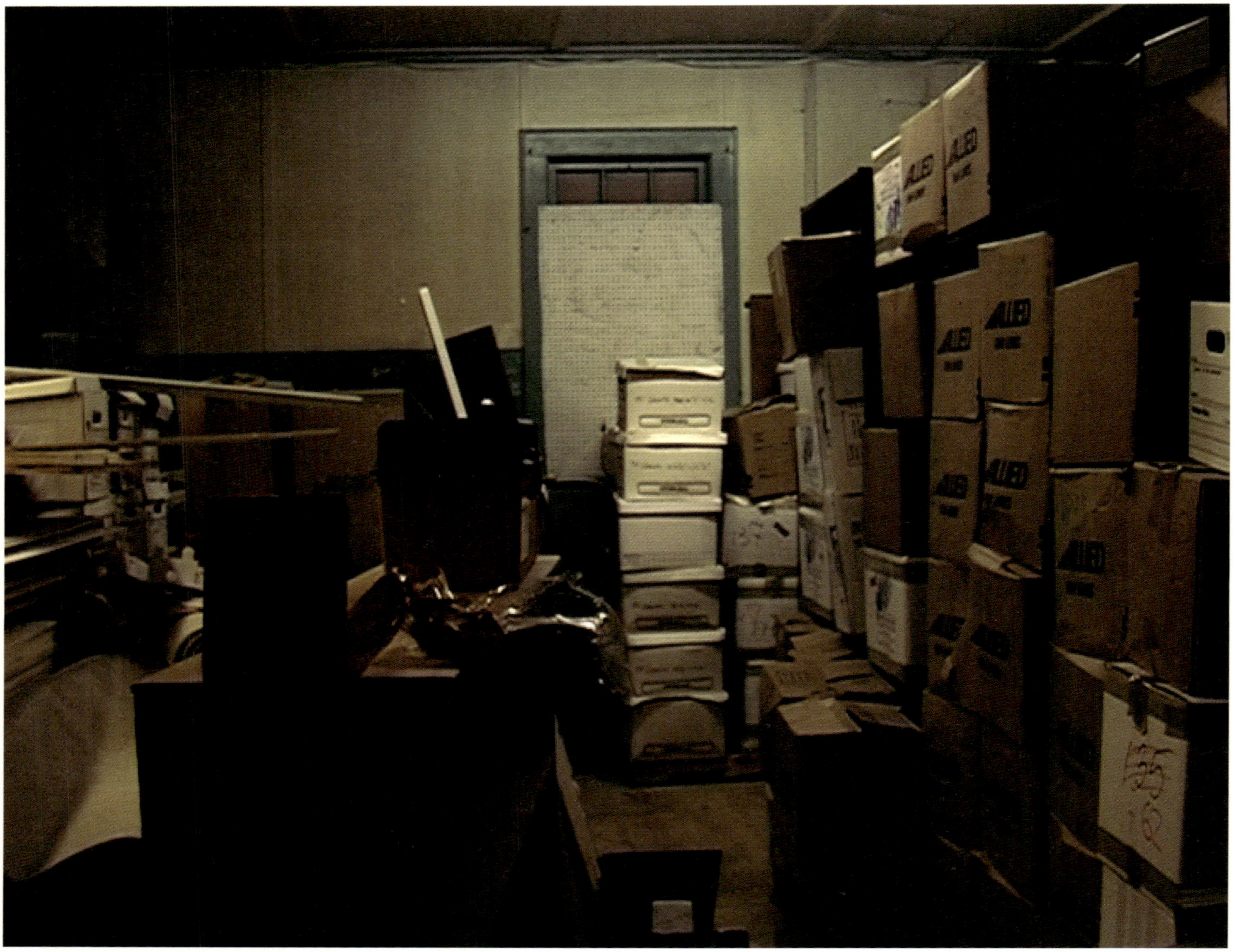

the psychic fluid appeared to be losing its energy much in the same way as a vertical jet of water, projected upwards against its own weight only, inevitably loses impetus and falls back. For whatever reason, Crawford failed to reproduce the photograph to support his verbal account, though it appeared in his posthumous book, *The Psychic Structures at the Goligher Circle,* published not long after he committed suicide in 1920. The plate is cracked. The "psychic rod" resembles the column of spectral light in Susan MacWilliam's *Library,* though admittedly it curves back on itself at its end.

Elsewhere Crawford, groping around in the dark under the medium's feet, reported that he had felt a substance which had a cold, clammy reptilian feeling, an observation which tallies with other accounts of the phenomena. Crawford referred to it as "plasma", a version of the more common term "ectoplasm". Baron Albert von Schrenck Notzing, in *The Phenomena of Materialisation,* his exhaustive study of the medium Eva C, noted that its movements could be "slowly undulating, sometimes in zigzag, or in wavy lines, comparable with the creeping of a snake, or the progress of a jelly-like material".

Sometimes the ectoplasm assumed more elaborate forms. Dr Gustave Geley, in experiments endorsed by Sir Arthur Conan Doyle, often saw complete representations of faces, fingers, hands, often with all the properties of a living organ: fingers with perfectly modelled nails, complete hands with their bones and joints, heads with palpable skulls under thick hair. Sometimes the forms appeared flat and two-dimensional, but then would blossom into

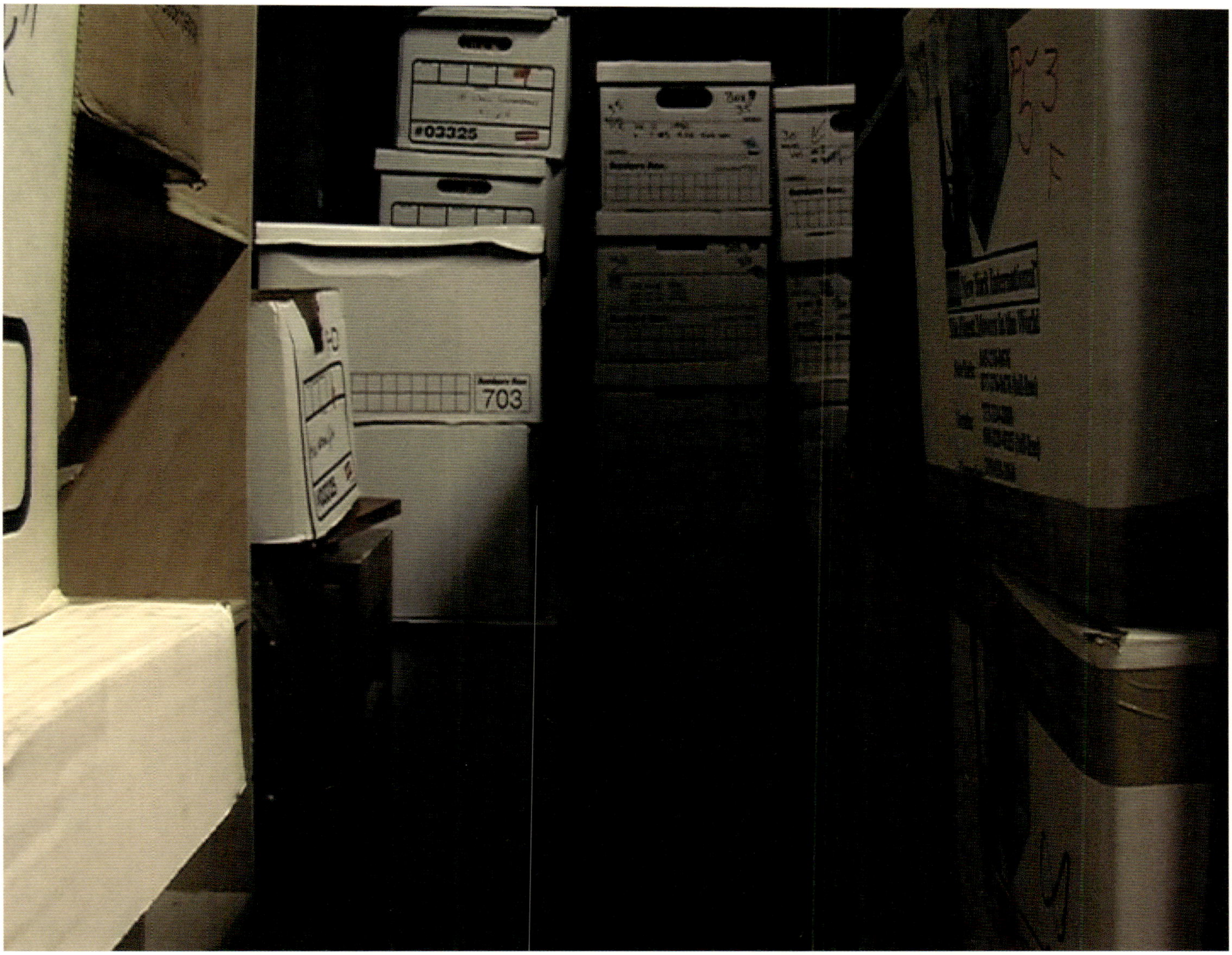

three dimensions under Geley's eyes. At other times, the images retained this cardboard cut-out quality, or assumed bizarre, incomplete forms, like botched imitations or unconvincing simulacra of organs: faces like masks, with tufts of hair sticking to them, and hands like gloves.

Geley compared these to the strange formations called "dermoid cysts", in which are found hair, teeth, viscera, and even more or less complete foetal forms. Supernormal physiology, he argued, like normal physiology, has its finished products, but also its dermoid cysts, abortions and monstrosities. It was clear to him that the formations materialised in séances arose from the same biological process as normal birth. Their production was no more miraculous than the miracle of normal life. The analogy extended to details such as the generation of an umbilical cord connecting the medium to the ectoplasm. Geley had sometimes seen a hand wrapped in a membrane closely resembling that of the placenta; and he had often noted the pain connected with the birth of ectoplasm, the moans and movements of the entranced medium reminding him strangely of a woman in travail.

Common to many accounts of ectoplasm is its ability to sometimes assume a textile form: threads, strings, cords, braids, ropes, pleats, radiating folds and fabric or woven material were all observed. As it happens, Kathleen Goligher was a textile worker in one of Belfast's spinning mills. To a modern observer, the suspicion arises that she and her Circle were spinning a yarn, a narrative taken as "nothing but the truth" by those who wanted desperately to believe in it.

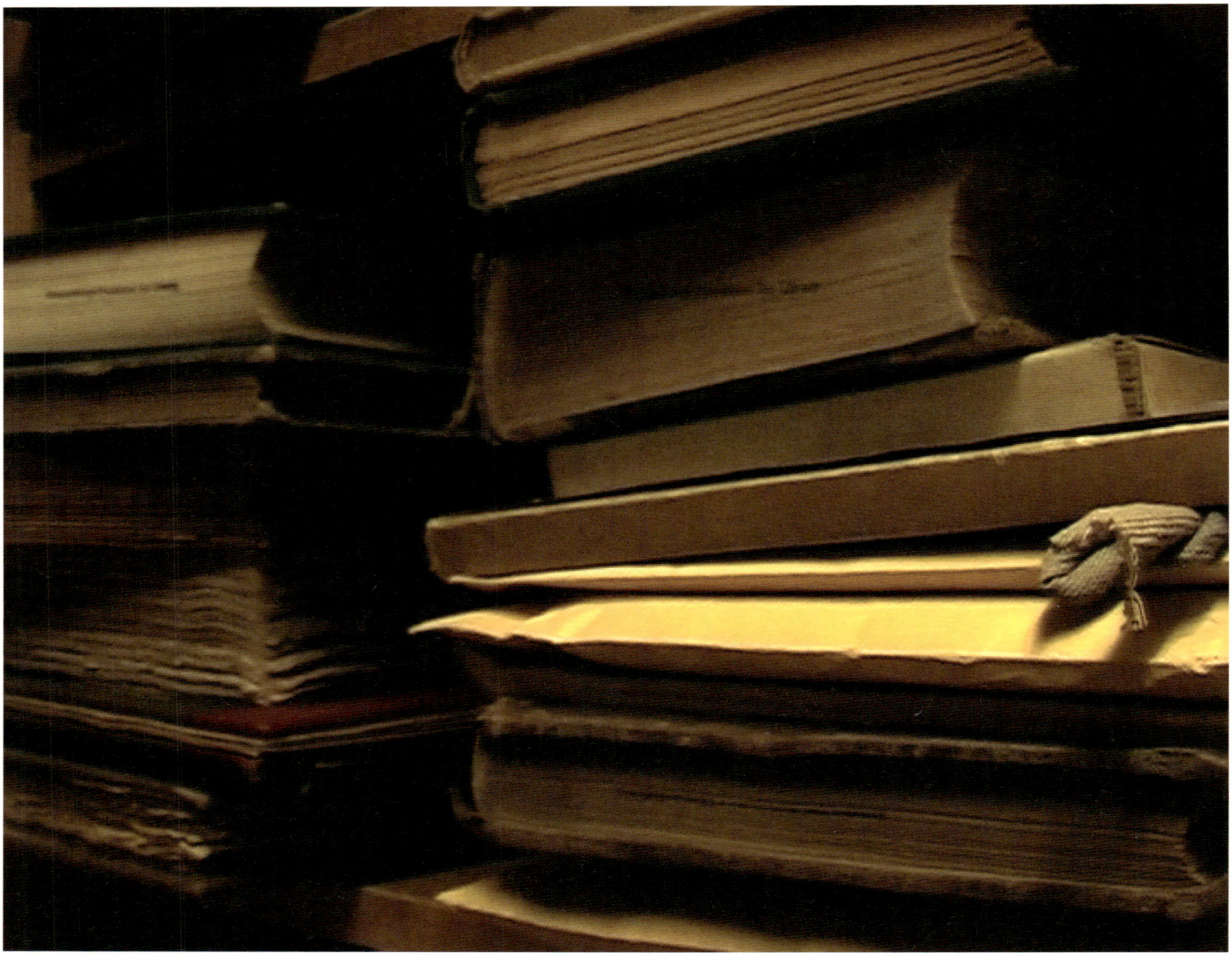

From time to time, in Susan MacWilliam's *Library,* we detect a tremor in the image, for instance when the white walls of a store-room seem to shimmer as if responding to windblown sunlight passing across an unseen window, suggesting a world beyond the library. But we cannot be sure if that is not just an effect of the video reproduction, or of the computer monitor I am viewing it on. If *Library* is a 'motion picture', it is a strange one, since the only thing which moves for certain in it is the chain-pull switch of the banker's lamp.

In this it resembles Chris Marker's film *La Jetée*, 1962, which is assembled entirely from still photographic images except for one moment when one of the protagonists opens her eyes to look into the camera, and smiles. It is a moment which never fails to send a shiver up the viewer's spine. In an interview Marker traced his

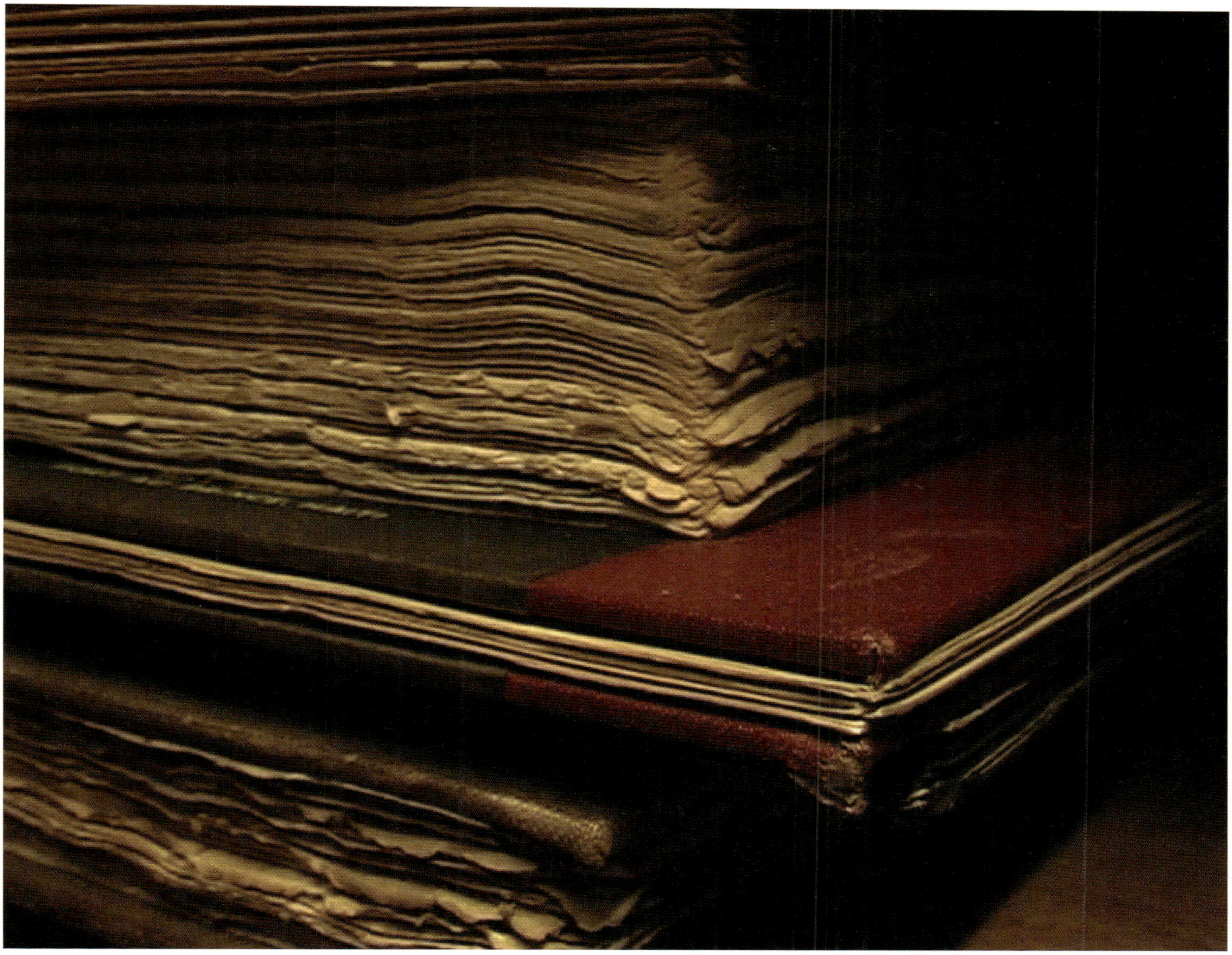

method to a childhood memory of an optical toy called the "Pathéorama", essentially a hand-cranked zoetrope. Marker set to work drawing his own filmstrips, but his attempts were scorned by a school-friend who announced that "nobody can do a film with still images". *La Jetée* also owes much to the French tradition of *bande dessinée* (literally, "drawn strip"), a hommage brought into focus when *La Jetée* was made into a *"ciné-roman"* graphic novel in 1992.

In *La Jetée,* the hero of the film is haunted by an image from his childhood, a memory of the observation jetty at Orly airport and a woman's face, then a man falling and the later realisation that he has seen this man die. Some time after, the city of Paris is destroyed by a nuclear explosion, and the survivors take refuge in the labyrinth of subterranean galleries under the Palais de Chaillot. The hero of the film, because of his strong attachment to this moment in the past, is chosen from a prison camp to be the subject of time-travel experiments by the 'victors' of the war. He is sent into the past where he meets the woman and begins to inhabit her world. The experiments having been deemed to be a success, he travels to the future where Paris has been rebuilt, and is given a power supply to restart the earth's industry. He now realises that the experimenters are finished with him and that he will be killed. He receives a visit from the men of the future, who also travel in time and invite him to join them, but he asks instead to be sent back to the jetty at Orly. As he runs towards the woman, he recognises a guard who has followed him from the camp and who shoots him. The man realises that there is no escape from Time, and that the image that has

haunted him from childhood was the moment of his own death. *La Jetée* is a closed, self-referential loop, a series of moments endlessly replayed.

La Jetée deals with the manipulation of time and memory, as does all film. The illusion of motion in a series of still images is due to the phenomenon of the eye known as "persistence of vision", by which even nanoseconds of exposure to an image result in milliseconds of reaction from the retina to the optic nerves. Watching a film is a kind of remembering. Perhaps all film is a kind of elegy.

I turn again to *Library* and run it through again, asking myself again what it is I am listening to, what it is I am seeing, what it is I am imagining, what it is I am remembering.

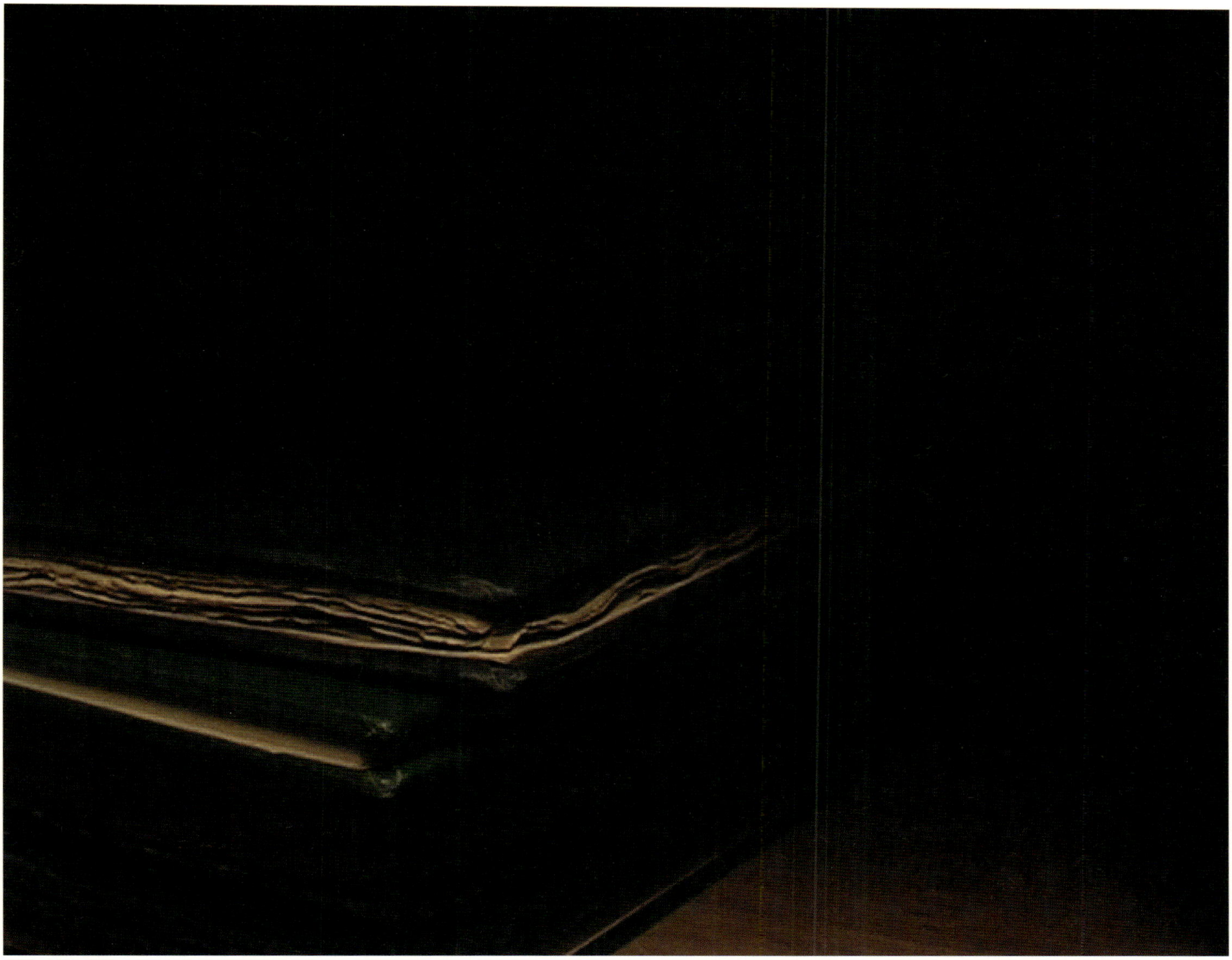

2008, Synchronised three-channel video installation, Colour, Stereo, 28mins 53secs

EILEEN

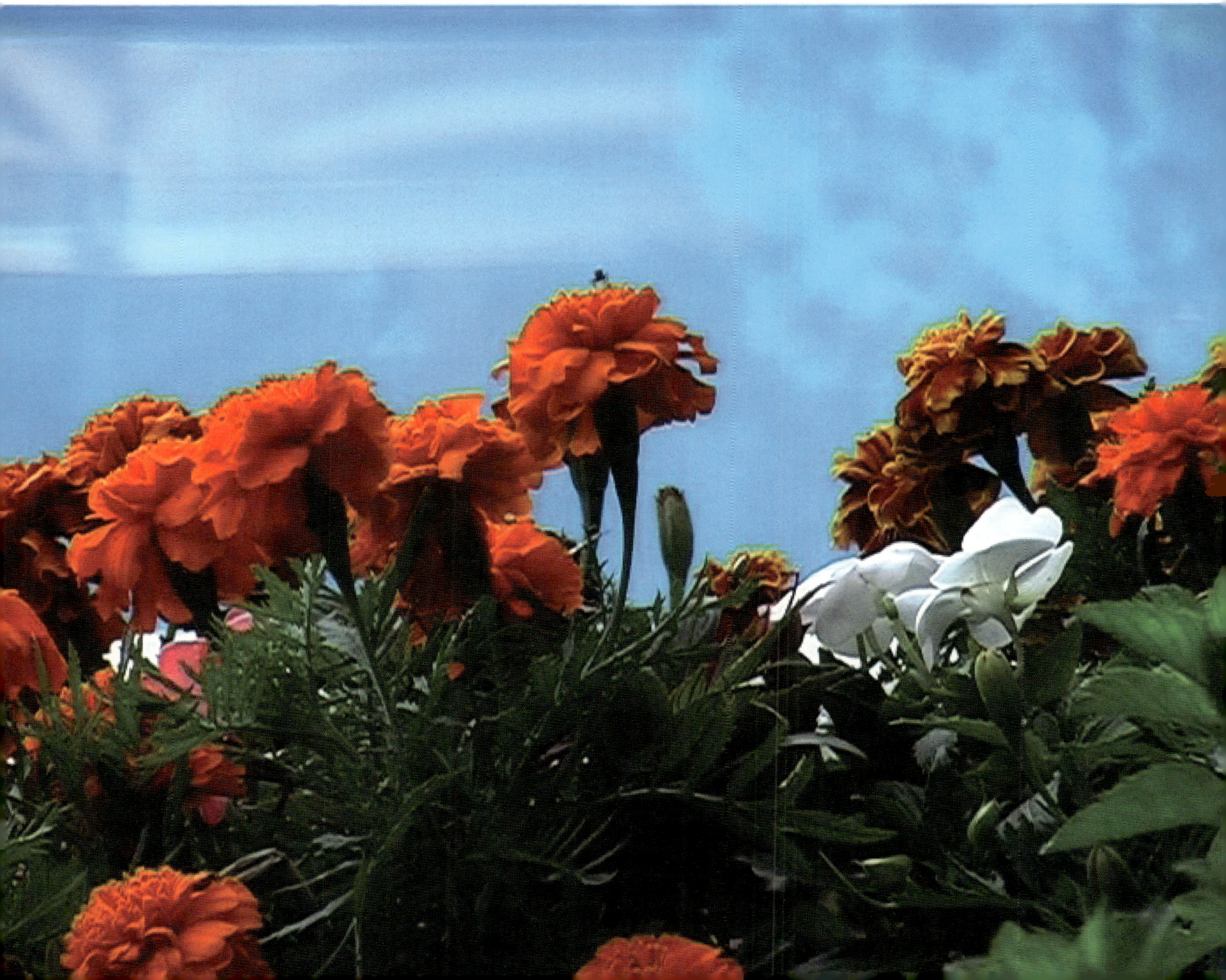

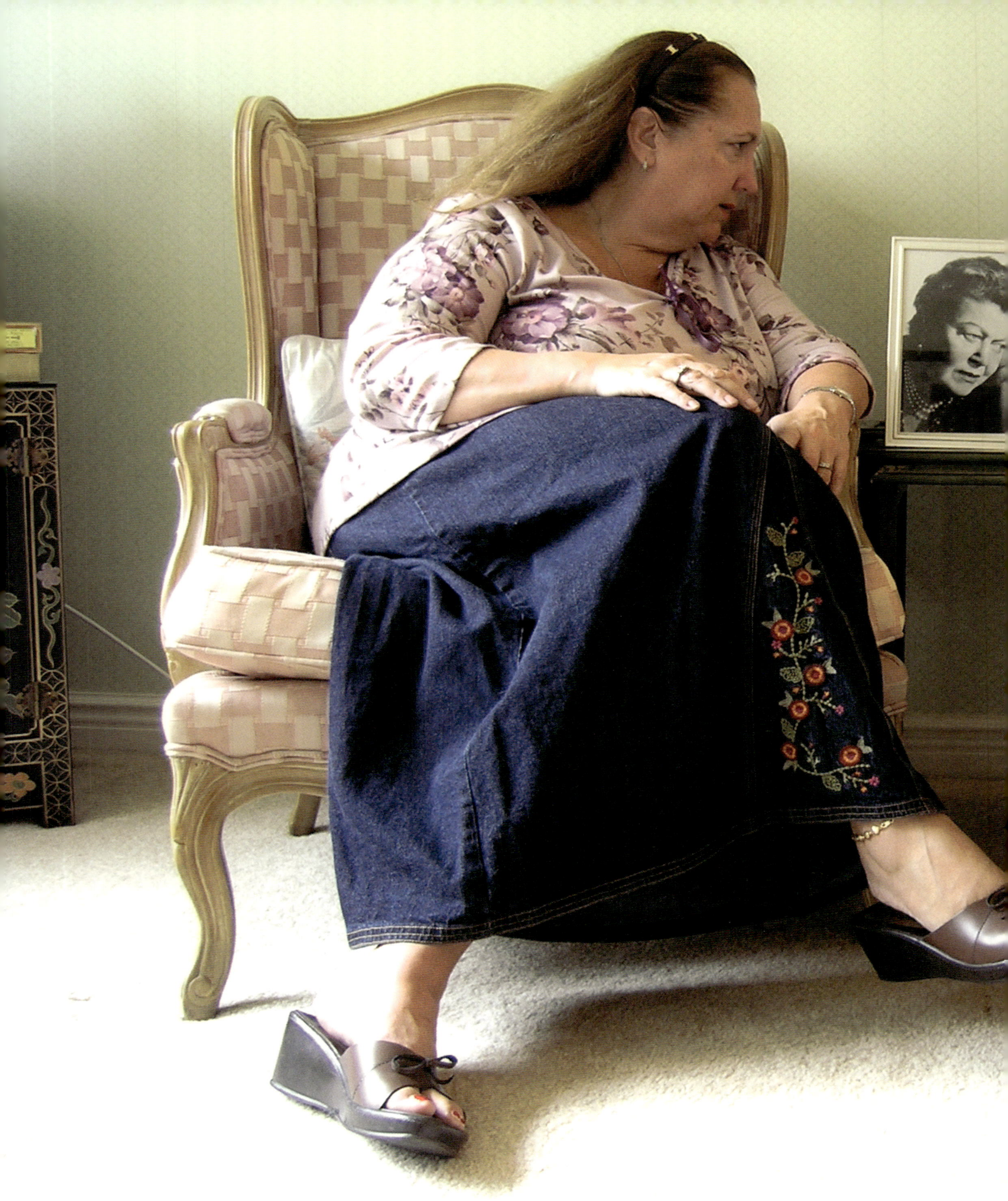

Garrett Girls, 2006, Photograph, Manhattan, New York, left–right: Lisette Coly, Eileen J Garrett, Eileen Coly

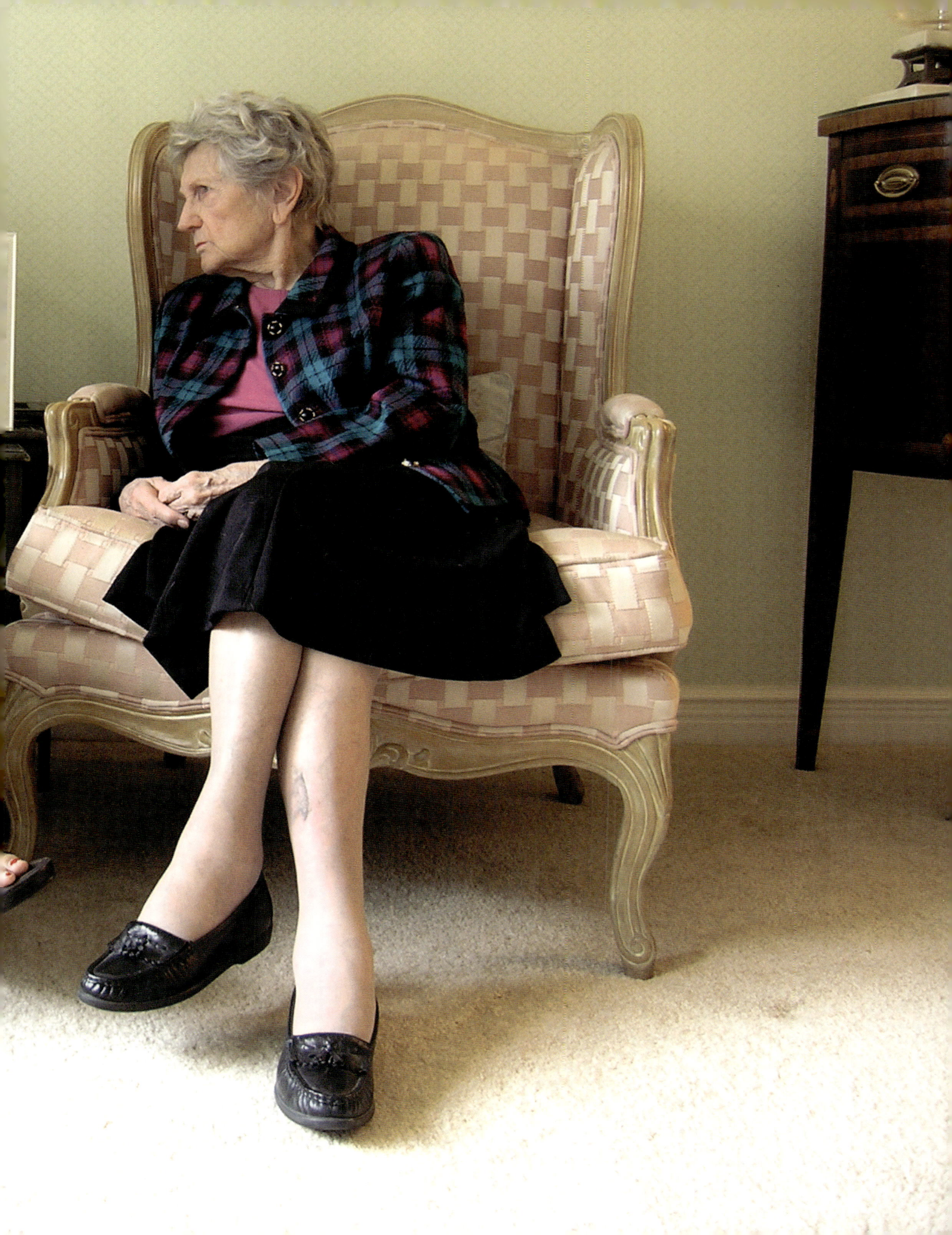

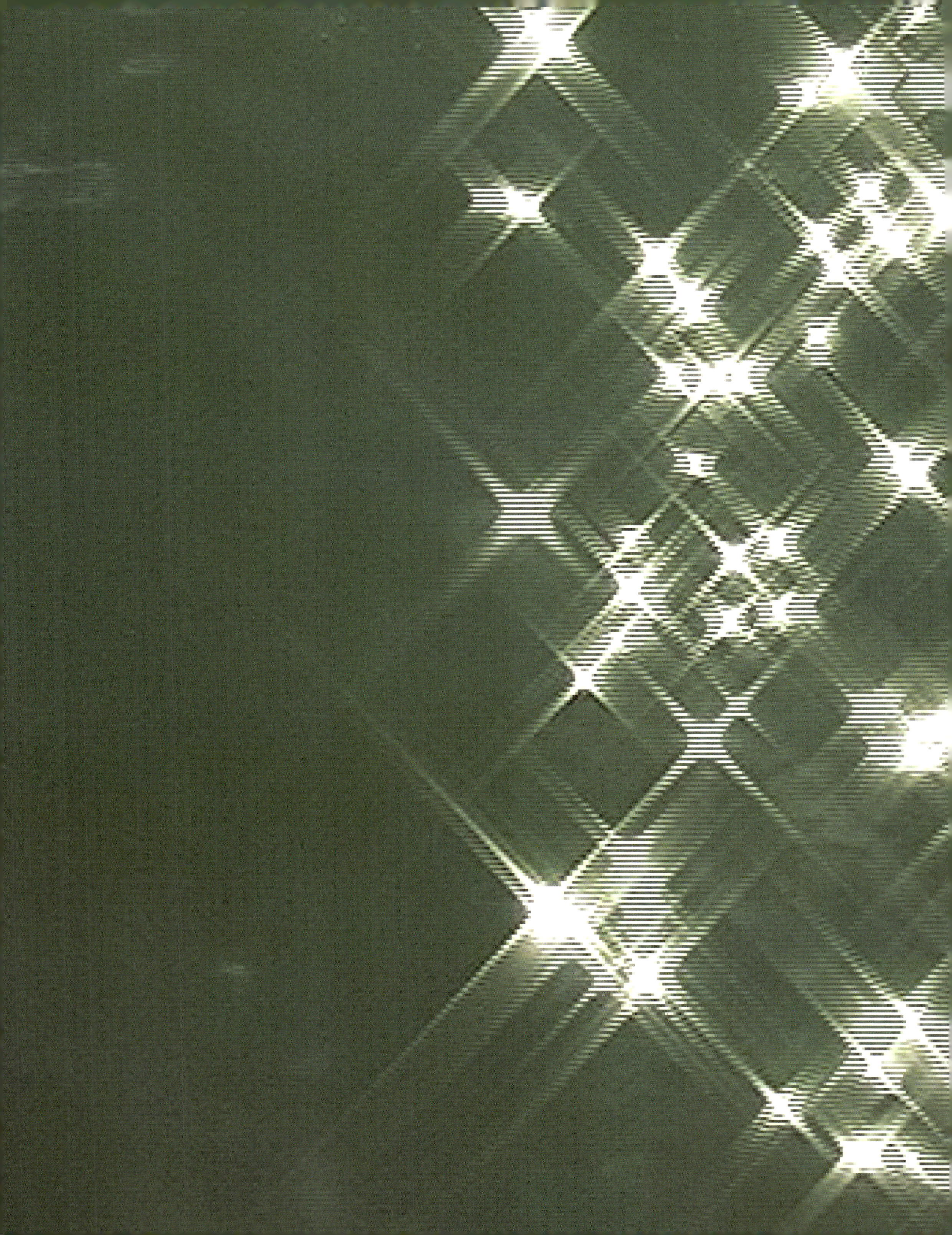

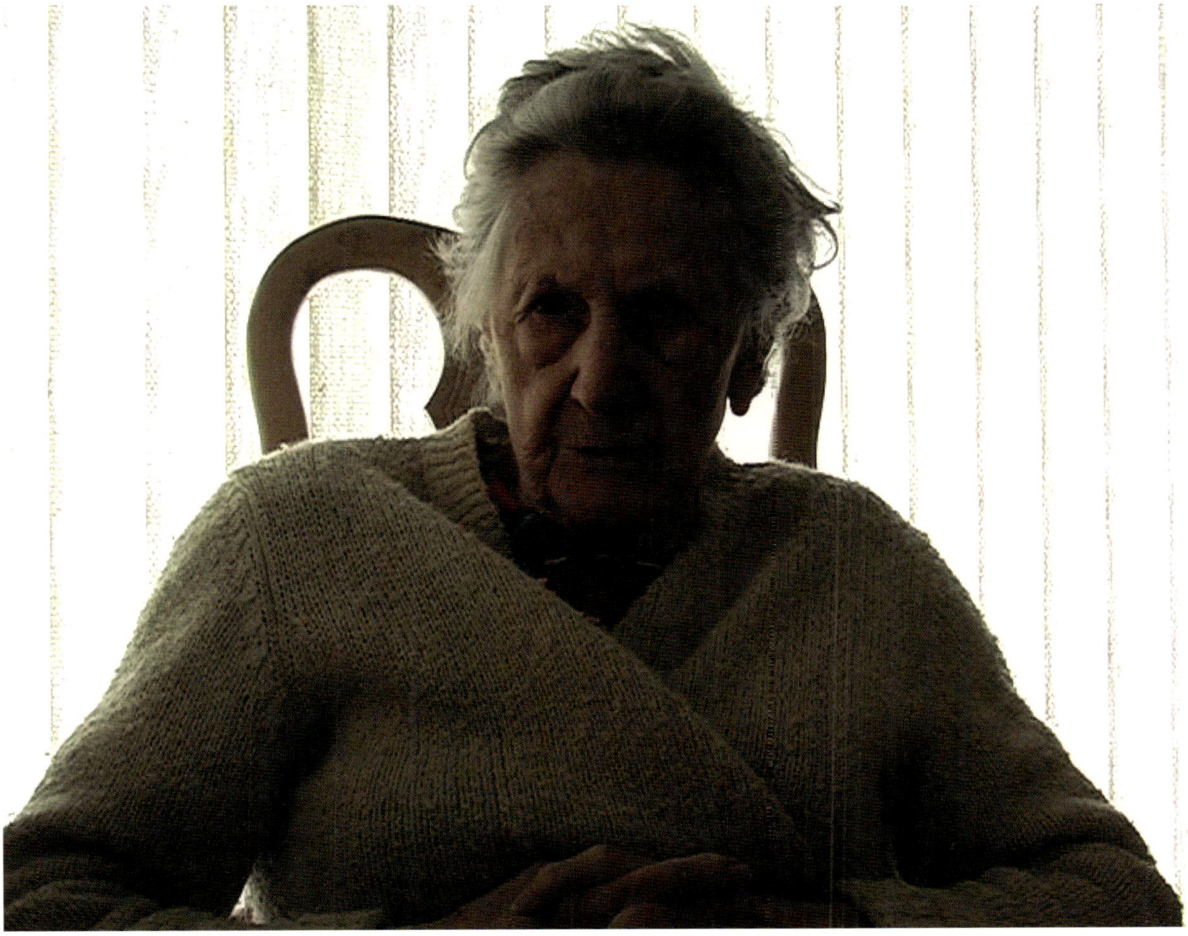

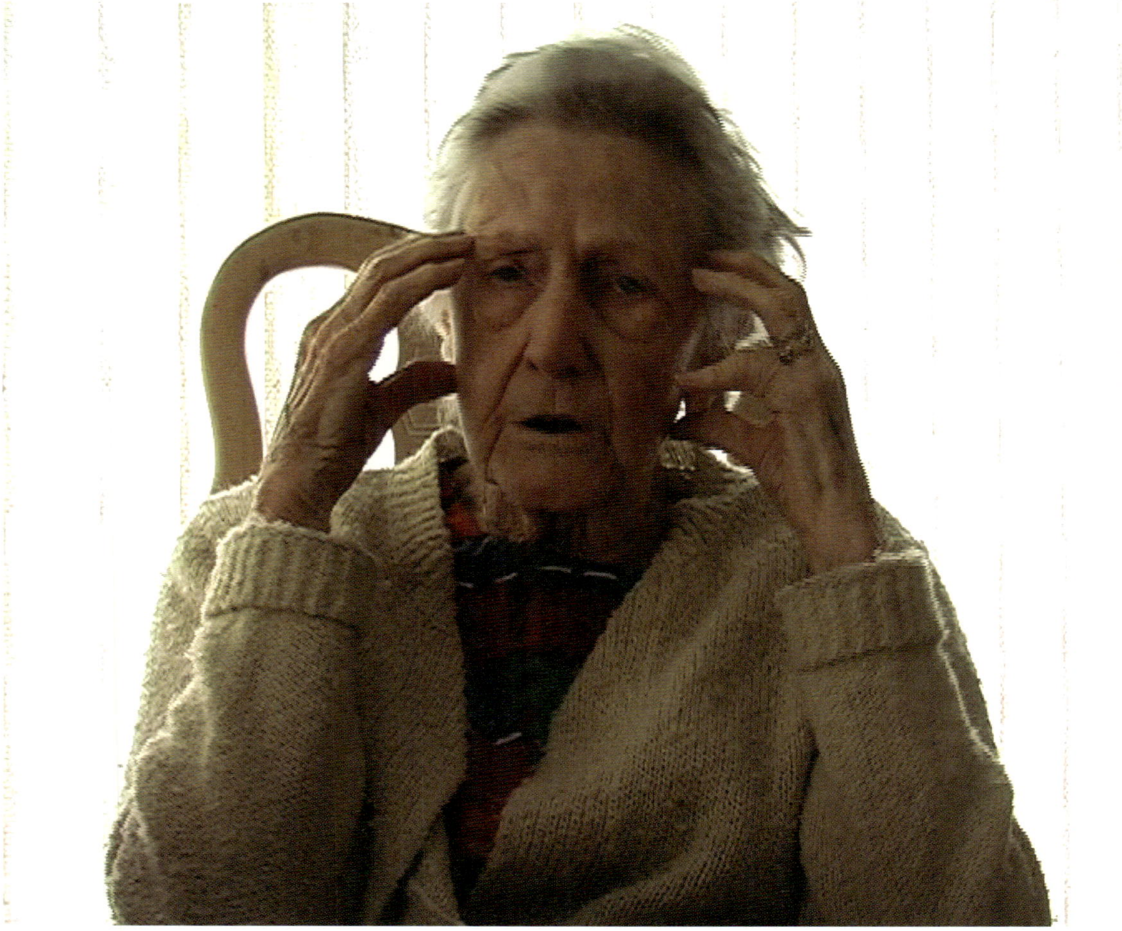

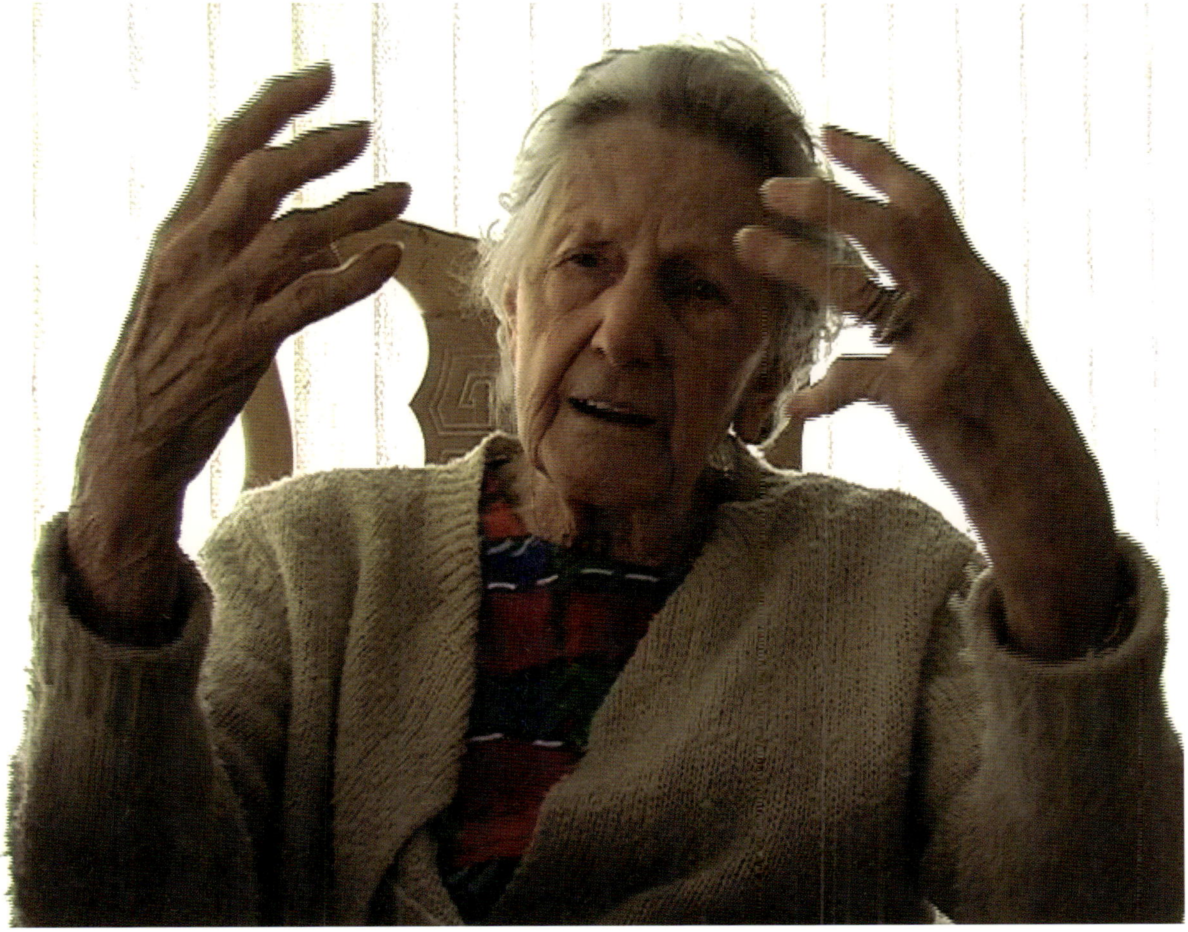

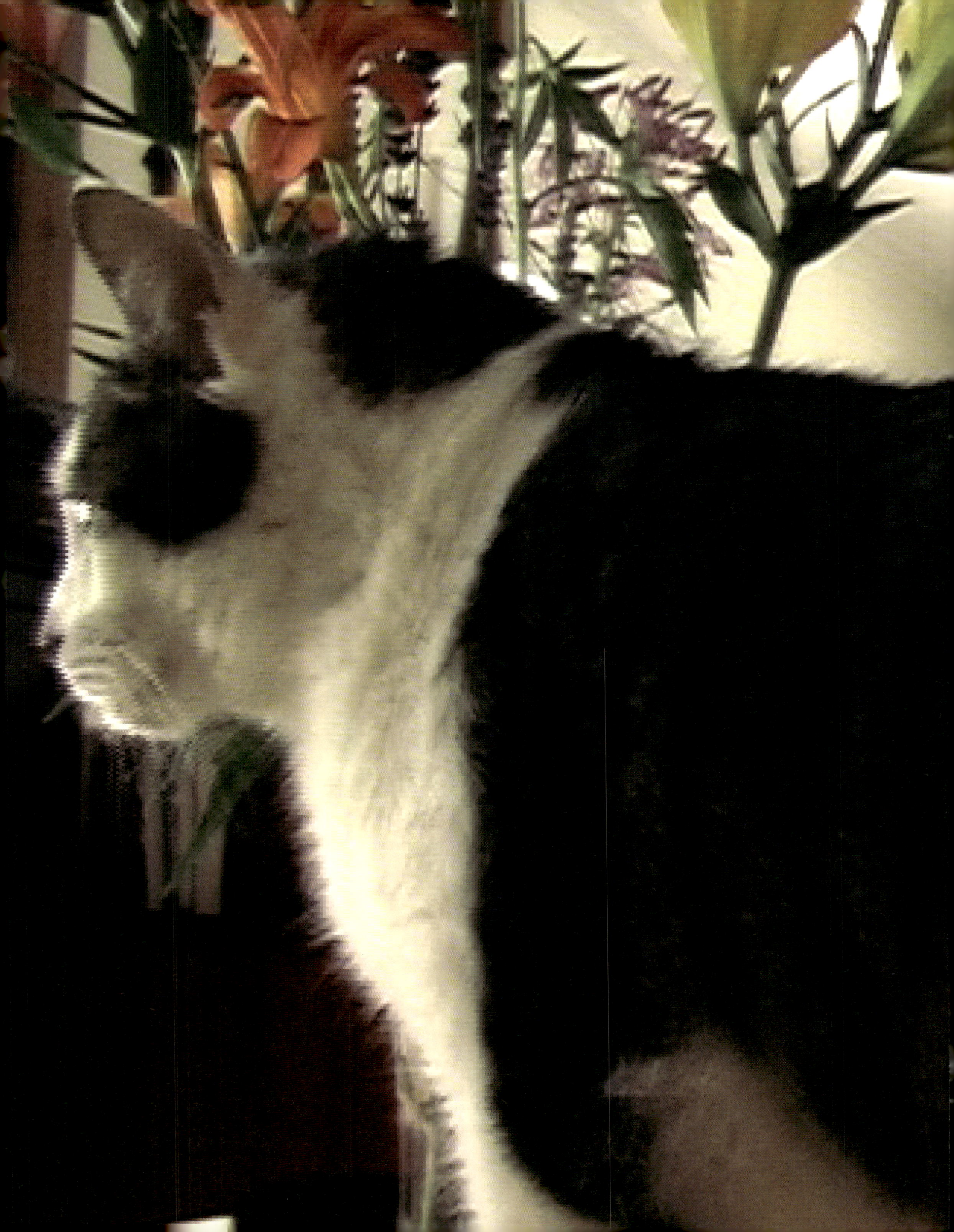

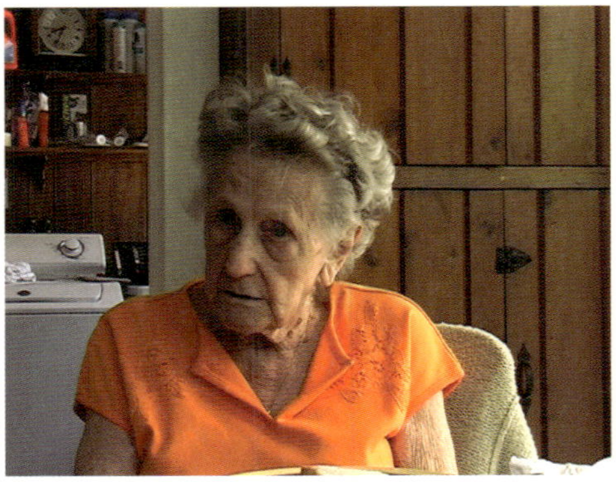
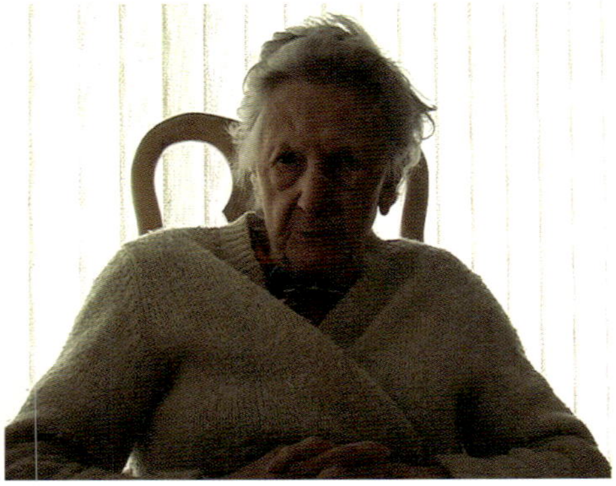
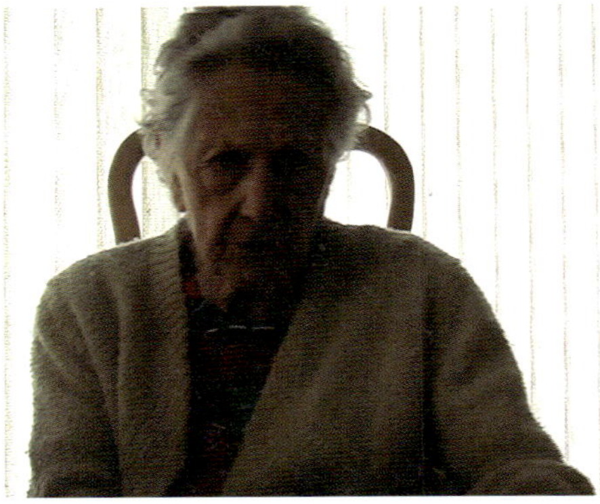
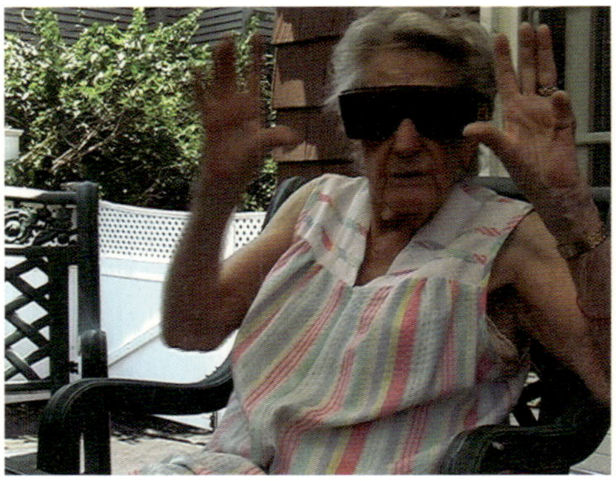
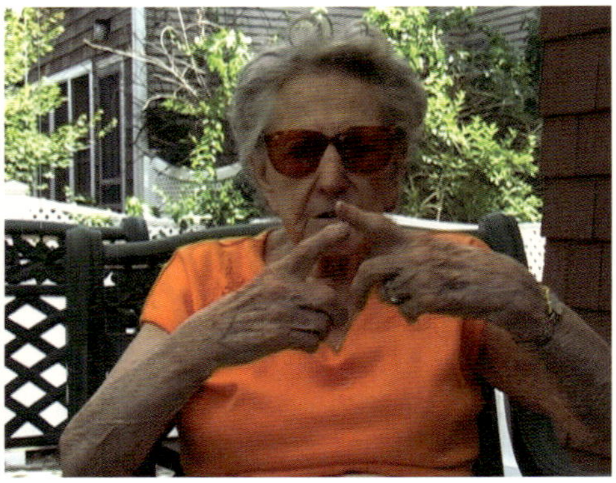
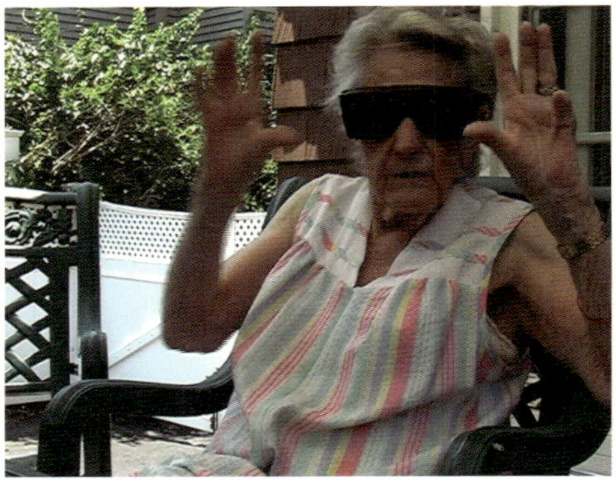
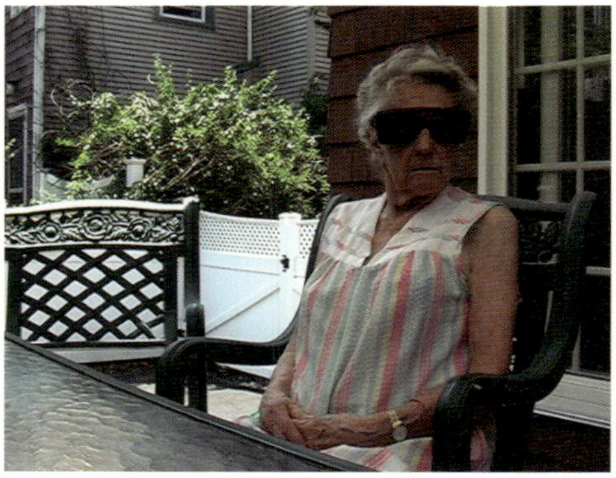
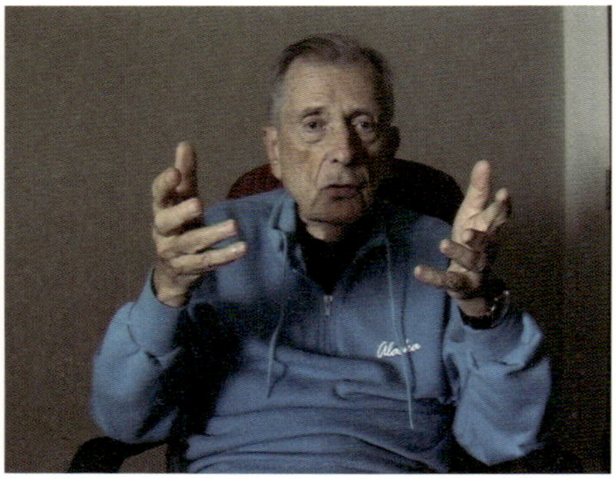
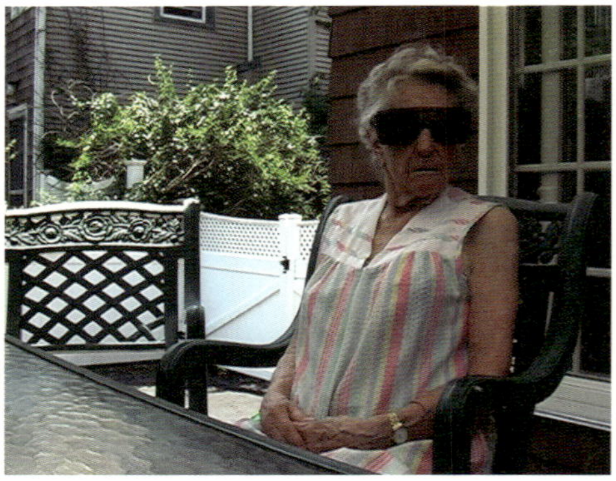
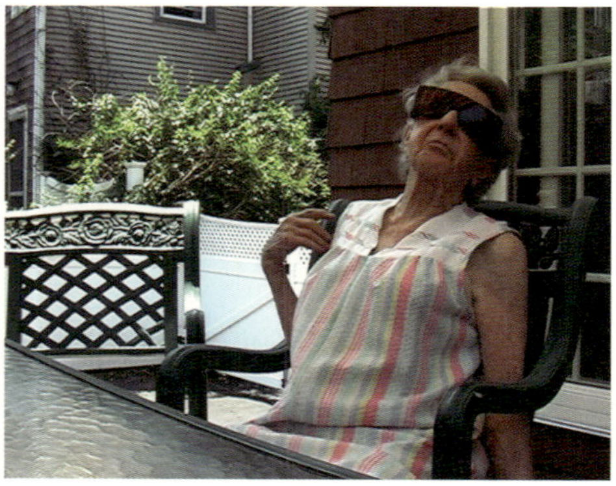
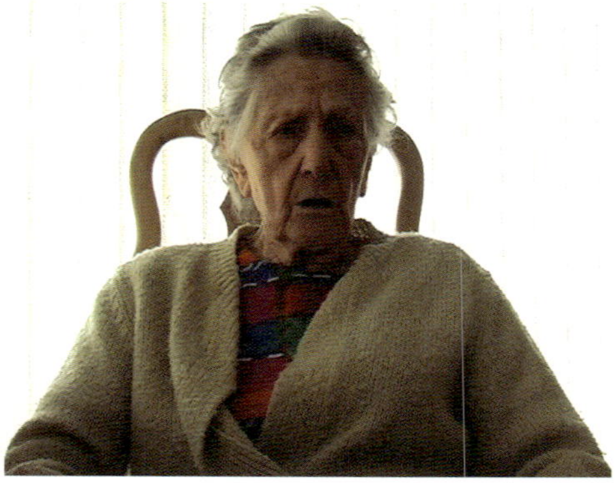
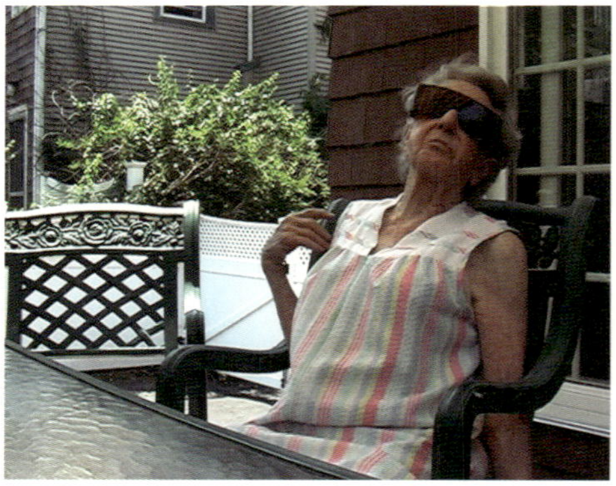

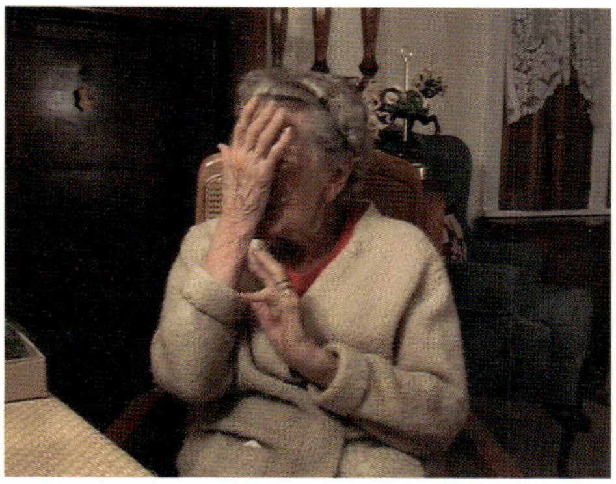
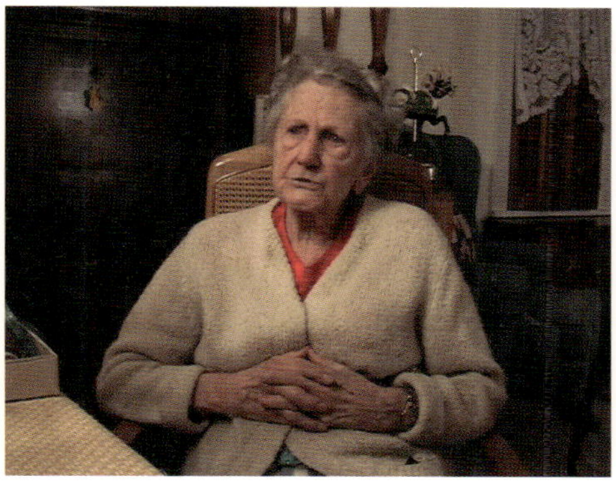
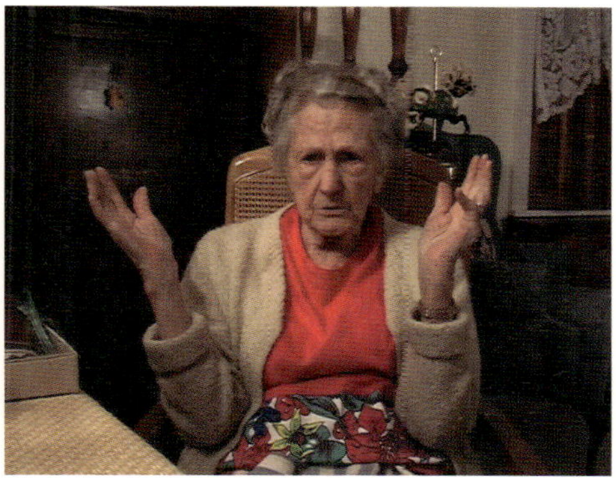
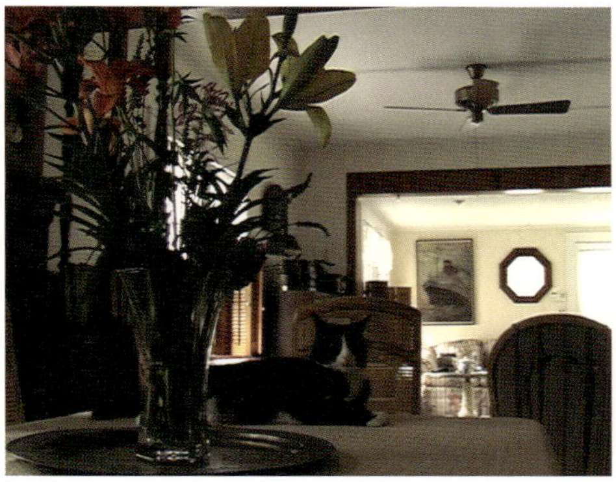
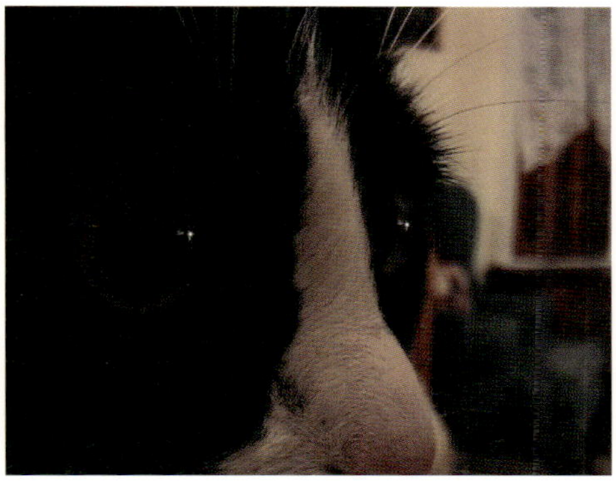
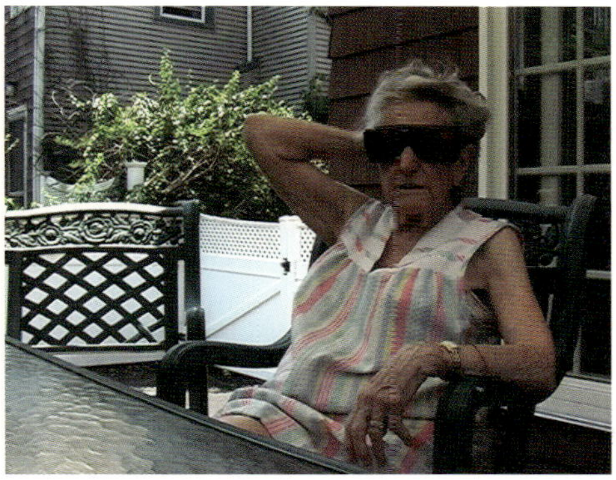
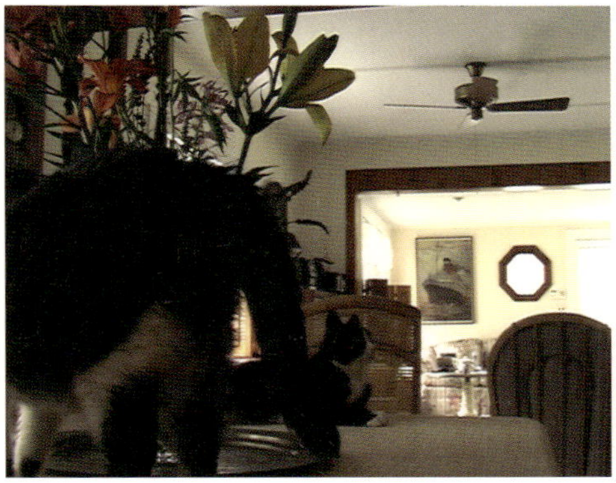
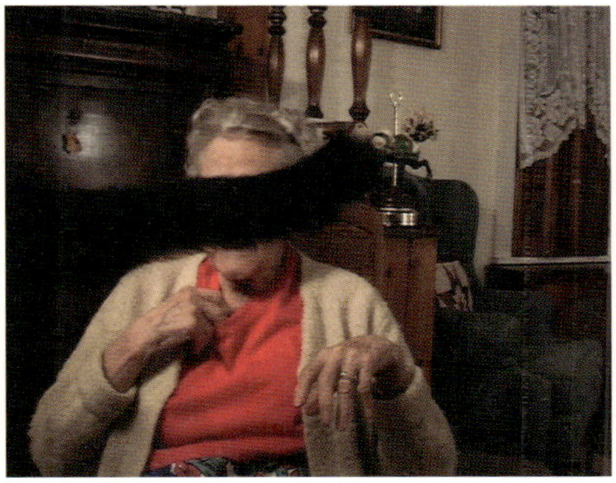
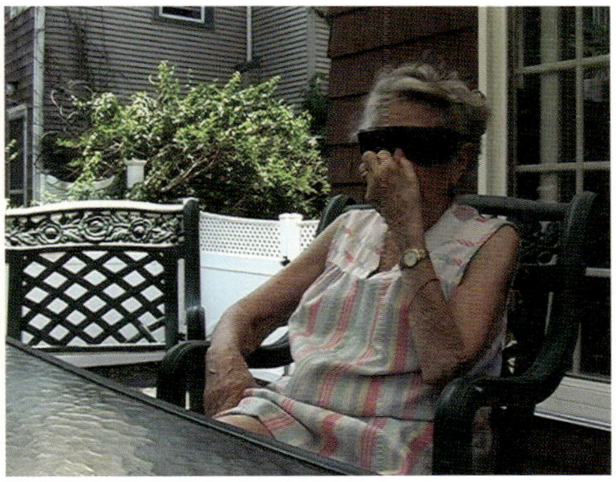
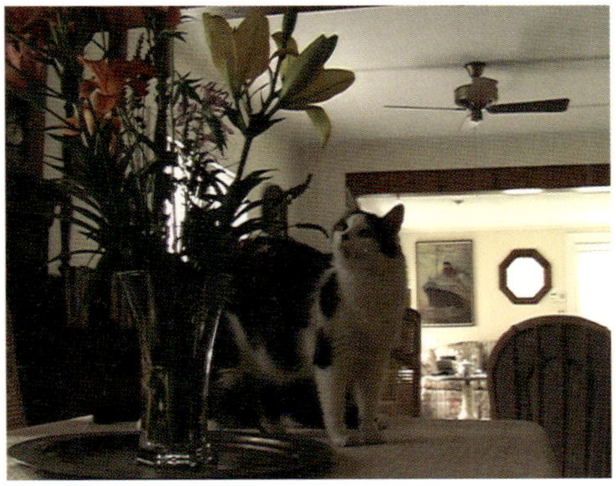
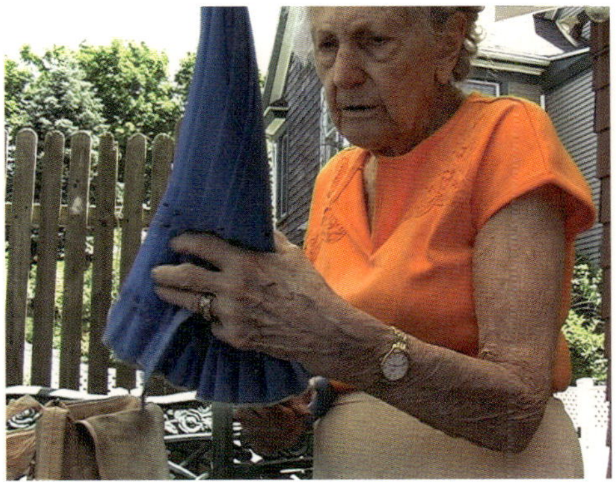
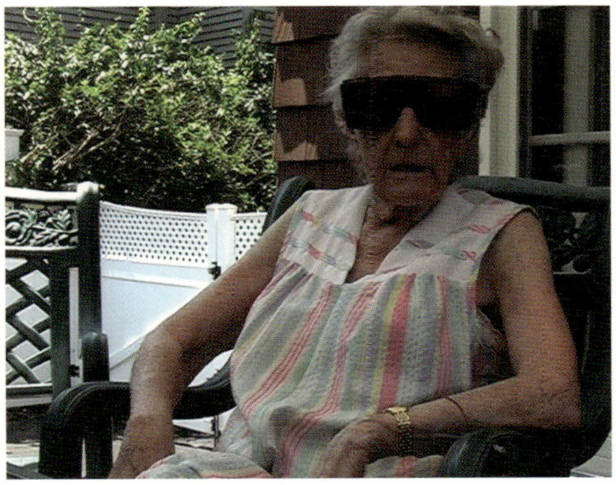

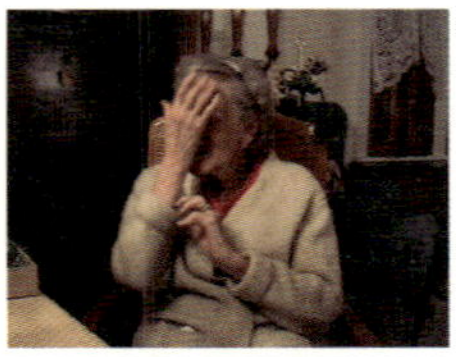

THIS PSYCHIC THING

Eileen Coly *Why in the, in the fingertips particularly—but she just did that—but then—her hands were very important to her—like the business with the cat nose—or—noses—animal noses were important—because a dog—she'd go for his nose—a nose was very—a cat nose on her, on her hand—but then a dog she'd—yes she liked noses—on animals—now I don't know—I don't remember any particular—on human noses*

Lisette *Often times if you have an apparition or whatever there's an olfactory sense—you'll hear—smell smoke or, or very perfumy flowers*

Eileen Coly *Oh that, that's true—yes—yes—I hadn't thought of that association of Garrett*

Lisette *But Garrett, yes Garrett she would really like an animal sniff people—I think when it came to sixth senses she had senses*

Eileen Coly *Oh we always—because her nose would be pinched*

Lisette *would be pinched*

Lisette *And she would have a sense of if she didn't like the smell or whatever, she would sniff—sniff someone*

Eileen Coly *Oh you could tell—if she didn't like someone—you could see there was a little sort of a pinch—(*Lisette*—And god forbid if there was any body odour) you could spot it—knowing her as we did*

Lisette *yeah yeah yeah—So it's interesting about the, the floral sense and the sense of smell (Eileen Coly—yeah—yeah) and sniffing things out—which is true*

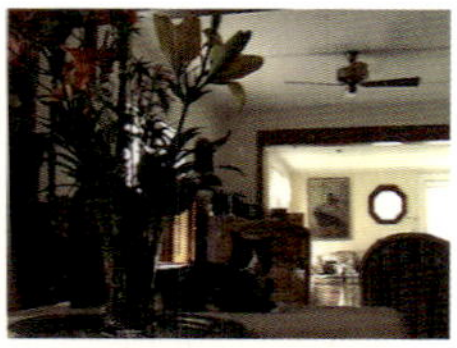

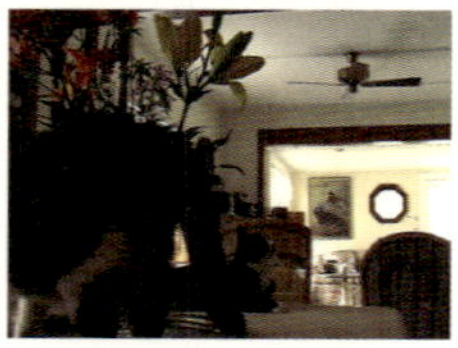

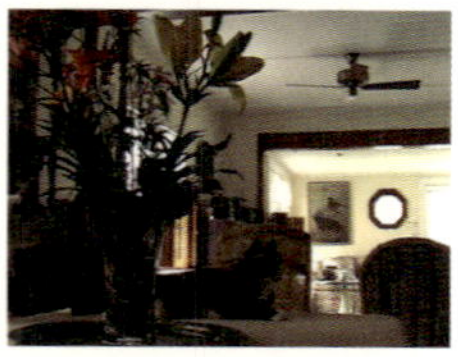

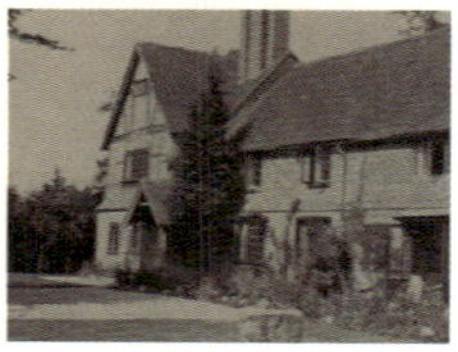

THE ASH MANOR CASE

Eileen Coly *But then he became so involved in chasing poltergeists, poltergeists particularly—because that intrigued him and when he heard of these noisy ghosts—as—as as what they've interpreted as poltergeist*

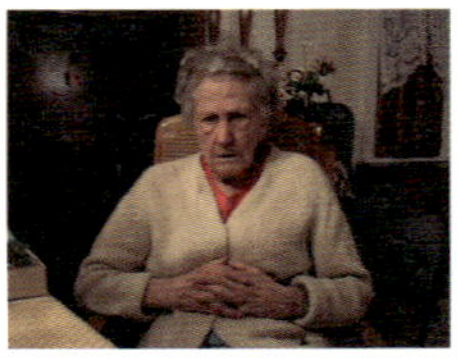

THIS PSYCHIC THING

Eileen Coly *You see there was this psychic thing, which she really preferred to deny all her life and did for her early life because it was, er—its nuisance value was very distressing—and certainly nuisance value was rather, er—an important way of looking at it—because it did enter unwanted upon occasion.*

Eileen Coly *She had been, well not a counsellor but I mean she had been a publisher, she'd had this weird psychic gift to deal with—she'd always had to deal with people in various stages of discomfort with their lives and their human approach to the world—so you've got so much to try and convey and as I said before one hell of a job. And how to—to get it out of someone and you're only left with two people who actually knew her well enough to live with her and to see her in her different moods and then to realise that those different moods were god about ten different characters.*

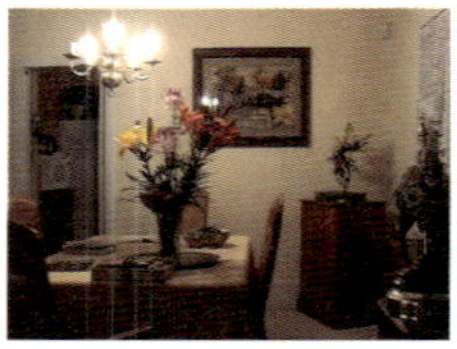

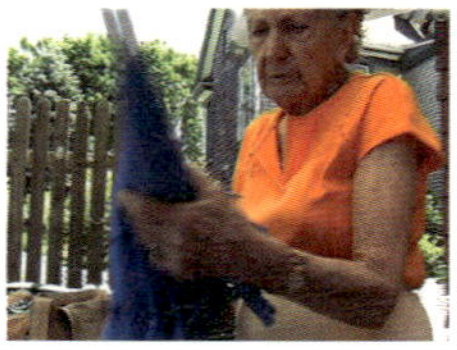

IN LIKE FLYNN

Lisette *Not that she was a fool because she certainly didn't suffer fools lightly—(Eileen Coly—Oh no no no) it wasn't an easy interview but having—and again—if she fell back against her psychic quotient—if she felt like, that there was something there—You were in like Flynn and off you go. So many, many people career wise have said that she gave them their start I mean Rhine himself said he wouldn't have been able to carry on if—and I don't think it was just a cause of money I think it was really the support and added encouragement to take off and, and look at anything because basically she felt and I think the Foundation certainly operates under the thought that psychical research—the study of that phenomena is really a multi-disciplinary approach because you can have a biologist that says that maybe your psychic because it's an over abundance of the endocrine system or whatever or it's your hypothalamus—you can have a quantum physicist who'll talk to you about quantum wave theory—you have a psychologist who thinks that you need some Thorazine because you're hearing voices and talking to a tree and I think again part of the legacy of Garrett apart from the money and the nurturing was trying to get people from different disciplines to come together—we've had so many conferences...*

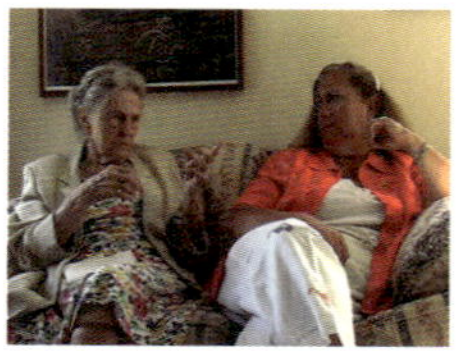

THE ASH MANOR CASE

Eileen Coly *I only went on one of that particularly fantastic one that was the (Lisette – Ash Manor) Ash Manor – Lord Henley and that we went with Nandor Fodor who was a well known (Lisette – ghost*

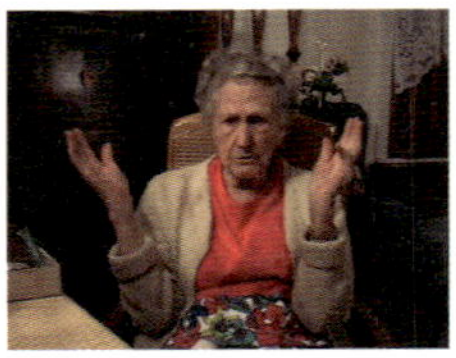

THIS PSYCHIC THING

Eileen Coly *Well travelled, character who knew all the other well known, well travelled characters—but that there was something more that she had the ability to not only listen to—not all their troubles—the one thing that is driving them into a desperate state—that kind of pinpoint it right away and somehow or other—how the devil she did it we've never known—she certainly wouldn't tell anybody.*

The nose is very important—but then this—Garrett always used to say oh it's because she grew up on a farm—I don't know if she was actually on the farm or beside it—but she was close enough to the animals anyway and that's what she said—that an animal sniffs you out which of course they do—it's their nose that's their main object—the sight plays a big a part maybe but the nose is the thing—so we always teased her and literally I think that really did pinch slightly because there was something in the nose—and that statue we have of her—where is it now—who has it? Oh its down here in the library here—very often if Lisette and I go by we'll pinch our nose—because the nose was always—she said she sniffed people out—that, that it was an animal instinct and that a lot of her psychic thing—and that's why when I was telling you about the business of this half hour with her—that this poor dejaded soul would go in and half an hour later he would come out ready to face the world—what the hell she said to them she never told us—But that was all part of growing up and the usefulness of the Garrett nose—so that you learned in your own way to smell them out which Lisette demonstrated there's the nose.

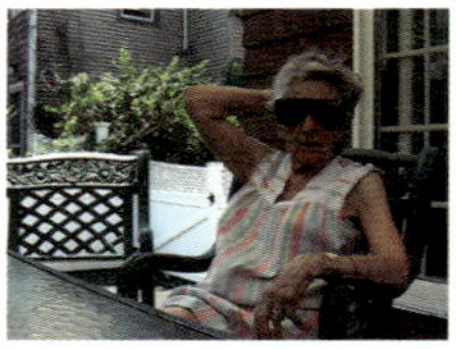

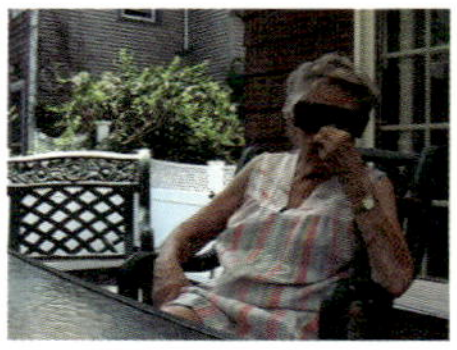

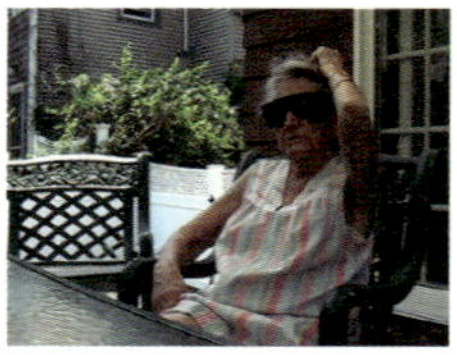

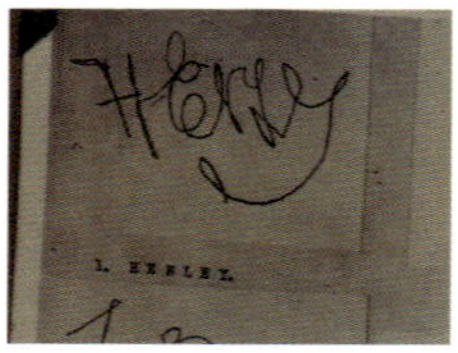

THE ASH MANOR CASE

Eileen Coly *But he had particularly opened up to see if he could find out what was bothering them through the use of this mediumship since he discovered that, that was a noisy ghost, was an entity that had passed out of this*

as meaning—er—so he had quite a lot of cases....
Eileen Coly *Who had no understanding of anything —but is still in some hell hole—under the influence of these (Lisette—trapped) terrible people—trapped*
Eileen Coly *and he found that with the use of a medium, who could go into a trance and find the, the object of the—the person who was causing the disruption and what's bothering them—if you can solve their problems—by telling them that that problem—usually somehow convincing them that that problem no longer exists and that nobody that they knew before lives in that house anymore—not even trying to tell them that they're talking—that we're living two centuries later or something—just tell them that the occupants of the house have changed and it doesn't happen anymore (laughs)*

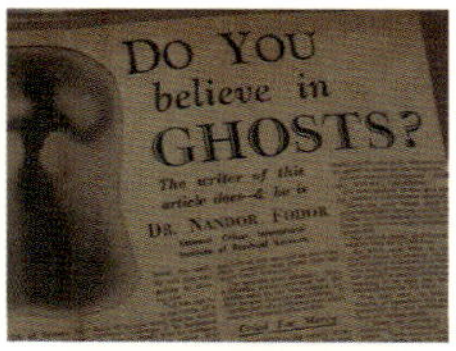

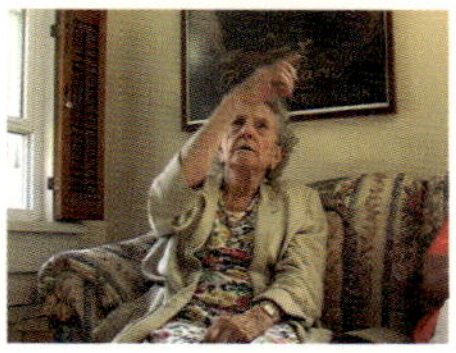

HIGHER AND HIGHER

Eileen Coly *And imagine a spiral—keep it in proportion—increasing of course as it goes higher and higher and higher and then we just leave it going off into space somewhere... a spiral winding up*

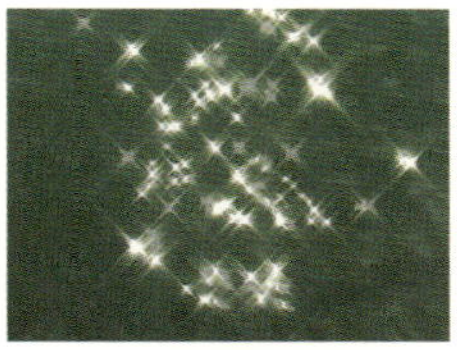

THE HORSE RIDING INCIDENT

Eileen Coly *Nowadays that same bunch perhaps wouldn't have been quite as straight laced in the same way and given the attention to young people of that age that is given today—I could possibly have leaned over to my hostess and said you know honestly my mother isn't quite right—I do not know that much about—you know horse riding and everything—but there was no way that I could approach that woman in those days—so all I had to do was—and she was too far away so that I couldn't even make any facial or any kind of sign to her that I was going to be in trouble*
Eileen Coly *I got the reigns somehow or other in one hand (Lisette—so it looked good) and—sort of hanging on—so we're just barely even walking not even cantering yet—but she's in such a bloody hurry—I mean the woman was born on a horse.*
Eileen Coly *I said for god sakes help me—I got stuck in this by my mother—I couldn't get out of it I don't know what I'm doing.*
Eileen Coly *But strangely enough there was no further contact with that family and that was the end of my riding. But that was the most horrible experience.*

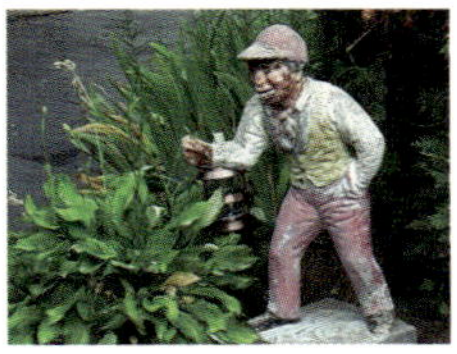

investigator) ghost investigator, another man who had done many of these cases just out of interest—Dr Elmer Lindsay—he was a dentist but it was useful to have a sort of partly medical man around anyway and I forget a couple of others anyway
Lisette *Well you acted as the secretary—as the stenographer—*
Eileen Coly *Well I was the note taker*
Lisette *Wasn't he walled in or something?*
Eileen Coly *Yeah and tortured and god knows what*
Eileen Coly *So that was it and he—anytime he heard of these annoyances then he would track them down*
Eileen Coly *So this would go on—I think it went on for two hours or so and gradually he could feel this entity or whatever it was—*
Eileen Coly *beginning to understand that there was a sort of freedom being offered from this terrible internment (Lisette—purgatory) torture, purgatory that—gradually opening up of a sort of freeing of the body and the spirit and in this time period becoming sort of more lucid even grateful to find a friend and we insisted on trusting us—so agreed that yes—you know, just a little after thought...*

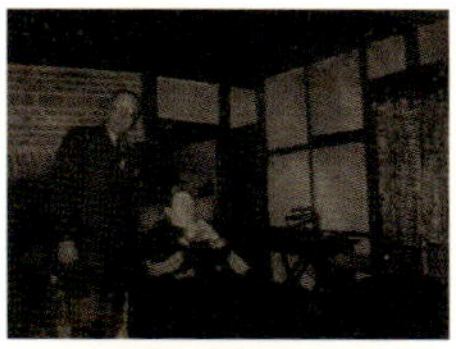

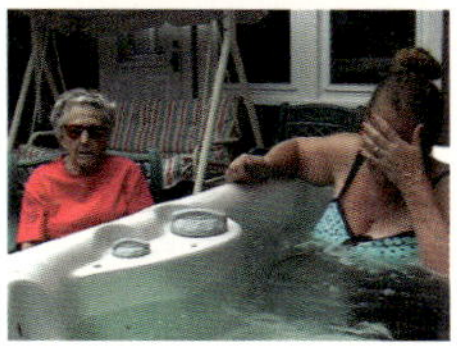

THE HORSE RIDING INCIDENT

Eileen Coly *My famous bloody horseback thing*
Eileen Coly *Well I was at a dinner party—stuck as usual because people felt that they had to invite the daughter as well if they wanted La Garrett. And the wife had recently had a baby and was crowing with the fact that oh boy she's going to be out riding again she missed riding so much while she was pregnant etcetera, etcetera. She said oh yes my dear and turns to me and said and Do you ride dear? and I said No, no, no I lived in the city all—Oh well that doesn't matter I mean I'm sure you ride no? So—Garrett at the end (Lisette—old cloth ears) of this long table—cloth ears—pipes up and said Of course you ride dear don't you remember?*
Eileen Coly *So I sort of said (Lisette—What was it a pony trap?) No mother*
Eileen Coly *She said yes don't you remember last year in Bournemouth—so I nearly fainted—in Bournemouth where they have these pony rides along the beach*
Eileen Coly *I don't even know which side you mount a horse—I sort of dithered around—but they had grooms and everybody there so somehow I just watched others and managed to get my foot in the stirrup, hoping to god someone would goose me to get up there but I managed to climb up*
Eileen Coly *She starts really cantering pretty fast, speeding up and I knew if she goes into a gallop and looks back and says shall we gallop I'm dead—so the, the (Lisette—the groomsman) the groom or whatever sort of falls real close beside me and says—Would you mind telling me what you're doing on a horse? I said—For gods sake help me—I got stuck in this by my mother, I couldn't get out of it—I don't know what I'm doing. And this guy was nice enough to realise that I was in all kinds of*

world into another but they just couldn't settle down over there because they hadn't settled their problems over here.
Eileen Coly *All this—aaarh—trying to speak—aaarh aaarh—not being able to speak as if being choked and gradually through this very difficult speech pattern—to shorten the story it would seem that it was a man who had been (Lisette—had been strangled) strangled at this site—and proceeded with all this difficulty of the—and overcoming the throat problem and finally getting through and with questioning giving a name.*

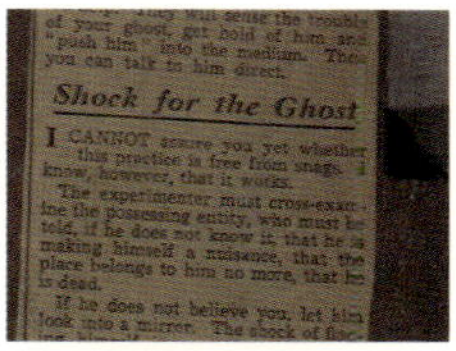

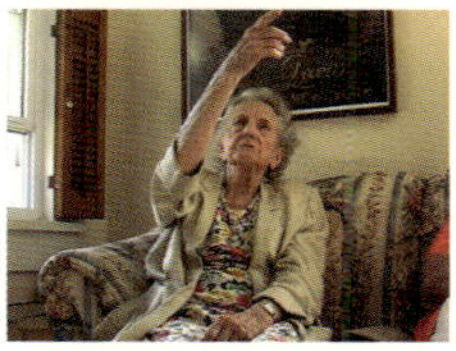

HIGHER AND HIGHER

Eileen Coly *And imagine a spiral—keep it in proportion—increasing of course as it goes higher and higher and higher and then we just leave it going off into space somewhere... a spiral winding up*

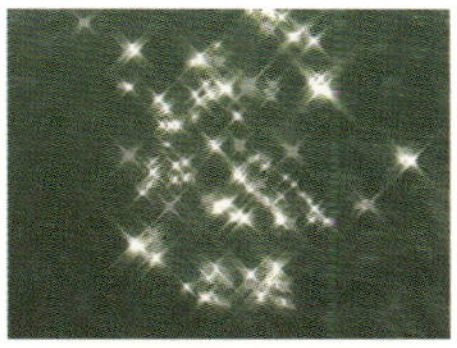

THE HORSE RIDING INCIDENT

Eileen Coly *Nowadays that same bunch perhaps wouldn't have been quite as straight laced in the same way and given the attention to young people of that age that is given today—I could possibly have leaned over to my hostess and said you know honestly my mother isn't quite right—I do not know that much about—you know horse riding and everything—but there was no way that I could approach that woman in those days—so all I had to do was—and she was too far away so that I couldn't even make any facial or any kind of sign to her that I was going to be in trouble*
Eileen Coly *I got the reigns somehow or other in one hand (Lisette—so it looked good) and—sort of hanging on—so we're just barely even walking not even cantering yet—but she's in such a bloody hurry—I mean the woman was born on a horse*
Eileen Coly *I said for god sakes help me—I got stuck in this by my mother—I couldn't get out of it I don't know what I'm doing*
Eileen Coly *But strangely enough there was no further contact with that family and that was the end of my riding. But that was the most horrible experience.*

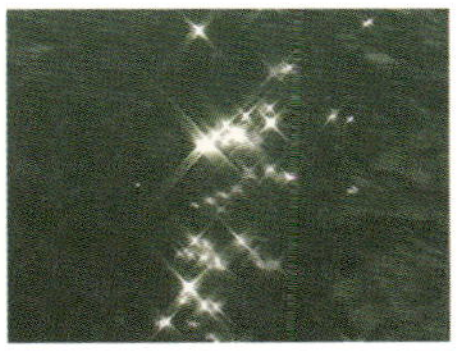

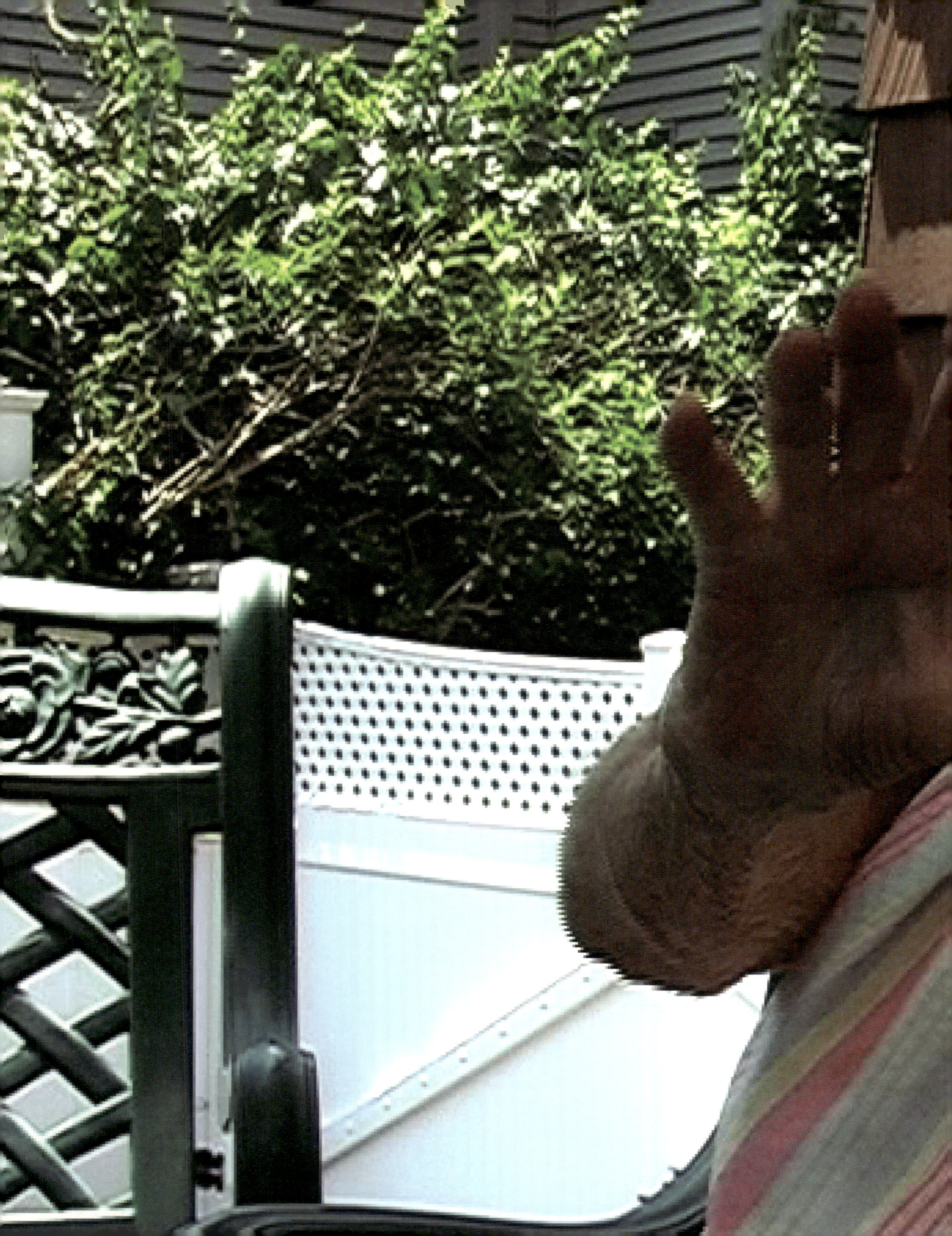

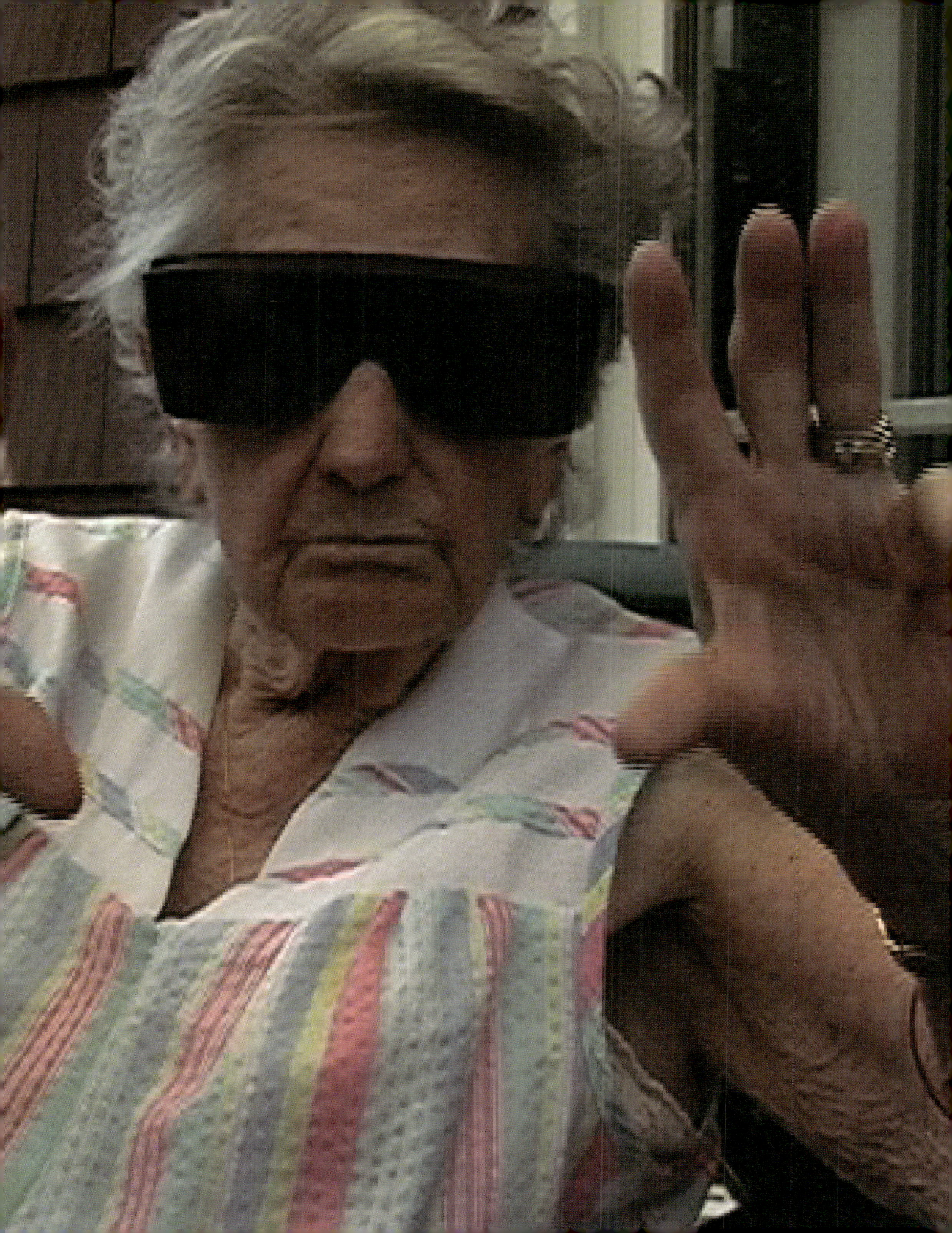

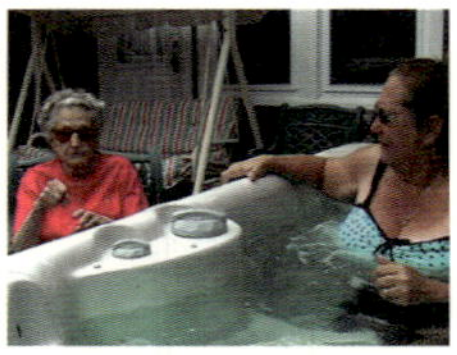

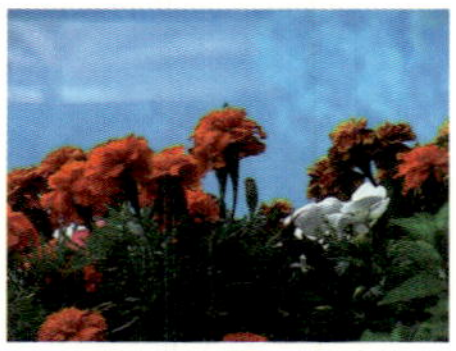

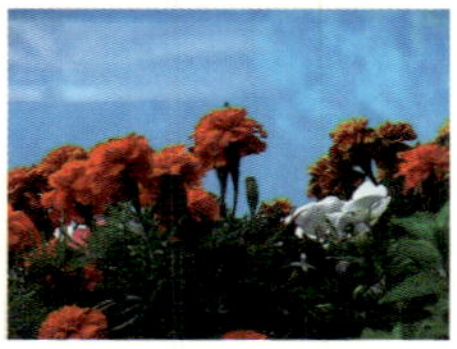

DEAD DUCKS

Eileen Coly *That's right—yes—the ducks—well go ahead—do ducks*

Lisette *She went down to the pond and rang their little necks and as she was appalled at the moment that she had gone and done that and she saw their little bodies lying by the shore—She was taken to see these whispy, vaporous emanations from the little dead bodies spiralling upwards—which all throughout her lifetime she would see this at the moment (Eileen Coly—yes she felt that there is something, something that—spirals upwards) Yes so she was always taken with that*

Lisette *And when She, in a, in a paroxysm of—a fit of pique, did that—she writes that she saw the little bodies on the grass and she was taken with this grey emanation of smoke like, wraith like essence that was rising out of their bodies.*

Eileen Coly *And that was the idea of the spiral because the rising became—became bigger as it wafted up.*

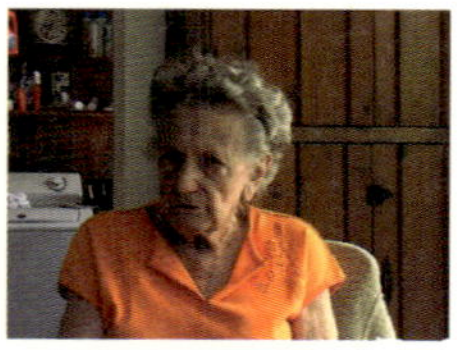

SPIRIT CONTROL

Eileen Coly *'cause Garrett had only practiced this damn thing—under the aegis of the—what was known as the British College of Psychic Science. And that was controlled by this dour Scotsman who was not about to have any kind of nonsense of any kind in his care so it was all very rigorously controlled.*

Lisette *And turn it off when*

Eileen Coly *Usher them into the office—the door would close—and this poor rather depressed soul would sort of tentatively enter the room and half an hour later a smiling wonderful person would appear as though there are no more worries in the world—what she did to them, what she said to them, what impression she was doing, what she brought out of them, what she gave of herself to them—we never knew.*

Eileen Coly *I only actually witnessed a trance thing a couple of times and for that she would sit in a pretty straight chair—no lounging—she never lounged in a chair either—She always sat straight, always, yeah, even in a comfortable chair—she still would never flop into a chair she would sit in it in a ladylike fashion and remain in a ladylike fashion—so for this trance thing she would be sitting in her comfortable office chair and it would have a soft back so she would lean on it and she'd just be silent she'd talk to them for a minute and say nothing more—so they not knowing perhaps what to expect*

trouble plus the fact he didn't want me to fall off or he'd be in trouble. So he did the best he could and together we got back alright. But mother said how did you enjoy it—I said it was the most God awful experience—the next day the lady is on the phone (Lisette—to who?)—to my mother. And she said—oh something—how is your daughter today? (Lisette—eating off the mantelpiece) Oh mother is gushing away, you know—oh it was so wonderful of you to invite her—she had such a wonderful time

Lisette *For a psychic that's a pretty strange response*

Eileen Coly *So the woman was obviously a little cool. But strangely enough there was no further contact with that family and that was the end of my riding. But that was the most horrible experience.*

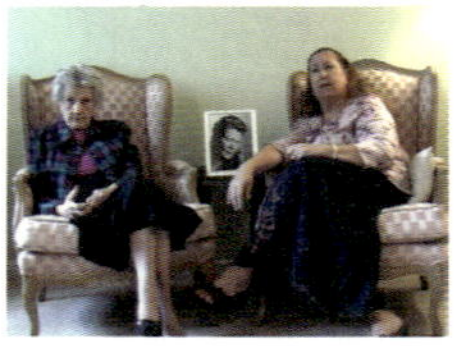

DEAD DUCKS

Eileen Coly *The ducks*

Lisette *The ducks, that's right*

Lisette *The aunt had been raising prize ducks and after being called—I think following the premonition of the dead aunt she went down to the—after the aunt had been calling her the devils spawn and kicking up a ruckus she went down to the pond and the prize ducklings were there and she happily went and drowned—wrung their necks whatever, which is really very cruel*

Eileen Coly *Which she knew would be the one thing (Lisette—that's one way to get to auntie) that would touch that horrible aunt*

Bill Roll *Her unhappy childhood and her need to escape her childhood in her case landed her in a different and very interesting world. So we have to thank her awful aunt for that (laughs)*

Eileen Coly *I automatically sort of do this to embrace whatever it is that she found up there*

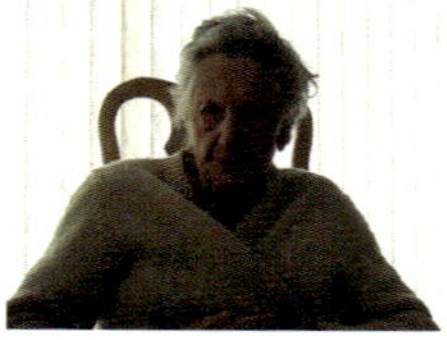

SPIRIT CONTROL

Mrs C *If you imagine having this psychic ability that anyone who walks by (Lisette—who needs that) you suddenly realise that there's some awful disaster or something worrying them or maybe they're suicidal or whatever—that you can't have that invading you all the time*

Lisette *Well you'd go mad*

Mrs C *Dour Scotsman*

Eileen Coly *She could control when to presumably invite this psychic feeling to—to operate and other times like opening and closing the eyes as it were but certainly opening and closing the mind to the invasion of this particular facility taking over her conscious mind*

Eileen Coly *So that people would come to her but whatever—however she handled it—she must have pinpointed the particular problem and somehow given them the solace or even a spot of a direction that they hadn't thought of that they pick up and it succeeds but because of this psychic sense she happens to have just hit on that one spot—mentioned it and that's the thing that they said My God now if I do that, maybe it'll work—so she wasn't just foretelling future or even giving advice by saying yes now you yes go out and meet so and so and they'll introduce you to so and so—she'd simply say had you thought that if you did it this way, maybe—they would go out and do it and it would work*

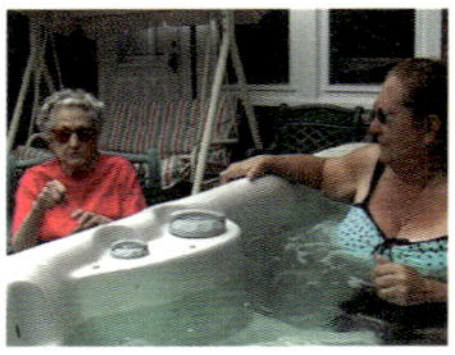

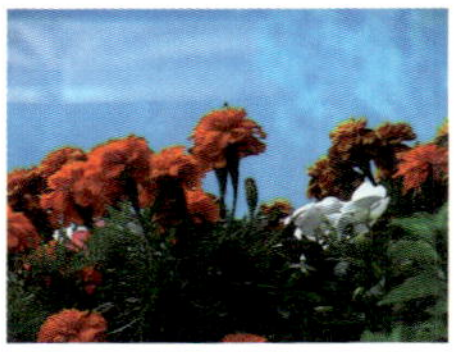

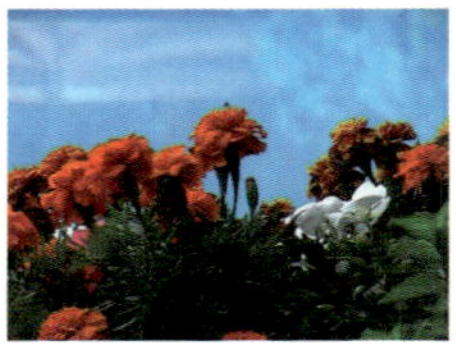

DEAD DUCKS

Lisette *Well the spiral that's very evocative I think when she would see—well I think she writes that the first time she saw the spiral (Eileen Coly—from the ducks) was when she in a fit of pique she drowned her nasty aunt's ducks (Eileen Coly—yes—I think you're right)—to vengefully hurt her aunt as much as her aunt had just recently hurt her. The spiral always had to be going up never hopefully going down (Eileen Coly—Oh no, no always winding up) because she used that in Creative Age—the symbol and of course people would deride her and I've heard it—I think somebody from either was it Life Magazine or Time—I don't remember—referred to it as—Mrs Garrett's bedspring (Eileen Coly—bedspring yeah—because it looked like a spring) So apart from it representing possibly the survival question I think for Garrett it comes to also represent the creative force and perhaps this—the great oneness of spirit right?*

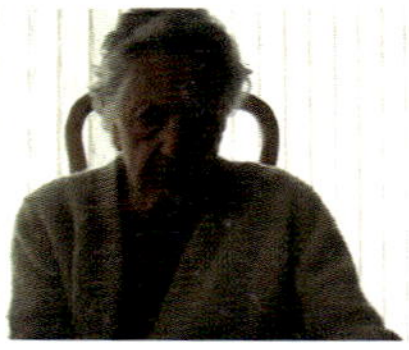

SPIRIT CONTROL

Eileen Coly *Dour Scotsman*

Lisette *She could just turn it on*

Lisette *when she wanted to*

Eileen Coly *She had the ability to not only listen to—not all their troubles—the one thing that is driving them into a desperate state—that kind of pinpoint it right away and somehow or other—how the devil she did it we've never known—she certainly wouldn't tell anyone. But I have seen people go into her office in a state of trying to pick up the pieces of themselves as they went in and half an hour later that door would open and a composed almost smiling character would come out and Garrett would be there saying—well it's so nice—telephone me again sometime—with just being a polite lady—it's just extraordinary this power she had*

Eileen Coly *I only actually witnessed a trance thing a couple of times and for that she would sit in a pretty straight chair—no lounging—she never lounged in a chair either—She always sat straight, always, yeah, even in a comfortable chair—she still would never flop into a chair she would sit in it in a ladylike fashion and remain in a ladylike fashion—so for this trance thing she would be sitting in her comfortable office chair and it would have a soft back so she would lean on it and she'd just be silent she'd talk to them for a minute and say nothing more—so they not knowing perhaps what to expect would be silent and the head would go down a little—and there would be silence she wouldn't talk anymore—there'd be no groaning or anything but if you watched it I think the breathing rate might change to a rather different breathing but not visibly—aaa aaa—or anything like that and then the head would come up and then a rather different tone—it wouldn't be an imitation of a, of a male voice at all but just a rather different, slightly different accent—that this wasn't the normal Garrett intonation and it would look at you and say—I think it was something like—I give you greetings friends—peace be with you and how may be I—how may I be of assistance to you or can I be of some help to you—not just what is your problem but how may be I, I be of assistance. Very politely and just very gentlemanly just as someone you don't know—as you might in a business interview you sit there and say—can I be of assistance without leaning forward but just, just I'm paying attention so obviously the person then would probably blurt out well if they're in dire need—I wanted to know this that or the other and whatever would follow who knows—and she never, never divulged what was going on…..*

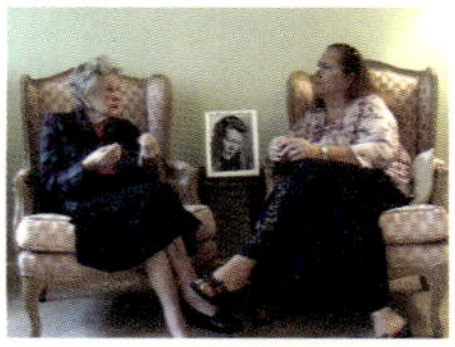

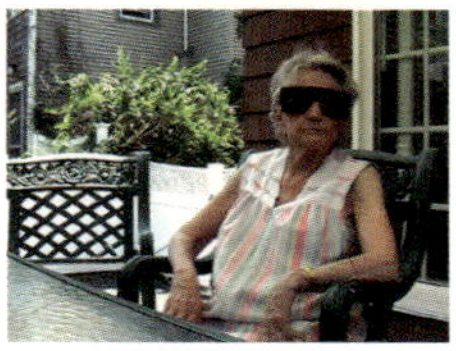

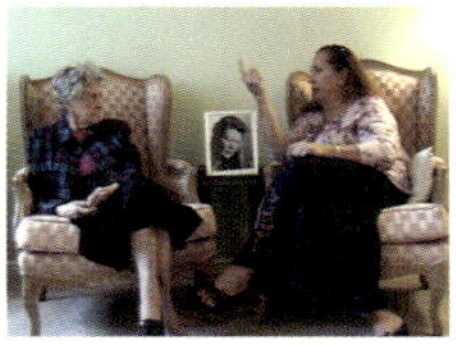

DUCK-BILLED PLATYPUS

Lisette *She well deserved the story she used to tell about her friend Aldous Huxley—who said to her once—there are three creatures which really ought not to be—the giraffe, the duck billed platypus and you Eileen Garrett—She apparently was very pleased to find herself classified among such marvels of evolution—The spiral always going up as her, as her logo*

Lisette *The duck billed platypus and you Eileen Garrett—She apparently was very pleased to find herself classified among such marvels of evolution—The spiral always going up as her, as her logo*

Lisette *The duck billed platypus and you Eileen Garrett—She apparently was very pleased to find herself classified among such marvels of evolution—The spiral always going up as her, as her logo*

Lisette *The duck billed platypus and you Eileen Garrett—She apparently was very pleased to find herself classified among such marvels of evolution—The spiral always going up as her, as her logo*

Lisette *The duck billed platypus and you Eileen Garrett—She apparently was very pleased to find herself classified among such marvels of evolution—The spiral always going up as her, as her logo*

Lisette *The duck billed platypus and you Eileen Garrett—She apparently was very pleased to find herself classified among such marvels of evolution—The spiral always going up as her, as her logo*

Lisette *The duck billed platypus and you Eileen Garrett - She apparently was very pleased to find herself classified among such marvels of evolution—The spiral always going up as her, as her logo*

Lisette *The duck billed platypus and you Eileen*

Eileen Coly *Garrett had a psychic ability pretty much unrivalled by any*

Eileen Coly *As a young woman it intruded—she had these visions and things and then finally she found - how she found him—I don't know I think she went to an association—there were several of them in those days—well I guess there still are. They build up on finding people who have psychic abilities and don't know what to do with them and if they have some developed way of producing this phenomenon of speaking with or to the departed and all that kind of thing and they would so called develop this*

Eileen Coly *so she would lean on it and she'd just be silent she'd talk to them for a minute and say nothing more—so they not knowing perhaps what to expect would be silent and the head would go down a little—and there would be silence she wouldn't talk anymore—there'd be no groaning or anything but if you watched it I think the breathing rate might change to a rather different breathing but not visibly—aaa aaa—or anything like that and then the head would come up and then a rather different tone—it wouldn't be an imitation of a, of a male voice at all*

Stanley Krippner *Then at the appointed time Eileen Garrett called upon her spirit control—she had several of them and in this case it was Uvani—who I never looked at as an actual personality or an actual person but as a process, as a manifestation of some sort*

Eileen Coly *and how may be I—how may I be of assistance to you or can I be of some help to you—not just what is your problem but how may be I, I be of assistance. Very politely and just very gentlemanly just as someone you don't know—as you might in a business interview you sit there and say—can I be of assistance without leaning forward but just, just I'm paying attention so obviously the person then would probably blurt out well if they're in dire need—I wanted to know this that or the other and whatever would follow who knows—and she never, never divulged what was going on…..*

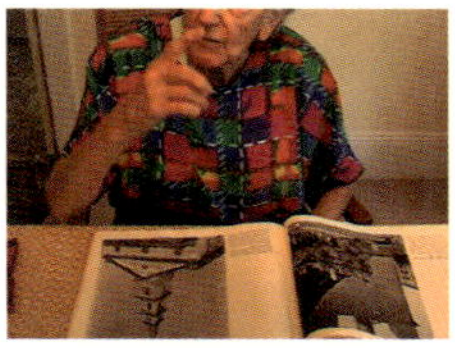

DUCK-BILLED PLATYPUS

Lisette *She well deserved the story she used to tell about her friend Aldous Huxley—who said to her once—there are three creatures which really ought not to be—the giraffe, the duck billed platypus and you Eileen Garrett—She apparently was very pleased to find herself classified among such marvels of evolution—*

Eileen Coly *Oh of the spiral—of Garrett's spiral—yes I don't really know of the origin of that spiral except that it of course was the story of her life—a small beginning and winding—always with the degree of the unexpected, obviously the necessity for curiosity, for continuing for enlarging the experience—for just going on and on, and it was always the symbol to her and she used it perhaps even in describing things slightly but then she used it as a symbol for her publishing house—and it has remained as far as Lisette and I are concerned the symbol of anything to do with Parapsychology Foundation, the old days of Creative Age Press which of course Garrett herself created. But it was always the spiral and of course the spiral expresses it—the symbolism. So yes it's, it's strange that you should have spotted that—but it has been so much a part of—and in a way she was very expressive in using her hands so that it would be I think symbolic of her—anything that she was always working on something that was evolving hence always the spiral effect in whatever she was doing—but always the—her hands she was so expressive and the thing is that—she wasn't—when you do—well at least sometimes to me if you talk about a woman who is so expressive physically you think of the long slender hands on a tall slender, beautiful woman or something—Garrett was not tall she was anything but splendor she was on the—for a*

would be silent and the head would go down a little—and there would be silence she wouldn't talk anymore—there'd be no groaning or anything but if you watched it I think the breathing rate might change to a rather different breathing but not visibly—aaa aaa—or anything like that and then the head would come up and then a rather different tone—it wouldn't be an imitation of a, of a male voice at all but just a rather different, slightly different accent—that this wasn't the normal Garrett intonation and it would look at you and say—I think it was something like—I give you greetings friends—peace be with you and how may be I—how may I be of assistance to you or can I be of some help to you—not just what is your problem but how may be I, I be of assistance. Very politely and just very gentlemanly just as someone you don't know—as you might in a business interview you sit there and say—can I be of assistance without leaning forward but just, just I'm paying attention so obviously the person then would probably blurt out well if they're in dire need—I wanted to know this that or the other and whatever would follow who knows—and she never, never divulged what was going on…..

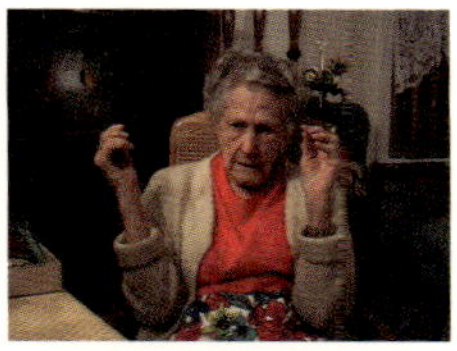

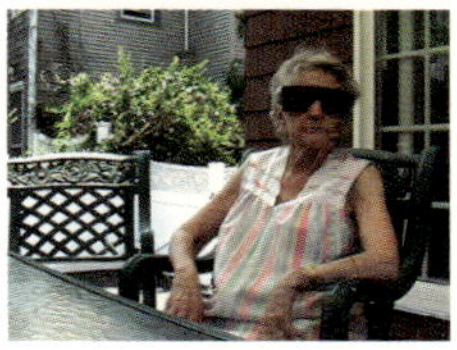

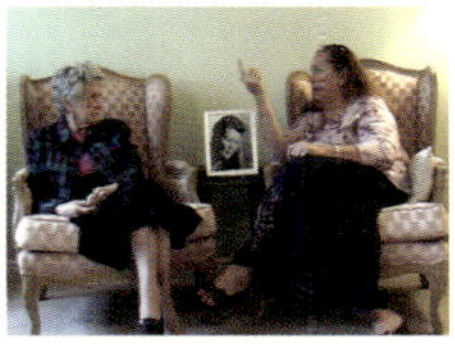

DUCK-BILLED PLATYPUS

Lisette *She well deserved the story she used to tell about her friend Aldous Huxley—who said to her once—there are three creatures which really ought not to be—the giraffe, the duck billed platypus and you Eileen Garrett—She apparently was very pleased to find herself classified among such marvels of evolution—The spiral always going up as her, as her logo*

Lisette *The duck billed platypus and you Eileen Garrett—She apparently was very pleased to find herself classified among such marvels of evolution—The spiral always going up as her, as her logo*

Lisette *The duck billed platypus and you Eileen Garrett—She apparently was very pleased to find herself classified among such marvels of evolution—The spiral always going up as her, as her logo*

Lisette *The duck billed platypus and you Eileen Garrett—She apparently was very pleased to find herself classified among such marvels of evolution—The spiral always going up as her, as her logo*

Lisette *The duck billed platypus and you Eileen Garrett—She apparently was very pleased to find herself classified among such marvels of evolution—The spiral always going up as her, as her logo*

Lisette *The duck billed platypus and you Eileen Garrett—She apparently was very pleased to find herself classified among such marvels of evolution—The spiral always going up as her, as her logo*

Lisette *The duck billed platypus and you Eileen Garrett—She apparently was very pleased to find herself classified among such marvels of evolution—The spiral always going up as her, as her logo*

Lisette *The duck billed platypus and you Eileen*

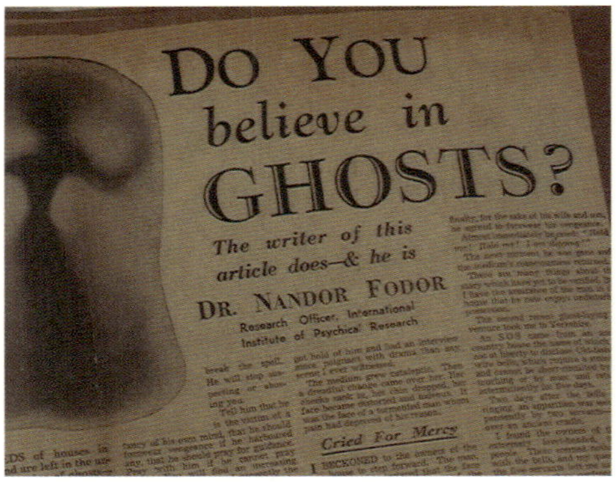
DO YOU
believe in
GHOSTS?
The writer of this
article does—& he is
DR. NANDOR FODOR
Research Officer, International
Institute of Psychical Research
Cried For Mercy

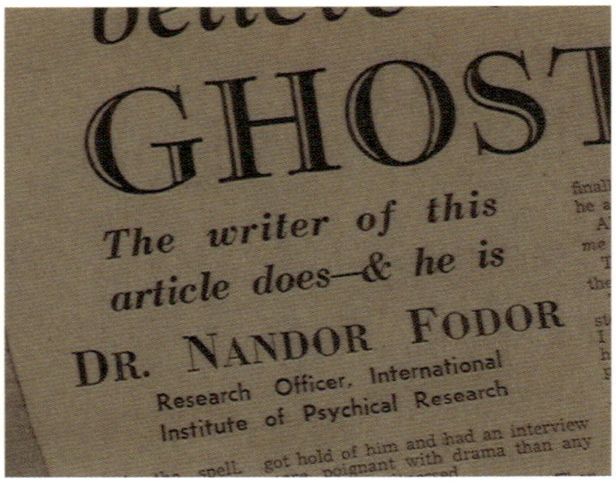
GHOST
The writer of this
article does—& he is
DR. NANDOR FODOR
Research Officer, International
Institute of Psychical Research

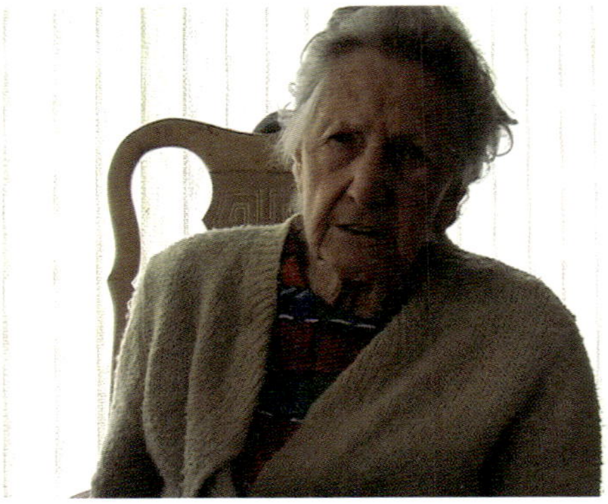

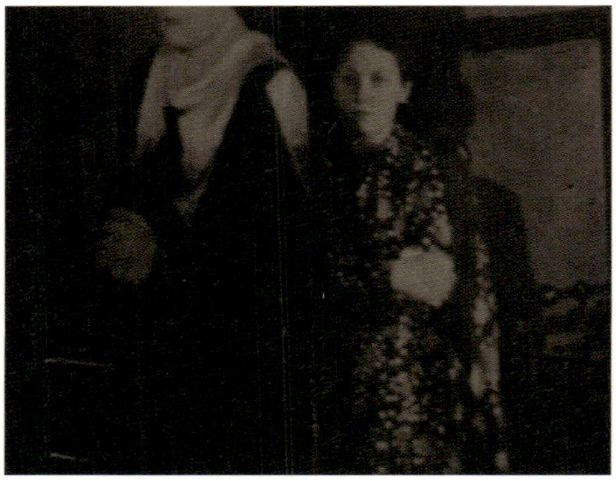

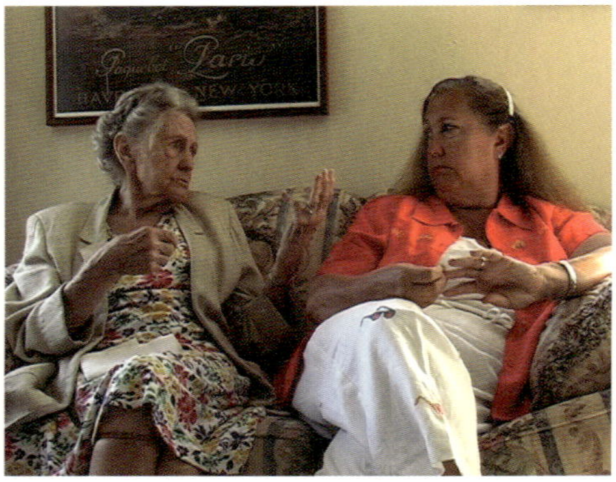

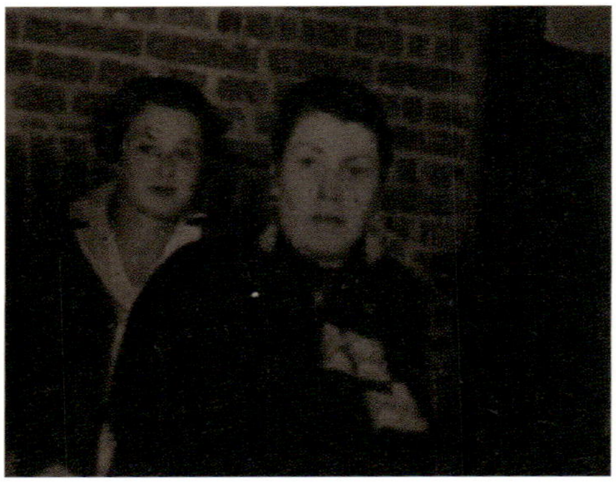

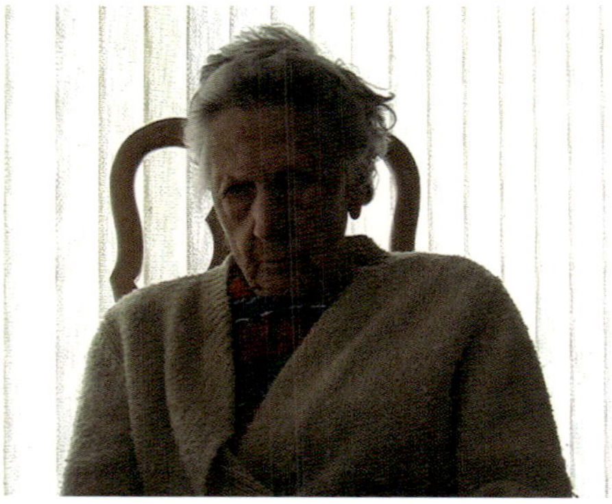

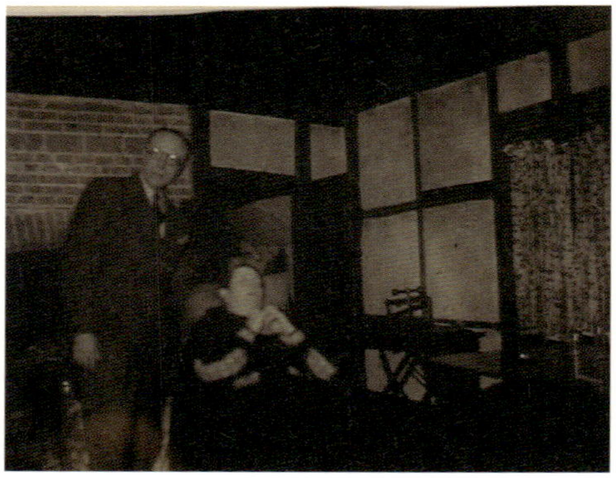

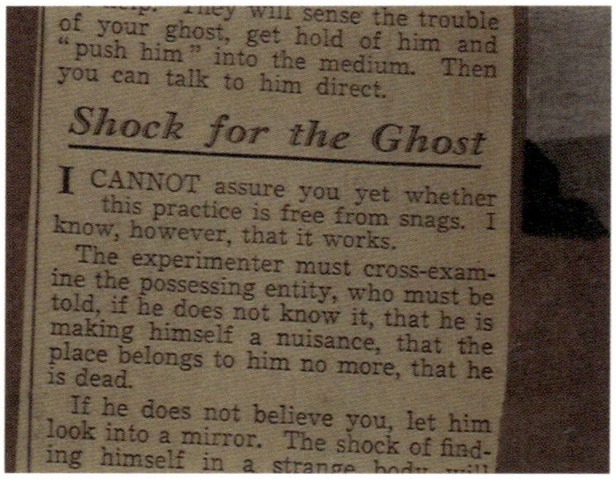
of your ghost, get hold of him and
"push him" into the medium. Then
you can talk to him direct.
Shock for the Ghost
I CANNOT assure you yet whether this practice is free from snags. I know, however, that it works.
The experimenter must cross-examine the possessing entity, who must be told, if he does not know it, that he is making himself a nuisance, that the place belongs to him no more, that he is dead.
If he does not believe you, let him look into a mirror. The shock of finding himself in a strange body will

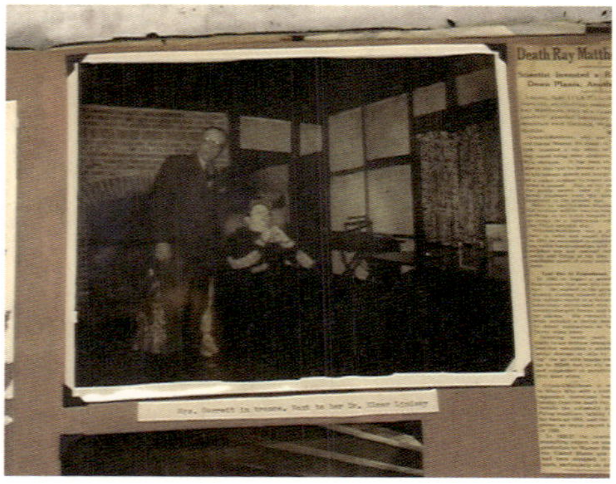

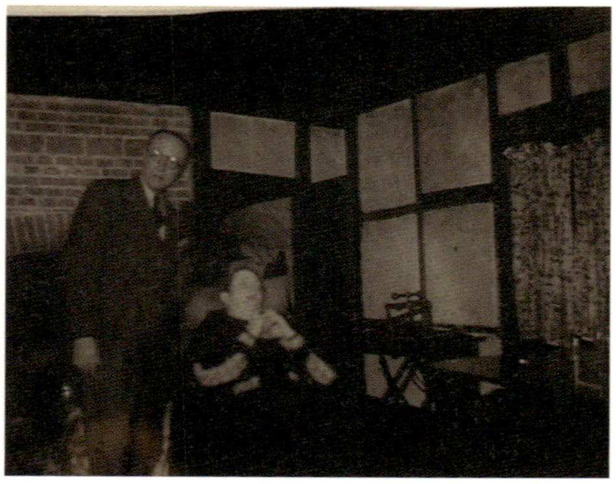

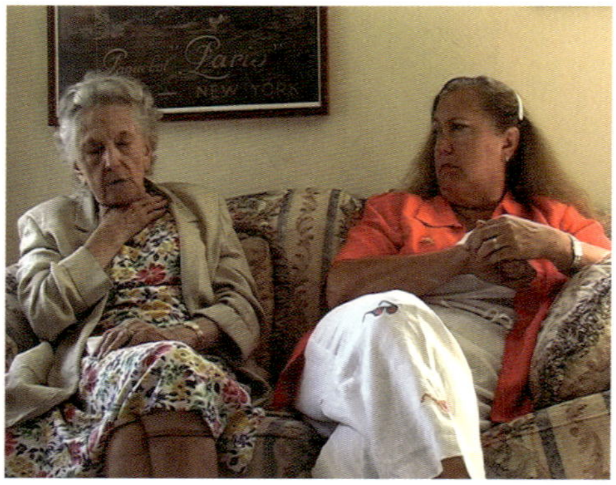

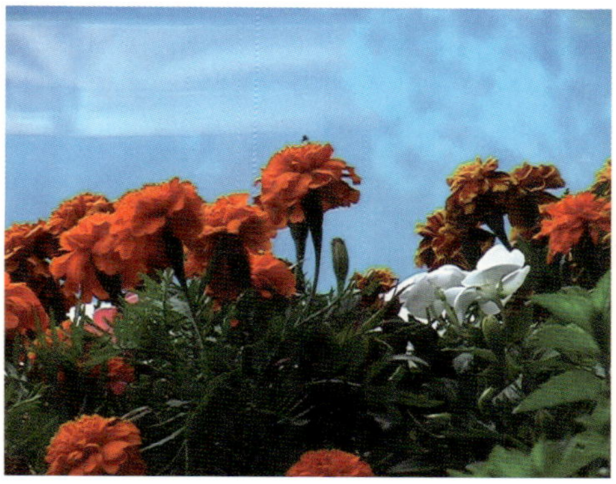
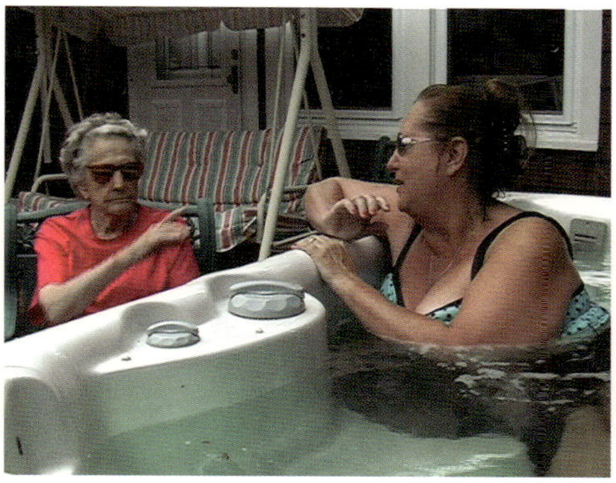
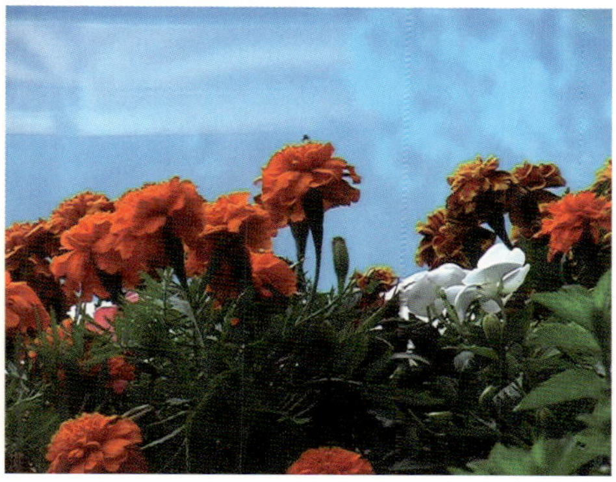
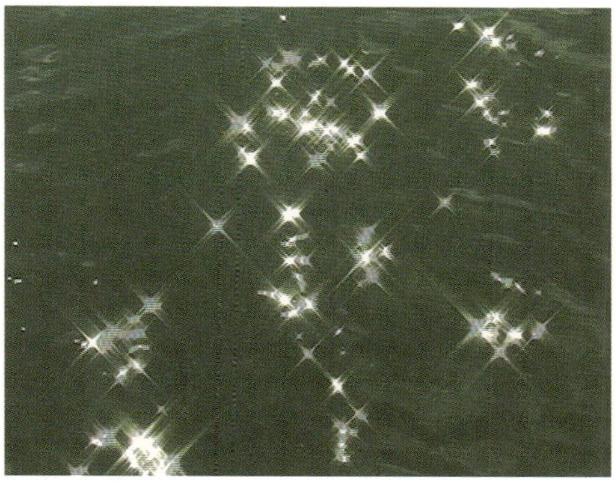
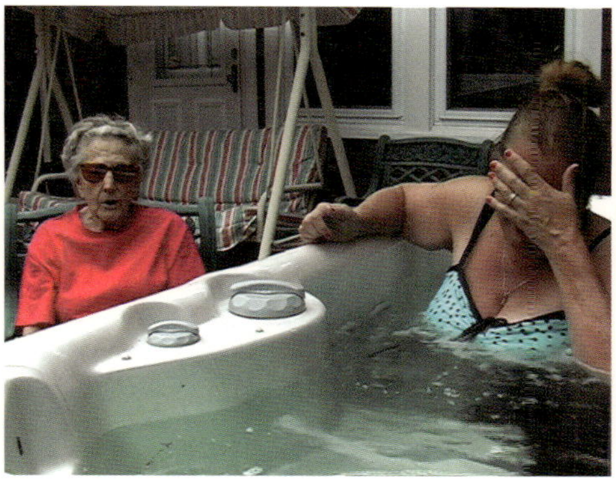
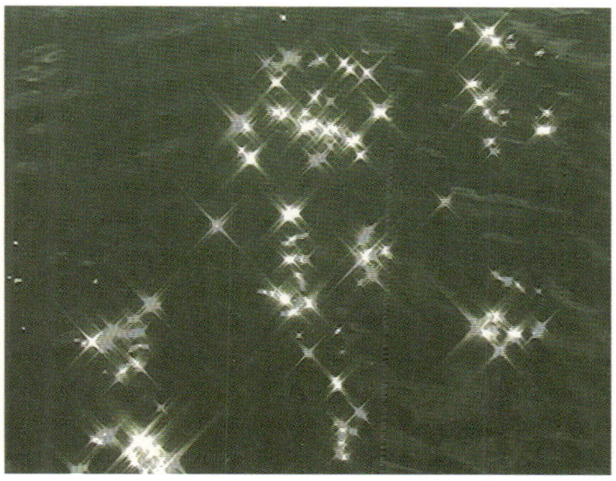
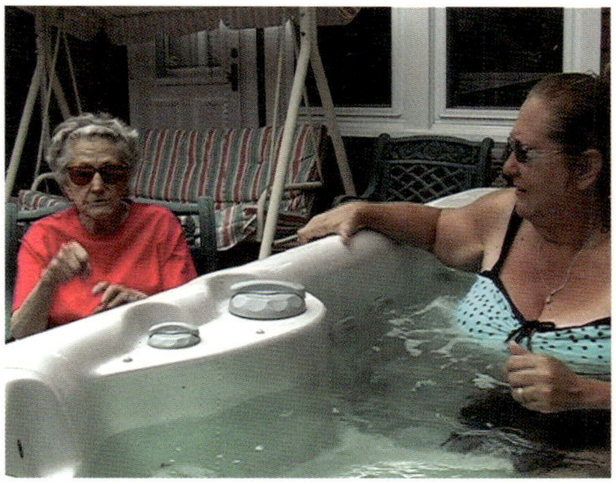
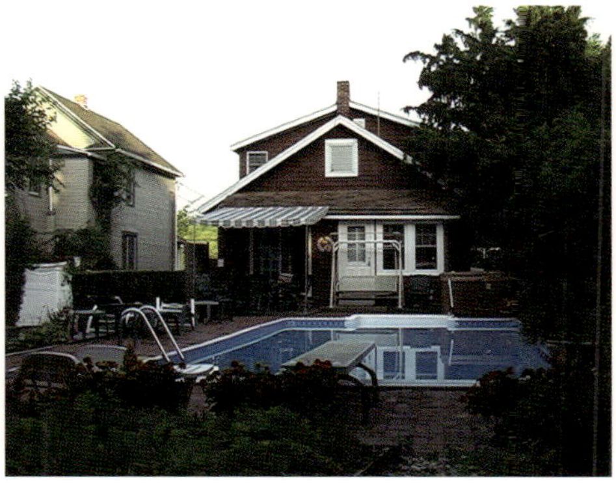
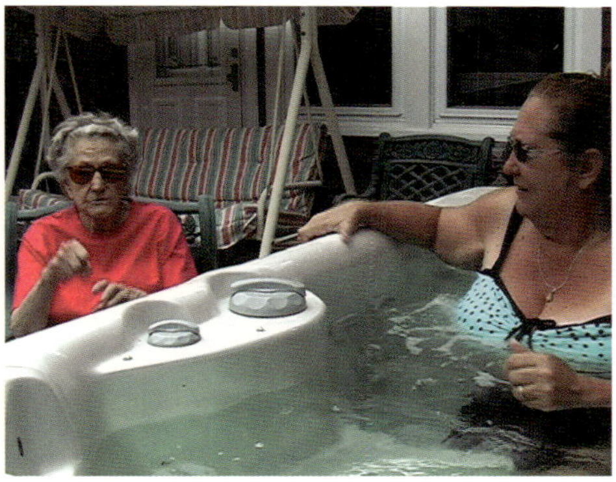
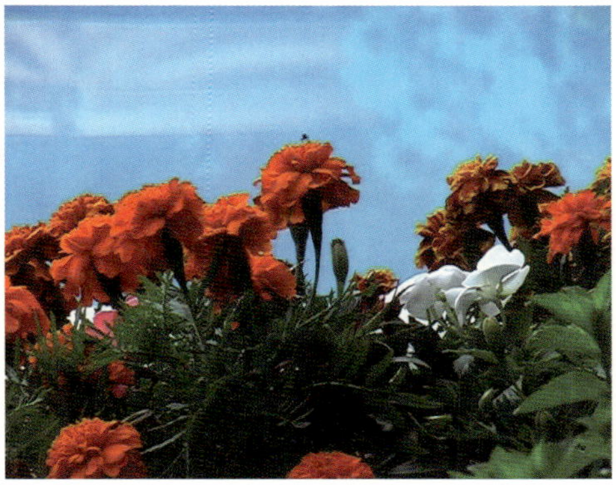
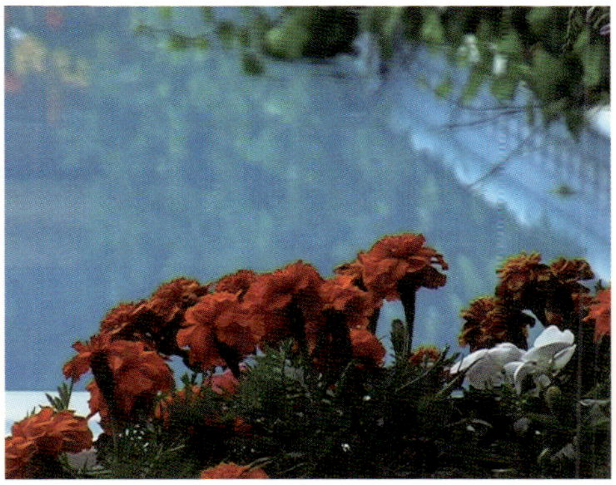
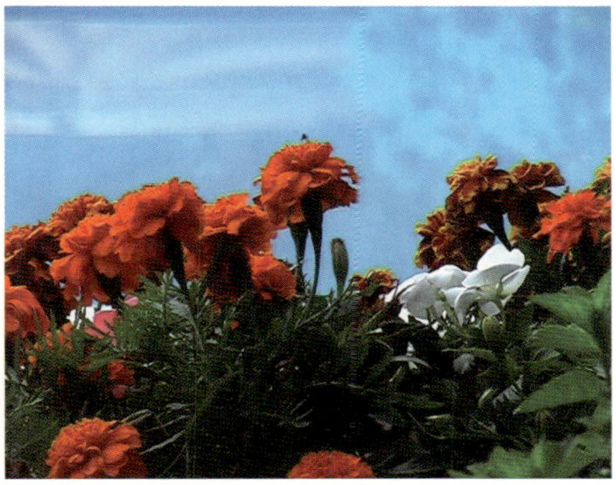

Garrett—She apparently was very pleased to find herself classified among such marvels of evolution—The spiral always going up as her, as her logo

Lisette *The duck billed platypus and you Eileen Garrett—She apparently was very pleased to find herself classified among such marvels of evolution—The spiral always going up as her, as her logo*

Lisette *The duck billed platypus and you Eileen Garrett—She apparently was very pleased to find herself classified among such marvels of evolution—The spiral always going up as her, as her logo*

Lisette *The duck billed platypus and you Eileen Garrett—*

Eileen Coly *She was stroking the tips, the very tips of her fingers, and somehow that was linked to some—some perception—something that was emanating—I don't know whether it was necessarily—she was concentrating on something coming from you or just what was percolating all around her—I think more probably what was around her and she was sorting out what that was—was it good was it evil was it—you know—that sort of thing. But I don't know why—why in the—in the fingertips particularly but she just did that—but then—her hands were very important to her—like the business with the cat nose—or noses—animal noses were important because—a dog she'd go for his nose—a nose was very, a cat nose on her hand—but then a dog she—yes she liked a—noses on animals—now I don't know—I don't remember any particular on human noses—but the—the animal noses she liked.*

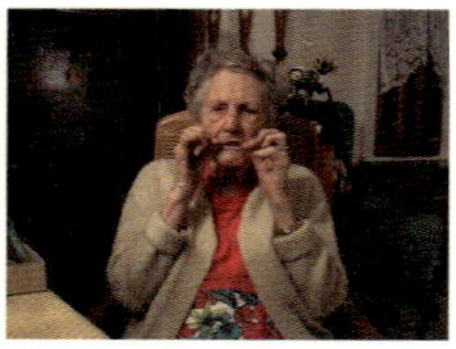

HUXLEY, DALI, DIETRICH

Eileen Coly *But all kinds of people would automatically just pounce on her and they'd find a way to get to her—that was just their main objective—*

Get to Garrett

Get to Garrett

Get to Garrett

Get to Garrett

Lisette *She had an eclectic mix of people.*

Eileen Coly *So she had an absolute kaleidoscope of all kinds of people.*

Lisette *Fellini apparently wanted to do a film about the psychic—surreal—and I laugh*

Lisette *Theatre people would also be drawn*

Eileen Coly *Oh very, very much*

Lisette *Or it's not the theatre—it's just the artistic temperament I think*

Eileen Coly *I think all, all creative people*

Lisette *Didn't she date Randolph Scott for a while—when you were—yeah Randolph Scott?*

Eileen Coly *Oh no she was amused because....*

Lisette *Or was he gay?*

Eileen Coly *Oh no he was always running around with...*

Lisette *When she would, knew, met Lucky Luciano*

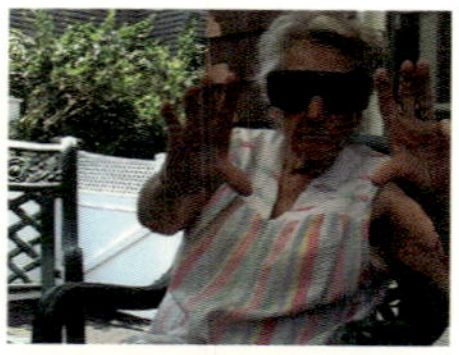

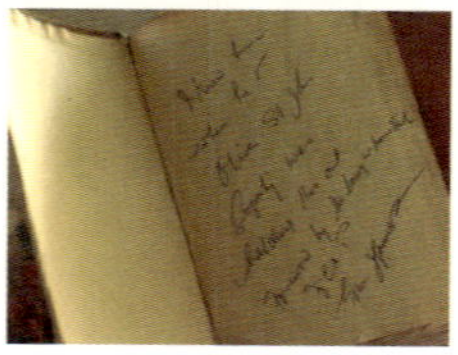

lot of her life on the plump side but she had those eye which once you've taken a look at her face everyone was drawn to her eyes—they were so expressive and just drew people to her so that everything—She used her hands so beautifully—she did have lovely small hands, beautifully shaped but not the impression that using them so much they were long graceful fingers at all—because nothing about her was built long and gracefully—but it was all so expressive so the hands were very much a part of her and of course the eyes—I think many people have said that once they've met her—the eyes, it was just the eyes that attracted them immediately and stayed there as her main attraction—you just, have to take notice of them—so what made me think so much of that—now I've lost the—oh again the hands—the spiral—it all, this spiral was very much a part of her whole being because anything that she undertook—there was a system of working, of unwinding—of processing something in this unwinding as well as the creation, but it was an unwinding process—so the spiral was very important to her and became the symbol in a lot of her printed work which of course we continue to this day as I told you before...

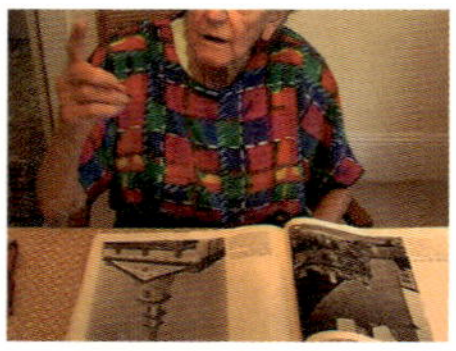

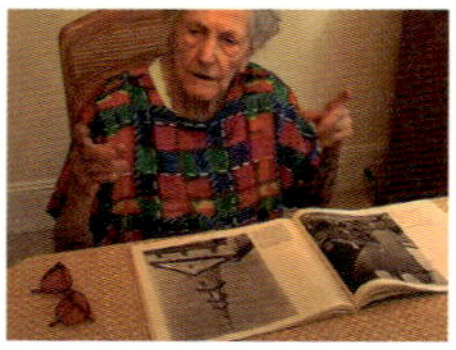

HUXLEY, DALI, DIETRICH

Lisette *What a motley crew—the hairdresser, Muriel Hankey, a spy and Garrett—you never knew who you'd find at her table*

Lisette *And it's not too easy to get rid of Salvador Dali*

Eileen Coly *But all kinds of people would automatically just pounce on her and they'd find a way to get to her—that was just their main objective—*

Get to Garrett

Get to Garrett

Get to Garrett

Get to Garrett

Eileen Coly *And some of these acquaintances, strangely enough would be very, very short—for instance I'm not sure when it comes to—Gore Vidal even*

Lisette *So this is James Joyce—Ulysses—and Garrett what, wrote in it that "I knew him when he and Sir Oliver St John Gogarty was hatching this out—forward by the lawyer Maurice Ernst of Creative Age Press"*

Lisette *She had an eclectic mix of people*

Lisette *The doors were always open to Aldous Huxley*

Eileen Coly *So of course the Huxley work—and with all the LSD—the idea of how do we compare the effects of LSD—what has that to do with psychic trance, with imposing psychic visions, observing—whatever—all that stuff*

Eileen Coly *So she had an absolute kaleidoscope of all kinds of people*

Lisette *"Who taught the Duke of Windsor to dance the Charleston—the Prince of Wales"—that's the one who abdicated, right?*

Eileen Coly *Yes*

Lisette *And he's writing "To Eileen, my darling, anytime, anywhere, and how! always Barry"*

Eileen Coly *But a pure meeting, meeting of souls or something—and she had that, that drew people to her.*

Lisette *So did you ever get used to interfacing with these famous people—I mean, god like Marlene Dietrich? or Tallulah Bankhead?, (Eileen Coly—No) Henry Miller?*

Garrett - She apparently was very pleased to find herself classified among such marvels of evolution—The spiral always going up as her, as her logo

Lisette *The duck billed platypus and you Eileen Garrett—She apparently was very pleased to find herself classified among such marvels of evolution—The spiral always going up as her, as her logo*

Lisette *The duck billed platypus and you Eileen Garrett—She apparently was very pleased to find herself classified among such marvels of evolution—The spiral always going up as her, as her logo*

Lisette *The duck billed platypus and you Eileen Garrett—*

Eileen Coly *She was stroking the tips, the very tips of her fingers, and somehow that was linked to some—some perception—something that was emanating—I don't know whether it was necessarily—she was concentrating on something coming from you or just what was percolating all around her—I think more probably what was around her and she was sorting out what that was—was it good was it evil was it—you know—that sort of thing. But I don't know why—why in the—in the fingertips particularly but she just did that—but then—her hands were very important to her—like the business with the cat nose—or noses—animal noses were important because—a dog she'd go for his nose—a nose was very, a cat nose on her hand—but then a dog she—yes she liked a—noses on animals—now I don't know—I don't remember any particular on human noses—but the—the animal noses she liked.*

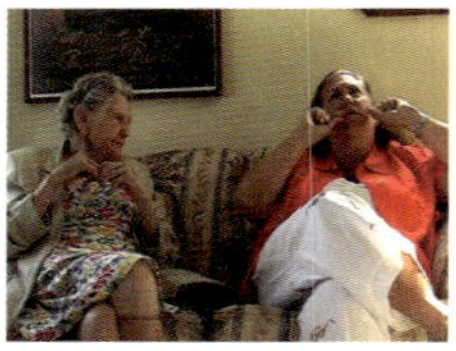

HUXLEY, DALI, DIETRICH

Eileen Coly *But all kinds of people would automatically just pounce on her and they'd find a way to get to her—that was just their main objective—*

Get to Garrett

Get to Garrett

Get to Garrett

Get to Garrett

Lisette *She had an eclectic mix of people.*

Eileen Coly *So she had an absolute kaleidoscope of all kinds of people.*

Lisette *But then film was particularly interesting—the visuals—Fellini apparently—Federico Fellini was quite a fan*

Eileen Coly *Oh, very, very much*

Lisette *Or it's not the theatre—it's just the artistic temperament I think*

Eileen Coly *I think all, all creative people*

Eileen Coly *Was it Cary Grant?—I think it was Cary Grant*

Lisette *I don't know dear*

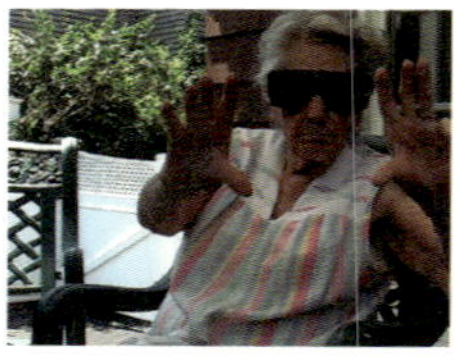

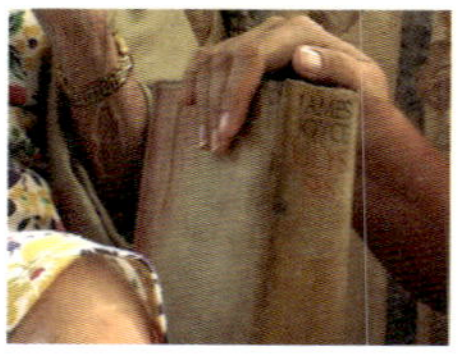

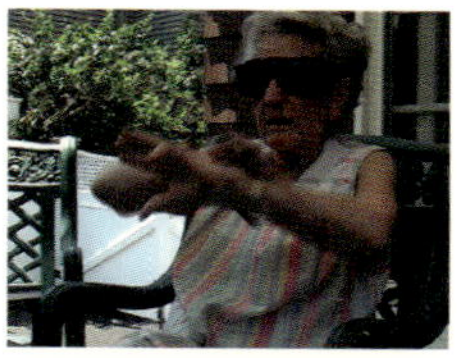
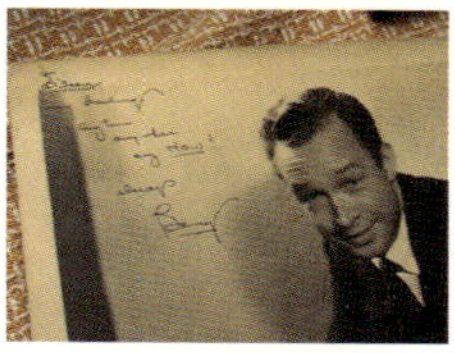
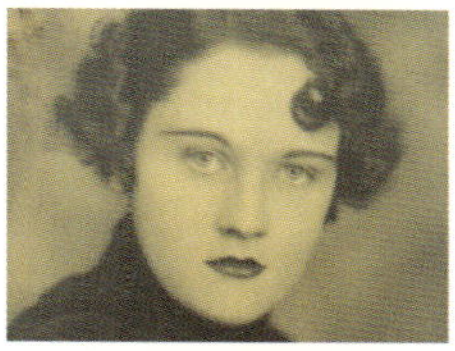
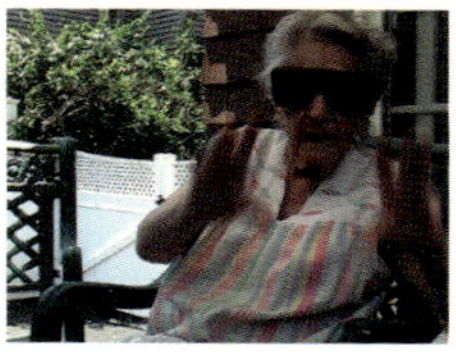

Lisette *Because I think—boy—Fellini and Garrett now that fits being a Fellini film*
Lisette *Would also be drawn*
Eileen Coly *Oh very, very much*
Lisette *Or it's not the theatre—it's, it's just the artistic temperament I think*
Eileen Coly *I think all, all creative people*
Lisette *Look at that, that is so cool, you look like Theda Bara "The Vamp" or something—what year is that?*
Eileen Coly *That hair business—that was all perms, because*
Lisette *This is all the, the Rita Hayworth stuff. Oh god very smoky. (Eileen Coly—Good God) Now when would, that would have been the 30s, these aren't dated mama. Oh and Angus McBean in '36*
Eileen Coly *Oh well yes that's why we had a lot of these fancy things from Angus (Lisette—so you had a short hair...) a personal friend too.*
Lisette *In the office you would one day have a, a movie star—you know Jackie Gleason or (Eileen Coly—yes, oh yes) or she'd be friends with Gloria Swanson*
Eileen Coly *Whether or not they were both gay, or not—I don't know*
Lisette *Then again there's all the gangsters*
Eileen Coly *In the early '30s*
Lisette *And you used to go to the Cotton Club up in Harlem right?—She used to love to dance—Garrett*
Eileen Coly *Yes you could go, go to Harlem in those days and go to the Cotton Club*

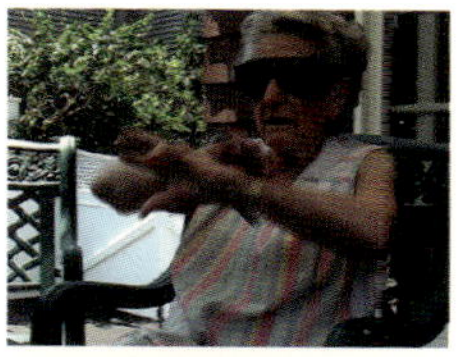
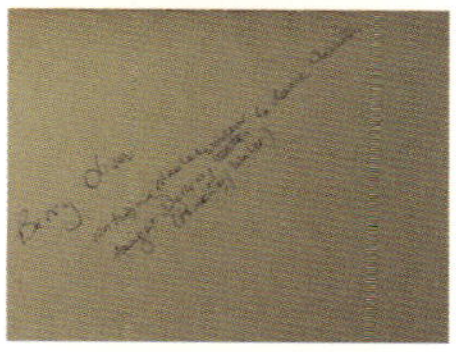
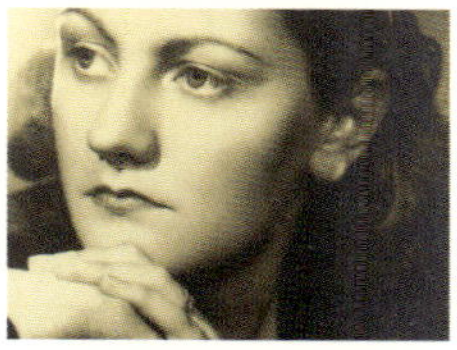
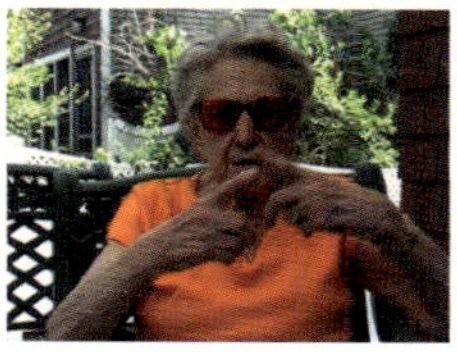

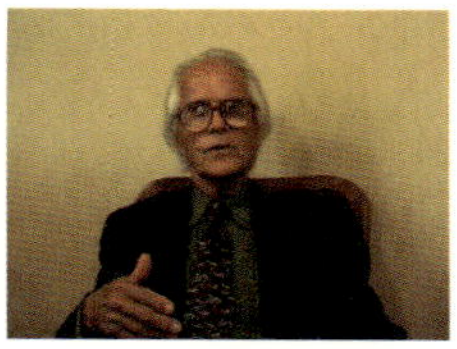

PARAPSYCHOLOGISTS

Bill Roll *Mrs Garrett—who was a kind of—I would consider a kind of meditation master—because she emphasised the importance of the breath and breathing for the development of her psychic abilities and—er—and so that's another respect in which she has been important and helpful to me and to the field as a whole. So she is very, a considerable contribution of course—she was as well a subject and whenever anybody wanted to do experiments with her of any type she always agreed and as a result we have some very interesting findings. Eileen Garrett, Mrs Garrett played a major role in my life as a Parapsychologist in fact she helped me get a start in the field financially—she supported me for several years while I was at Oxford and then she invited me to the first Parapsychology conference I ever intended which was at Utrecht in 1953—on the occasion of the appointment of Tenhaeff—Dr Tenhaeff to the chair in Parapsychology at the University of Utrecht.*
She came to Oxford where we had—where I was studying and I'd set up a little Parapsychology reading room—a laboratory in my house and she came to visit that and I think that was the first time I actually met her—and of course she is a very—when she enters a room you know it—(laughs) she's a kind of—a sun around whom planets rotate—(laughs) you know who's the centre—she's the centre—so she was a very visible presence always (laughs)

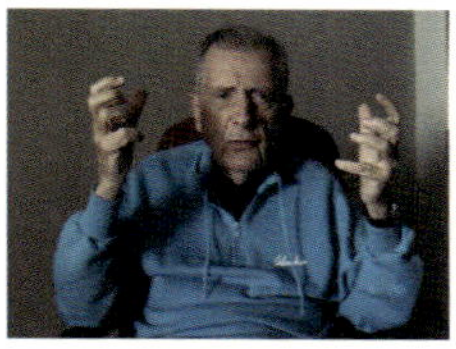

PARAPSYCHOLOGISTS

Stanley Krippner *Then Eileen said 'Oh I think that I have the, I think that I have the spirits with me now—give me the film' and so Walter Panky gave her the film and he said 'put this against the most vibrant part or your body—the part of your body that's radiating the most energy' and she clasped it to her ample breasts and held it and then Douglas said 'Oh I feel the energy too' and Walter said 'put it to the part of your body where you feel the most energy' and Douglas put it against his crotch. Well we were having great expectations for the film—alas the film was black on both occasions and didn't show any exotic figures, but it was a good try.*
I had the great pleasure of attending Eileen Garrett's annual conference in Le Piol, France on two occasions in the 1960s—on one of those occasions the topic was Drugs and Altered States of Consciousness and on another occasion—one of the foci was Dreams and I remember very well the excellent food that this marvellous restaurant served—best food that I've had in France or just about anyplace else as a matter of fact. Eileen Garrett was always right at the breakfast table and when I came in she would always ask 'how did you sleep?' and I would say 'Very well—Merci'.
And I think that she is a sort of a role model for people with special sensitivities who do know how to bring in some money but also know how to invest it wisely for the good of the field—let's face it the mediums who are on television today—I don't know how they spend their money but it's not to help Parapsychology, it's not to create scholarships, it's not to stimulate research—So Eileen Garrett is almost alone in terms of a psychic sensitive who really devoted energy, time and money to propagate the field and to fostering Parapsychology as a science.

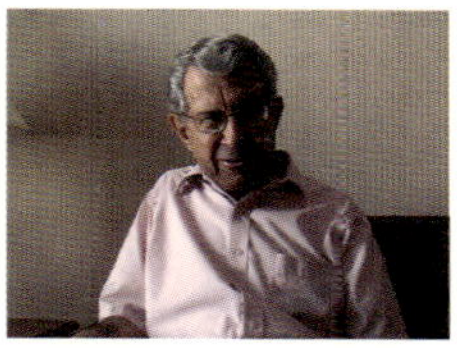

PARAPSYCHOLOGISTS

Rex Stanford *Well I had one meeting with Eileen Garrett—but it's a meeting I certainly remember—I'd been looking forward to it for years and my wife and I attended that meeting—it was in New York City up in their head-quarters. And I remember—that—what I'd heard about her was—it was hard to believe that she was up to it—as a woman who, who was very attentive and very strong and her, in her ability to present herself she was a person who sort of immediately commanded your attention—even, probably even if you didn't know who she was. But I was really looking forward to it because she was that paradox to me of the person who just—well she was obviously a medium and she had a spirit control and yet she had been curious enough to want to find out what that was all about and I just wanted to meet someone like that, it was hard for me to even imagine what a person would be like in that way—Well I found a very straight forward kind of practical person—not a—she didn't seem to be dreamy out in outer space or anything like that. This was, this was over twenty years ago I don't even remember the exact date and I had only one meeting with her with my wife with her and there were several other Parapsychologists who were on that occasion—I do not remember who was with us—but—er and not much of a conversation—it was more the impression of Mrs Garrett. But here's the point—here was a person who was very sympathetic to the field not just as one part of a more vast research programme who had focused their support in one single area and she was very eager to see that the field be promoted and the projects she supported—every one I ever heard of seemed to be a worthy project—and of course I like to believe that mine were—but I—I had a number of grants from the Parapsychology Foundation and am very grateful but I remember Eileen Garrett—as—there are some people who hold a special sense of a niche in your mental existence and I've never met one before, I'd never met one before or since that time who had those—that unique set of characteristics and I know that there are many people in the field of Parapsychology who feel that grateful...*

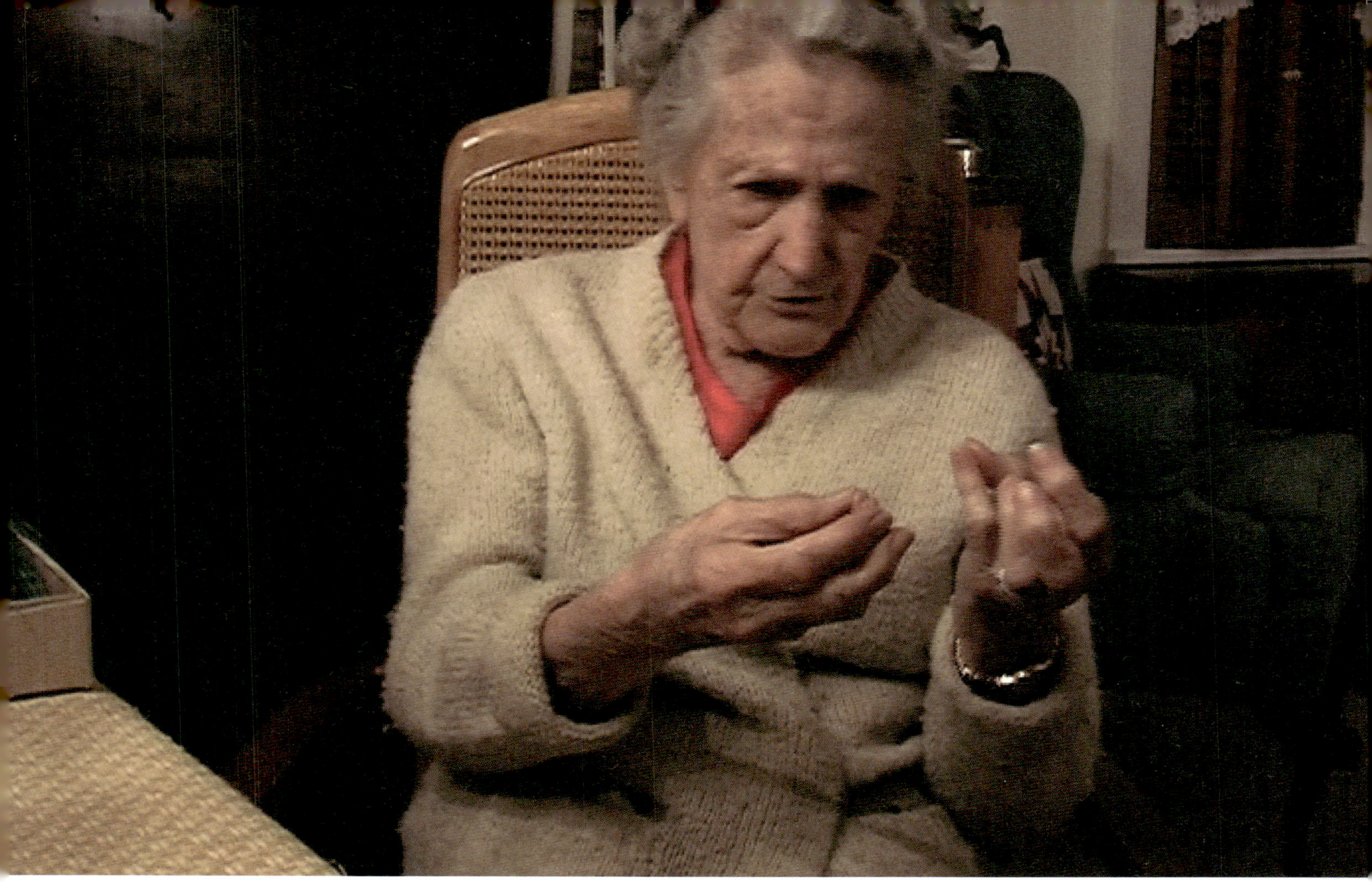
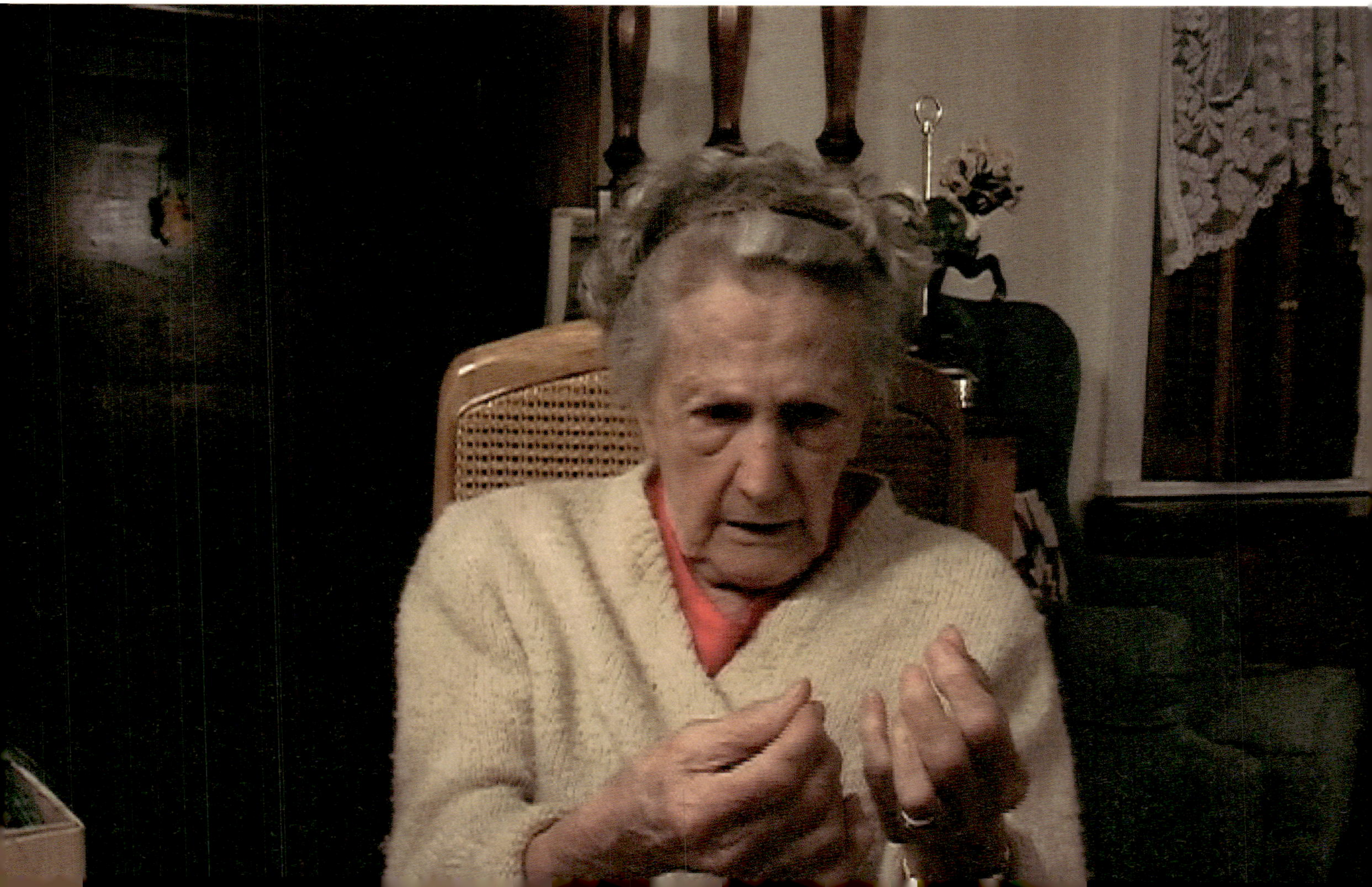

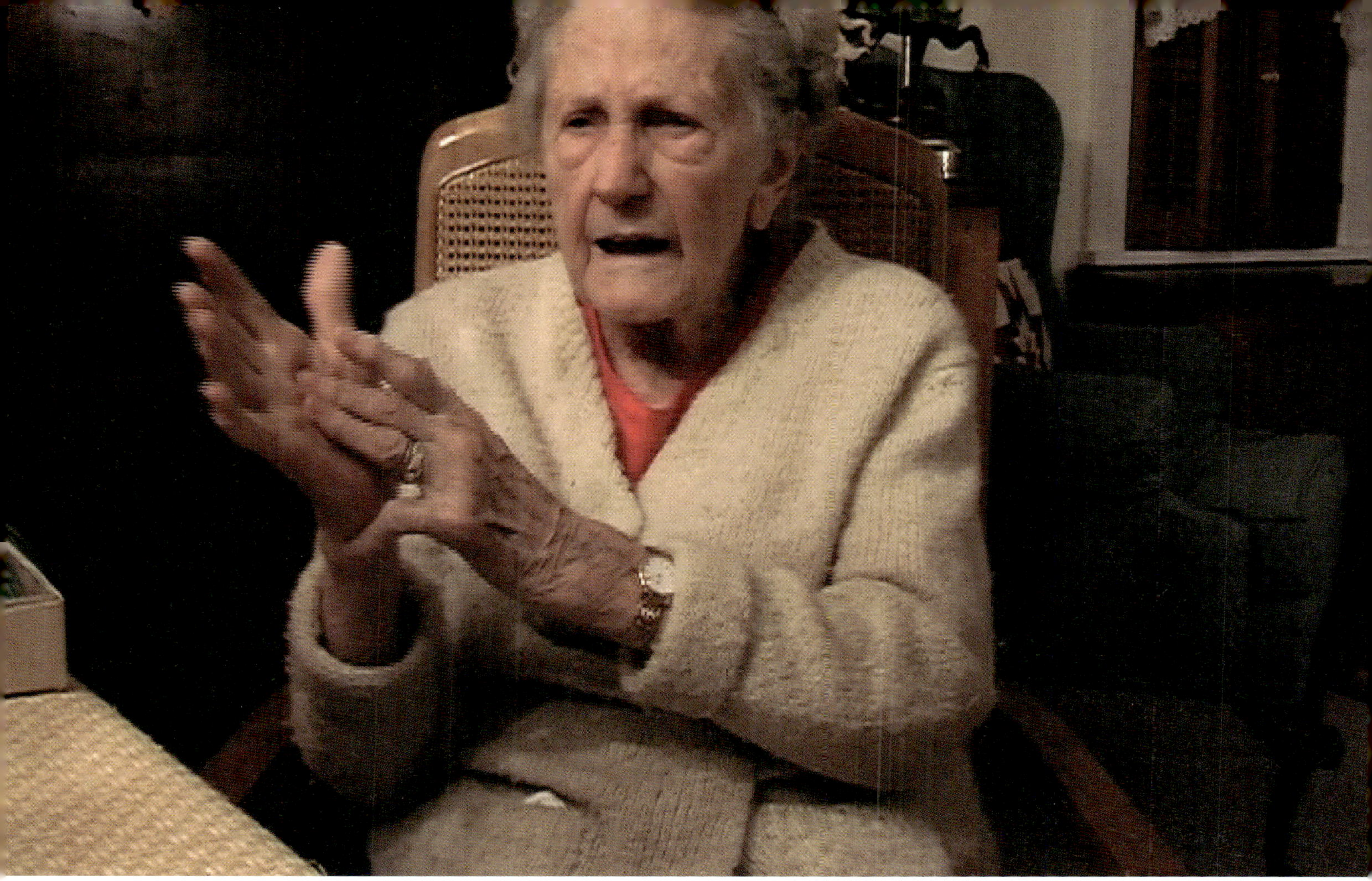

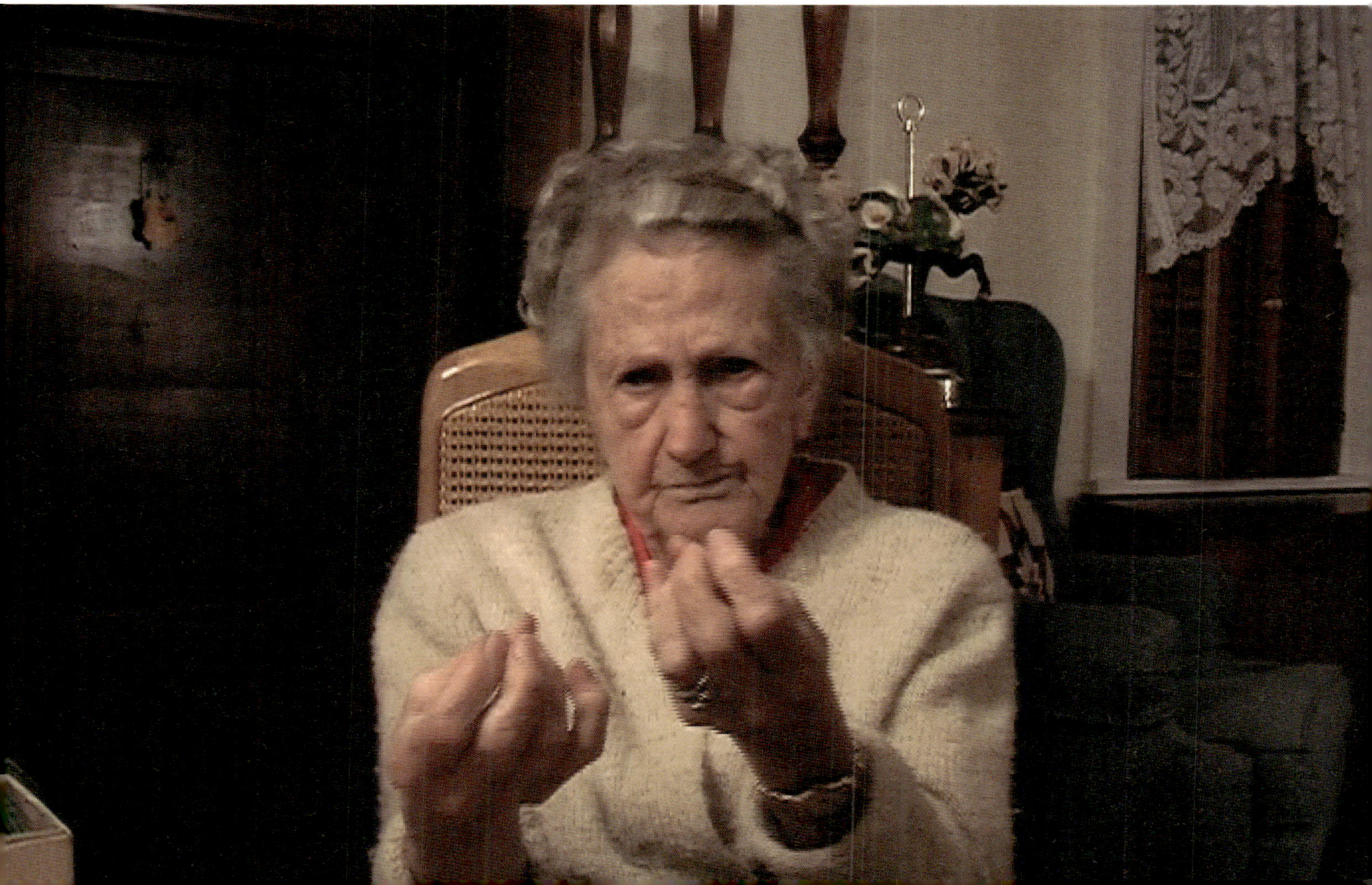

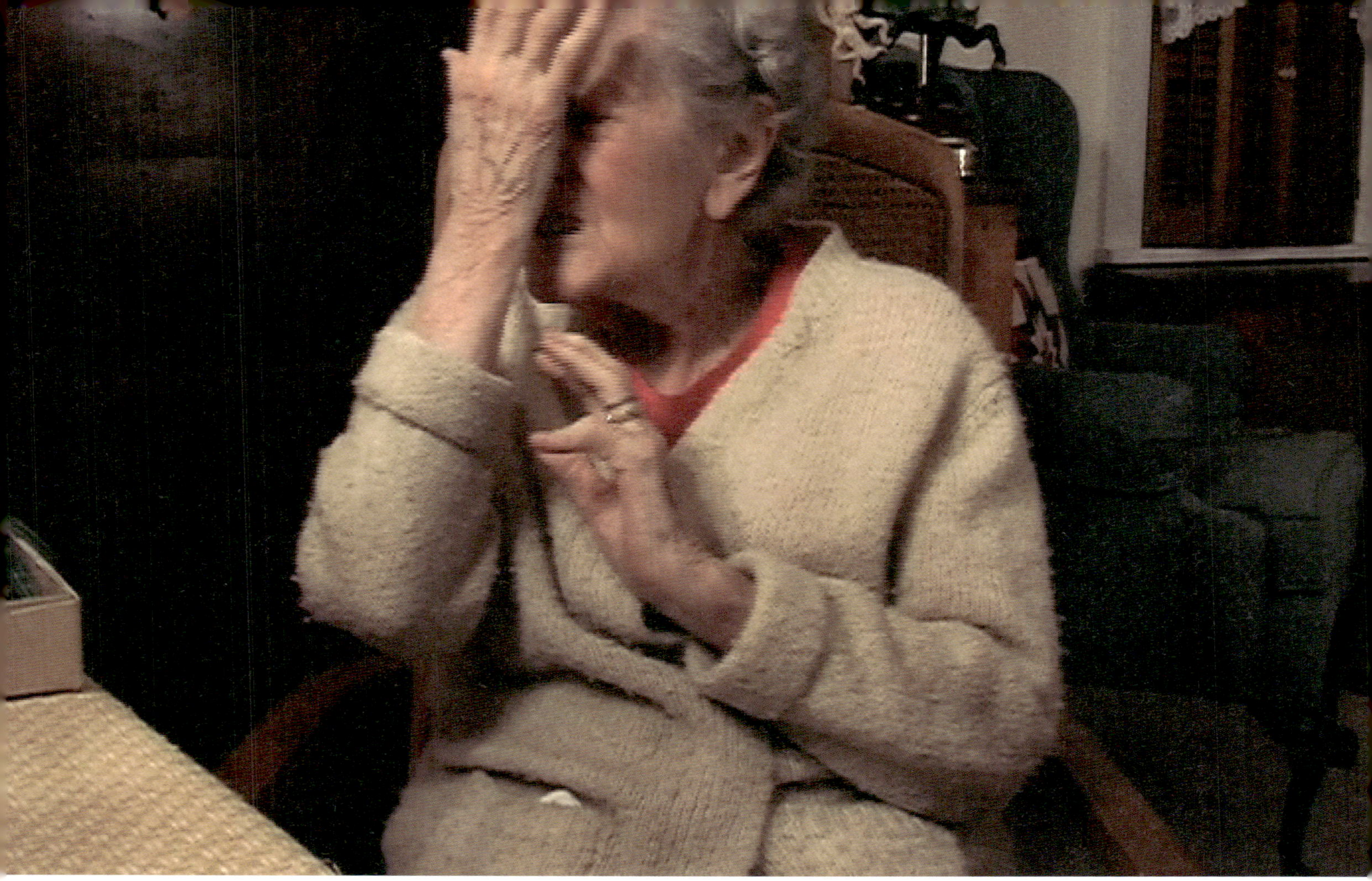

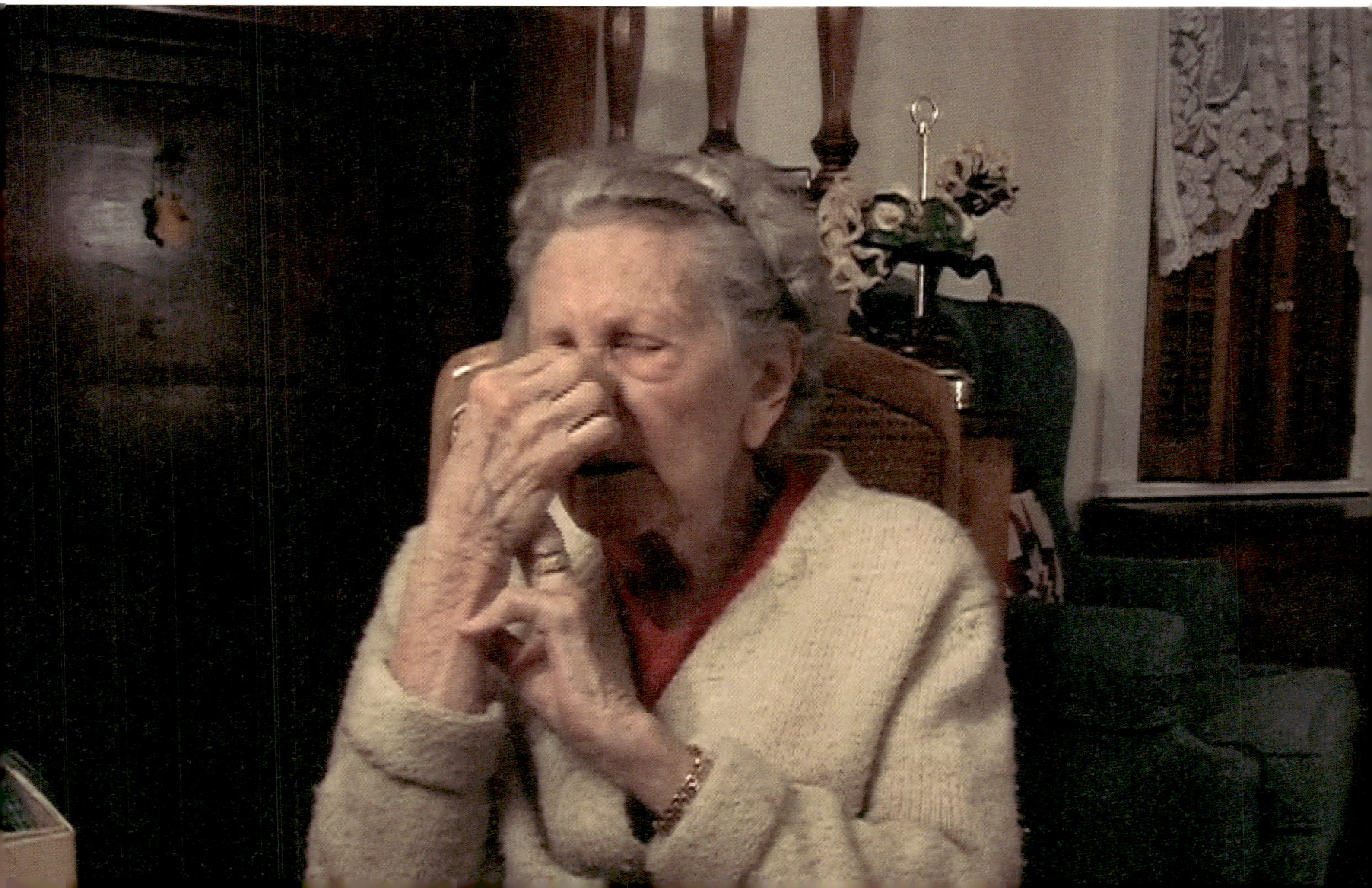

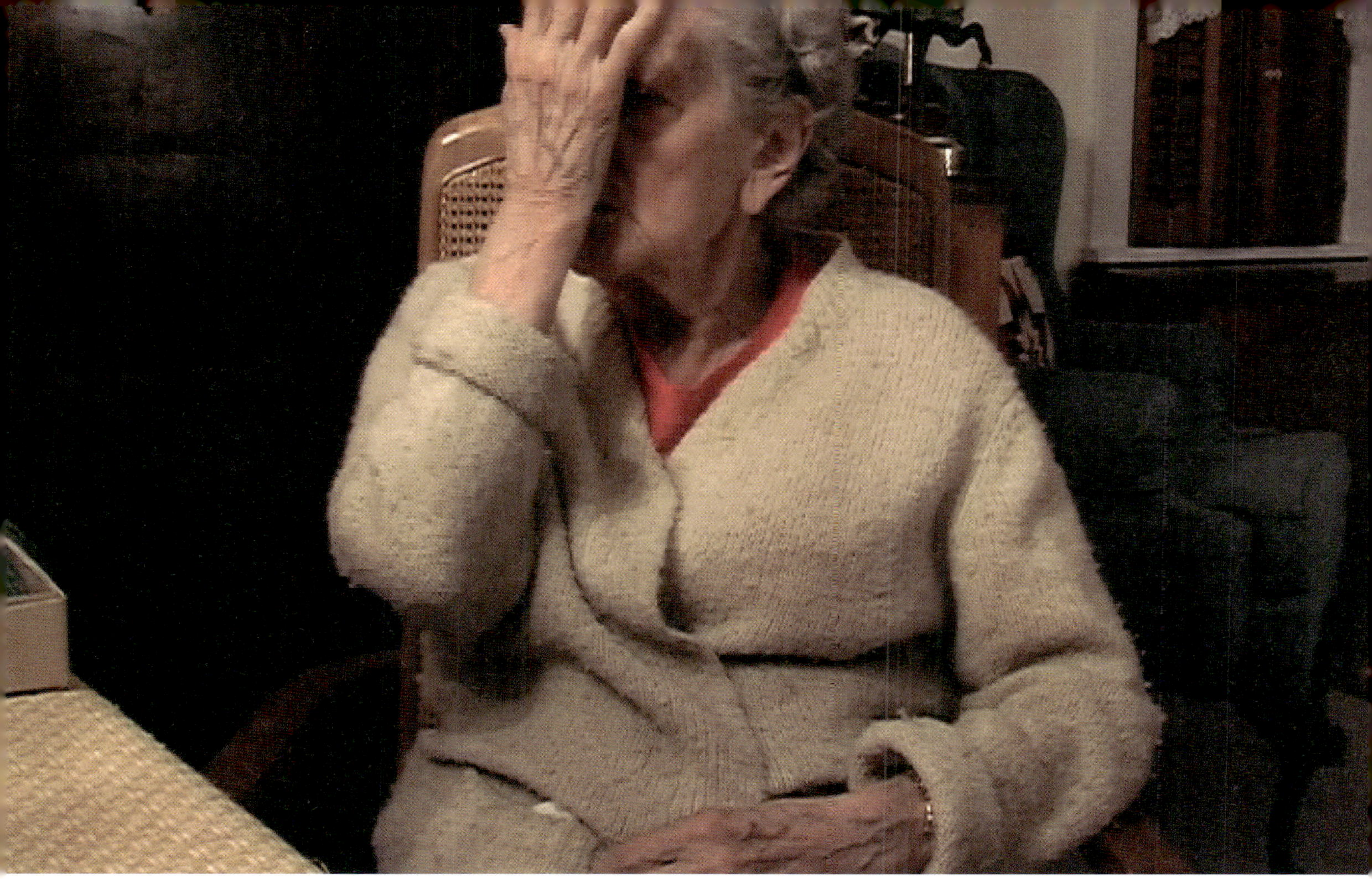
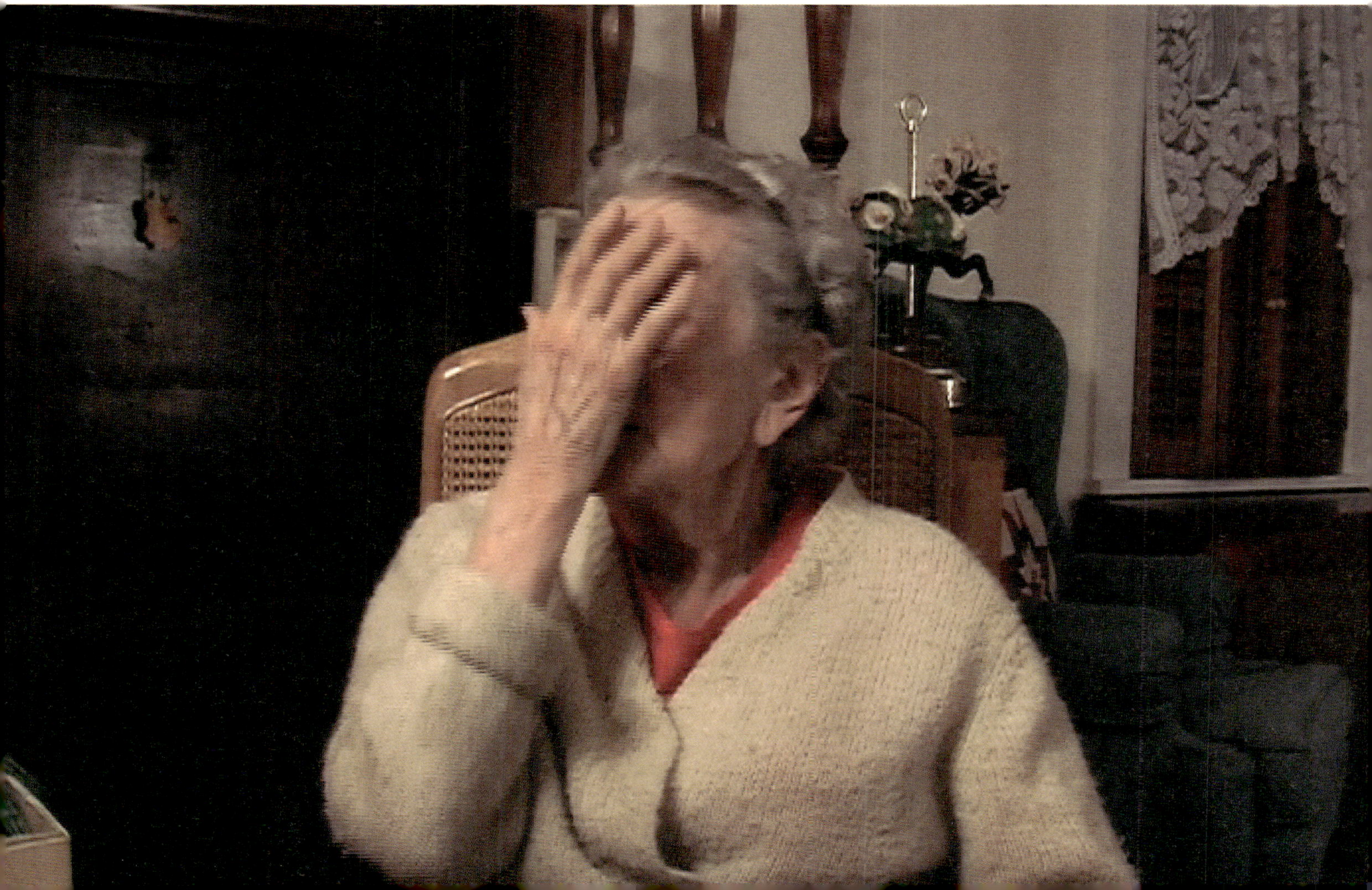

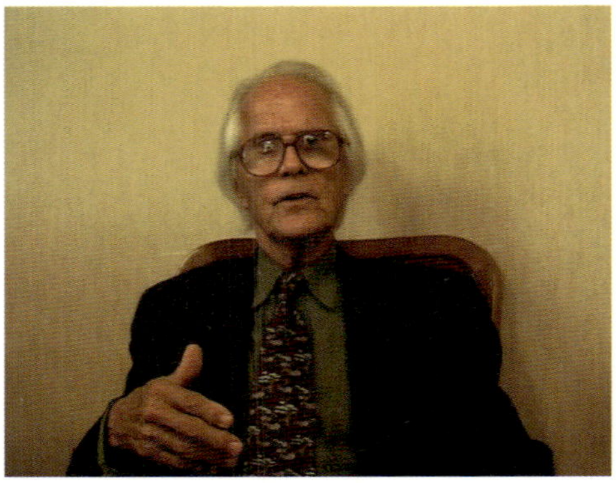
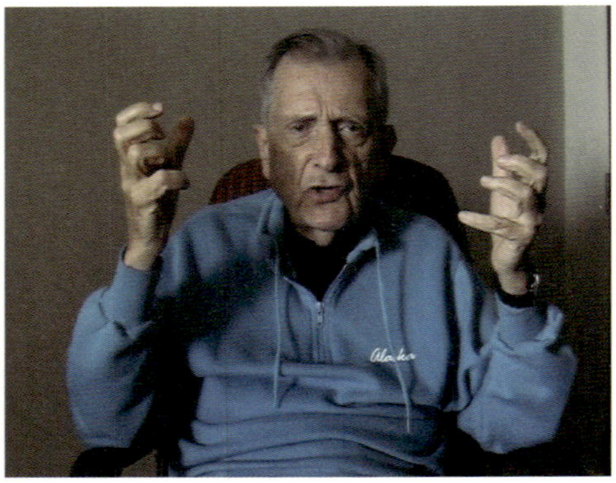
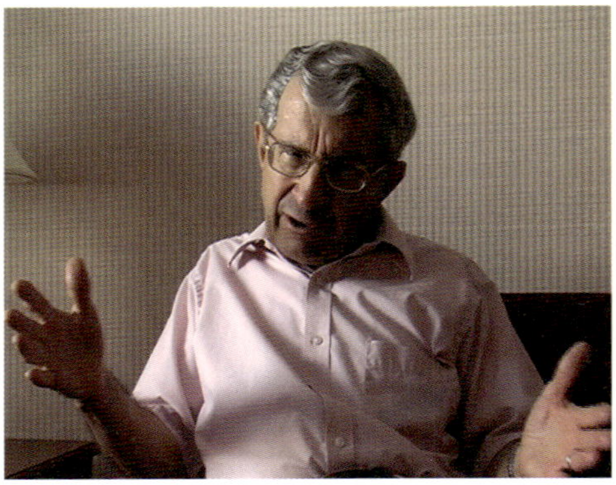
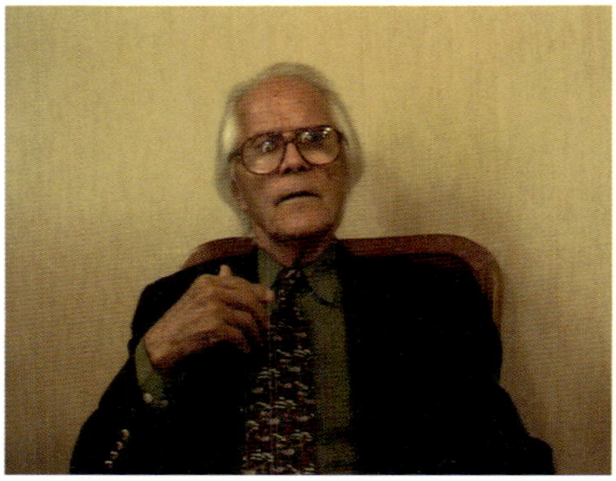
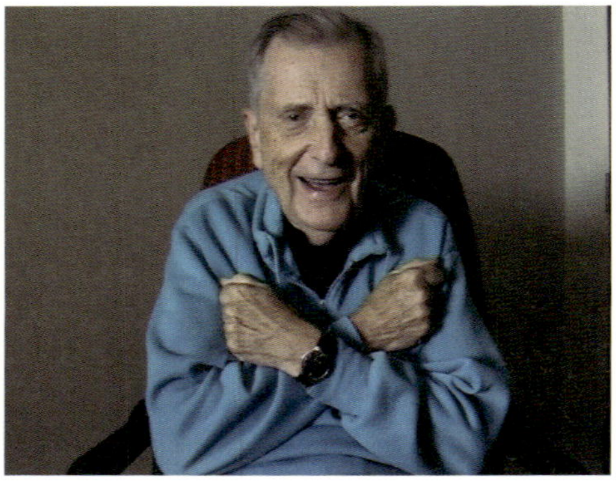
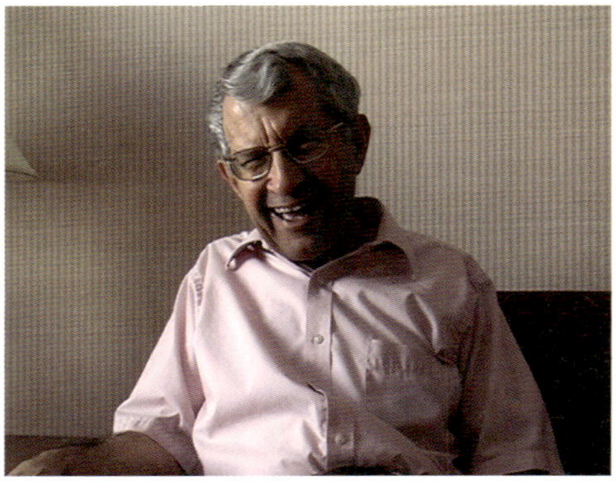
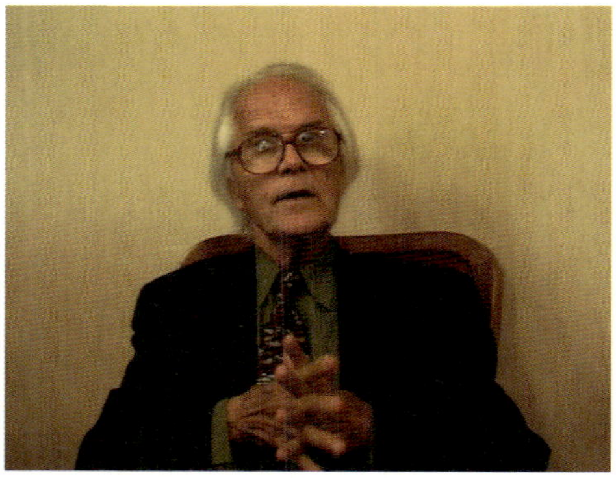
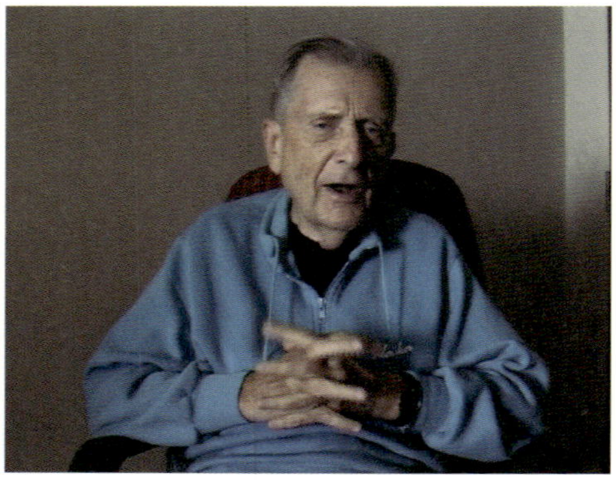
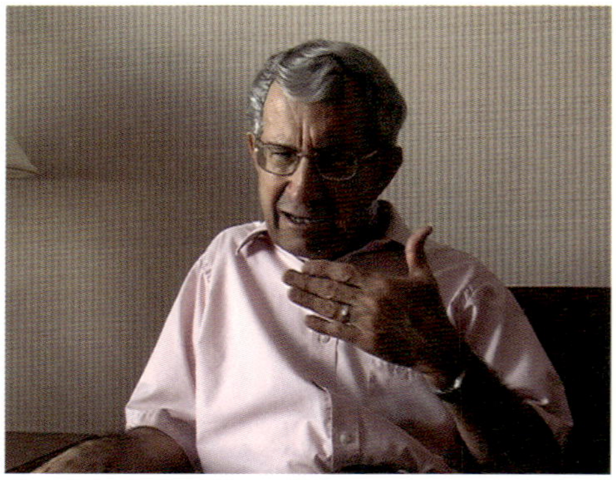
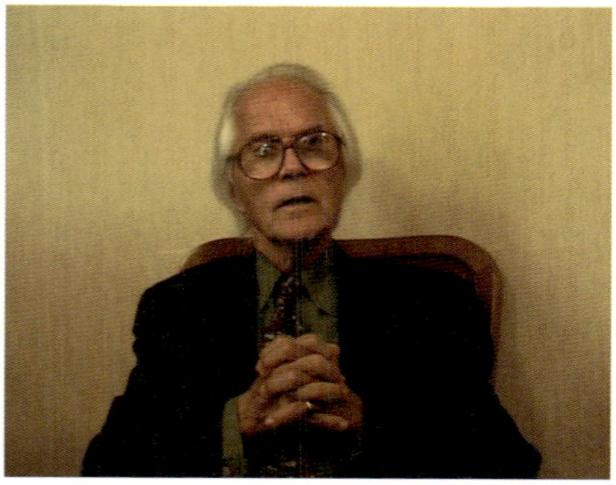
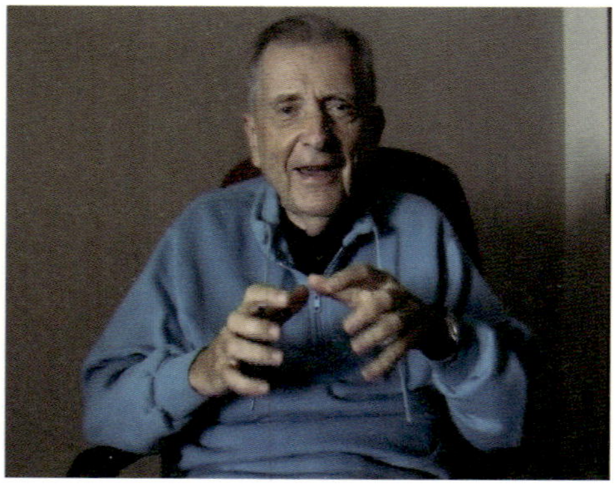
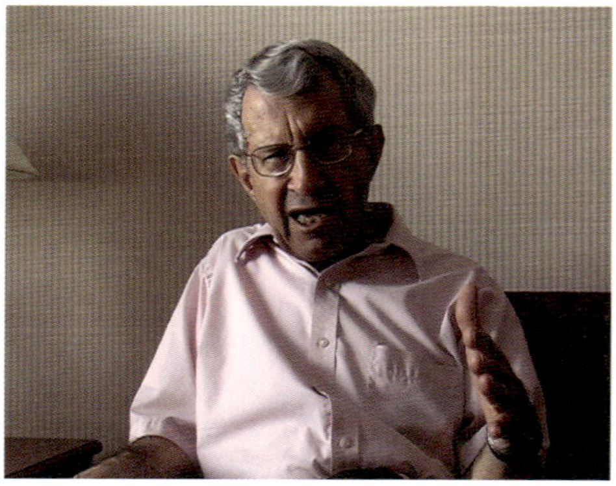

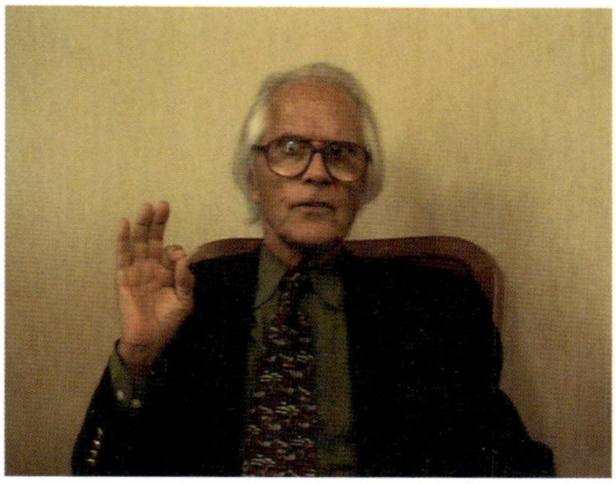
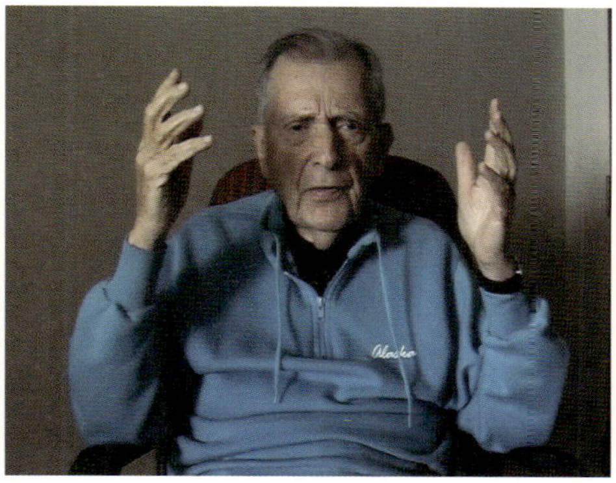
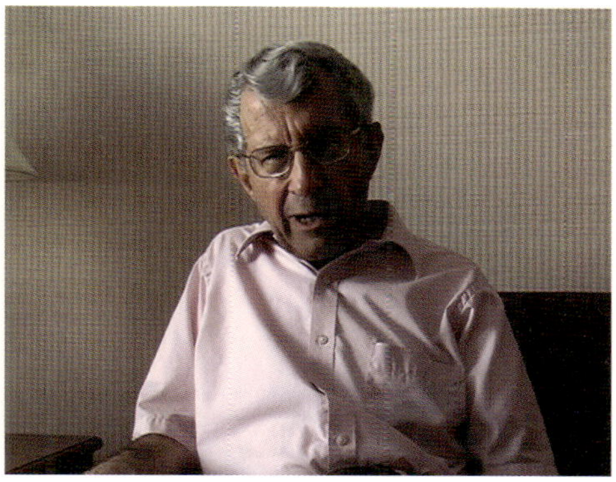
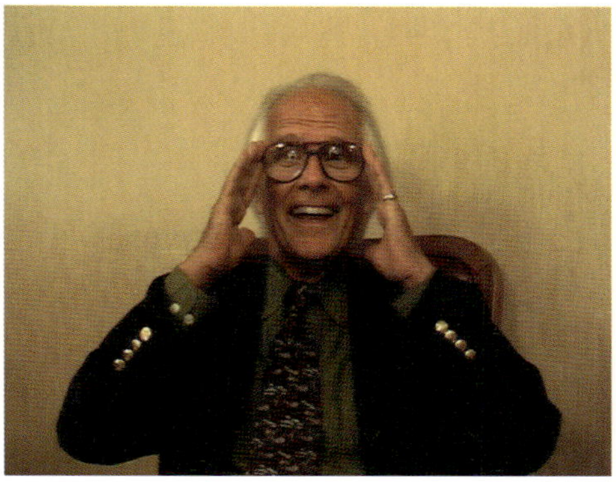
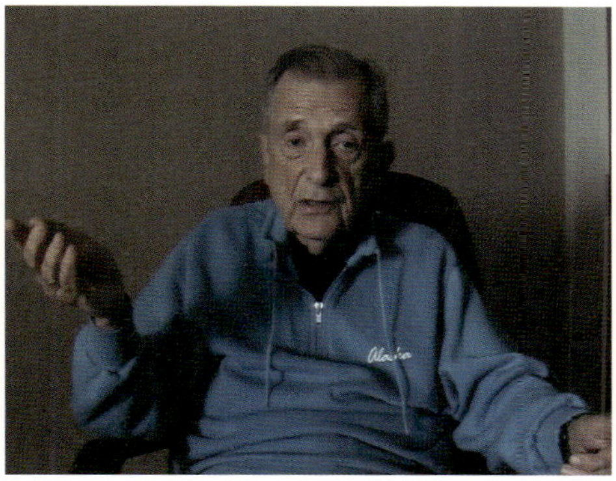
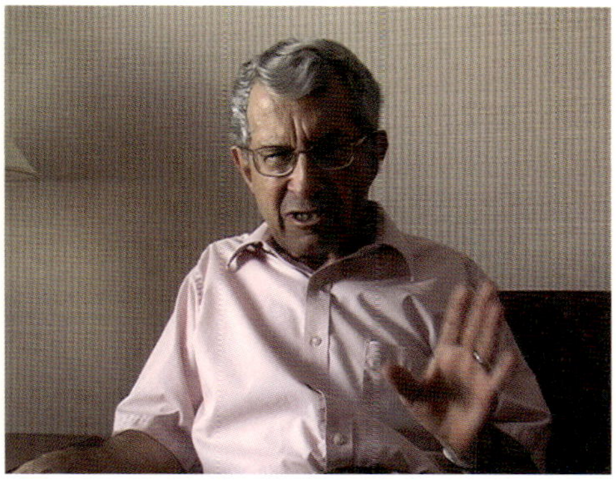
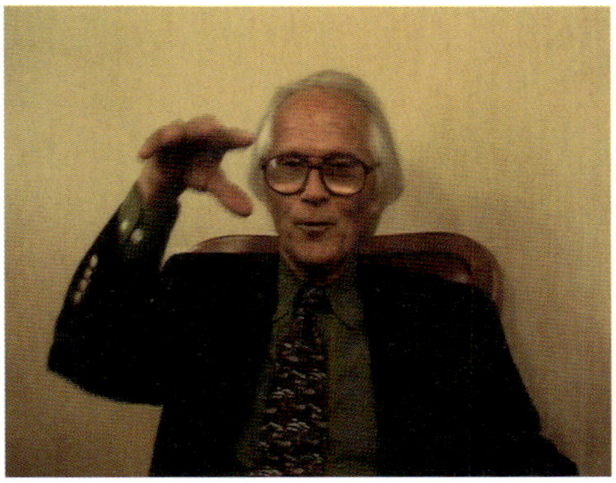
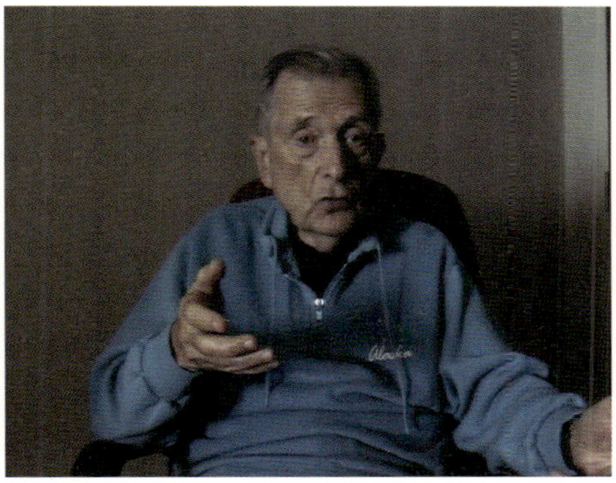
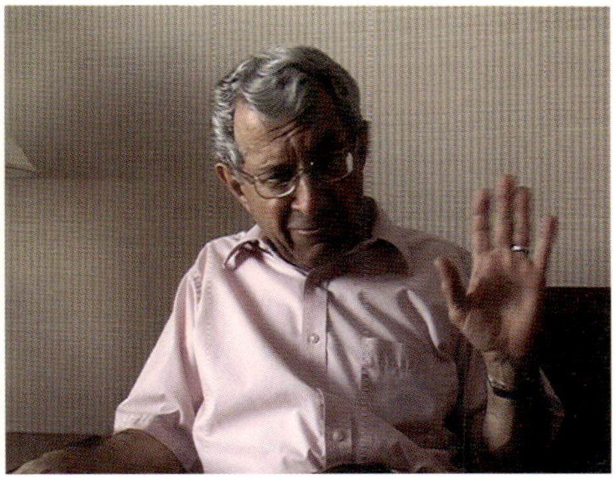
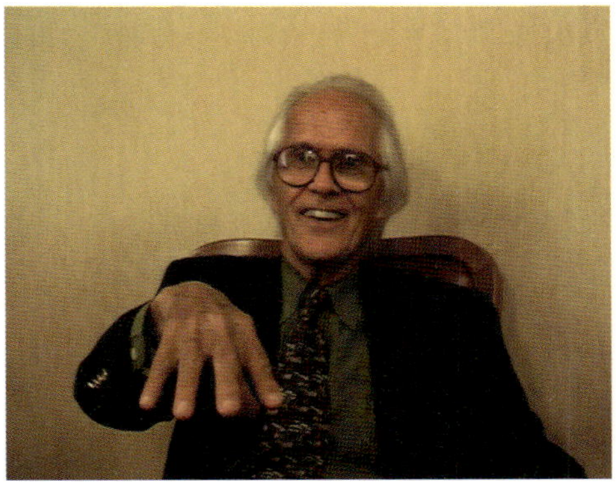
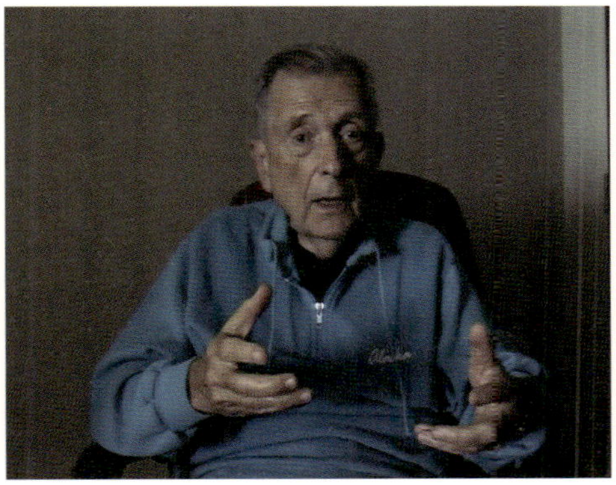
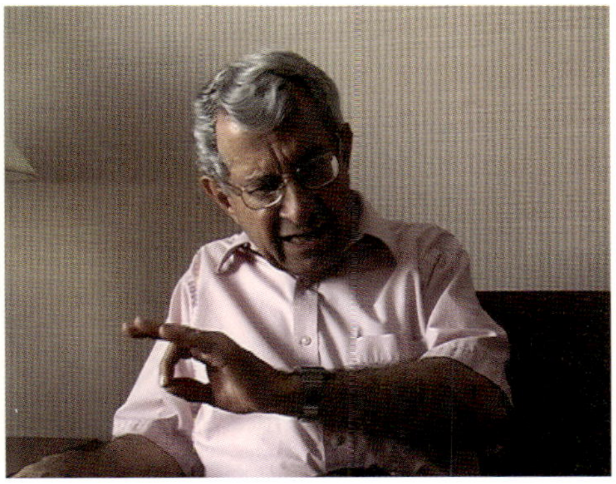

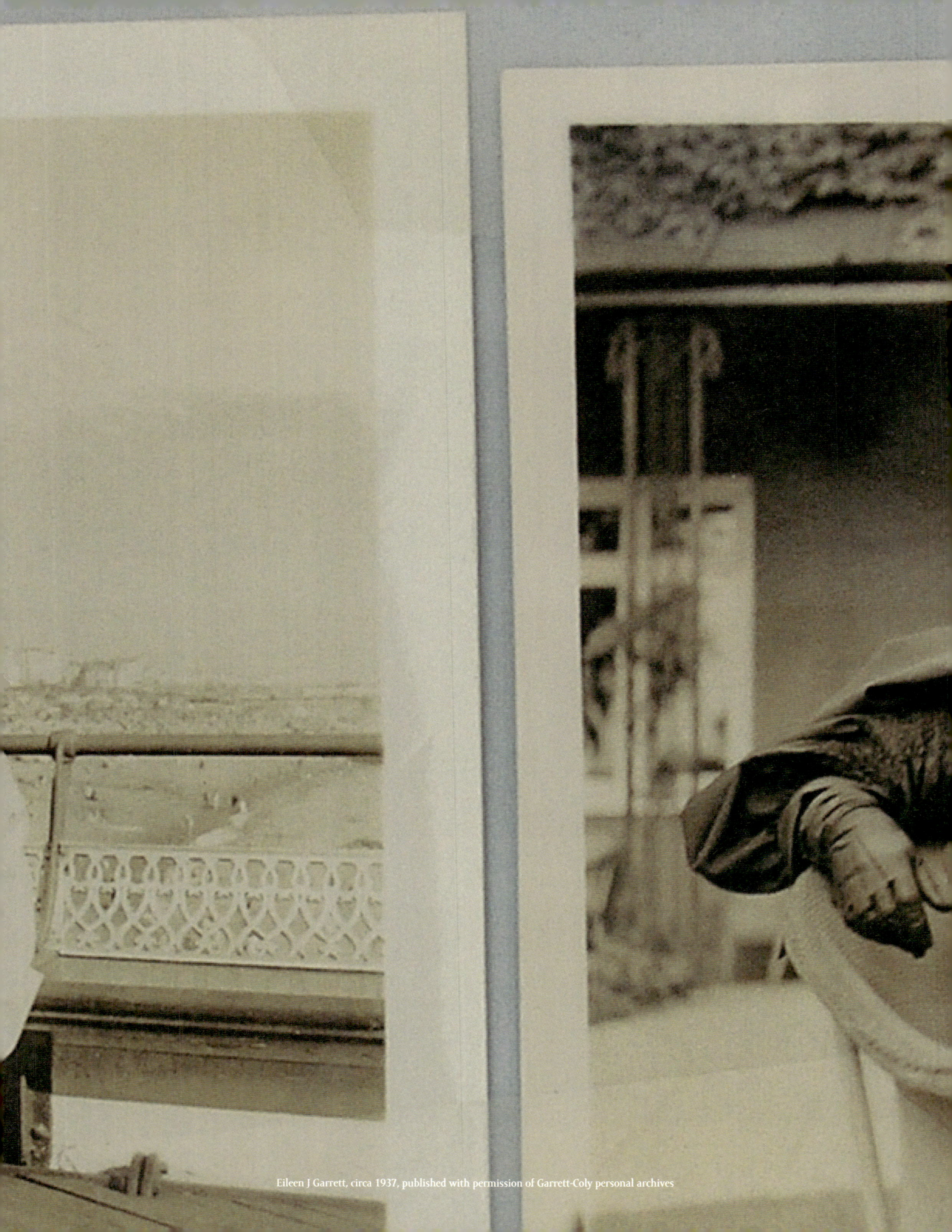

Eileen J Garrett, circa 1937, published with permission of Garrett-Coly personal archives

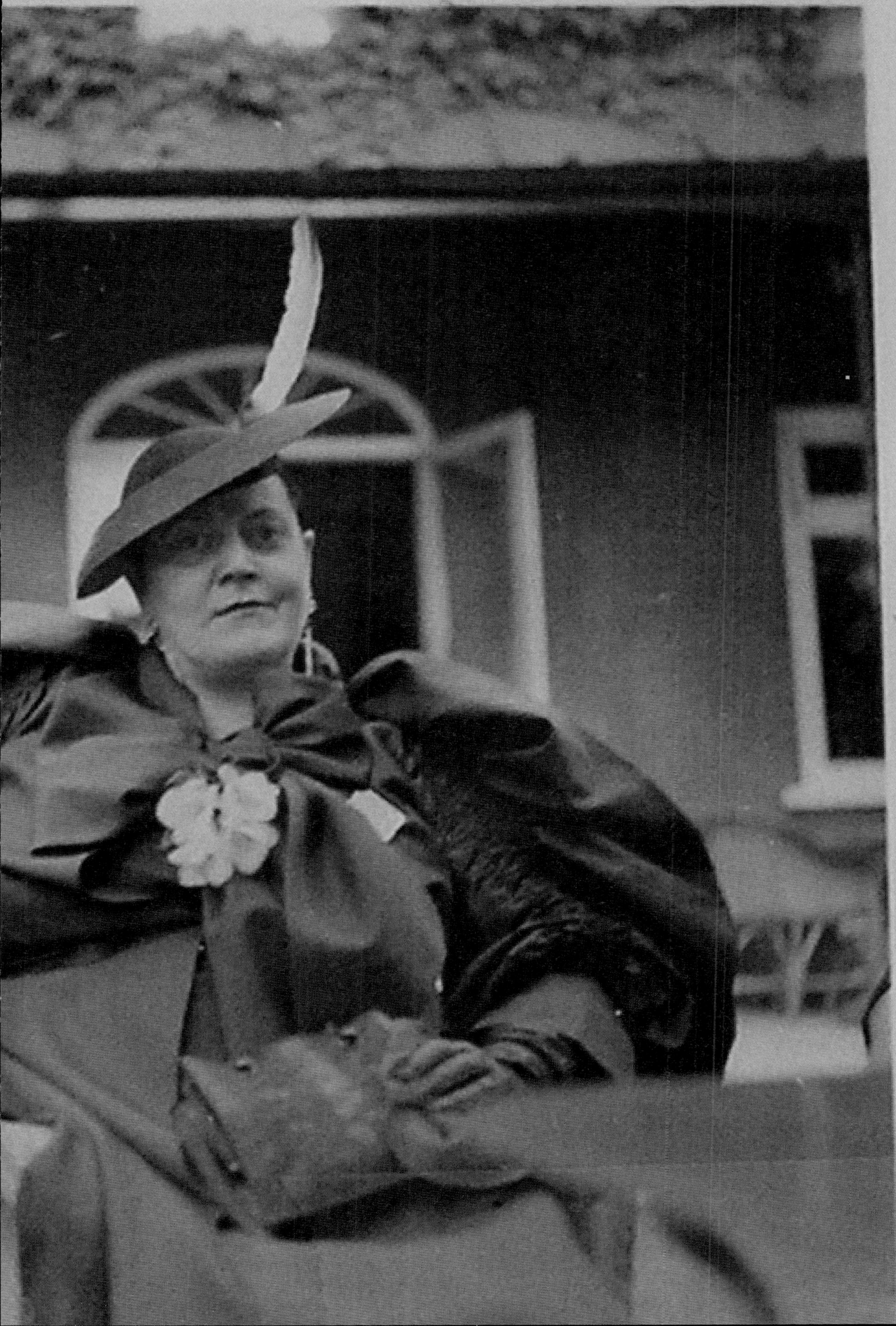

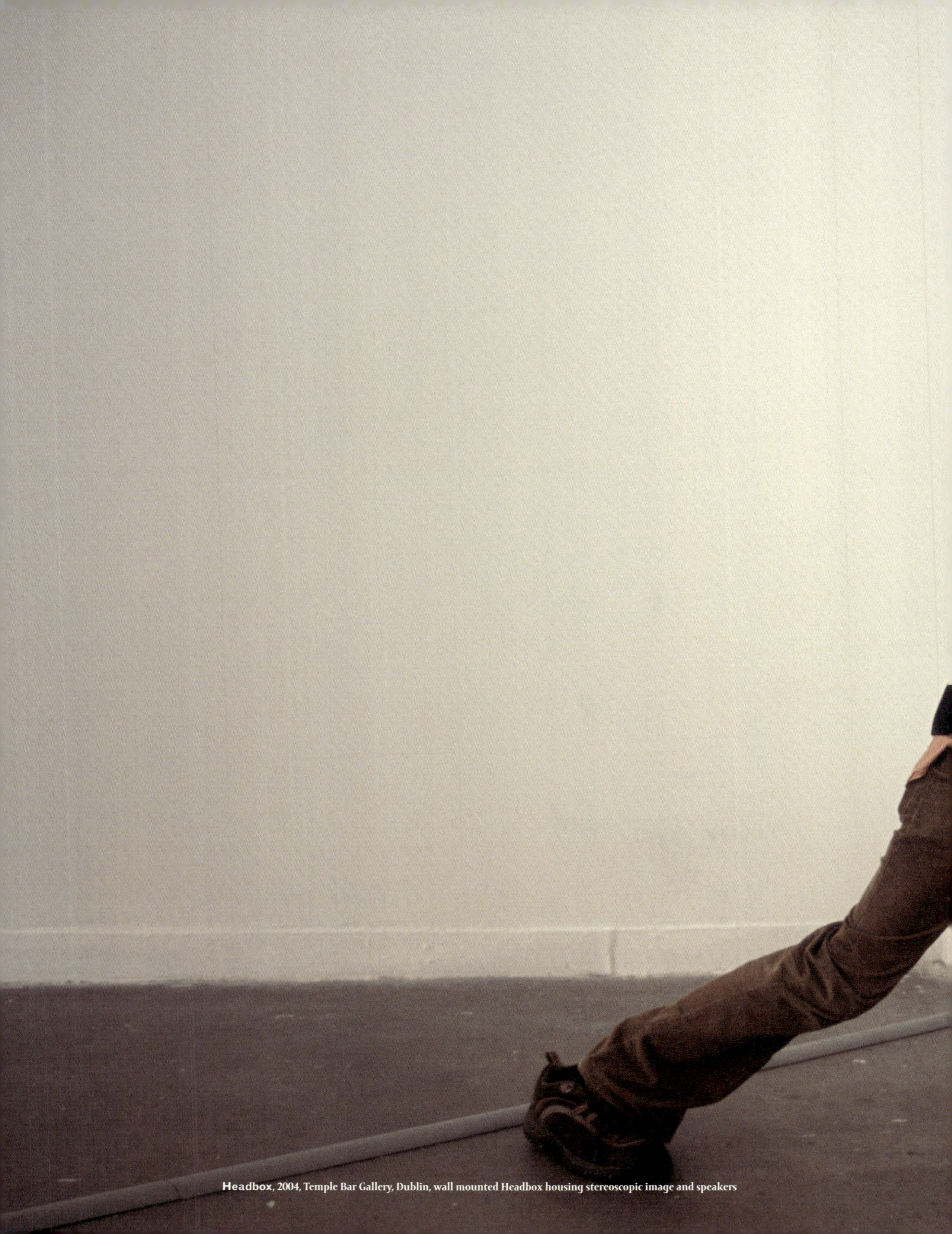

Headbox, 2004, Temple Bar Gallery, Dublin, wall mounted Headbox housing stereoscopic image and speakers

Dr Slavka Sverakova

SUSAN MacWILLIAM

PORTRAYING A WORLDVIEW

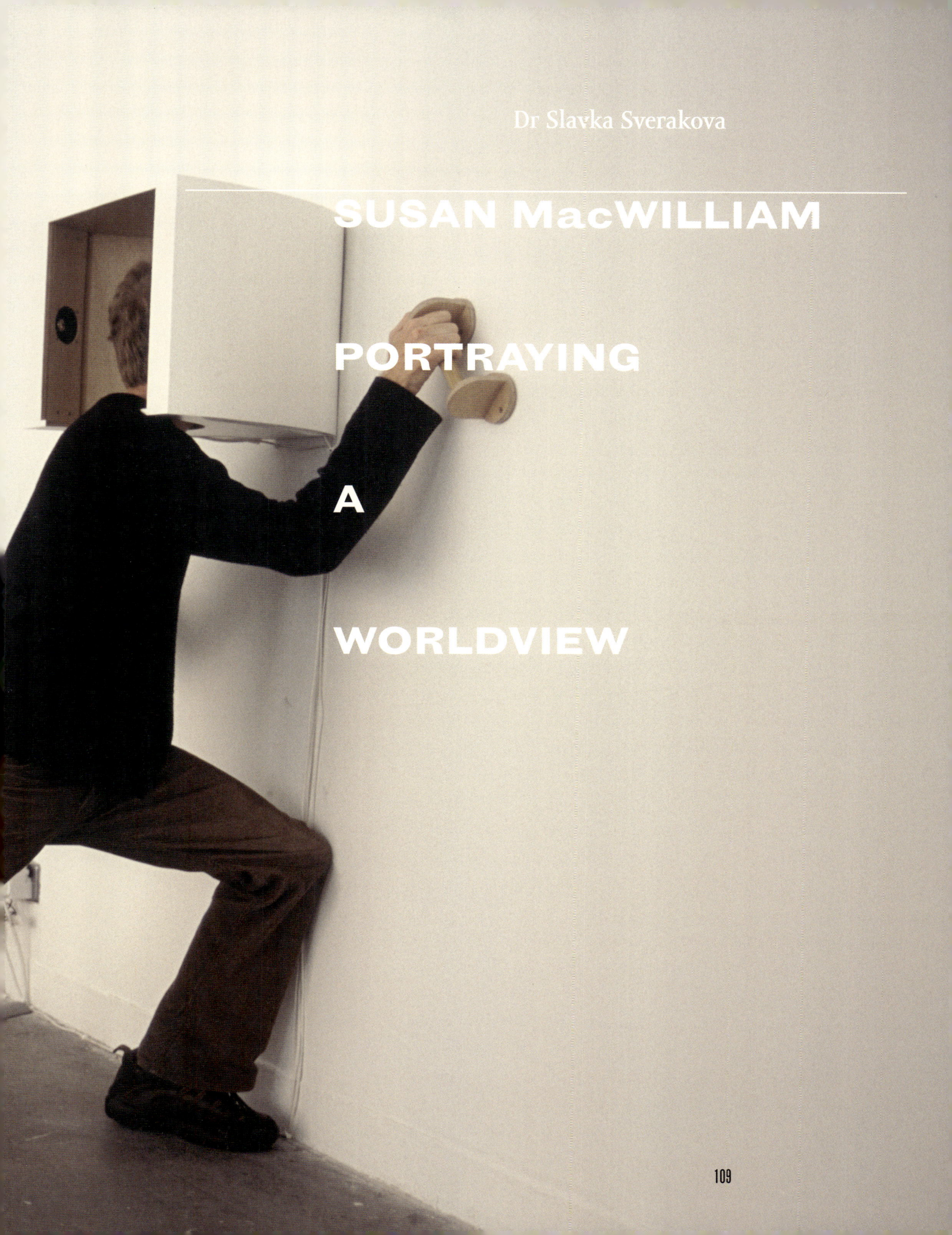

Each person has a worldview, a skeleton of cognitive assumptions encompassing notions of existence or non-existence of the supernatural and of deities, of morality, and of values and questions about the origin of life and of the universe.

A classical text on cosmology, Plato's *Timaeus*, describes the Demiurge cutting, placing, turning, dividing, bending and connecting sameness and difference to obtain the visible world.[1] Susan MacWilliam cuts, places, divides, connects, replicates, reconstructs, imitates, performs, builds, evokes, provokes, copies and documents perceptions to create the world of her subject.

MacWilliam's art reflects evocative and nuanced differences between scholarly and artistic research, and focuses on not only what we know, but also how we know it.

Her work appears as a document, but to see it as such would lead to an erroneous perception. Through a variety of strategies, most specifically a skilfully subversive approach to editing, the artist defends the autonomy of her art.

While MacWilliam offers lead through composition and editing, she allows her subject to sit on the seam of epistemology and belief. She does not make a judgement on the belief held, but keeps strictly, and without critique, to the evidence as a base for knowing.

MacWilliam's art is trans-disciplinary, capable of nurturing other disciplines and accepting nurture from them. The terms of such exchange are significant, not only because artists reserve the right to work on their own terms, but also because the complex interdependence of different, previously unconnected, subjects and elements produces so many levels of experience and knowledge.

Through carefully considered approaches and precise methodologies, MacWilliam delivers *ambivalence*. The tension between uncertainty and clarity breeds a conviction that both the existence and character of a worldview depend on the acquisition of knowledge about the world. There are many ways to do this, but art is considered an efficient way, not only to obtain knowledge, but also generalise it.

Thinking of visual art, neurophysiologist Samir Zeki admits: "... I hold the somewhat unusual view that artists are neurologists. Studying the brain with the techniques that are unique to them and reaching interesting but unspecified conclusions about the organization of the brain." He maps out three significant functions of art in relation to the 'connectivity' of the brain.

i) A major function of art can thus be regarded as an extension of the function of the brain, namely to seek knowledge about the world.[2]

ii) Visual art contributes to our understanding of the visual brain because it explores and reveals the brain's perceptual capabilities. As Paul Klee once wrote "Art does not reproduce visible, it makes things visible."[3]

iii) In analysing the distinct attributes of images the brain invents a visual world.[4]

Séance Cabinet and Teleplasmic Ship, 2009, Sculpture

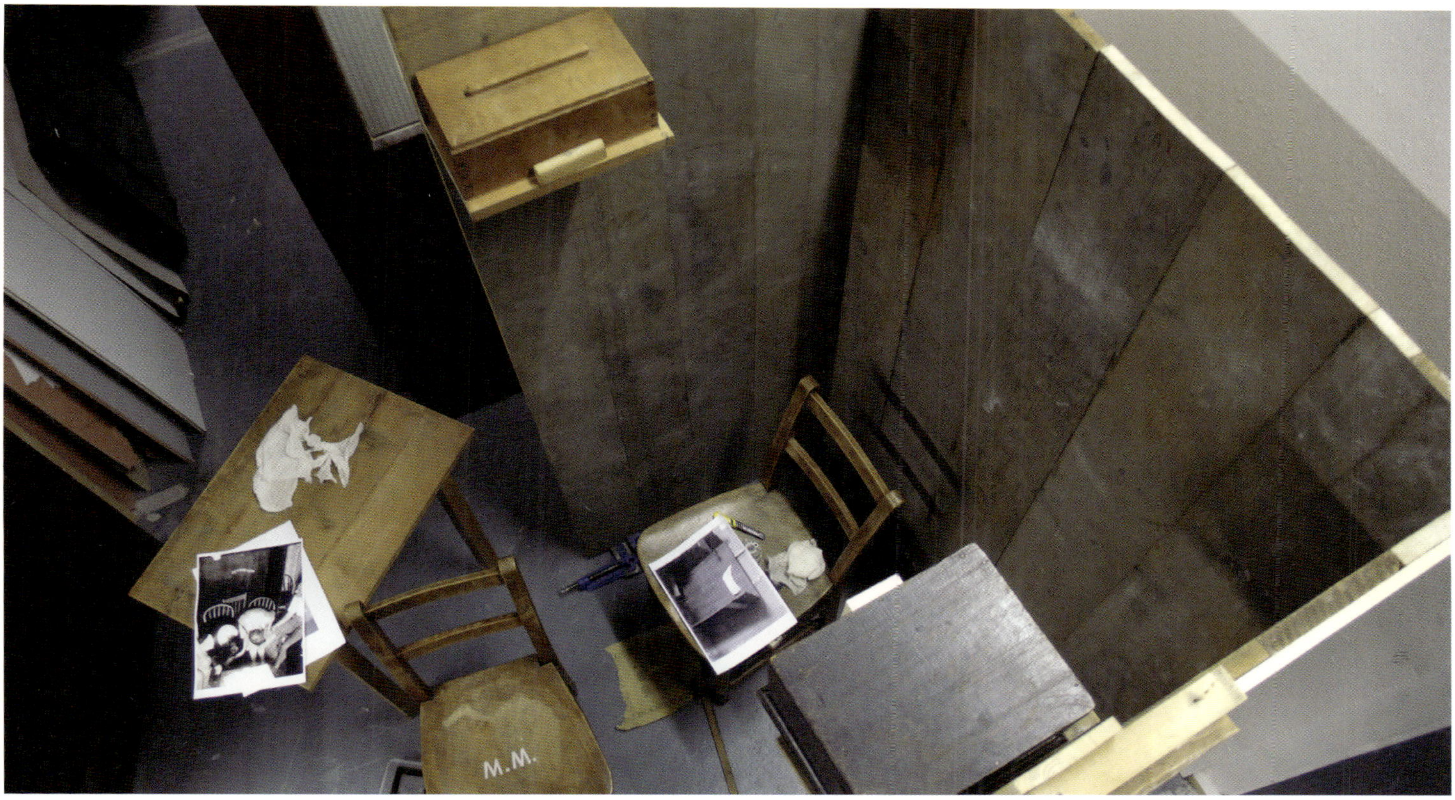

HER EYE IN THE SOURCE:
F-L-A-M-M-A-R-I-O-N, 2009

At the time of writing Susan MacWilliam offered a concept of this work: "I am making a séance cabinet in the studio based on that of Thomas Glendenning Hamilton. I have always thought the process of manifestations and materialisations of the séance room to be similar to the realisation of ideas and objects in the studio." (e-mail to me, 21/12/2008, 14:32.)

MacWilliam developed her reading of sources into a remake of three significant objects: the séance cabinet, *teleplasmic* letters and a *teleplasmic* ship. Over the years, MacWilliam has developed another strategy connected to archival sources: she invites *guests*. One of them, Dr William G Roll appears in two previous works, *Eileen*, 2008, and *13 Roland Gardens*, 2007. In *F-L-A-M-M-A-R-I-O-N*, Roll delivers three mini-performances: he browses through Hamilton's book, repeats words to the camera and describes his experience of levitation. By filming the interaction of her guests with her sources and reconstructions, MacWilliam puts herself in a position parallel to that of her main source, Dr Hamilton and his sitters. Arla Marshall and Dr Howard Reed are filmed examining the archive of Dr TG Hamilton at the University of Manitoba, where MacWilliam spent a month working with the collection. Among other comments they voice their perception of the image of the *teleplasmic ship*: "Does it look like a ship to you?" "No." Their judgement coincides with Dr Roll's observation that the ship appears as a random arrangement of cheesecloth, and that the *teleplasmic letters* seem to be held together by a wire. The guests stand for themselves, and also as mediators, both interpreting a fragment of a world and becoming a fragment in it. MacWilliam records their views and then goes on making the materialisation visible: "Last night, at 11pm, I found myself on the sitting room floor stitching a teleplasmic ship using muslin and working from the photographs from the Hamilton archives." (e-mail to me 21/12/2008, 19:29.)

To intensify meanings suggested by her guests, MacWilliam employs a variety of viewing angles: over the shoulder, from above, from below from the side.... It is somewhat parallel to Dr Hamilton's use of 12 to 14 cameras to get multiple views of the séance. In *F-L-A-M-M-A-R-I-O-N*, an en face portrait exudes authority, dignity and detachment. An acute angle is favoured for close attention and surprises, for example, "this is my grandmother!" It is also used for doubt; "he

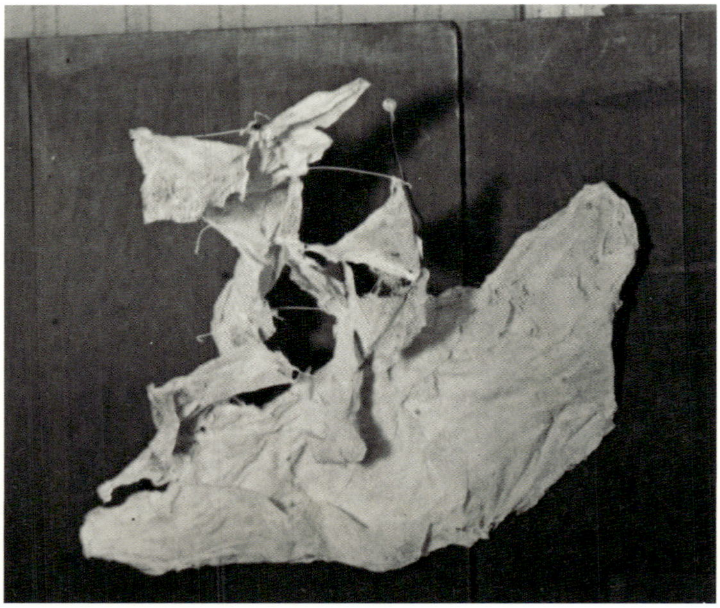

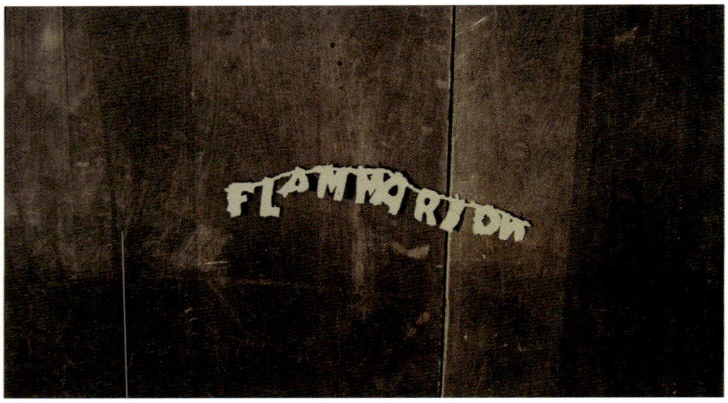

Teleplasmic Ship, Courtesy Hamilton Family fonds, University of Manitoba Archives

F-L-A-M-M-A-R-I-O-N, 2009, Video, Colour, Stereo

put his hands over the face of the medium, and said he felt nothing there" and for assurance (hands hovering above the table when describing levitation). The editing respects the linear narrative, in most cases. Departures, such as the use of stereoscope or a loop, intensify the visual force. I am reminded of Thomas Schütte, who said: "I think the job of the artist is to tell continuous stories with colour, light, lines, form and volume. It is about developing and making work that is independent and convincing."[5]

GET TO GARRETT

"While I had been aware of Eileen Garrett prior to meeting Lisette and Eileen Coly, I had never been taken with the idea of using her as a subject for my work—however, when I met the family it was hard to get away from her... 'Get-to-Garrett'—I feel it rings true for me, in that, if others felt the pull to Garrett that I feel to her family, I can well understand [it]." (e-mail MacWilliam to me 02/01/2009.)

The research phase for *Eileen*, started in October 2006 when MacWilliam met Lisette Coly, the granddaughter of the medium Eileen J Garrett, and recorded footage of her and her mother, Eileen Coly, seated in formal pink easy chairs with a photograph of Garrett on the table between them. The image appears in the "duck-billed platypus" vignette of *Eileen*. MacWilliam showed them *Dermo Optics*, 2006, a video account of the artist's visit to the Dermo Optical Laboratory of Yvonne Duplessis in Paris. In a happy coincidence, Lisette and Eileen had funded Duplessis' research, through the Parapsychology Foundation, some 30 years earlier. Over the next two years the artist met the two women six times, in New York, London, Utrecht, Dublin and in Co Meath, where they traced Eileen Garrett's birthplace.

F-L-A-M-M-A-R-I-O-N, 2009, Video, Colour, Stereo

Eileen, 2008, Synchronised three-channel video installation, Colour, Stereo, 28mins 53secs

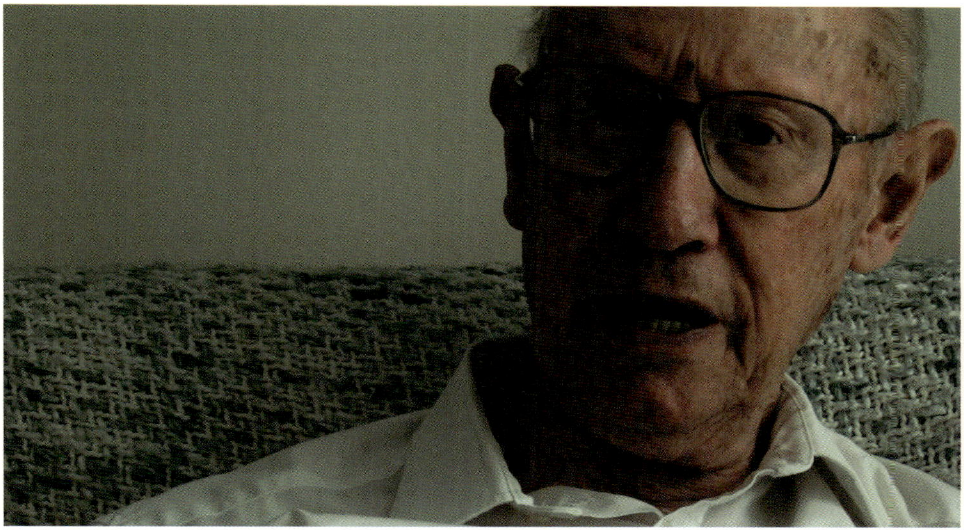

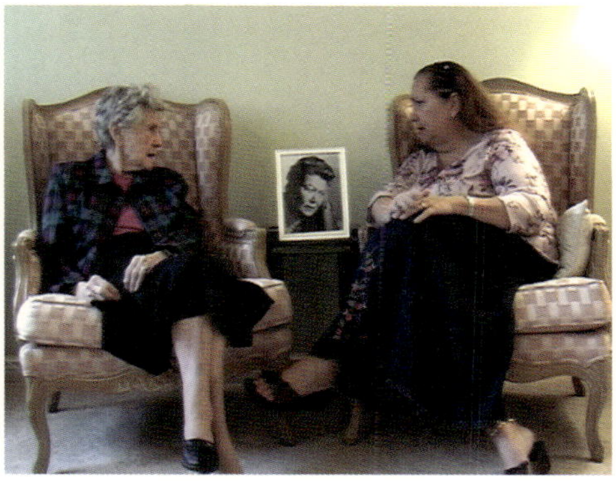

At some of the meetings more footage was made, enabling the life story of the famous medium to be narrated by her daughter through the ten vignettes that make up *Eileen*. Each vignette lasts as long as it takes to tell the story. MacWilliam stays superbly attuned to the visual force of repeats, rhythm, absences, eye contacts and, above all, gestures.

In *F-L-A-M-M-A-R-I-O-N*, the gestures of the guests tell polite, additional stories: a finger runs alongside a line on a page, points at a detail, a book quivers between two palms like a nervous offering. With big, slow gestures, Dr Roll tells of his "truly amazing experience" witnessing a levitating kitchen table. In *Eileen*, both Eileen and Lisette display a great range of gestures. In one loop, Lisette repeats ten times: "The duck billed platypus and you Eileen Garrett" each time drawing a spiral in the air. The following vignette, "Huxley, Dali, Dietrich" develops into an extraordinary staccato sequence, accentuating Eileen Coly's exclamation "get to Garrett", accompanied by four stabbing hand gestures. MacWilliam focuses on the motif, speeds it up, repeats it, splits it between screens and distresses the original continuity of the narrative by—silent experience. A new connection between gestural rhetoric and the subject's state of mind grows in intensity and threatens to get out of control. In this instance the general urge to "get to Garrett"—to understand how she did what she did, is presented as an undesirable trespass of privacy. *Eileen* is a portrayal of both the medium and her daughter.

Gestures play an undisputable cognitive role in recalling the past. For example, in *13 Roland Gardens*, 2007, Eileen Coly 'draws' the layout of an apartment in the air and on the table, helping the viewer to 'see' it too. *13 Roland Gardens* was produced following MacWilliam's residency with the Parapsychology Foundation, New York in 2007. It was exhibited in *Seeing is Believing* at the Photographers Gallery, London, alongside photographs from the Harry Price Collection (housed at Senate House Library, University of London). Price also lived at 13 Roland Gardens and documented Garrett's R101 séance. The séance refers to the crash of the R101 airship at Beauvais two days earlier. Eileen Coly speaks of Garrett's trance, her psychic contact with the airship flight lieutenant Irwin, and the mediation of his technical explanation for the disaster.

The glorious failure of "getting-to-Garrett" demonstrates the artist's level-headed recognition that not all can be known and accessed. However, MacWilliam relishes the playful insistence of coincidences. When

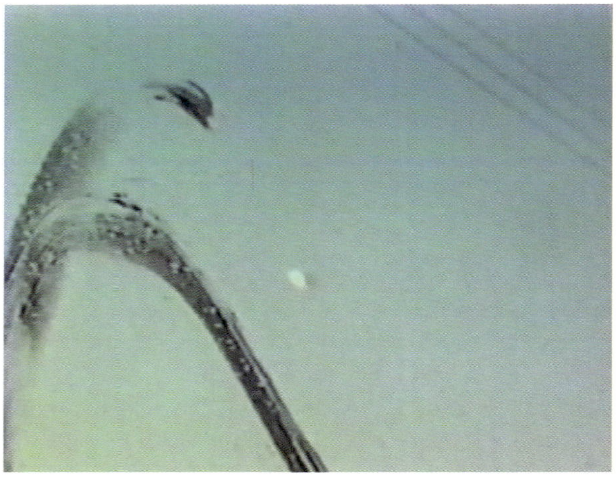

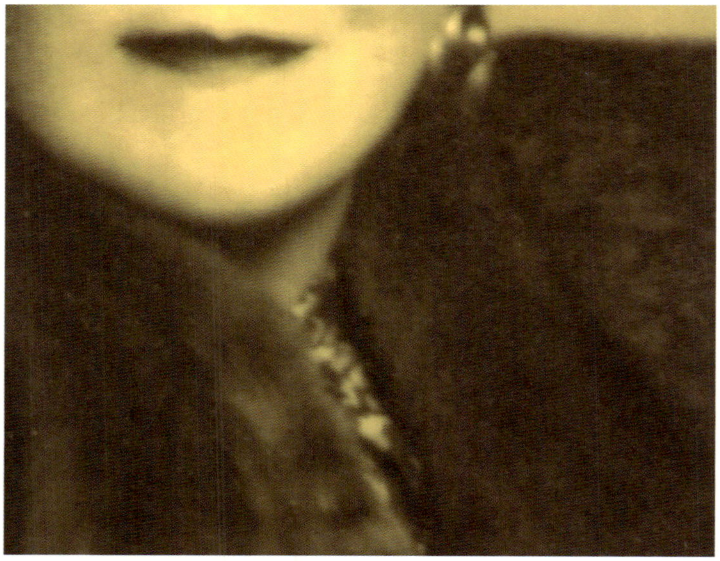

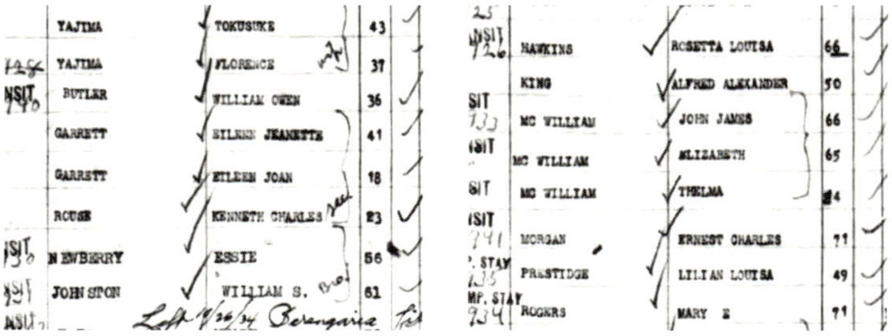

Psychic Edit, 2008, Colour, Stereo, 14secs, Continuous Loop

Shipping records from **The Only Way to Travel**, 2008, Video, Colour, Stereo, 38mins 30secs

Psychic Edit, 2008, Colour, Stereo, 14secs, Continuous Loop

working on an ancestral research website for the video *The Only Way to Travel*, 2008, she came across a page with a link between Eileen Garrett and herself: "the MacWilliam/Garrett crossing was on the SS Majestic in 1934—I discovered this in the shipping records that I was researching… my relatives were entered onto the same page …". Another coincidence occurred when a gallery showing MacWilliam's work booked her into a hotel in Cartwright Gardens, Bloomsbury. There, in 1916, Eileen Garrett opened a hostel for soldiers wounded during the Great War 1914–1918. Is the subject circling the artist while the artist is circling her?

An interesting portrait of Eileen Garrett is also offered in the 14 seconds of *Psychic Edit*, 2008. Garrett's disembodied smile from one photograph is placed over another image, recalling Man Ray's *Observatory Time, The Lovers*, 1935, and Surrealism's devotion to dreams. So does the image of a 'headless Garrett' in summer dress and sandals descending a narrow crevice in a rocky terrain. MacWilliam turns the possible inexpert framing into a powerful metaphor: Garrett's body can follow only a narrow defined path, her head/mind out of the frame, out of the box. In another shot, Garrett is wearing a white hat and white pearls, both emphasising her face. Her hand gesture addresses the viewer and reflects some, undefined, insight.

There is ongoing research at several universities studying the connections between language, thinking and memory which focuses on gestures.[6] The research proposes that gestures intensify the representation of experience. This is significant in relation to the Safir-Whorf hypothesis—which has been both supported and decried—that the language we speak influences the way we think and understand the world. The advantage of gestures over language is that they appear, to some extent, universal and unaffected by differences between languages. The observation by Francis Bacon, 1561–1621, that gestures are "transitory hieroglyphs" still feels valid. Even more so when watching the vignette "parapsychologists" in *Eileen*. The three men are giving their accounts of meeting Eileen Garrett. Their gestures are easily understandable. Their words melt into simultaneous delivery. Such a de-activation of a crucial element of the narrative signals the essence of this art: it does not matter if it does not add up in a rational sense; it does not matter if the evidence is not convincing. What matters, is that the art works on its own terms and effectively taps into the observer's

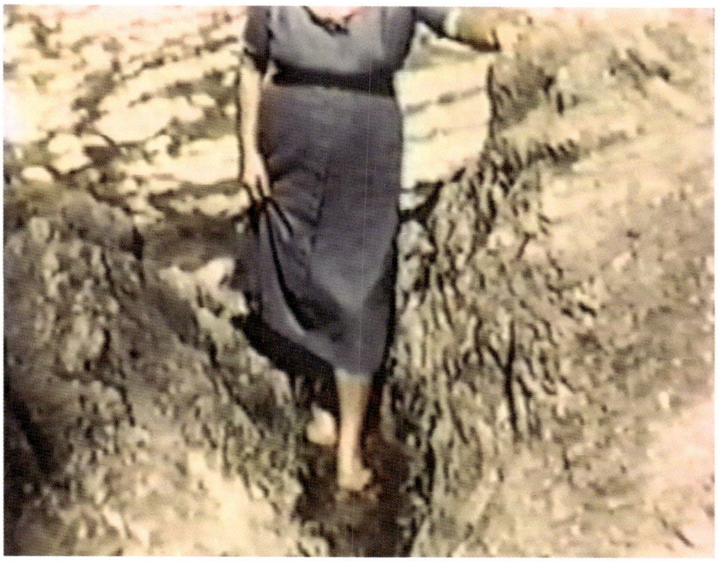

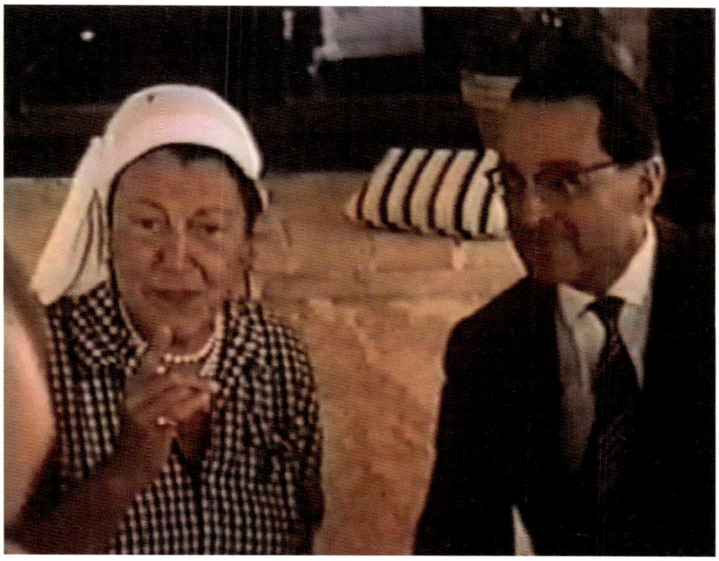

willingness to connect its ambiguities and incongruities to a sense of surprise or disbelief. These biographies and portraits keep making detours into the extraordinary world of magic, an enhancer of the brain's intimate encounter with the impossible.

1. Plato (427BC–347BC), *Timaeus* ca 360BC, accessible on www.forgottenbooks.org, pp. 20–21.
2. Zeki, S, *Essays on Science and Society: Artistic Creativity and the Brain*, accessed on http::/www.sciencemag.org/cgi/content/full/293/5527/5.
3. Zeki, *Essays*.
4. Zeki S, "The visual image in mind and brain", *Scientific American*, 1992. In addition, a survey of the research facilitated by new imaging techniques has been given in a special issue of the *Journal of Consciousness Studies*, vol. 6, no. 6–7, 1999.
5. See http://www.Thomas-Schuette.de/website_content.php. and scroll to interview with Adrian Searle, or http://arts.guardian.co.uk/art/visualart/story/0,,2207206,00.html.
6. Dr Susan Goldin-Meadow (goldin-meadow-lab.uchicago.edu); Elena Nicoladis at the University of Alberta, Canada; Susan Wagner Cook at the University of Iowa, USA; Richard Byrne at the University of St Andrews, Scotland; to name just the few.

DERMO OPTICS

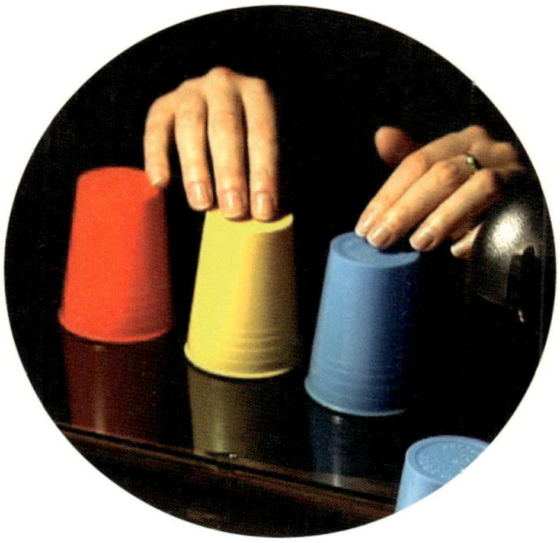

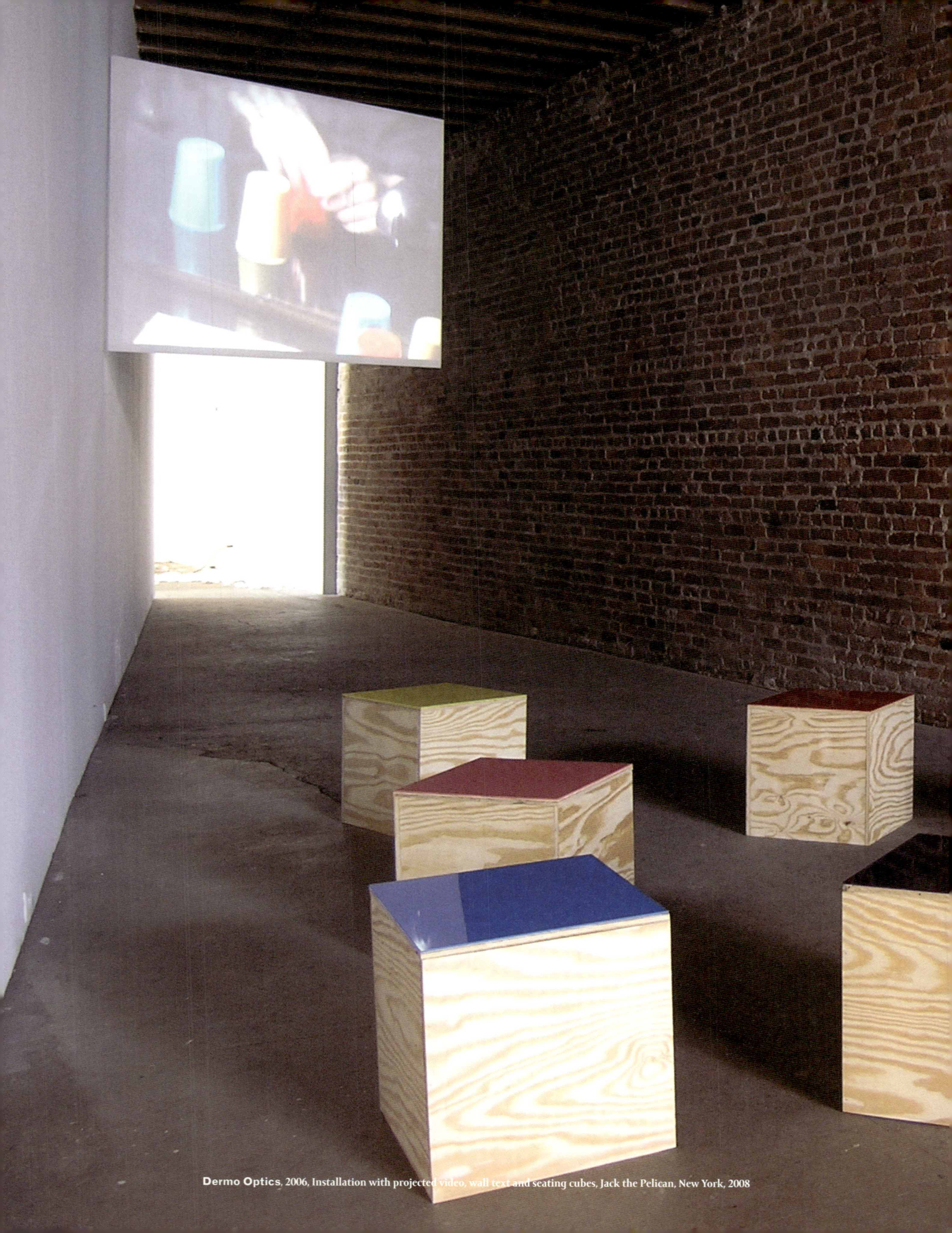

Dermo Optics, 2006, Installation with projected video, wall text and seating cubes, Jack the Pelican, New York, 2008

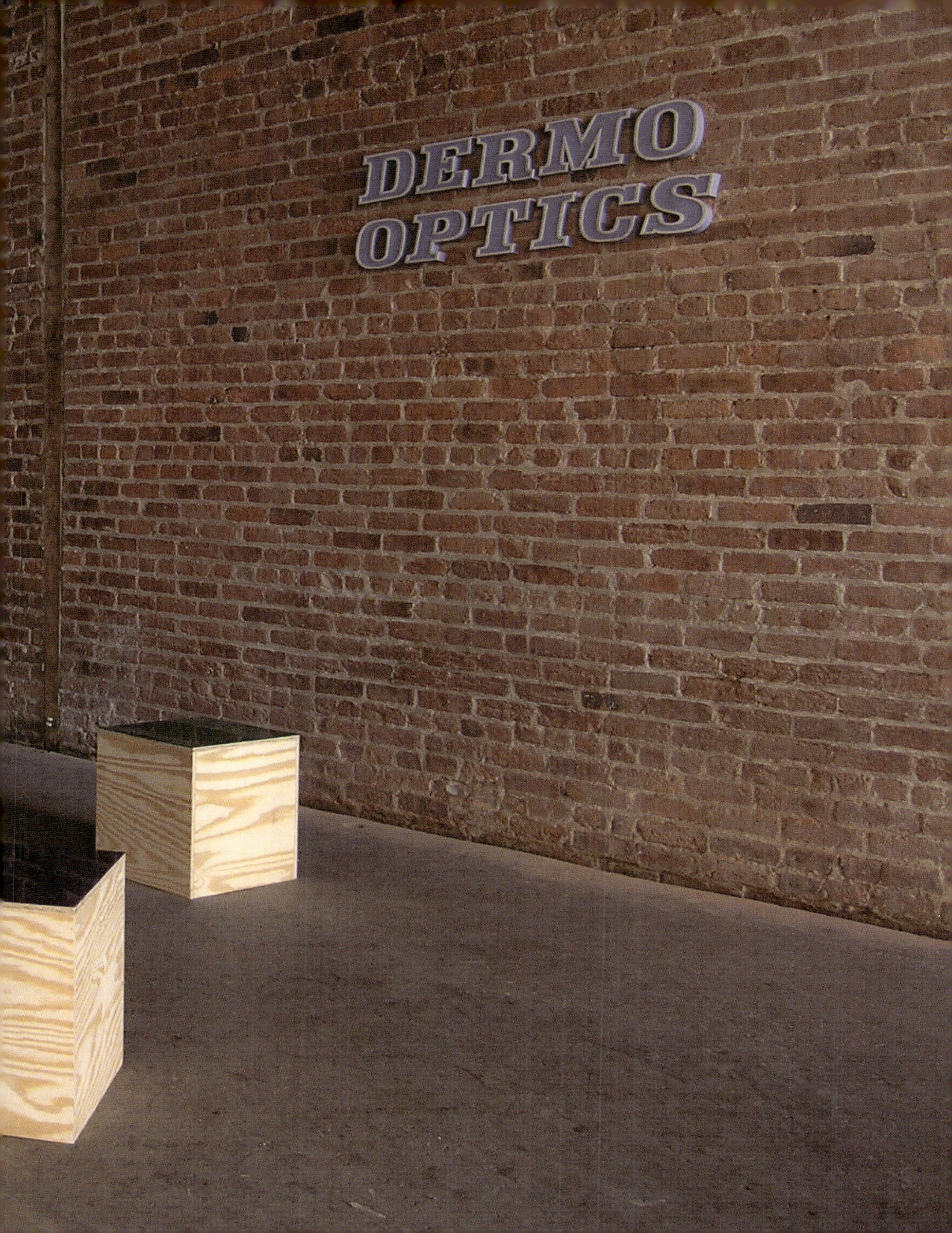
DERMO
OPTICS

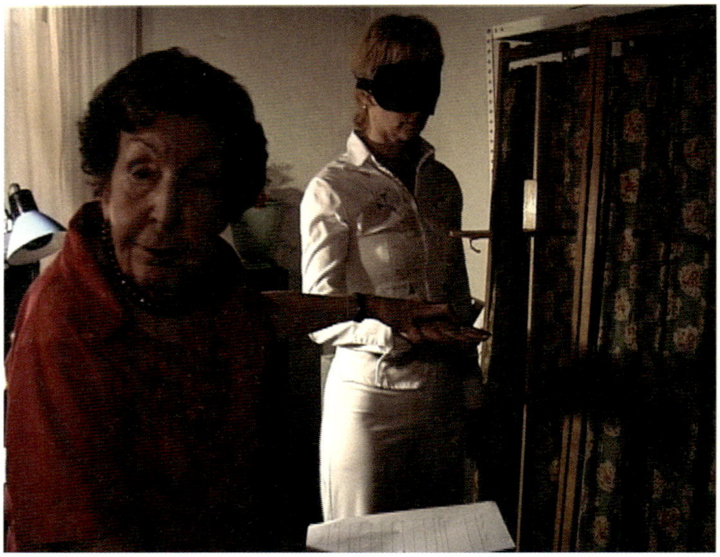

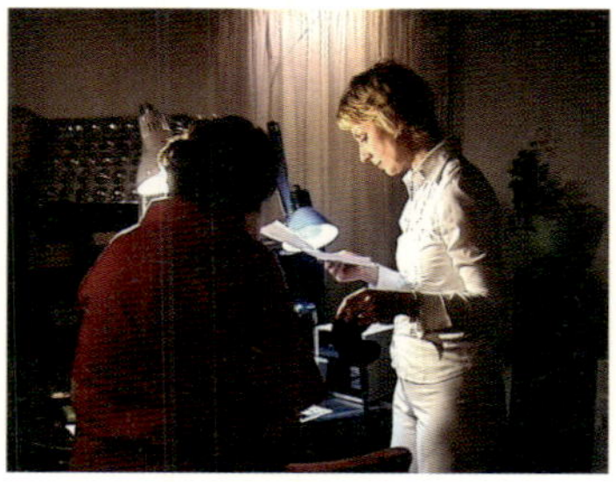

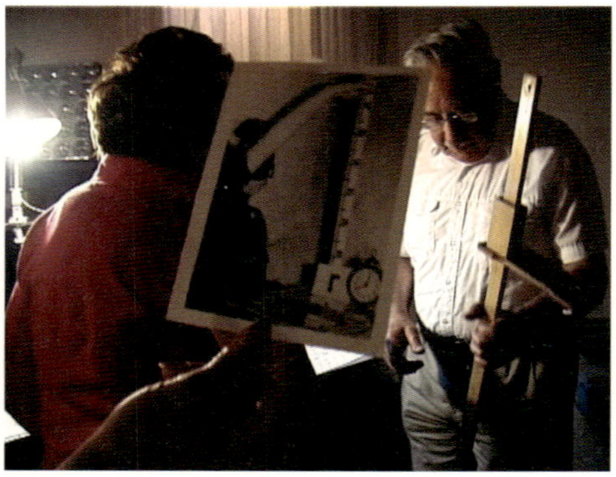

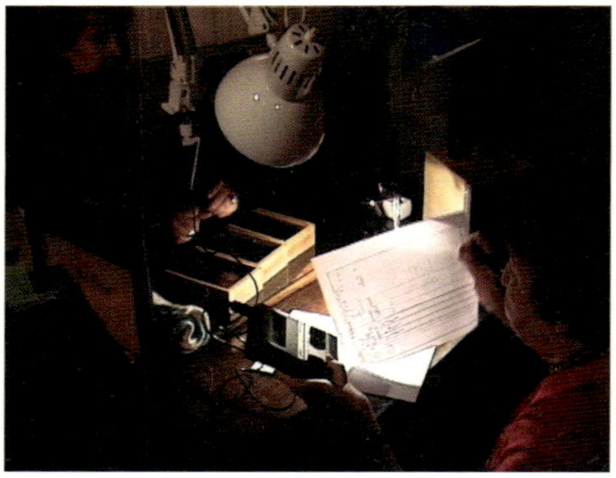

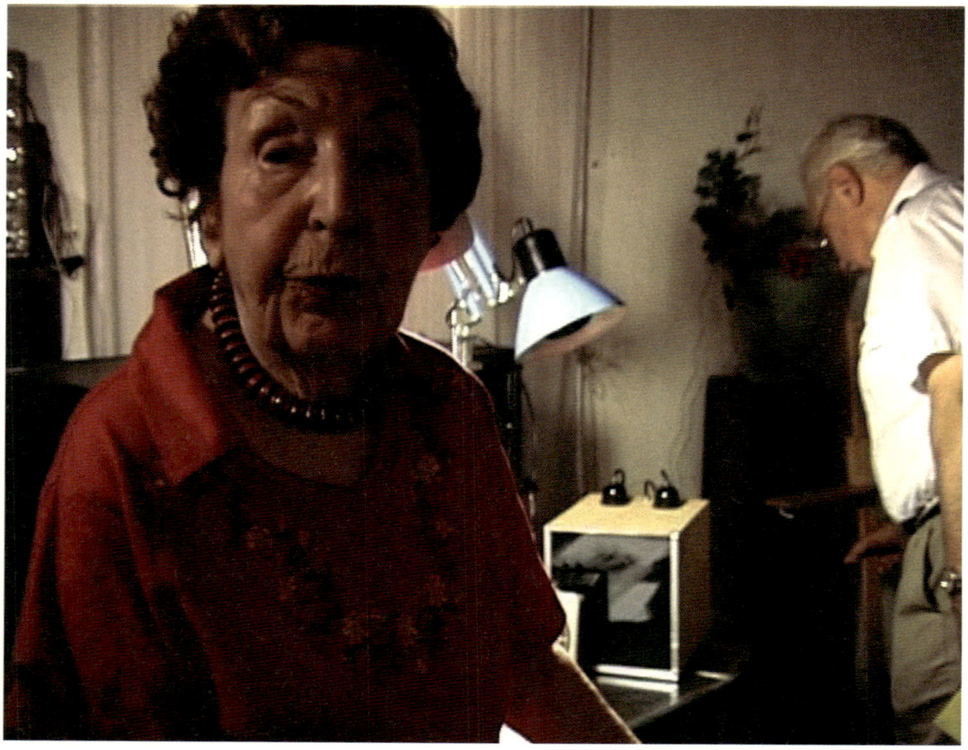

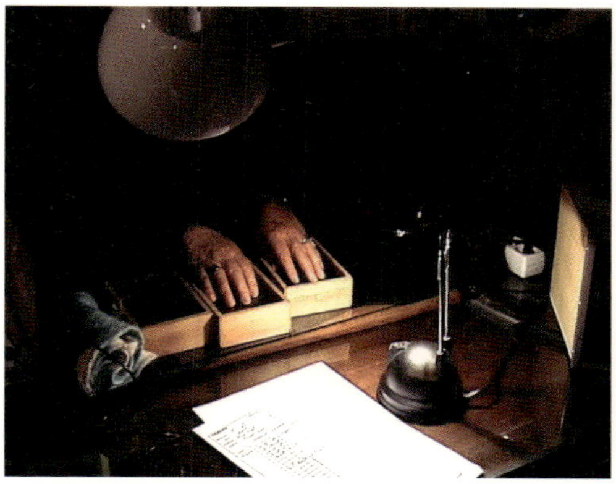
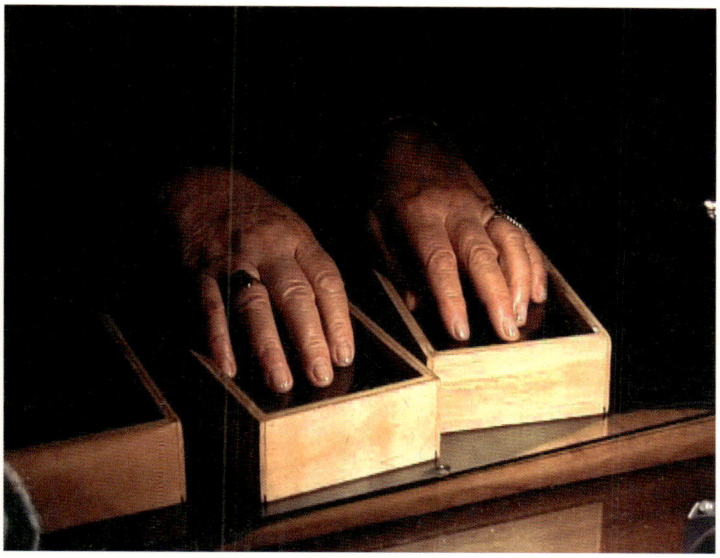
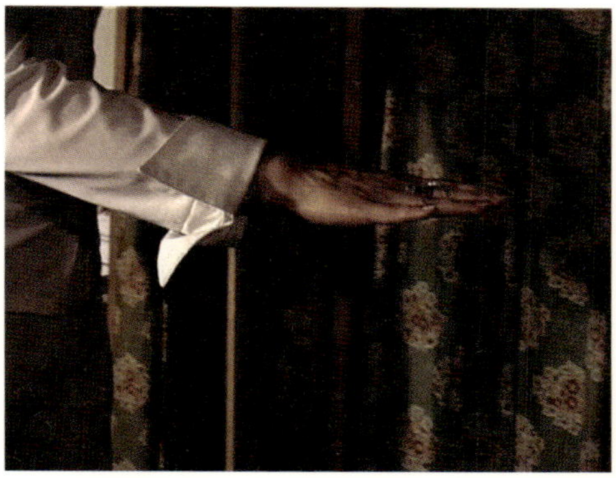
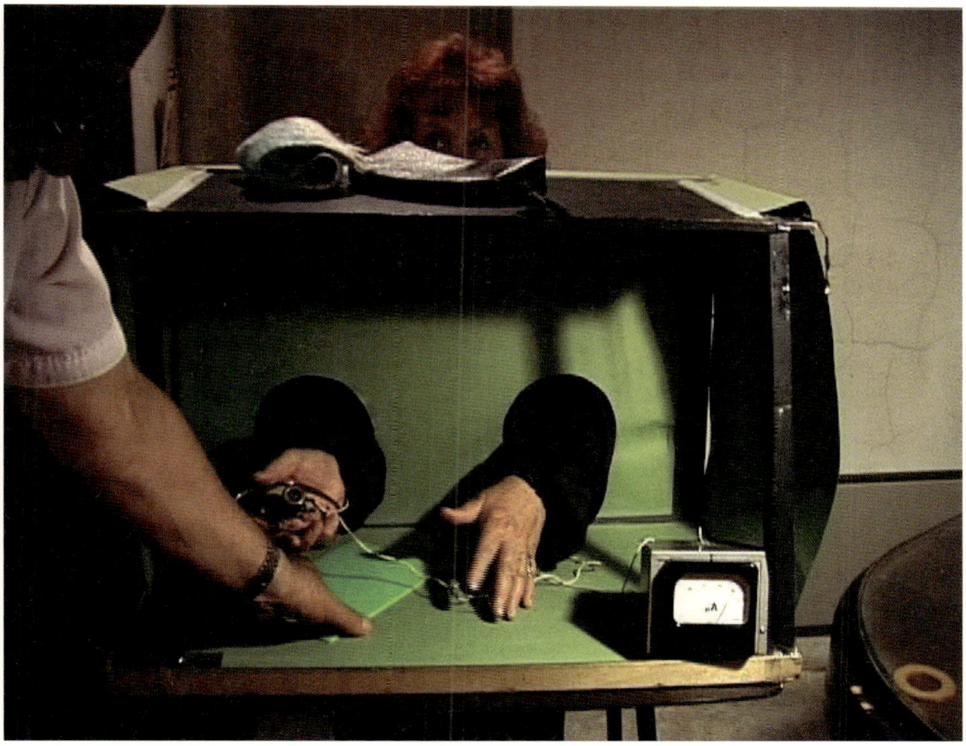
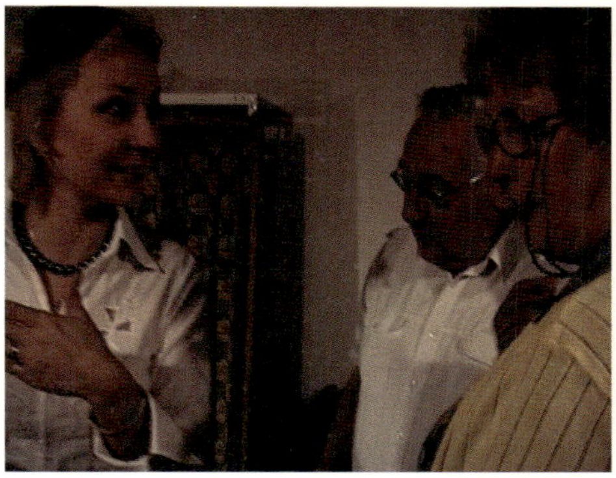
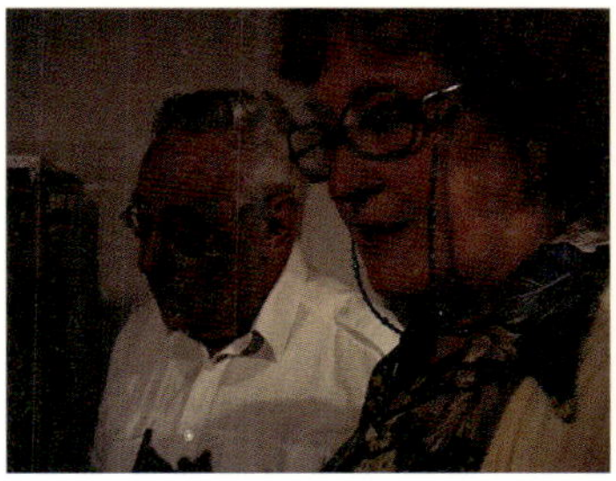
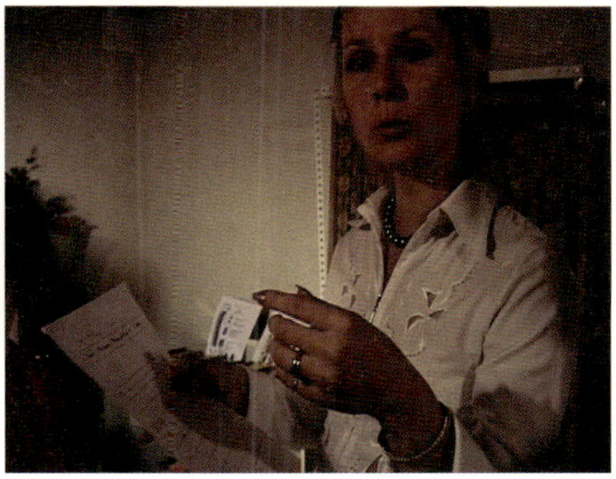

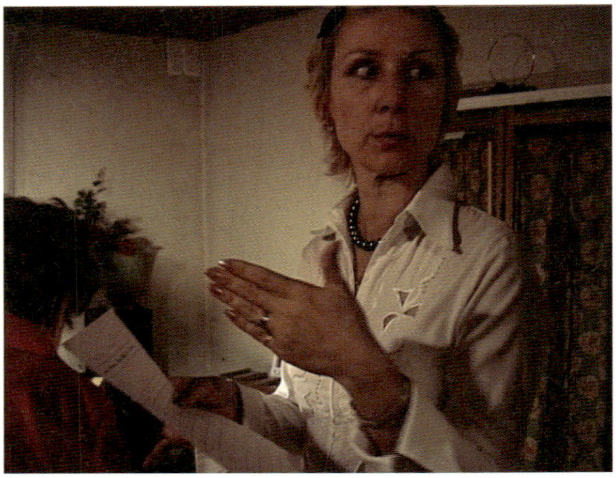

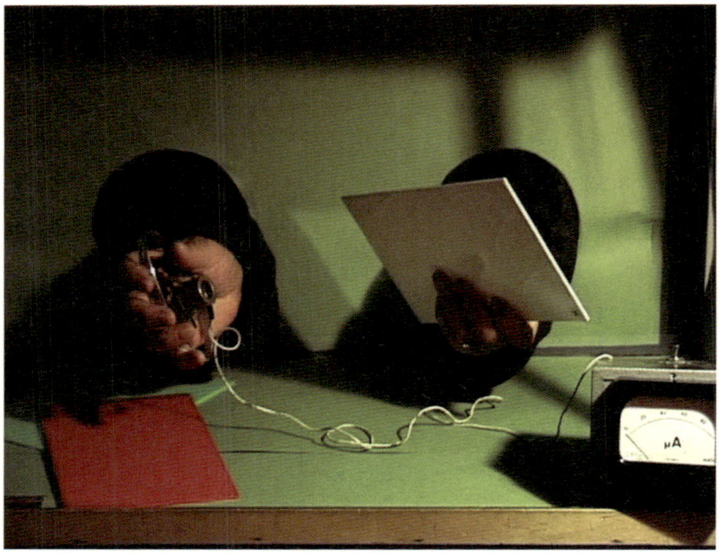
μA

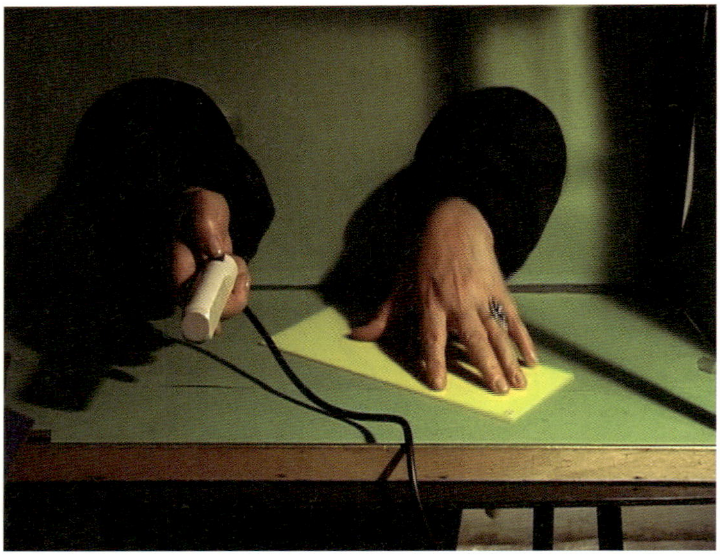

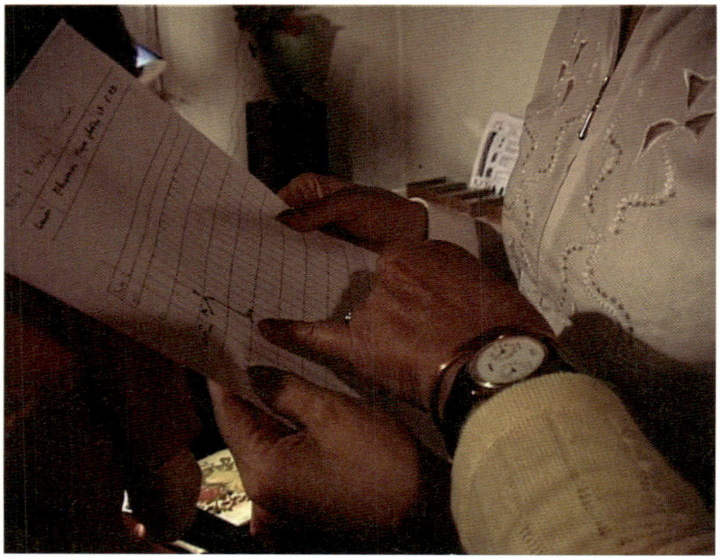

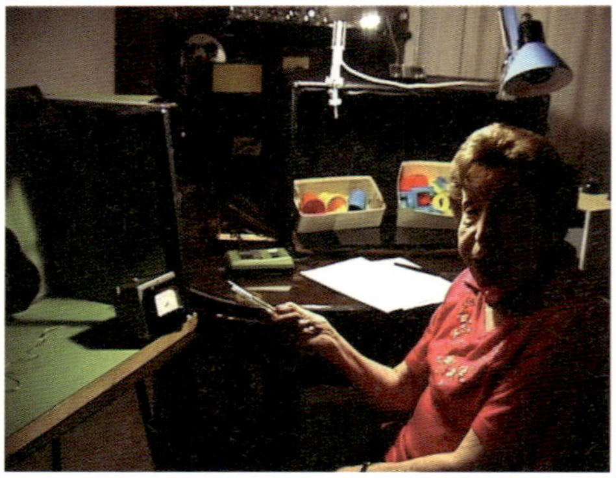

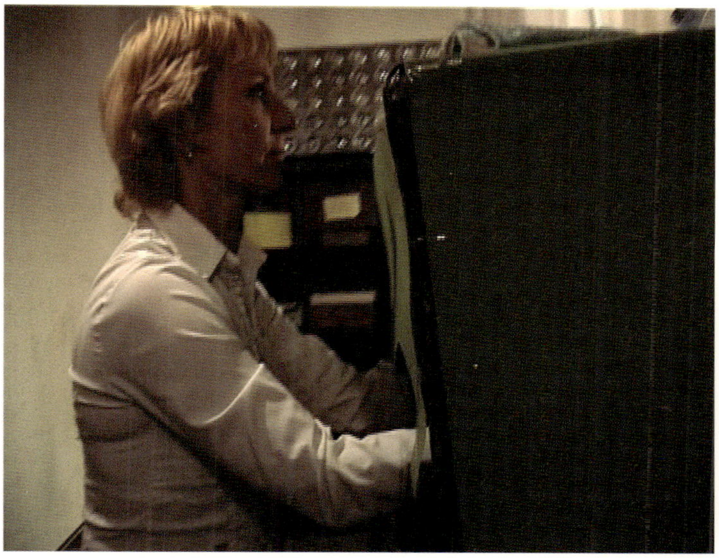

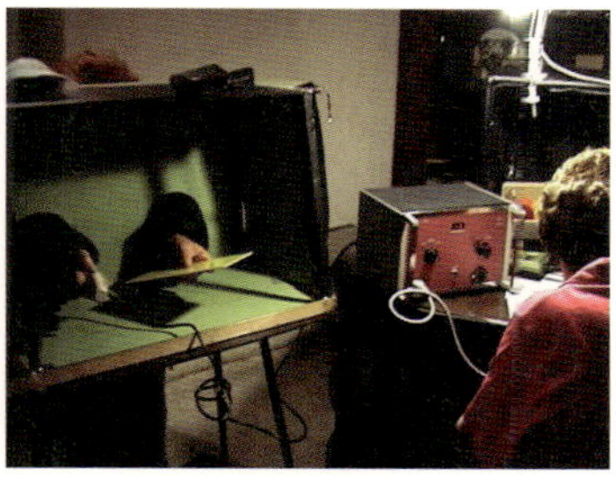

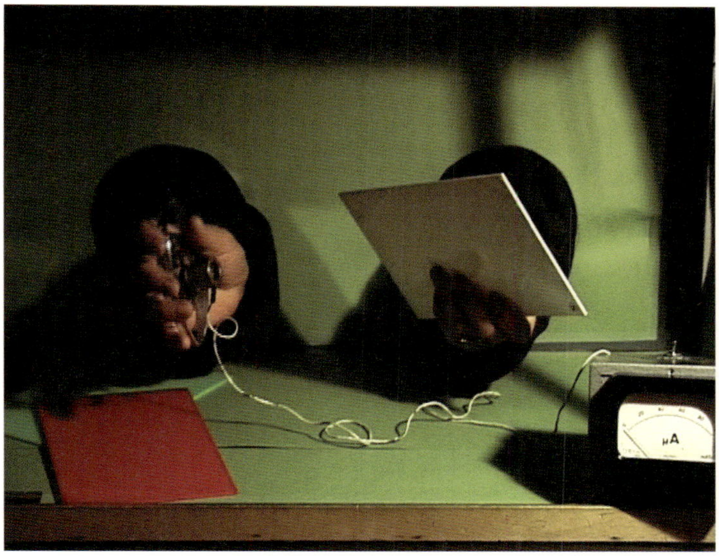
μA

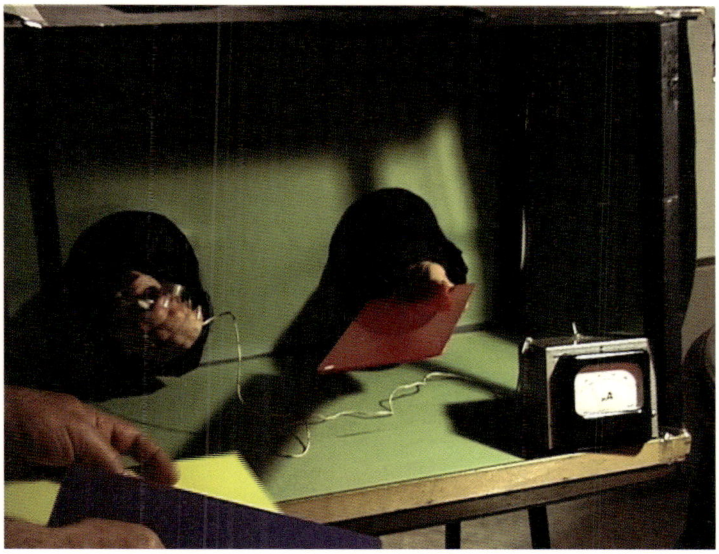

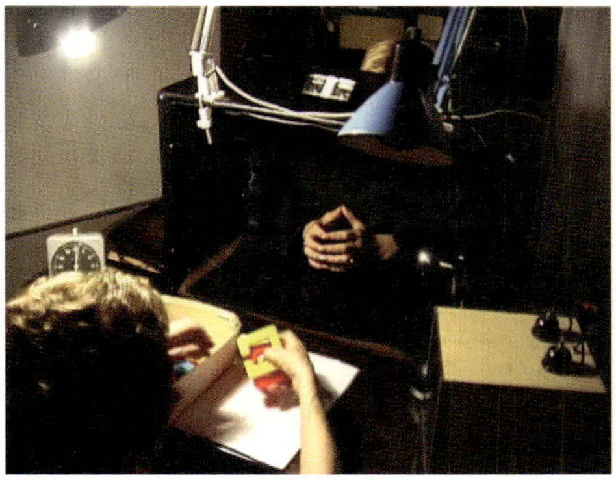

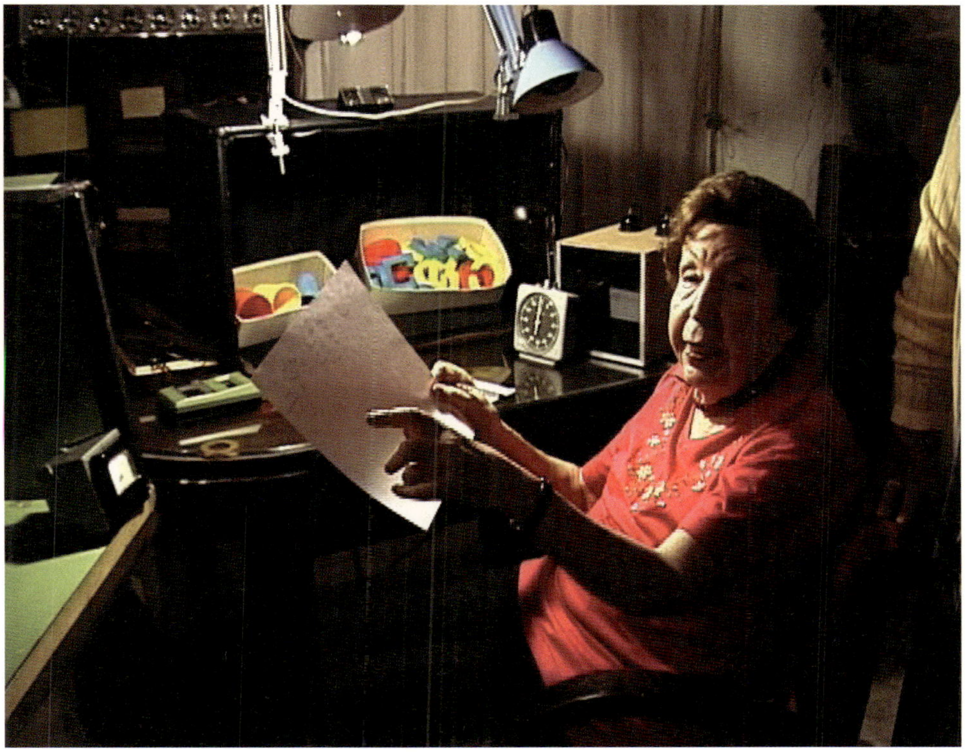

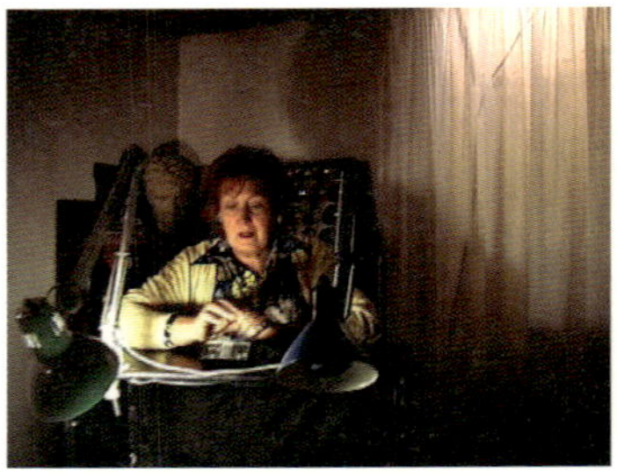
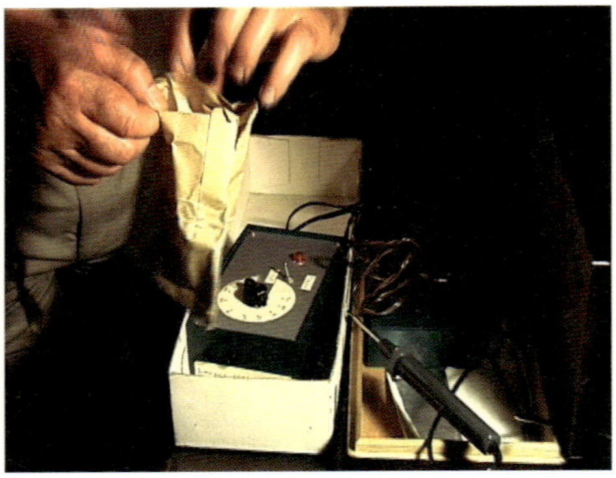
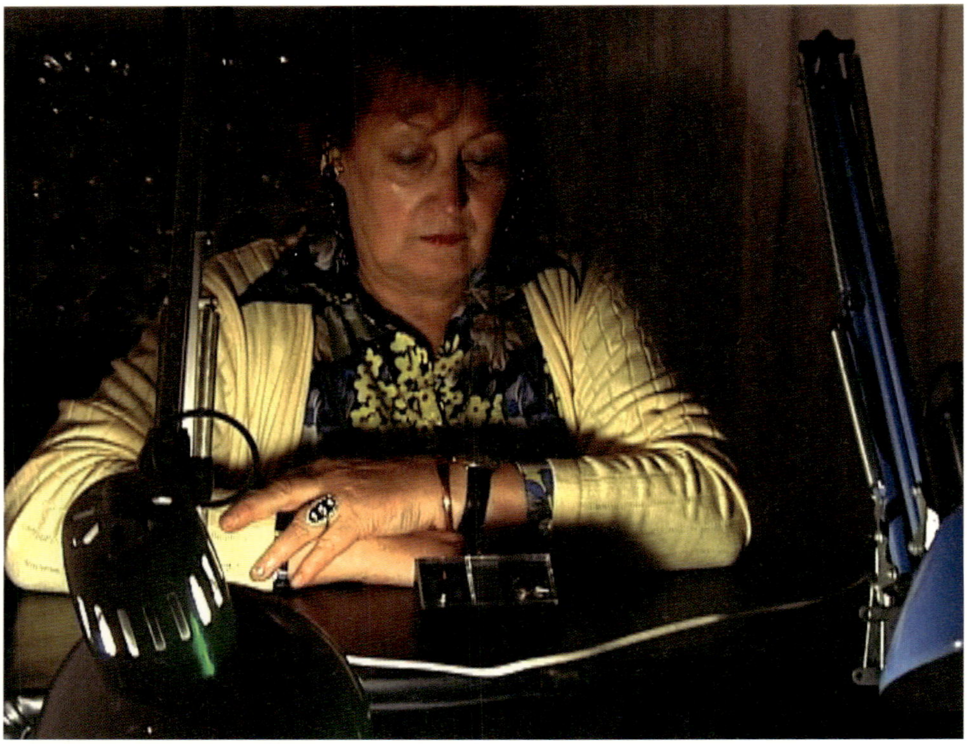
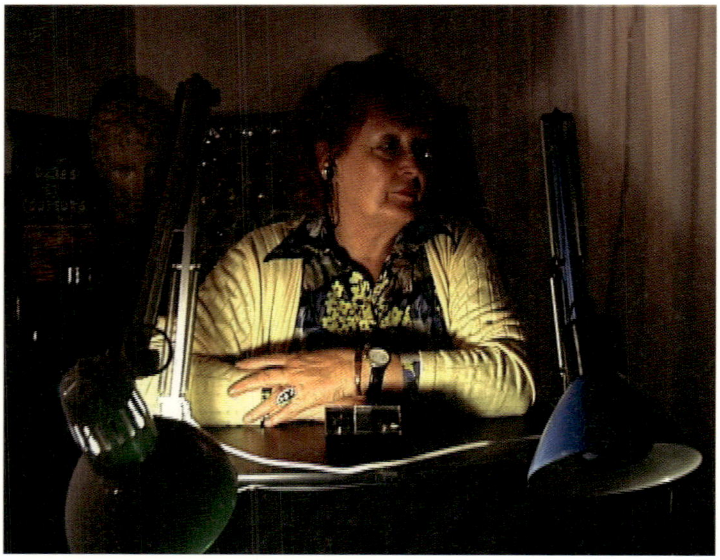
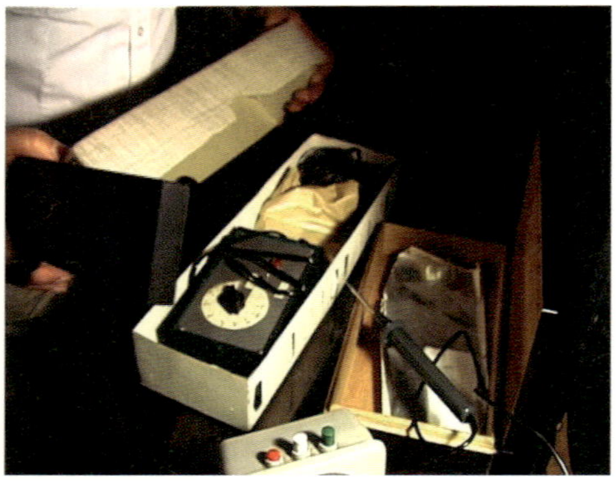
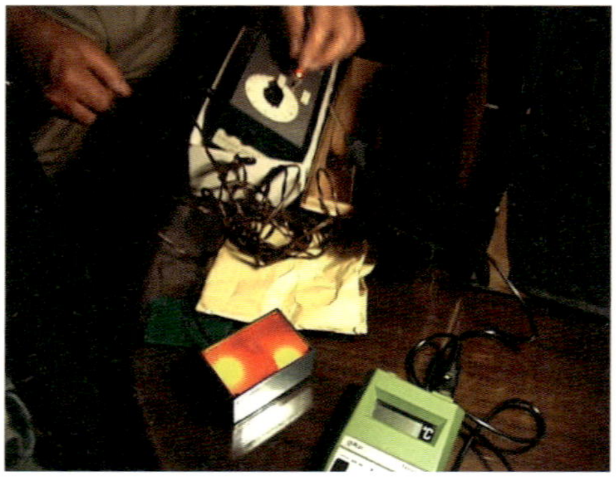

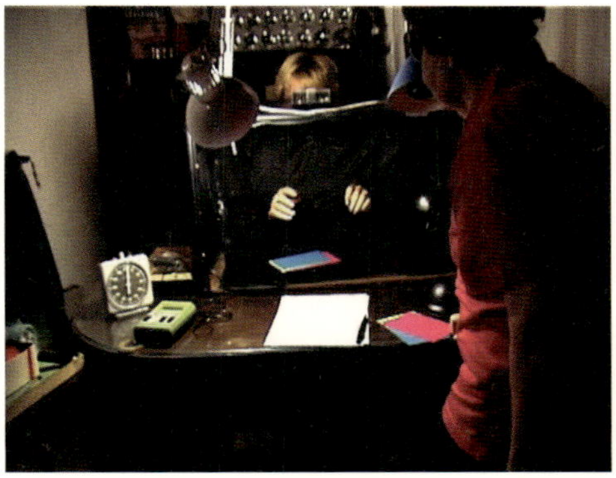

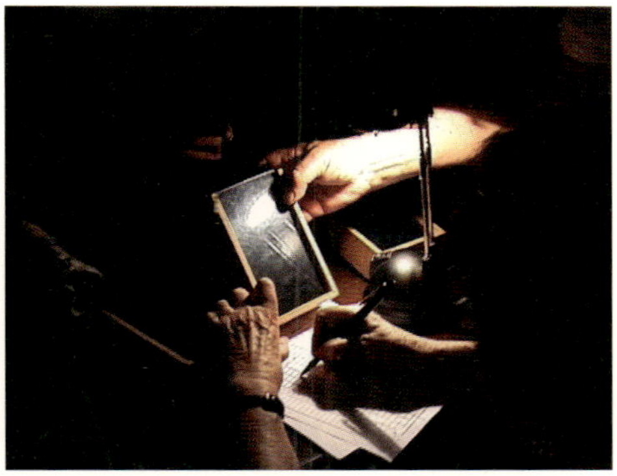

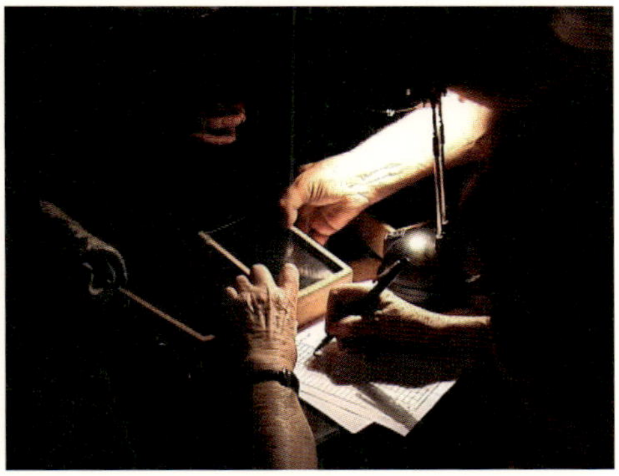

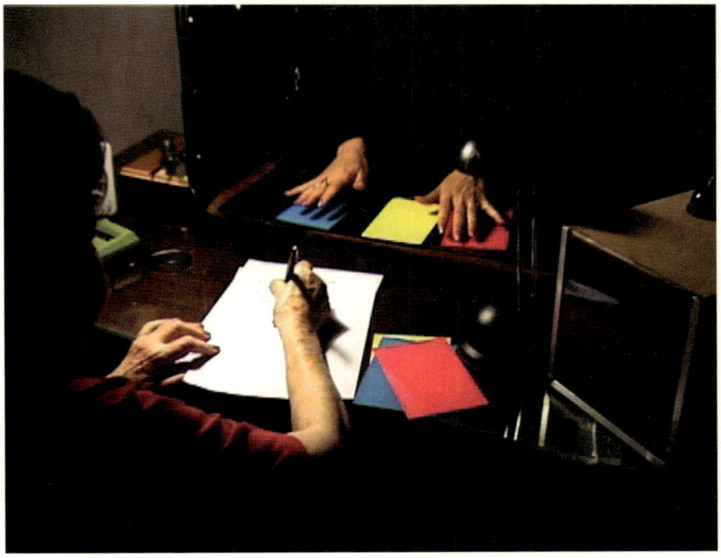

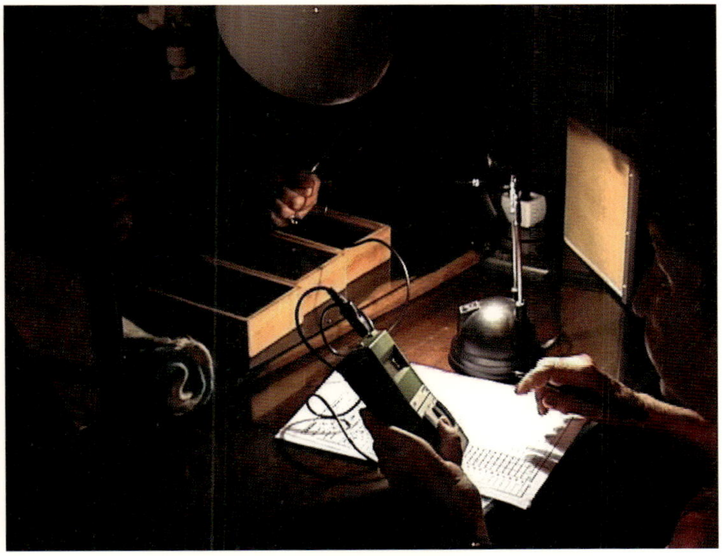

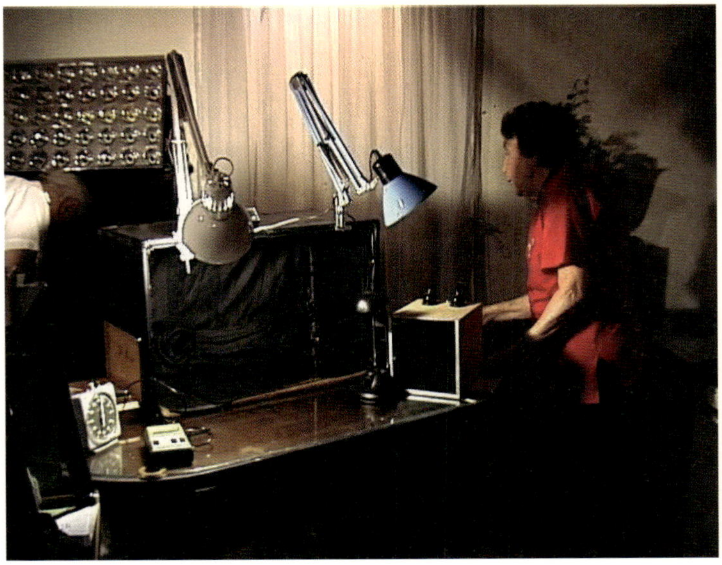

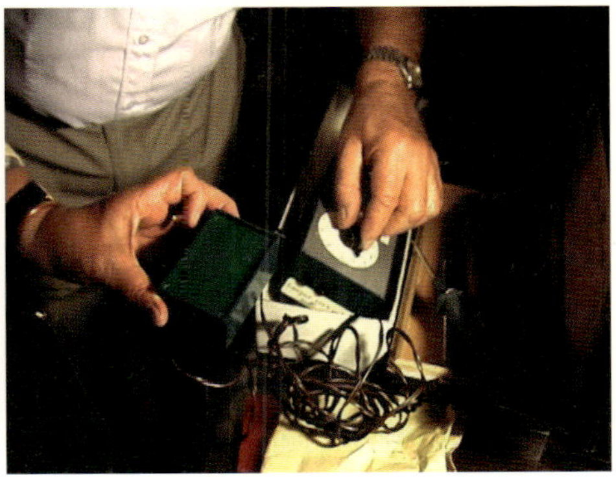

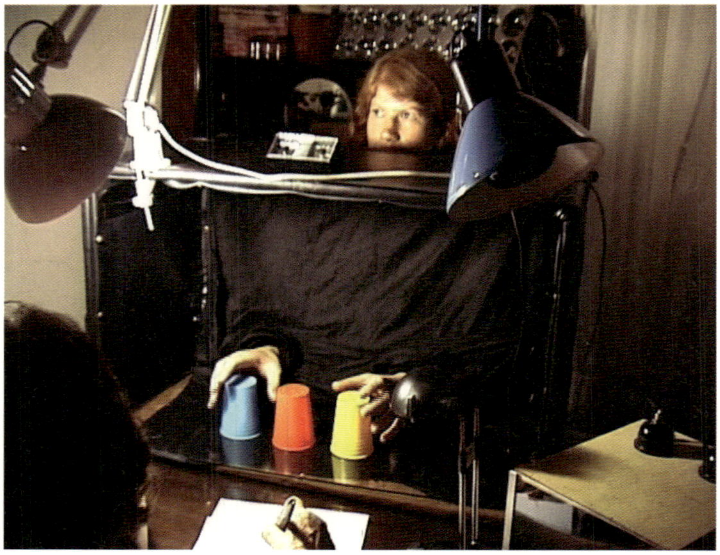

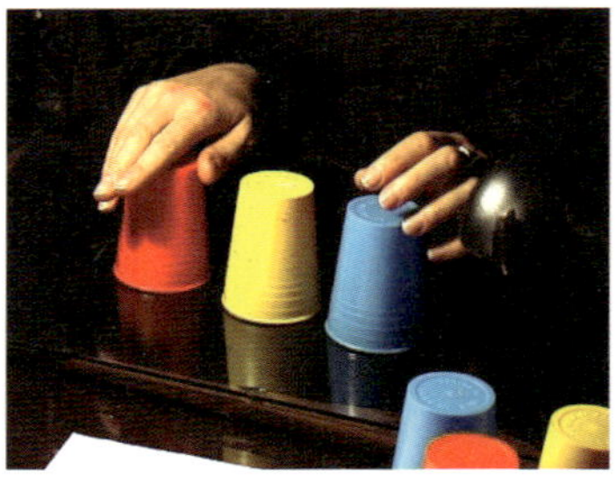

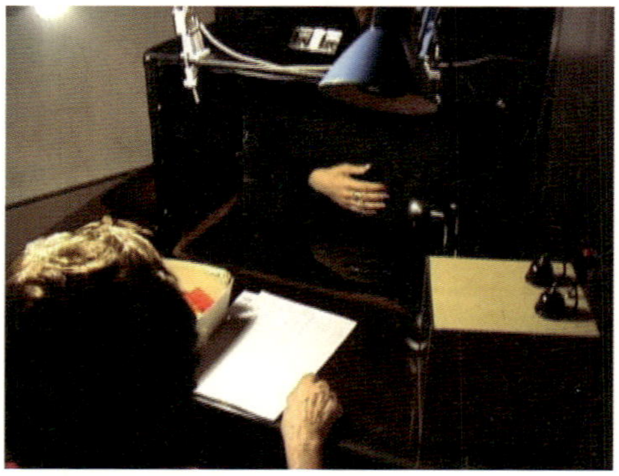

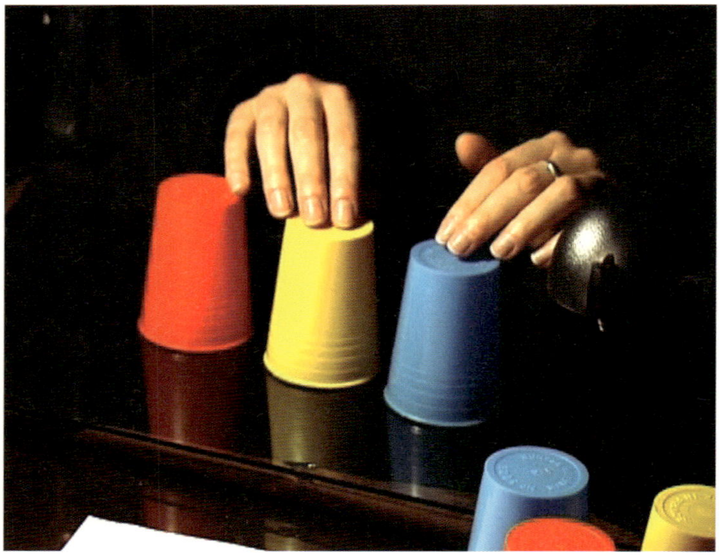

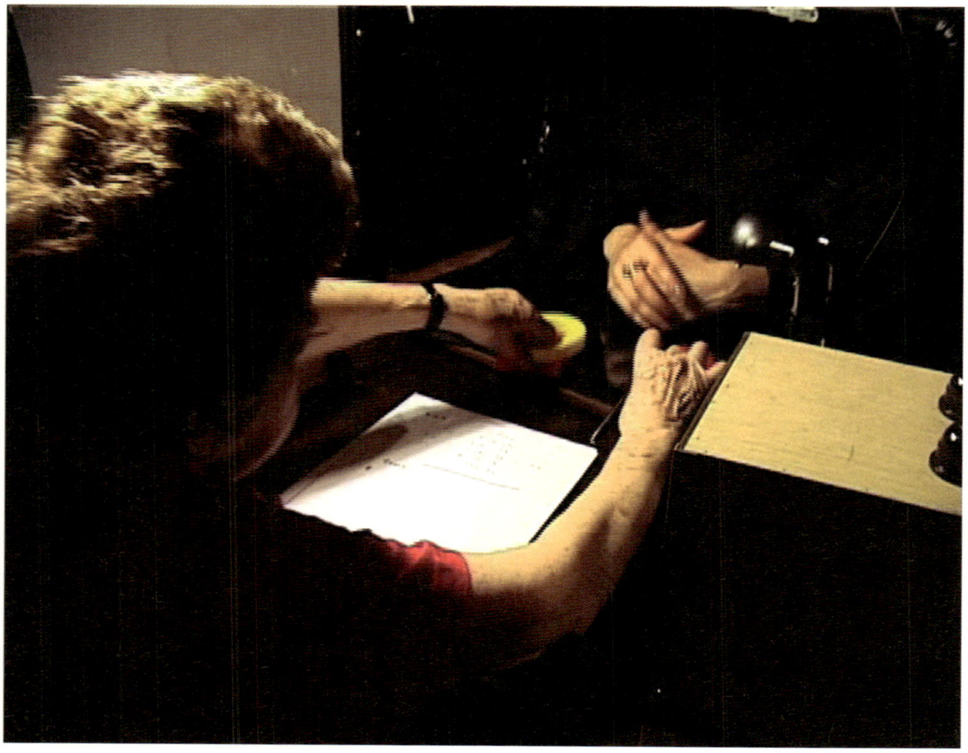

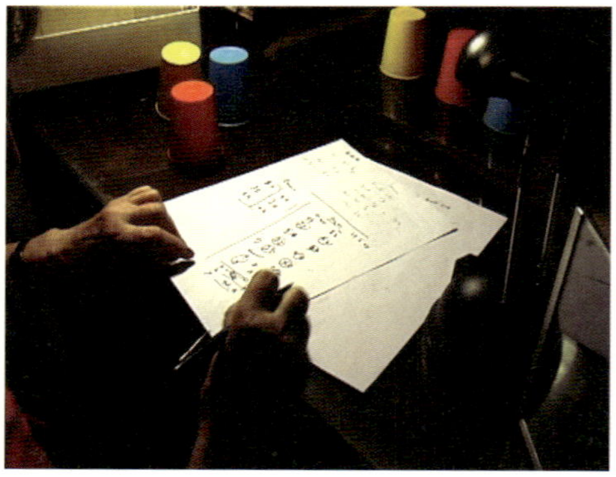

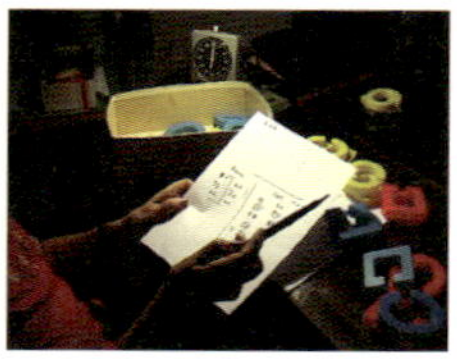

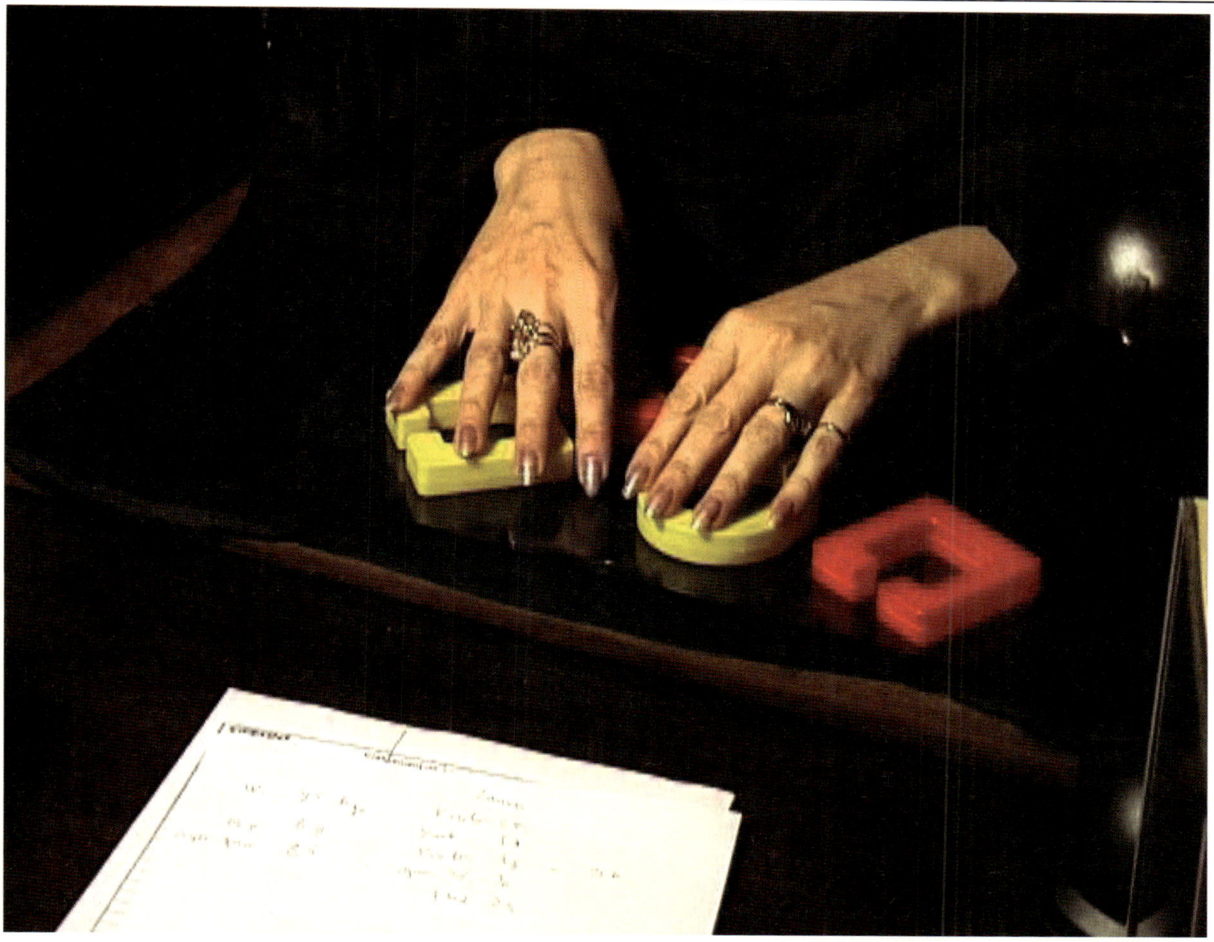

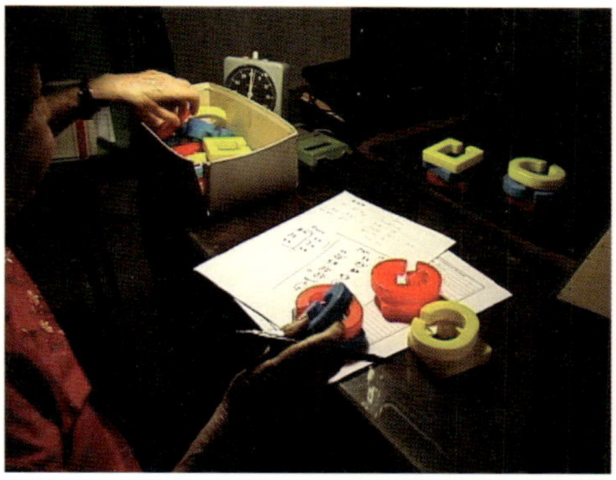

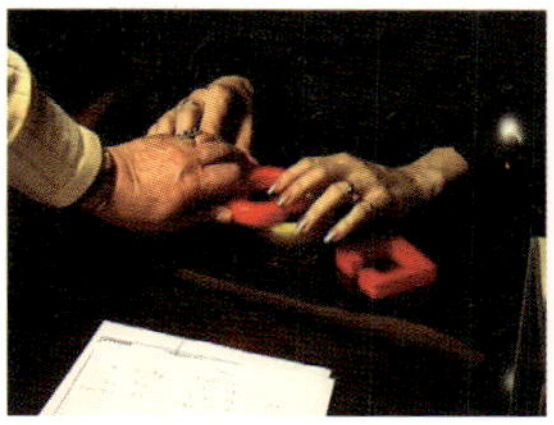

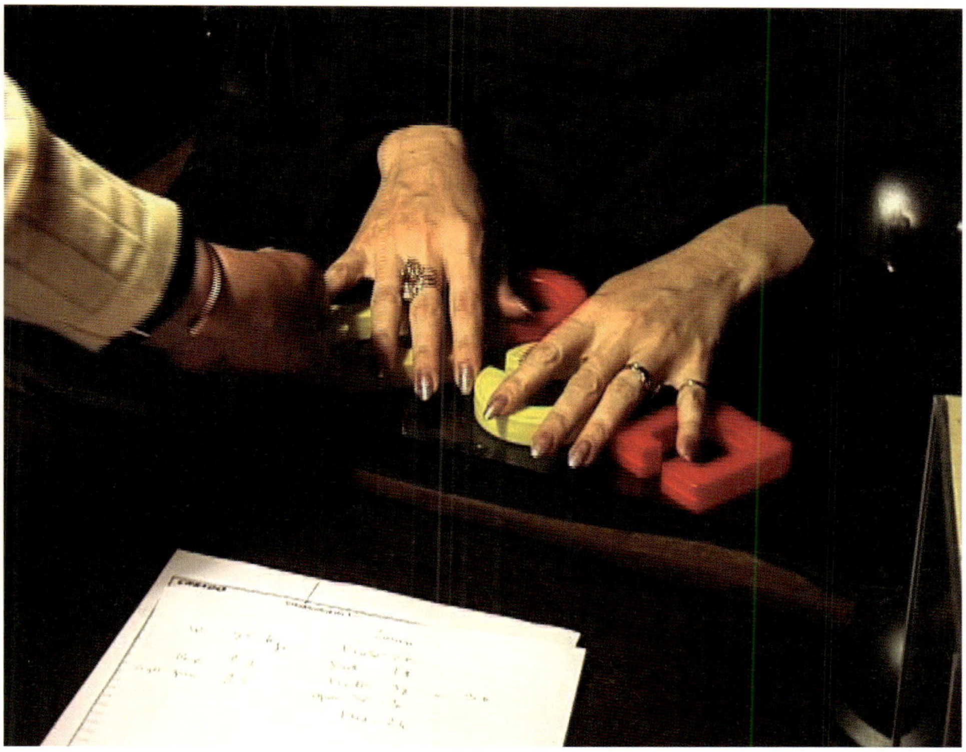

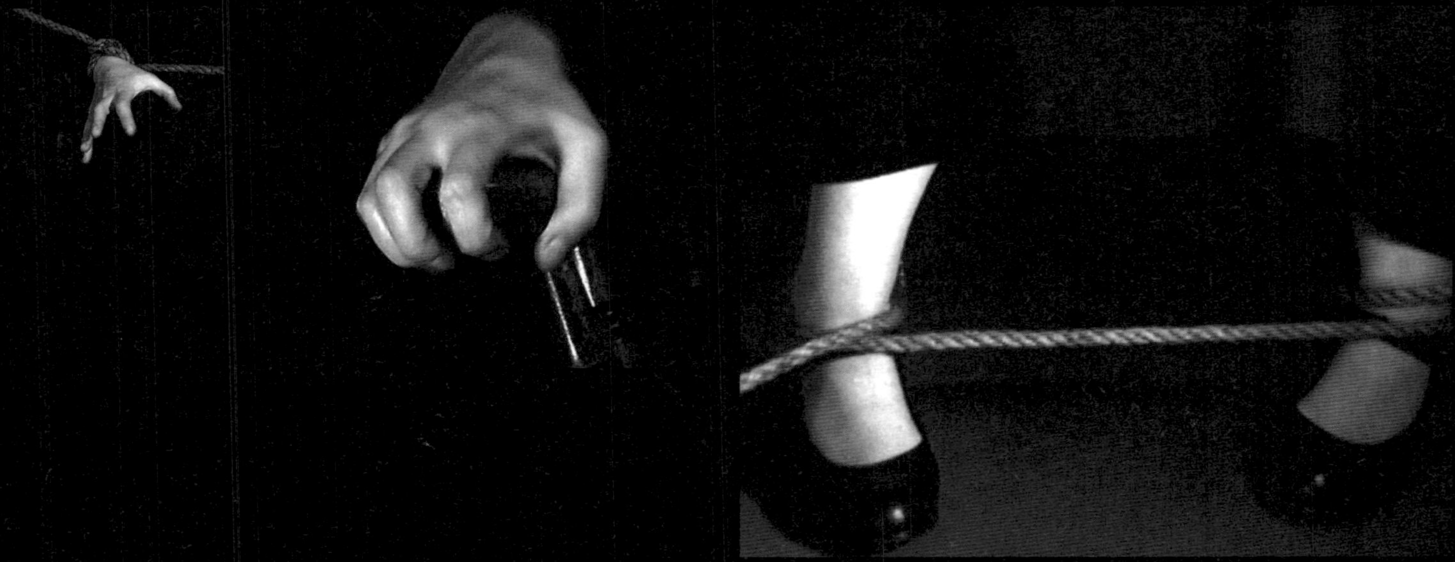

The Last Person, 1998, Video, Black and White, Silent, 10mins 30secs

Martha Langford

A MURDER OF WHITE CROWS: SUSAN MacWILLIAM'S VARIETIES OF PSYCHICAL EXPERIENCE

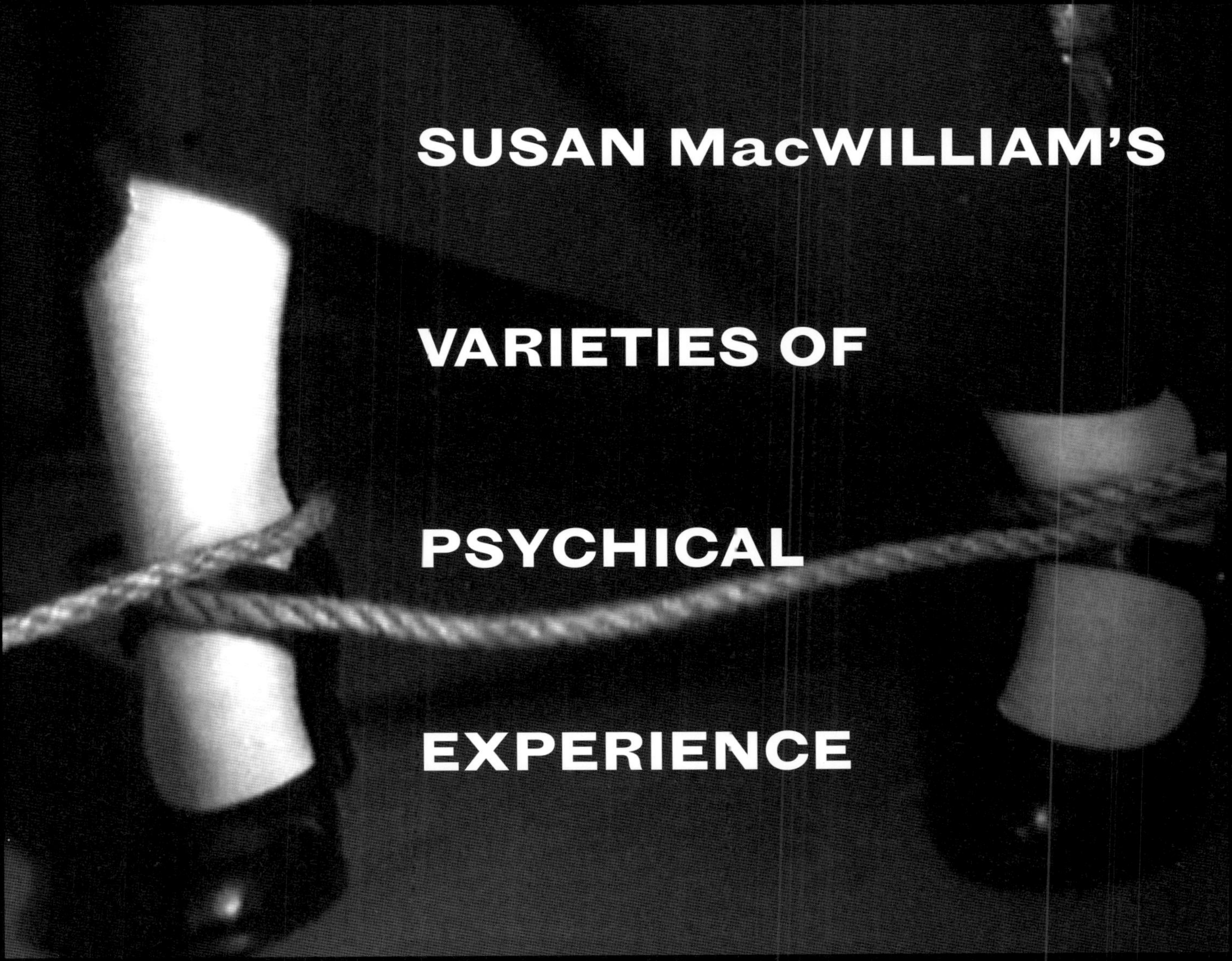

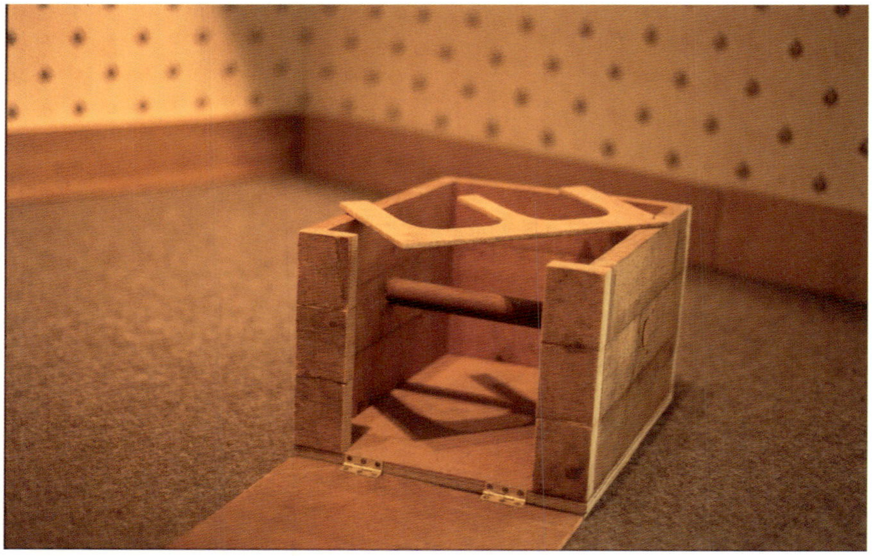

The varieties of psychical experience brought to life in Susan MacWilliam's video and installation work draw on the recorded histories of the paranormal. At the centre of these histories are charismatic individuals and the circles that formed around their wondrous abilities. Most of the players are gone, at least in body, and their language, though copiously preserved in journals of psychic societies, scientific bulletins and volumes of experimental work, has fallen into disuse. We hear no fresh reports of communicating raps, ectoplasmic extrusions, violent optograms, lucid planchettes, and stiff psychic rods. Actors and heiresses have siphoned off the celebrity once accorded mediums, controls, mentalists, memorists, mystics, spiritualists, and operators.

MacWilliam puzzles these communities together from archival traces; she reactivates their power for contemporary observation. Textual fragments, brittle snapshots, and first-hand accounts are nested in her creative reconstructions of the past, her visual and aural tellings that emulate the workings of personal memory. This is no trick, but the result of total immersion. MacWilliam has been travelling in paranormal circles since 1997, when she became interested in nineteenth century spirit photography, the representation of ghostly figures and their materialised messages on photographic plates. Historian Martyn Jolly explains the appeal of spirit photographs as an antidote to the morbidity associated with the still photography: "they were material witnesses to the possibility of endless emergences, returns, and simultaneities.... The images were performative."[1] Loved ones were not just seen, but summoned in the desires of the bereaved whose active participation was crucial.

From the first, MacWilliam seems to have felt the same things. She began to use video technology and performance strategies as seeking, sifting, reanimating devices. Her experiential approach, first essayed in *The Last Person,* 1998, was a significant breakthrough. Drawn to the story of Helen Duncan, 1898–1956, a Scottish medium convicted in 1944 for witchcraft, MacWilliam pored over the court records and newspaper stories of the trial. They fed her performance as Duncan and they directed the attention of the camera, to the mouth, to the hands. The effect of total embodiment is as American psychologist William James described the trance state of the medium Mrs Piper: "great muscular unrest, even her ears moving vigorously in a way impossible to her in her waking state".[2] Such energy must be controlled: MacWilliam ties her protagonist (herself) to an institutional wooden chair —the camera observes how her hands grip and stroke the armrests, how her feet twitch against the rope. This crude and ineffective binding touches me more deeply than the pathos of a woman masticating, swallowing, and regurgitating her cheesecloth prop—a woman fettered to prevent her from displaying her talents is, in a way, so *ordinary*.

Across the spectrum of her work, MacWilliam seizes hold of a fundamental aspect of magic, its embeddedness in everyday life experience. Considering what he had heard through the mediations of Mrs Piper, James moaned about "the extreme triviality of most of the communications. What real spirit, at last able to

Experiment M, 1999, Installation, foot box, EV+A, Limerick, 2001

Experiment M, 1999, Video, Black and White, Silent, 5mins, 43secs

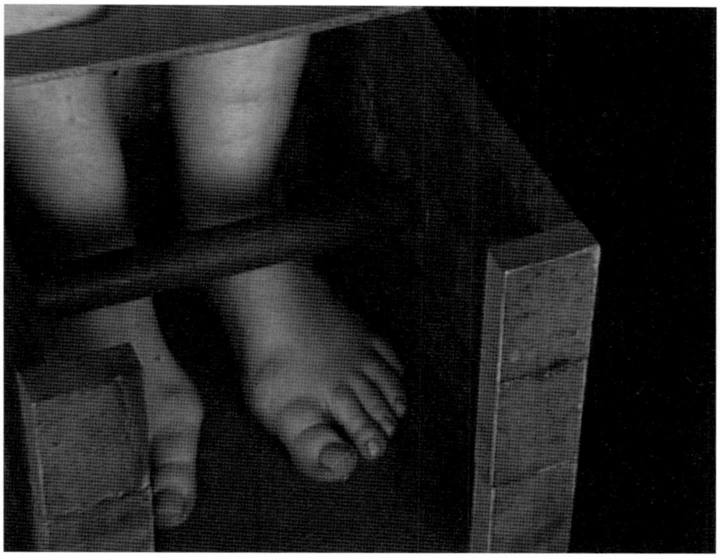

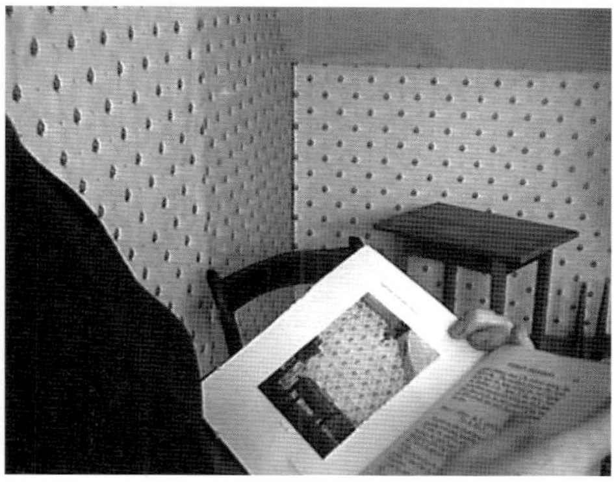

revisit his wife on this earth, but would find something better to say than that she had changed the place of his photograph?"[3] What did he expect? Rigorous and consoling scientific proof: James came wounded from grief and doubt to his religious and psychic investigations. I too carry baggage. Confirmed skeptic, fallen Catholic girl that I am, the spiritual is for me a MacGuffin. So what did I expect from this art, if not the warp and woof of postmodern media discourse, a display of tension between fact and fiction? That critical tension presents, of course, but the hook in MacWilliam's work is her consistent ability to commandeer my senses. This is done through an impressive array of mediations. MacWilliam *channels* many ways of working; by assuming different shapes, her work worms its way into different pockets of cultural memory. Her strategies include recreation, appropriation and materialisation—each method of mediation carefully constructed in form and process, and rigorously disciplined, with unsettlingly compelling results. Evidence of *something* is observed through tiny tears in the cinematic curtain: a cat slinks into the frame, teasing the mechanical eye; an interlocutor's hands form spirals of power over uncleared lunch dishes; magic is explained in the breakfast nook, at the edge of a swimming pool, or in front of the laundry room. Sound, or sometimes its absence, is an important agent of this mesmerising dailiness; so is touch, activated imaginatively through the observation of experiments and physically through real objects that are on screen and also part of the display. To gather up this evidence is an intriguing, immersive task that suspends judgement. This is how time travel begins.

Experiment M, 1999, is an installation based on investigations of medium Kathleen Goligher (born 1898), and the Goligher Circle, conducted by Dr William Jackson Crawford, a lecturer in mechanical engineering at Queen's University, Belfast, and published in a series of books, beginning with *The Reality of Psychic Phenomenon*, 1916. The installation consists of a set modelled on the attic room in the Goligher house, where most of the experimental séances took place, and two key props, made according to Crawford's measurements: the table levitated by the "operators" and the "foot box" he designed to prove that her busy feet were not the cause. There are two monitors showing black and white tapes: one is a series of Crawford's observations scrawled on a chalk board; the other is an episodic montage of scenes drawn from his descriptions. This tape is a contagion of restlessness: a woman's feet being fitted into the box; her clenching unclenching hands; her roiling skirts; the hypnagogic pattern of the wallpaper; a plate of putty impressed by telekinesis with marks resembling oversized fingerprints (the subjects declined on this occasion to reach out with their psychic rods). The camera roves close to the ground, under the table where Crawford crawled in the dim red light to make his closest observations. His notes, drawn from four volumes, fling off his confusion and desire: "touches are sometimes experienced", "spasmodic jerking", "trembling and vibrating sinuously", "softish and elastic", "noises in spasms", "medium wore clean white knickers", "rise and fall of her flesh", "involuntary trembling and shivering".

Crawford committed suicide, but there is nothing agonistic in his text; rather it is cheerful and geekish in

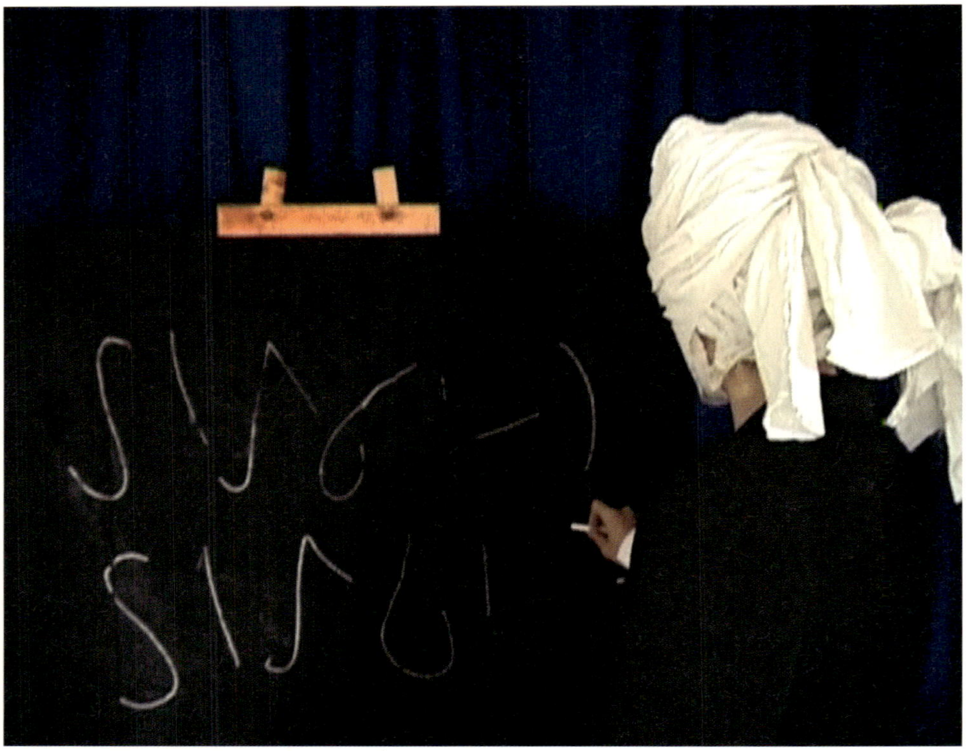

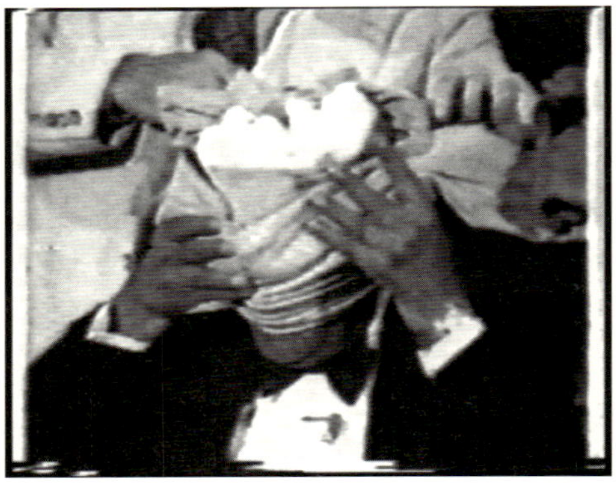

Kuda Bux, 2003, Video, Black and White and Colour, Stereo, 10mins 40secs

Kuda Bux, courtesy Mary Evans Picture Library

Head Box, 2004, Rosa and Collar Model, Video, Colour, Stereo, 14mins

tone: "I recommend an experimenter, if he has a levitating medium at hand, to carry out this experiment [number 54]. It is simple and also effective, for the observer can take a stroll round the circle while it is going on, can see the table levitated, can hear the bell ringing, and can see that all hands are held in chain order and that feet are on the floor."[4] MacWilliam's installation is equally effective, though not so simple: it efficiently combines archival references that prove the accuracy of her set with absorbing passages of fluid camera work, these heightened by the continuous feed of thoughts and feelings emanating from the mind of the experimenter. Her images are seized from events set imaginatively in flow, then technically recorded, or could it be the reverse? Has her instrument set the dial? The fitting of form to imaginative experience is perfectly engineered (rather like the foot box). James performs a similar imagistic feat, automatically drawing a picture of table lifting, when he argues for open-mindedness: "All of us live more or less on some inclined plane of credulity. The plane tips one way in one man, another way in another; and may he whose plane tips in *no* way be the first to cast a stone!"[5]

Hands and ears figure significantly in MacWilliam's imagery, and centrally in her explorations of eyeless sight and dermo optics. These closely connected themes are the basis of a number of installations, including *Kuda Bux*, 2003, and *Headbox*, 2004. *Kuda Bux* is unique in MacWilliam's oeuvre on a number of levels, not least of which is gender. This scene shifts from the domestic sphere of the private séance into the public sphere of popular entertainment, a culture of magicians and mystics. There we find Kuda Bux, 1906–1981, a man born Khudah Bukhsh in Kashmir, and active mainly in the United States, from the 1930s through the 50s, as a stage and stunt performer, "The Man With X-Ray Eyes", as well as a film actor. Kuda Bux performed many tricks, including fire walking and reading newspapers while blindfolded. In the opening sequence of MacWilliam's video, a woman's hand pulls back a curtain to reveal appropriated black and white archival footage of Kuda Bux in his stage act. Contemporary spectators can only be astonished to see the performer, elegantly attired in black tie, having great gobs of bread dough applied to his eyes before his head is wrapped in gauze and tape. MacWilliam underscores the bizarre effect by speeding it up, turning the mystic's speech into electronic garble. Temporal shifts heighten the disorientation of the

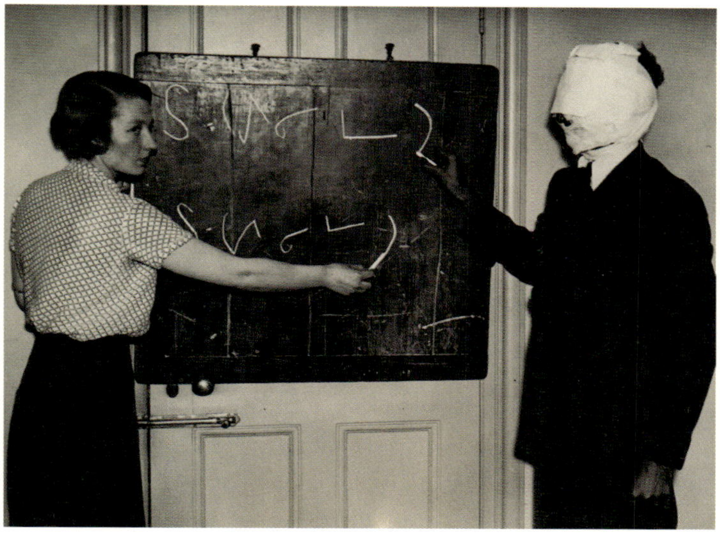

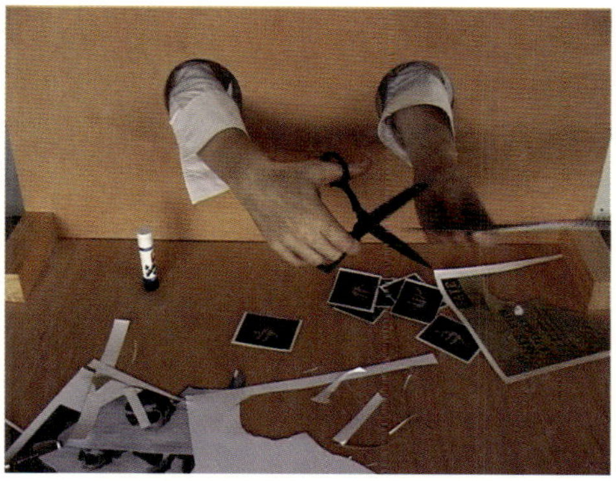

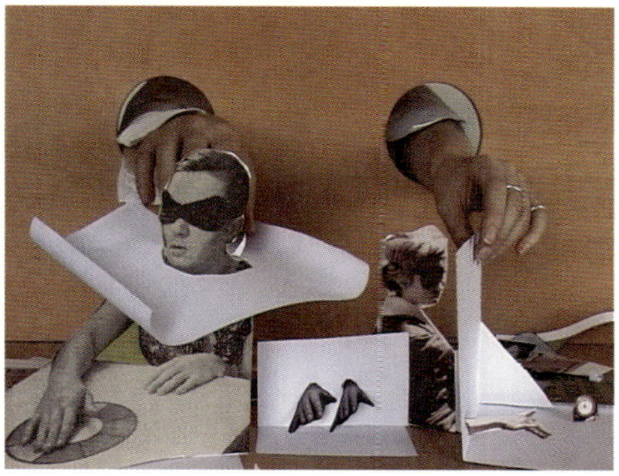

experience. Visitors to the installation watch the video in full colour on a 50s television, while lounging in a 30s armchair. A chalk board, wooden table, glasses, and a vial labelled "hydrochloric acid" are copied from Kuda Bux's rather primitive stage props, while retro-signage puts his name in lights. The video is episodic: texts and photographs flashing on the screen provide the backstory; the materiality of certain objects—chalk—is patiently explored; slow but sure performances make the crowd roar. All kinds of sounds permeate this work: carnival barkers, applause, traffic, bird song, chalk moving across the board, dough being mixed in a bowl, darts hitting a board, a banjo being strummed, and a balloon exploding. Silence, when it comes, feels like sensory deprivation; perhaps the audience is holding its breath.

Something strange is occurring. In a work concerned with sight and touch, the most forceful address is coming through another part of the sensorium—sound is overwhelming vision. Is distraction the secret behind Kuda Bux's power? In this carnival setting, am I a *mark*, literally touched on the shoulder with chalk? MacWilliam doesn't answer these questions. Rather, she presents more examples of unexplained sensory phenomena, rather like pulling rabbits from a hat.

Headbox is concerned with fingertip vision. Simulating laboratory conditions for the re-enactment of tests and demonstrations, the installation breaks down into three complementary forms of experience, each delivering a different category of knowledge. The first, arranged like a historical exhibit in a science museum, is a reconstruction of the laboratory apparatus: the central element, a wooden table, is fitted with a screen that has armholes cut through, so that a seated test subject is blind to the objects on the table with which she or he must perform a series of tasks. The viewer gazes up at this strange contraption (like the foot box, it reminds us of stocks), possibly wondering how it could ever have served science. The second, wall-mounted as an art object, consists of boxes housing 3-D images and delivering sound. The visitor must commit to this experience, by inserting his or her head into the box, thereby embodying seeing and listening for other visitors. The third, accessed through monitors in a slick, information-type display, is a trio of video works in which the test table is seen to be in use. Here the visitor is exposed to trials and

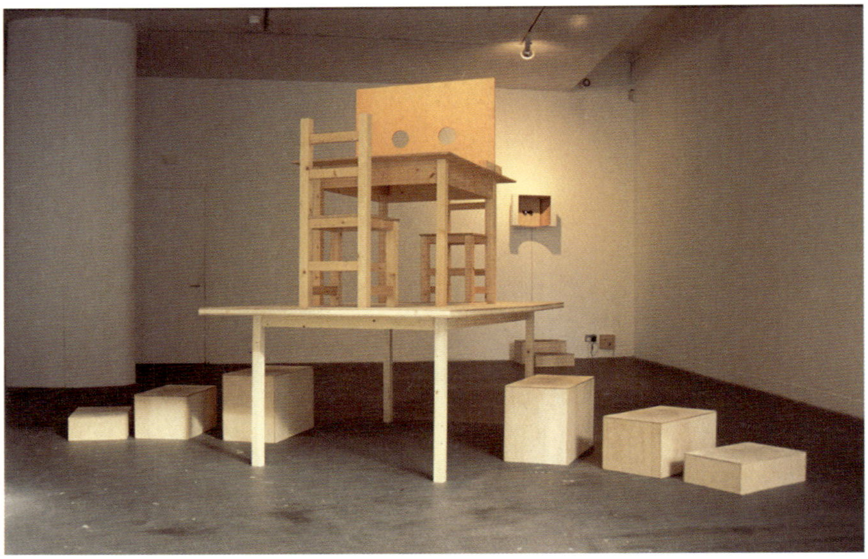

demonstrations, which are delivered in moving images and sound.

Turning to the video, I hear a warning that recurs and troubles me throughout: the movement of a flock of birds zigzagging across the sky is synchronised with the sound of moving traffic. A trick, I think, and one that alerts me to the possibility that I should not believe my eyes and ears, or suggests, more precisely, that my eyes and ears may conspire internally in some deception. Cautioned against myself, I begin to observe the first demonstration, which is shot from a fixed camera position, parallel to the wooden screen. A woman (MacWilliam) sits down at the table behind the wooden screen and, picking up a pair of scissors, begins to cut out a figure in a photograph. Such monstrous scissors! Such confident handling! The ground is cut away; the figure becomes a paper doll. This action continues. Plain white sheets are geometrically divided, cut, folded and glued. Paper sculptures rise up from the surface of the table, neo-Constructivist monuments to *Headbox*'s historical subject, a Russian psychic named Rosa Kuleshova, 1942–1978.

The editing of this work is very careful, so much so that the experience can be taken, like a piece of Performance Art, as occurring in real time—this continuity flies in the face of cuts, changes of camera angle and shot, even signs of interference in the tabletop collage. Sync sound, or what seems to be—buses and voices coming in through an open window; a cell phone insistently ringing; paper pushed across the grain; nails and skin scraping; and those awful scissors clipping, squeaking, and clanging when they hit the table—this steady feed concentrates the mind, building faith in these cinematic proceedings. And still more confirming are the movements of the test subject's body, the purposive gestures of those near sighted hands. They move with haptic drive and creative intelligence. Rosa imagined and re-embodied returns, appealing for accreditation.

The work that MacWilliam has accomplished through her connection with the Parapsychology Foundation in Greenport, Long Island, is the fullest demonstration of the remarkable elasticity, or mediumship, that she has brought to her project.[6] Five separate works to date compose a portrait of the Irish medium, or "sensitive", Eileen J Garrett, 1893–1970, as well as her circle and the research institute that she founded in 1951. Her daughter, Eileen Coly, who inherited no psychic powers, is a magnetic presence in these works, as the human conduit between "Garrett" (as even her daughter calls her) and MacWilliam, who conducts their synergy to us. Access to home movies and family albums sets the domestic stage for intergenerational transmissions of knowledge, some stories much rehearsed over the years, and others sparked by MacWilliam's research.

A three-channel video work *Eileen*, 2008, exquisitely captures the layered storage, random retrieval, and verbal rehearsals of memory that we call "storytelling". The shooting of *Eileen* refers formally to television talk shows and documentaries. In edit, it becomes an electronic choral work, structured as a series of motifs. Here, as everywhere in MacWilliam's work, we find a symbiotic relationship between dailiness and wonder.

Headbox, 2004, Installation, experimental table and chairs on viewing platform. Temple Bar Gallery, Dublin, 2004

13 Roland Gardens, 2007, Video, Colour, Stereo, 22mins 30secs

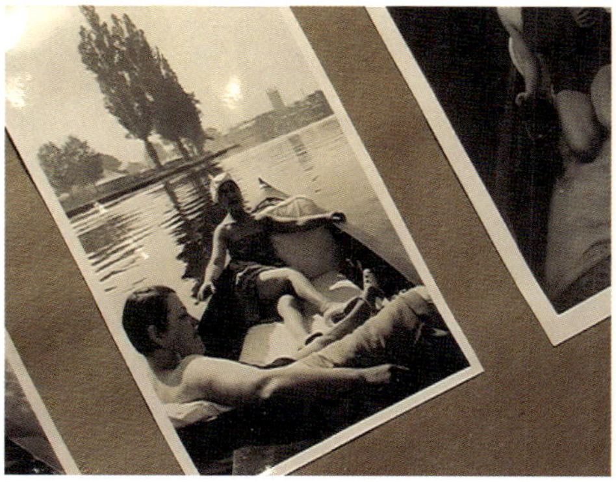

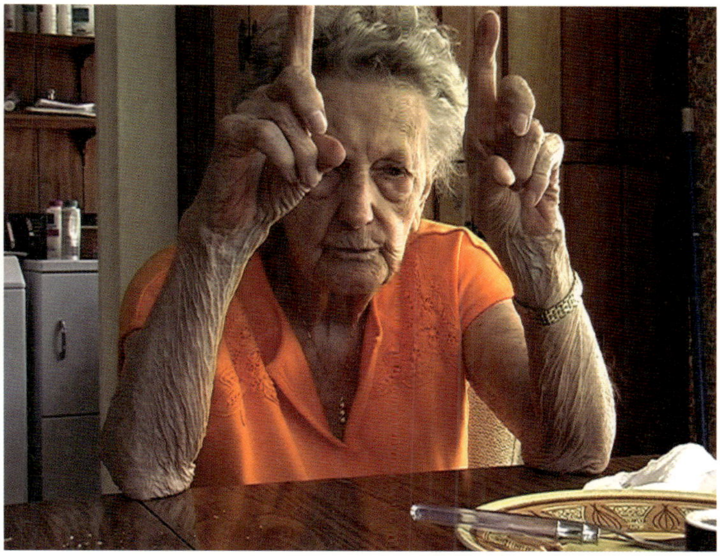

Her artistic mediation—the right degree of technological separation—is the fairy dust that transforms conversation into revelation. Garrett said it herself:

"But such séance room encounters are charged with psychological elements that are simply not present in everyday meetings. For a living person to speak to the departed is, no matter what, quite different from an ordinary conversation. We know that even things said over the telephone, and even more so in letters, may carry weight that they would not have in a face-to-face conversation."[7]

The transmitter matters. MacWilliam's formal articulations, speaking many different formal languages, have produced an oeuvre of remarkable coherence and dramatic punch. Her recuperation of psychic histories is both revelatory and referential, as a contribution to knowledge. MacWilliam has sent me back to the beautiful writings of James whose systematic investigations of religious and mystical experience led him to identify one person whose uncanny abilities could not be explained away. This Mrs Piper became James' proof of exception to the laws of knowledge—his white crow.[8] Faith follows form; perhaps Mrs Piper knew that; Garrett certain did. To the degree that beliefs are confirmed performatively, by mediated experience, MacWilliam's artistic progress across time and space has generated a murder of white crows. Her work communicates the mystery and authority of phantasmic lives lived.

1. Jolly, Martyn, "Spectres from the Archive", in Martha Langford, ed., *Image & Imagination*, Montreal: McGill-Queen's University Press, 2005, p. 176.
2. James, William, "A Record of Observations of Certain Phenomena of Trance (1890)", in his *Essays in Psychical Research*, Cambridge, MA and London: Harvard University Press, 1986, p. 82.
3. James, "A Record of Observations of Certain Phenomena of Trance (1890)", p. 83.
4. Crawford, WJ, *The Reality of Psychic Phenomena: Raps, Levitations, Etc.*, second edition London: John M Watkins, 1919, p. 134. http://www.archive.org/stream/realityofpsychic00crawrich/realityofpsychic00crawrich_djvu.txt. Last consulted 17 February 2009.
5. James, "What Psychical Research Has Accomplished (1892)", in his *Essays in Psychical Research*, p. 100.
6. For a history of the Foundation, including an impressive bibliography, see Alvarado, Carlos S, Eileen Coly, Lisette Coly and Nancy L Zingrone, "Fifty Years of Supporting Parapsychology: The Parapsychology Foundation (1951–2001)", *International Journal of Parapsychology* 12:2, 2001, pp. 1–26. posted at http://www.parapsychology.org/dynamic/010000.html. Last consulted 19 February 2009.
7. Garrett, Eileen J, "The Ethics of Mediumship", *Tomorrow*, 8:4, Autumn 1960. Posted on the First Spiritual Temple website http://www.fst.org/ethics.htm. Last consulted 19 February 2009.
8. James' point is worth quoting in full: "If you wish to upset the law that all crows are black, you musn't seek to show that no crows are; it is enough if you prove one single crow to be white." See James, "Address of the President before the Society for Psychical Research (1896)", in his *Essays in Psychical Research*, p. 131.

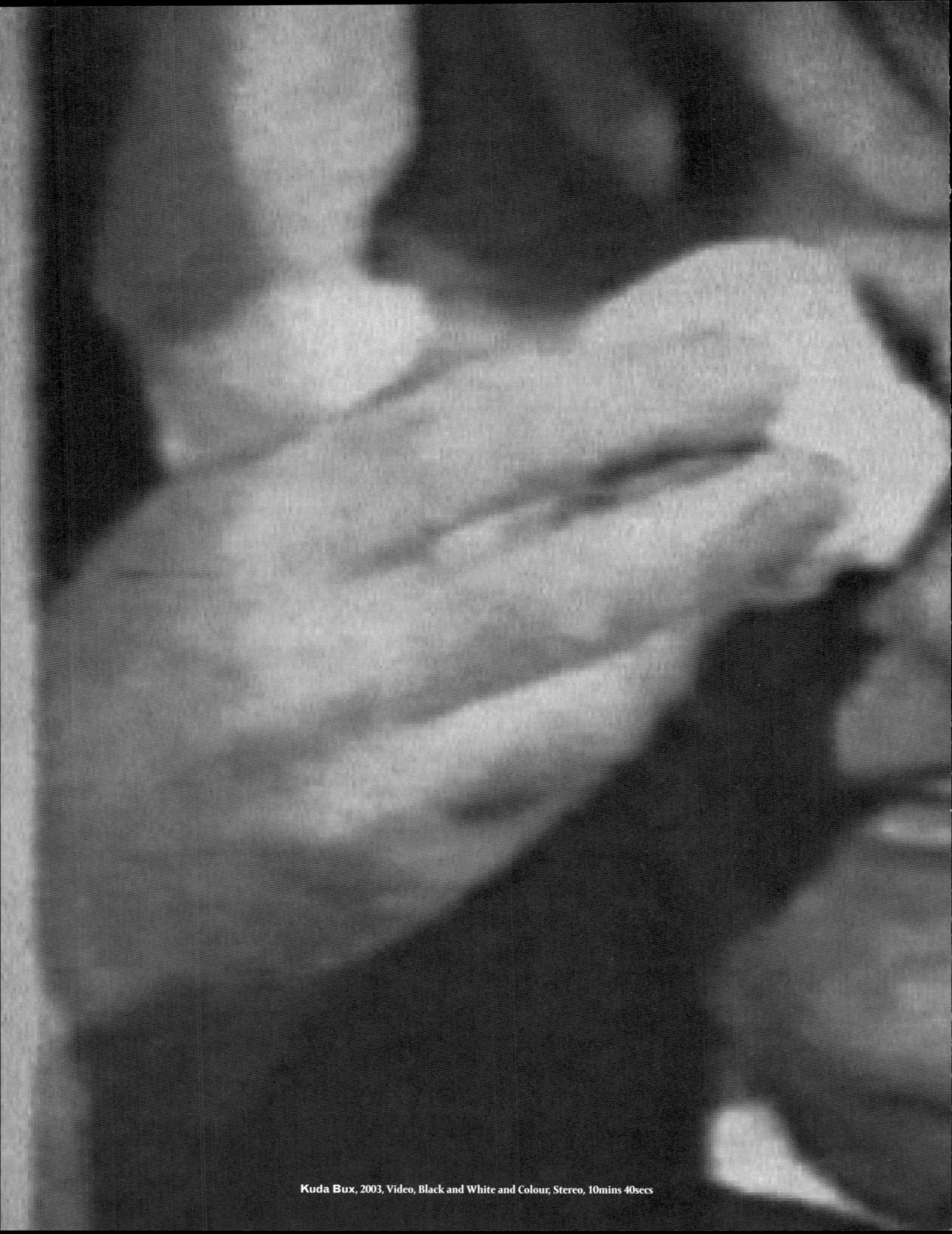

Kuda Bux, 2003, Video, Black and White and Colour, Stereo, 10mins 40secs

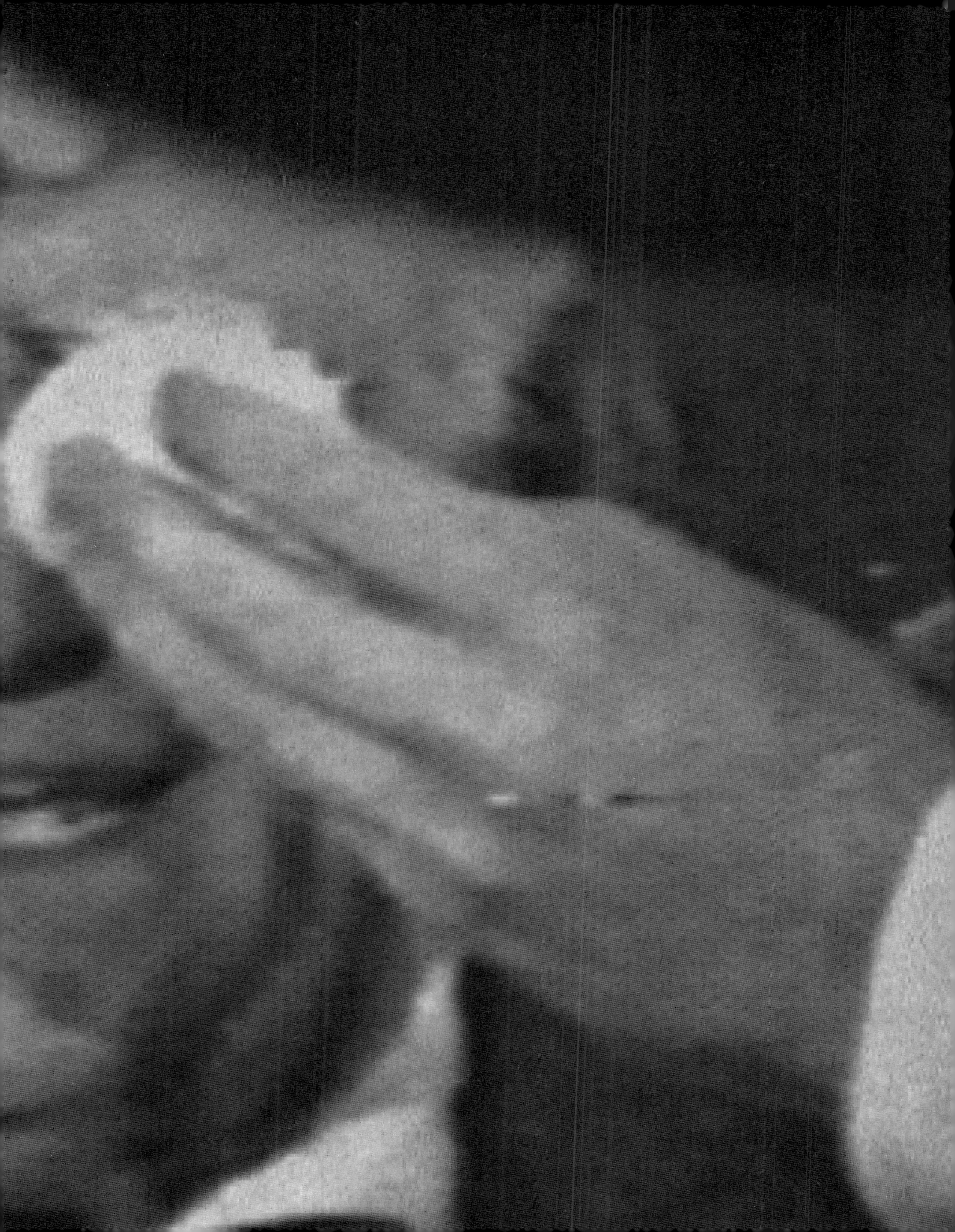

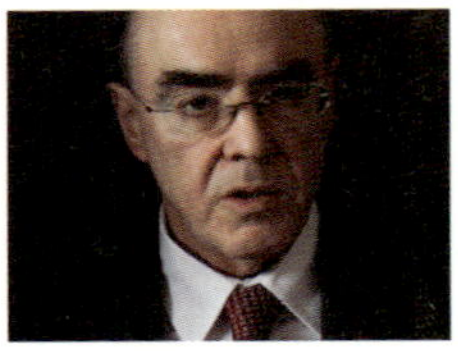

F-L-A-M-M-A-R-I-O-N
2009, Video, Colour, Stereo

In 1931 a 'teleplasm' spelling out the name Flammarion appeared on the wall of a cabinet at a séance in Winnipeg. Camille Flammarion, 1842–1925, was a French astronomer and psychical researcher and his name appeared at Thomas Glendenning Hamilton's sitting of 10 June 1931. *F-L-A-M-M-A-R-I-O-N* features a reconstruction of TG Hamilton's séance cabinet, the Belfast poet and writer Ciaran Carson, Atlanta based Danish American poltergeist investigator Dr. William G Roll and Arla Marshall, Canadian granddaughter of Hamilton's Scottish sitter Susan Marshall. Recorded in three cities across the globe Carson, Roll and Marshall come together in *F-L-A-M-M-A-R-I-O-N* and respond to the image of the teleplasm. Recorded in Winnipeg, Atlanta and Belfast.

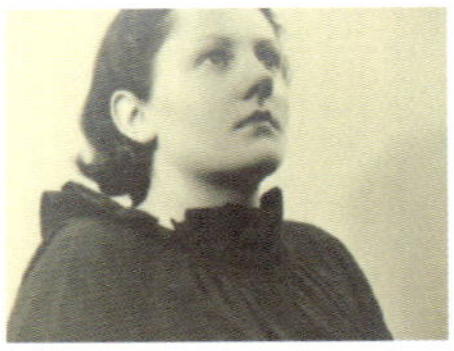

The Only Way To Travel
2008, Video, Colour, Stereo, 38mins 30secs

Eileen J Garrett first travelled to New York in 1931 upon the invitation of the American Society of Psychical Research. During the 1930s and 1940s, Garrett and her daughter Eileen Coly frequently travelled transatlantic from Europe to New York. *The Only Way To Travel* presents a world of 1930s high living, the cocktail hour, the rise of the New York skyscraper, and an era of glamorous travel, optimism and new horizons. Recorded in New York.

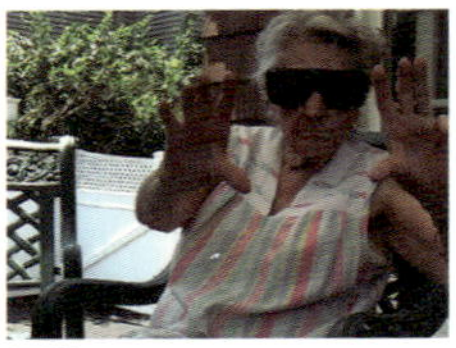

Eileen
2008, Synchronised 3 Channel Video Installation, Colour, Stereo, 28mins 53secs

The subject of *Eileen* is the Irish-born medium Eileen J Garrett, 1893–1970, one of the most celebrated psychics of the twentieth century and founder of Creative Age Press publishing house and the Parapsychology Foundation, New York. *Eileen* features Garrett's daughter Eileen Coly, her granddaughter Lisette Coly and parapsychologists Dr Stanley Krippner, Dr William G Roll and Dr Rex Stanford. Recorded in New York and Nova Scotia.

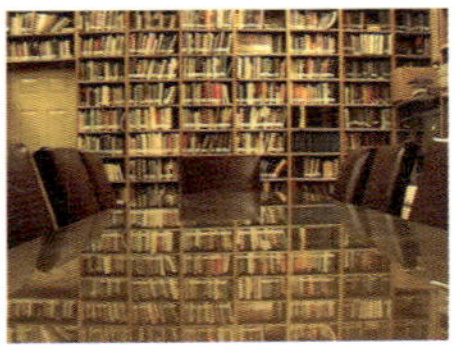

Library
2008, Video, Colour, Stereo, 14mins 10secs

Library is recorded in the Eileen J Garrett Library, Parapsychology Foundation, New York.

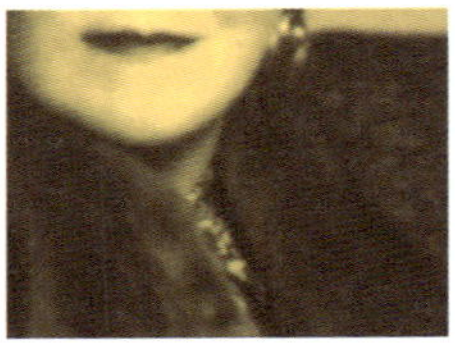

Psychic Edit
2008, Video, Colour, Stereo, 14secs, Looped Continuously

Psychic Edit presents a strobing edit of archival home movie footage of Eileen J Garrett from the Garrett-Coly personal archives.

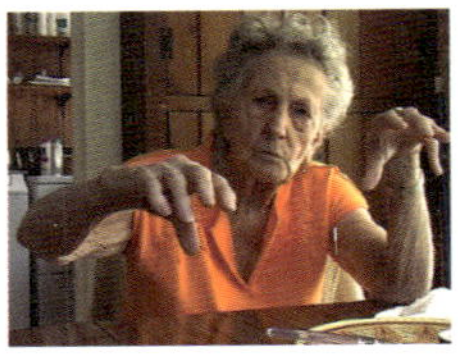

13 Roland Gardens
2007, Video, Colour, Stereo, 22mins 30secs

In *13 Roland Gardens,* Eileen Coly, daughter of the medium Eileen J Garrett, describes her mother's famous R101 Airship séance, 1930, and her experience living at 13 Roland Gardens, the site of Harry Price's Laboratory of Psychical Research in London. Recorded in New York and Nova Scotia.

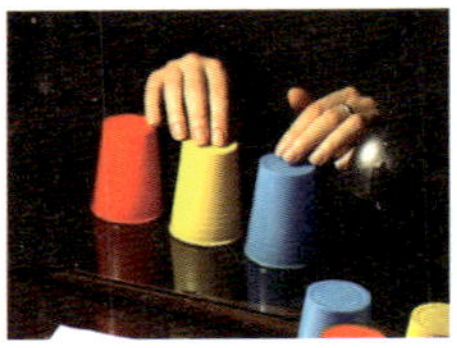

Dermo Optics
2006, Video, Colour, Stereo, 4mins 9secs
Installation with projected video, wall text and seating cubes

Dermo Optics is an account of the artist's visit to the Dermo Optical laboratory of Madame Yvonne Duplessis, Paris. Duplessis and her colleagues are observed as they demonstrate the experimental apparatus in the cellar laboratory. Dermo Optical Perception is the ability to read or perceive colour through touch or remotely without the use of the eyes.

ILLUSTRATED WORKS

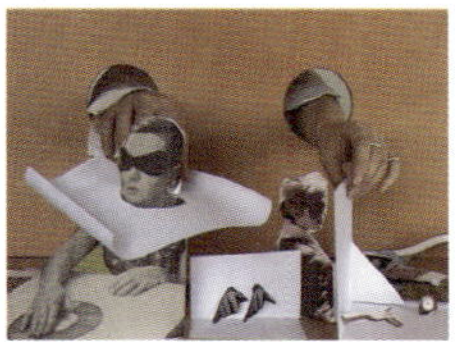

Headbox

2004, Installation of Objects and three Video Works
"Rosa and Collar Model", 14mins;
"Hands Through Screen Model", 12mins 55secs;
"Woman Behind Screen Model", 13mins 8secs

Headbox is based on the case of Rosa Kuleshova, a young woman whose ability to read with her fingertips made her the subject of scientific observation in Russia in the 1960s. The scientific research is reinterpreted though a series of videos and objects.

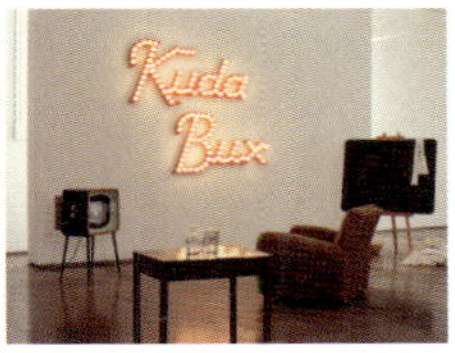

Kuda Bux

2003, Installation with Video, B+W, Colour, Stereo, 10mins 40secs

Based on the case of the New York mystic, Kuda Bux who was made famous in America during the 1930s and 1940s by his dramatic demonstrations of eyeless sight. Taking the form of an open set, *Kuda Bux* references the theatrical nature of Bux's performances and comprises illuminated text, video and gathered and constructed props.

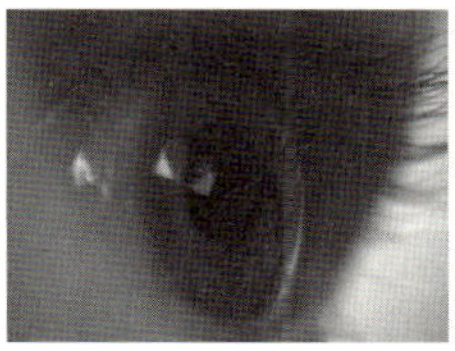

After Image

2002, Video, B+W and Colour, Stereo, 4mins 30secs

After Image explores the myth of the optogram and the nineteenth century theory that the last image seen before death is retained on the retina of the eye. *After Image* presents footage from *Four Flies on Grey Velvet* (Dario Argento, 1971, Italy) and Los *Muertos Hablan* (Gabriel Soria, 1935, Mexico) alongside footage shot by the artist.

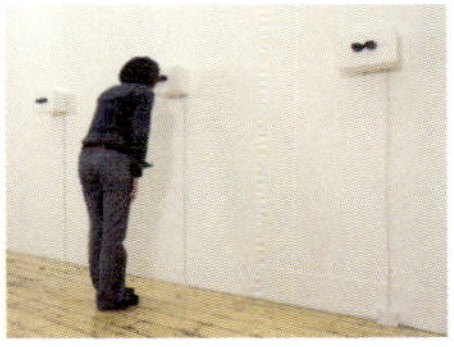

Stereoscopes

1999–2009, Illuminated Transparencies

The stereoscopes present 3-D images observed through special viewing glasses.

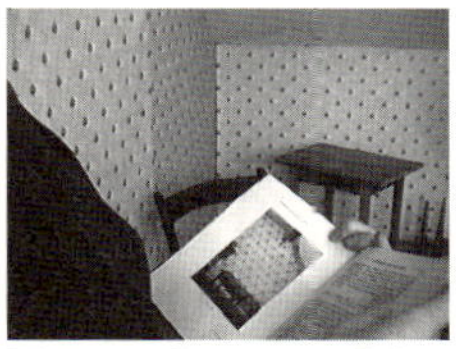

Experiment M

1999, Installation with two Videos, B+W, Silent, 5mins 43secs

Experiment M is based on the case of the Belfast table tilting medium, Kathleen Goligher and her researcher Dr. William Jackson Crawford. Between 1914 and 1920 Crawford researched the mediumistic phenomena occurring at the séances of the Goligher Circle, Belfast. *Experiment M* recreates the space where the séances and experimental research took place.

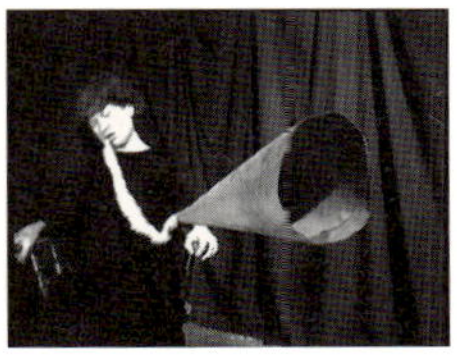

The Last Person

1998, Video, B+W, Silent, 10mins 30secs

The Last Person is based on the case of Helen Duncan, 1898–1956, a Scottish materialisation medium who in 1944 was the last person to be tried under the British Witchcraft Act of 1735.

SUSAN MacWILLIAM

1969 Born Belfast, Northern Ireland
Lives and works in Belfast and Dublin

Lecturer National College of Art and Design, Dublin

www.susanmacwilliam.com

EDUCATION

1987–1991 Manchester Polytechnic, England

SOLO EXHIBITIONS

2009
Remote Viewing, 53rd International Biennale, Venice
13 Roland Gardens, Golden Thread Gallery, Belfast
2008
Eileen, Gimpel Fils, London
Double Vision, Jack the Pelican Presents, New York
2006
Dermo Optics, Likovni Salon, Celje
2004
Headbox, Temple Bar Gallery, Dublin
2003
On The Eye, Golden Thread Gallery, Belfast
2002
On The Eye, Butler Gallery, Kilkenny
2001
Susan MacWilliam, Cornerhouse, Manchester
2000
The Persistence of Vision, Limerick City Gallery of Art, Limerick
1999
Experiment M, Context Gallery, Derry
Faint, Old Museum Arts Centre, Belfast
1997
Curtains, Project Arts Centre, Dublin
1995
Liptych, Crescent Arts Centre, Belfast
1994
Liptych, Harmony Hill Arts Centre, Lisburn

GROUP EXHIBITIONS (SELECTED)

2009
We Know More Than We Can Tell, Context Gallery, Derry
2008
Drawing a Line: Contemporary Survey of Northern Irish Art, Art Museum of the Heilongjiang Daily, China
Trickery and Illusion in Cinema, Tatton Park Biennial, Manchester
2007
Seeing is Believing, The Photographers' Gallery, London
The Fall Season, Jack The Pelican Presents, New York
Rigor Mort, Basement Gallery, Dundalk
The Double Image, Golden Thread Gallery, Belfast
New Art from Northern Ireland, Katzen Arts Centre at American University, Washington
2006
Flash on The Screen, Basekamp, Philadelphia
A Dark Noise, Golden Thread Gallery, Belfast
Vstop Prost, Likovni Salon, Celje
EV+A, Limerick
Smoke and Mirrors, Mac, Birmingham
2005
To Be Continued.../Jatkuu..., Helsinki Photography Festival
Red, White, Blue, Spencer Brownstone Gallery, New York
The Belfast Way: Young Art from Northern Ireland, Herzliya Museum of Contemporary Art, Tel Aviv
2004
Thinking of Ideas, Golden Thread Gallery, Belfast
Inter, Harris Museum and Art Gallery, Preston
Eye Test, Stephen Lawrence Gallery, London
2003
Think Over, Rialto Santambrogio, Rome
House of Science, Kino Central, Berlin
Afterlife, Chapter Arts, Cardiff
Afterlife, Guidhall, Newcastle
Exhumed, Museum of Garden History, London
Hindsight, Arnolfini, Bristol
LUX Open, Royal College of Art, London
EV+A, Limerick
2002
From Dusk to Dawn, Stephen Lawrence Gallery, London
Cluster, Bowes Bar, Dublin
Home + Away: Contemporary Irish Art, Haggerty Museum of Art, Milwaukee
Appropriation, Ormeau Baths Gallery, Belfast
EV+A, Limerick
2001
It's All Over, Again, Proposition Gallery, Belfast
Claremorris Open, Claremorris
2000
The Notice Day in This Factory is Thursday, Consortium, Amsterdam
D-Net Festival, LUX, London
Portobello Film and Video Festival, London
Clockwork 2000, The Clocktower, New York
Fantasy and Identity, Star67, Brooklyn, New York
1999
Glen Dimplex Artists Award, Irish Museum of Modern Art, Dublin
Haunted, S1 Artspace, Sheffield
1998
EV+A, Limerick
Video Soup, Collective Gallery, Edinburgh
1998
Fix '98, Catalyst Arts, Belfast
1997
Intermedia, Triskel Arts Centre, Cork
1996
Splatter, Crawfordsburn House, Crawfordsburn
1995
Subterraneans, Catalyst Arts, Belfast
1994
Belfast Young Contemporaries, One Oxford Street, Belfast

PUBLICATIONS (SELECTED)

2007
Rigor Mort, Basement Gallery, Dundalk, ed. Sally Timmons
2005
Dialogues: Women Artists from Ireland, IB Tauris, London/New York, ed. Katy Deepwell
Printed Project, Issue 5, Visual Artists Ireland, Dublin, ed. Alan Phelan
2004
Cat. *Inter,* Harris Museum and Art Gallery, Preston, text Shirley MacWilliam
Cat. *Eye Test,* Stephen Lawrence Gallery, London, text Kelly O'Reilly
2003
The Cities of Belfast, Four Courts Press, Dublin, ed. Nicholas Allen and Aaron Kelly, text Suzanna Chan
2002
Cat. *Appropriation,* Ormeau Baths Gallery, Belfast, text Richard West
2001
Cat. *EV+A 2001,* Gandon, Limerick, ed. Salah Hassan
2000
Cat. *Clockwork 2000,* PS1, New York, text Roxana Marcoci
1999
Out of Belfast, Denison University, Ohio, ed. Joy Sperling
Cat. *Glen Dimplex Artists Award,* Irish Museum of Modern Art, Dublin
Cat. *EV+A 99,* Gandon, Limerick, ed. Jeanne Greenberg Rohatyn
1998
Cat. *EV+A '98,* Gandon, Limerick, ed. Paul O'Reilly

REVIEWS (SELECTED)

2009
"Future Greats", Brian Dillon, *Art Review,* Issue 30, March
2008
"Susan MacWilliam, Eileen", Riann Coulter, *CIRCA* Issue 125
"Susan MacWilliam, Double Image", Michael Wilson, *ArtForum,* Summer
"Shaky Ground", *Garageland,* Cathy Lomax, Issue 6
2007
"Photography and the Unreal", Helen Sumpter, *Time Out,* London, 10 December
"The Spirit of Enquiry", Charlotte Cripps, *The Independent,* London, 14 November
"Belfast: Four Video Artists Exploring Consciousness", Slavka Sverakova, *Terminal,* Tel Aviv, April/May
"On Susan MacWilliam's *Dermo Optics* and

BIOGRAPHY

Explaining Magic to Mercer", Slavka Sverakova, *CIRCA Online*
2006
"An Outsider in her Native Town", Noel Kelly, *CIRCA*, Issue 118
"A Dark Noise", Slavka Sverakova, *Artists Newsletter*, December
"EV+A", Paul O'Brien, *CIRCA*, Issue 116
2004
"Susan MacWilliam", Niamh Ann Kelly, *Art Monthly*, October
"Susan MacWilliam", Aidan Dunne, *Irish Times*, 15 September
2003
"Perspective 2003", Aidan Dunne, *Irish Times*, 10 October
"Susan MacWilliam", Cherie Driver, *Sculptors' Society of Ireland Newsletter*, Summer
2002
"EV+A", Daniel Jewesbury, *Art Monthly*, May
"Controlled Explosion", Medb Ruane, *Sunday Times*, Culture Section, 5 May
"Images captured under an impossibly blue Ulster sky", Aidan Dunne, *The Times*, 24 April
2001
"Tripp/Kearney/MacWilliam", Robert Clark, *The Guardian Unlimited*, 15 October
"EV+A Expanded", Niamh Anne Kelly, *Art Monthly*, May
"Cutting Edge of Multi-Culturalism", Aidan Dunne, *The Irish Times*, 23 March
2000
"Ghostly Video Work", Elizabeth Martin, *Irish Connections*, Autumn
"The Persistence of Vision", Steph Pasquini, *NYarts Magazine*, July/August
"The Notice Day in This Factory is Thursday", Suzanna Chan, *Sculpture Society of Ireland Newsletter*, April/May
"The Notice Day in This Factory is Thursday", Phil Collins, *CIRCA*, Summer
1999
"Séance loaded with sexual overtones", Ian Hill, *Belfast Newsletter*, 7 September
"Dystopian Chic", Gavin Murphy, *Source*, Autumn
"Dominant Style/Variant Practices; Photography + Contemporary Art in Ireland", Justin Carville, *Source*, Issue 20
"Make-their-minds-up time", Aidan Dunne, *Irish Times*, 14 July
"Between Darkness and Light", Clare Doherty, *Contemporary Visual Arts*, June
"Susan MacWilliam: Faint", Maeve Connolly, *CIRCA*, Summer
"Susan MacWilliam: Faint", Gavin Weston, *Sunday Times*, Culture Section, 14 March
1998
"EV+A", Orla Ryan, *Variant*, Spring
"EV+A", Annie Fletcher, *CIRCA*, Winter
1997
"Susan MacWilliam", Mick Wilson, *CIRCA*, Autumn
"Susan MacWilliam", Mark Orange, *Art Monthly*, July/August
"Susan MacWilliam", Luke Clancy, *Irish Times*, 26 May
1999
"Subterraneans", Damien Coyle, *CIRCA*, Autumn
"Liptych II", Ian Hill, *Irish Times*, 1 March
1994
"Susan MacWilliam", Gavin Weston, *CIRCA*, Winter

RESIDENCIES

2008
University of Manitoba Archives and aceartinc Gallery, Winnipeg
2007
Parapsychology Foundation, New York
2006
New York, working with Parapsychology Foundation and American Society for Psychical Research
Zavod Celeia Centre for Contemporary Art, Celje, Slovenia
2001
Caribbean Contemporary Arts, Trinidad
1999–2000
PS1 International Studio Programme, New York
1998
Artists' Work Programme, Irish Museum of Modern Art, Dublin

AWARDS

2008
Visual Art Award, Arts Council of Northern Ireland
Winnipeg International Residency Award, Arts Council of Northern Ireland
2007
Claremorris Open, Curator: Ingrid Swenson
International Residency, Arts Council of Northern Ireland
2006
Visual Art Award, Arts Council of Northern Ireland
New York Residency, Arts Council of Northern Ireland
2005
EV+A, Limerick, Curator: Dan Cameron
Visual Art Award, Arts Council of Northern Ireland
2004
Commissions Award: An Chomhairle Ealaion/Arts Council of Ireland
2003
Perspective 03, Ormeau Baths Gallery, Belfast. Curator: Enrique Juncosa
Visual Art Award, Arts Council of Northern Ireland
2002
Visual Art Award, An Chomhairle Ealaion/Arts Council of Ireland
2001
Major Individual Award, Arts Council of Northern Ireland
Visual Art Award, Arts Council of Northern Ireland
EV+A, Limerick, Curator: Salah Hassan
2000
Visual Art Award, An Chomhairle Ealaion/Arts Council of Ireland
PS1/MOMA illy 2001 Collection
1999
PS1 International Studio Programme, New York
EV+A, Limerick, Curator: Jeanne Greenberg Rohatyn
Visual Arts Bursary: An Chomhairle Ealaion
Irish Museum of Modern Art/Glen Dimplex Artists Award, Short-listed
1998
Visual Arts Bursary, An Chomhairle Ealaion/Arts Council of Ireland
Visual Art Award, Arts Council of Northern Ireland
1997
Tyrone Guthrie Centre Residency
Visual Art Award, Arts Council of Northern Ireland
1994
Visual Art Award, An Chomhairle Ealaion/Arts Council of Ireland
Visual Art Award, Arts Council of Northern Ireland
1992
Visual Art Award, Arts Council of Northern Ireland

COLLECTIONS

Private Collections
The British Library Sound Archive, London: *Video works 1998–2008*
Arts Council of Northern Ireland

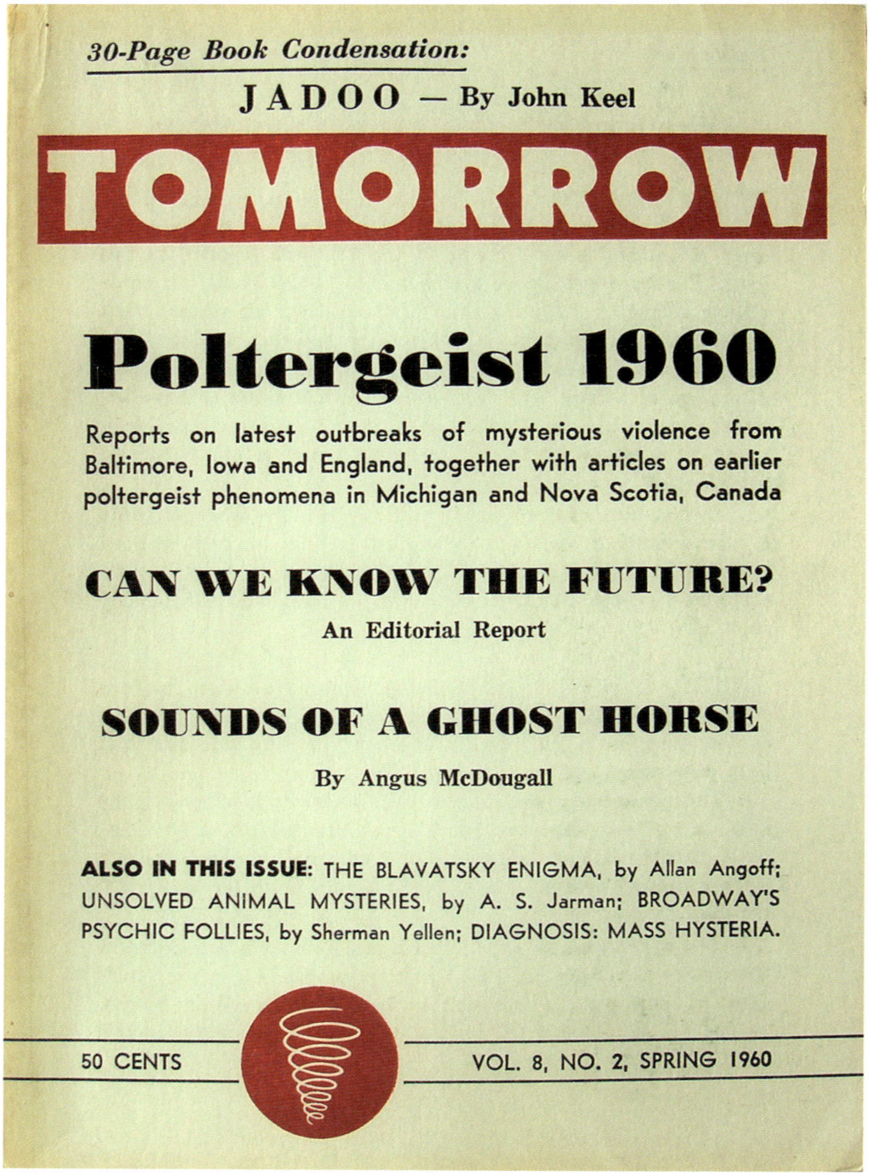
30-Page Book Condensation:

JADOO — By John Keel

TOMORROW

Poltergeist 1960

Reports on latest outbreaks of mysterious violence from Baltimore, Iowa and England, together with articles on earlier poltergeist phenomena in Michigan and Nova Scotia, Canada

CAN WE KNOW THE FUTURE?

An Editorial Report

SOUNDS OF A GHOST HORSE

By Angus McDougall

ALSO IN THIS ISSUE: THE BLAVATSKY ENIGMA, by Allan Angoff; UNSOLVED ANIMAL MYSTERIES, by A. S. Jarman; BROADWAY'S PSYCHIC FOLLIES, by Sherman Yellen; DIAGNOSIS: MASS HYSTERIA.

50 CENTS

VOL. 8, NO. 2, SPRING 1960

Tomorrow, Vol. 8, No. 2, Spring 1960, Published by Helix Press/Garrett Publications, Parapsychology Foundation Inc.

ACKNOWLEDGEMENTS

I would like to thank Karen Downey for her enthusiasm, ambition and professional and personal support in curating *Remote Viewing* and in developing this book. I would like to thank Ciaran Carson, Slavka Sverakova, Martha Langford and Brian Dillon for their commitment to the project; for their thoroughness with the work and for bringing so much to it through their detailed and thoughtful essays. To Ciaran I extend additional thanks for being in the work and for all the correspondences and books. Thank you to Marina Warner for her enthusiasm and generosity in offering to us excerpts from *Phantasmagoria*. Very special thanks to Niall Sweeney and Nigel Truswell at Pony Ltd., for designing this book—for always finding a solution and for so wonderfully reflecting the sources and forms of the work. I would also like to thank Duncan McCorquodale and the team at Black Dog Publishing.

I would most especially like to thank my continual collaborators and very dear friends Lisette and Eileen Coly—to them I extend my deepest gratitude and appreciation for their welcoming me into their family; for helping me *'get to Garrett'*; for opening so many doors to me and for all the shared adventures that started with that calamitous trip to the library in 2006. Thank you also to George Damalas. Thank you to Bill (Dr William G Roll) for the repetition, repetition, repetition and ever playful spirit. And a very special thank you to all my other subjects and for their role in making it such an enjoyable and exhilarating experience: Dr Stanley Krippner, Dr Rex Stanford, Dr Howard Reed, Arla Marshall, Madame Yvonne Duplessis, Edith, Larissa and Jean Paul. I would also like to thank Nic Roeg for taking the time—for his interest in the work and for his great conversation.

I would like to thank all those who have supported my work—Parapsychology Foundation, New York; Dr Shelley Sweeney, Head of Special Collections, University of Manitoba Archives, Winnipeg; aceart inc, Winnipeg; Denise Iredell—and all those who have helped with my queries and searches for documents; Dr Carlos S Alvaredos, Dr Nancy Zingrone, Peter Mulacz, Walter Falk, Jim Nickels. Thank you also to the granddaughters of TG Hamilton—Linda Hamilton Klassen and Margaret Hamilton Birston for their warmth and generosity in lending me their personal scrapbooks. I would especially like to thank the Arts Council of Northern Ireland for their continued support of my practice through awards and residencies and for their role in facilitating recent projects.

Thank you to my friends for their support and friendship—Theo Sims, Mairead McClean, Dan Shipsides, Lorraine Burrell, Liz Garlicki, Susan Kelly, John Duncan, Noel Kelly, Mark Orange, Peter Richards, Diana Copperwhite, Allan Hughes. Thank you also to Golden Thread Gallery, Kate McCollough, Oona Grimes, Tony Grisoni, Roger McKinley. To my friends and colleagues at the National College of Art and Design, Dublin—Robert Armstrong, Prof Brian Maguire, Declan McGonagle, Dr Siun Hanrahan.

Additional thanks to Penny Sychrava, Pearse Moore, Reto Stamm, The Nerve Centre, Derry, Joachim Reck and Robert Gorski at Eidotech. Darren Murray, Maria McKinney, Daniel Jewesbury, Mark McLaughlin, Brighdin Farren. Iain Davidson, Matthew Hendry, Arts Council of Northern Ireland, Department of Culture, Arts and Leisure, Colette Norwood, British Council, Caterina de Rienzo, Giulia Marabini.

Very special thanks to my family—to mum, dad, Shirley and Michael, for their love and support, and for always being prepared to help out at the eleventh hour.

Susan MacWilliam

COLOPHON

Black Dog Publishing Limited
10A Acton Street
London WC1X 9NG
info@blackdogonline.com

Published on the occasion of Northern Ireland's participation in 53rd Venice Biennale of Art.

Edited by Karen Downey.

Designed by Niall&Nigel at Pony Ltd., London

British Library Cataloguing-in-Publication Data.
A CIP record for this book is available from the British Library.

ISBN 978 1 906155 78 0

Black Dog Publishing Limited, London, UK, is an environmentally responsible company.

REMOTE VIEWING
is printed on Arctic The Volume Ivory, an FSC certified paper.

IMAGES

ALL IMAGES, UNLESS OTHERWISE STATED, ARE COURTESY THE ARTIST.

PAGES 2, 4, 5, 8, 9, 12, 13, 19 & 112
Hamilton Family fonds, University of Manitoba Archives & Special Collections (PC 12, A. 79–41)

PAGES 21, 67, 133
(Katie King, Goligher Structure, Kuda Bux): Mary Evans Picture Library

PAGES 104–105, 142
Published with permission of Garrett-Coly personal archives of Parapsychology Foundation, Inc. (www. parapsychology.org)
The Parapsychology Foundation was founded in 1951 by Eileen J Garrett (1893–1970) as a worldwide forum supporting scientific exploration of psychic phenomena. Eileen Coly, daughter of Eileen J Garrett currently serves as President with Lisette Coly, granddaughter of Garrett serving as Vice President and Executive Director.

TEXT

PAGES 56, 57
Reprinted by permission from Marina Warner, *Phantasmagoria: Spirit Visions, Metaphors, and Media into the Twenty-first Century*, Oxford University Press, Paperback Edition 2008. © Marina Warner.

architecture art design
fashion history photography
theory and things
www.blackdogonline.com

To Mum and Dad
Shirley and Michael
Lisette and Mrs C

and of course Garrett
Onwards and Upwards

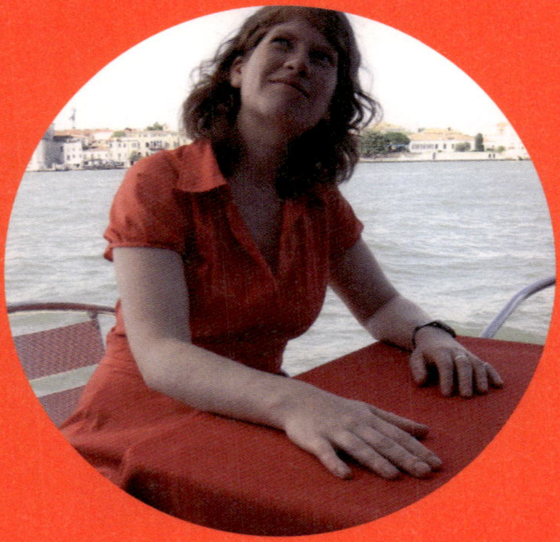

Table Tilting/Levitation, July 2008, Giudecca, Venice, Photograph Karen Downey